# Economic Wealth Creation and the Social Division of Labour

CW01091191

Robert P. Gilles

# Economic Wealth Creation and the Social Division of Labour

Volume I: Institutions and Trust

Robert P. Gilles
Management School
Queen's University Belfast
Belfast, UK

ISBN 978-3-319-76396-5          ISBN 978-3-319-76397-2   (eBook)
https://doi.org/10.1007/978-3-319-76397-2

Library of Congress Control Number: 2018945055

Printed on acid-free paper

This Palgrave Macmillan imprint is published by the registered company Springer Nature Switzerland AG
The registered company address is: Gewerbestrasse 11, 6330 Cham, Switzerland

# PREFACE

This book is founded on more than 30 years of reflection on the use and abuse of economic theory. During these years, I have considered myself to be a critical observer of developments in economics and in economic theory in particular. The impetus for my view of economics presented here was given, initially, during my studies as an economics student at Tilburg University and, subsequently, during research for my dissertation. My dissertation addressed the modelling of institutional constraints in Edgeworthian barter processes. During these initial years as a researcher in economics, I already found myself at odds with the main hypotheses put forward by leading economists. In particular, I lamented the state of general equilibrium theory and its singular focus on perfectly competitive markets, which I believe to be much too limiting.

During my subsequent career at Virginia Tech I turned my attention to several other areas in economic theory. Again, I found the practice in these other fields in economic theory lacking in critical self-reflection. I made several contributions to the general equilibrium theory of the provision of collective goods-better known as public goods. With my coauthors Dimitrios Diamantaras and Pieter Ruys, we have been able to apply this theory to understand the emergence of trade institutions, in particular market systems, that are subject to establishment and maintenance costs. Our conclusions from this research resulted in explanations that were different from the established theories in mainstream neo-classical economics.

Subsequently, I investigated the formation of networks and hierarchical authority organisations with various coauthors. In particular, I focused on the role of trust in the formation of networks under mutual consent. The main insight from this research is not only that trust removes ambiguity about networking decisions, but also that trust guides the various economic agents to form a social network with strong stability properties.

I first met Xiaokai Yang during a visit to Tilburg University in 1999. My reading of his 2001 book on the social division of labour triggered my interest in incorporating some of my own ideas in Yang's framework. It took a long time to truly understand the working of Yang's theory and its full potential. Only years after his death was I able to fully realise this potential in a mathematically correct theory of wealth creation through a social division of labour. The results have been beyond my expectations, and I have realised that this framework could unify many of my ideas from my previous research and introspection.

Immediately following the financial crisis of 2008, I returned from the USA to Europe and took up a professorship at Queen's University in Belfast, UK. The crisis strengthened my resolve to turn multiple strands of research and teaching material into a comprehensive vision of the functioning of an economy. This theory should be able to explain the crisis and make it possible to understand its effects.

During the past decade at Belfast I have developed and taught my emerging vision of the network-institutional nature of economic wealth creation through a social division of labour. This vision is presented in two volumes.

This first volume discusses the network-institutional foundation of economic wealth creation through a social division of labour. The theory put forward emphasises the role of socio-economic institutions in guiding the social division of labour. It brings together my thoughts on how institutions structure our economy and facilitate the production of goods and services. I discuss how this allows us to understand the financial panic of 2008 and what happened recently in the global economy. It also allows for a comprehensive understanding of the nature and role of trust and entrepreneurship. Both are essential elements in the functioning of wealth creation processes in a social division of labour.

While the nature of the first volume is very much in the realm of political economy, I turn to mathematical models of economies with a social division of labour in the second volume. There I am able to build on the framework laid out in the first volume to develop insights in the functioning of these economies. In particular, these theories explain that, if economic wealth is generated through a social division of labour, there is in principle no contradiction between the classical labour theory of value and the neo-classical market theory of value. This only emerges if institutions are assumed to implement a state of perfect competition and mobility: institutional imperfections allow the emergence of middlemen in the networks that make up the trade infrastructure of the economy. This, in turn, creates positions of power that can be exploited to create inequalities and deviations from the underlying value of the traded commodities.

## ACKNOWLEDGEMENTS

This book could not have been written without the helpful input of many of my colleagues and students. Many discussions over the years have shaped the research and philosophy presented here. Starting with my dissertation research at Tilburg University in the Netherlands in the 1980s and subsequently my work at Virginia Tech in Blacksburg, Virginia, and Queen's University in Belfast, UK, I have had many opportunities to shape my thoughts through interactions with colleagues and students and through lecturing to attentive audiences.

Above all, I acknowledge the contributions of my mentor, Pieter Ruys, to the material presented here. We have been debating the nature of the relational economy for 30 years and we continue this debate today. In the early days of my dissertation research at Tilburg University, Pieter gave me the freedom to find my own way and investigate networks and hierarchies well before these became fashionable. Pieter then gave and still gives me the inspiration to ask the hard questions and to demand that economists, and economic theorists in particular, should provide answers to these questions even though the search is tremendously difficult and demanding.

Second, I acknowledge the contributions of Dimitrios Diamantaras to the ideas and concepts presented here: Dimitrios was my coauthor in developing many of these theories. We spent a lot of time together to develop the demanding mathematical models and proofs that are required to address these questions properly. I thank Dimitrios and his student Marie Shorokey for detailed corrections and feedback on this first volume.

More recently, my work with Dimitrios and Marialaura Pesce on the endogenous emergence of a social division of labour in different institutional environments has been inspiring and is a major part of the ideas presented in the second volume. I thank Marialaura for hosting me in Naples these past years to develop these ideas more fully.

I also thank my former students, many of whom are now close colleagues and collaborators. In particular, working with René van den Brink and Emiliya Lazarova has given me much inspiration. We wrote many papers together, with René on hierarchical organisations and with Emiliya on the relational economy and institutions.

With Sudipta Sarangi I developed one of the most important concepts and models in this research programme, the model of network formation under mutual consent. Our model of trusting behaviour and the game theoretic solution forms in many ways a cornerstone of my research programme. This research extended into our work with Subhadip Chakrabarti on the many applications of networks in game theoretic models of economic behaviour.

Working with Kate Johnson has been a real inspiration. Together we explored the notion of social capital, Grameen banking and experimental game theory. Many of our discussions are hopefully reflected in this text.

Most recently, Owen Sims has contributed most prolifically to the discussion of how the social division of labour develops and, particularly, our understanding of entrepreneurship in such economies. Our debates and joint research has resulted in many ideas that are presented in this first volume. Chapter 5 on entrepreneurship is a joint work with Owen. His interest in historical cases of entrepreneurship matched my own and resulted in very insightful analysis that is used throughout this volume and Chap. 5 specifically. I thank Owen very much for these contributions. Without him this project would be much less complete.

I would also like to thank my former students Willy Spanjers, Kyungdong Hahn, Narine Badasyan and Zhengzheng Pan. Over the years, they gave me much motivation to keep on track with my work on the research programme that has resulted in these two volumes.

Finally, I thank my wife Jelena for putting up with my idiosyncratic state of mind and work ethic during the endless hours of working on this manuscript. I am very grateful to her for allowing me a more practical perspective on the functioning of the social division of labour through her lens of supply chain management. She complements me in more ways than I can express.

Belfast, UK                                                          Robert P. Gilles
January 2018

# Contents

# LIST OF FIGURES

# LIST OF TABLES

# CHAPTER 1

# The Principles of Economic Wealth Creation

"What are the causes of the human ability to create economic wealth?" This is one of the key questions that have occupied economists from the onset of their reasoning about economic activity and performance in a human society, exemplified by the title of the magnum opus by Adam Smith (1776), *An Inquiry into the Nature and Causes of the Wealth of Nations*.

The response to this fundamental question is not only the oldest, but also the most established economic theory: wealth is generated through a social division of labour that is encapsulated in a social trade infrastructure. Productive tasks are spread out among a multitude of individuals, who achieve collectively a higher output than when all of them remain non-specialised. Thus wealth generation is founded on "Increasing Returns to Specialisation". Through a social trade infrastructure these specialised productive individuals are brought together to exchange, barter and trade the fruits of their labour to allocate the collective output for consumptive purposes.

A social division of labour, therefore, *divides and integrates* simultaneously. In order to access the identified Increasing Returns to Specialisation, productive tasks have to be divided; similarly, these divided tasks can only be functionally implemented when they are integrated into a social environment that embodies an effective trade infrastructure. Human needs give rise to the double coincidence of wants that can only be resolved through such a trade infrastructure.

The ability to create such a complex social organisation and to let this organisation be sufficiently flexible is uniquely human. In fact, the human condition is exemplified by this unique social ability. Our hominin species *Homo sapiens sapiens* evolved biologically as well as socially to respond to environmental conditions in a cooperative manner, this is known as the "social brain hypothesis" (Dunbar 2003). The social brain hypothesis leads to the conclusion that this uniquely human characteristic naturally evolved into such a social division of labour.

© The Author(s) 2018
R. P. Gilles, *Economic Wealth Creation and the Social Division of Labour*,
https://doi.org/10.1007/978-3-319-76397-2_1

That the social division of wealth-generating tasks cannot be separated from its integration through a social trade infrastructure gives rise to questions about how a human society accomplishes such a difficult and complex objective. In this work I adopt the hypothesis that such an organisation is conducted and coordinated through socio-economic *institutions*. These institutions are understood as fictional narratives that build a parallel fictional reality in which humans interact and cooperate (Harari 2014).

Such an institutional perspective is, therefore, inalienable from the idea that wealth is generated through a social division of labour. This has been accepted by many social philosophers and economists, but has been neglected more recently in market-centred thinking about the human economy. I argue here that a return to a more institutional perspective is necessary to make economics relevant again and to address contemporary issues in the global economy in the twenty-first century.

The institutional perspective taken in this book is a very broad one, capturing many forms of the fictional narratives that guide human interaction. I include all forms of conventions, collective behavioural rules and forms of governance in the category of institutions. Institutions range, therefore, from simple human gestures, facial expressions and language to advanced governmental institutions and sophisticated financial instruments in our contemporary global economy.

In this chapter, I set out an axiomatic structure to underpin a thought framework in which one can meaningfully reason about the human economy centred around a social division of labour. Before doing this, I dwell for a short time on the historical roots of the fundamental theory that economic wealth is generated through a social division of labour that is encapsulated in an effective trade infrastructure.

**Some Historical Theories of the Social Division of Labour** The idea or principle that economic wealth generation is conducted through such a social division of labour was already proposed in ancient Greek social philosophical discourse. This is exemplified by the description of the ideal "polis" in Plato (380 BCE) as an urban economy that is structured through a clear social division of labour. This was expounded and expanded upon by Xenophon (370 BCE, 362 BCE), who emphasised the necessity of having a proper functioning institutional environment in which a social division of labour can flourish.

Aristotle (350 BCE) developed the conception of economic wealth creation through a social division of labour in its most complete vision during Greek antiquity. He emphasised the importance of specific socio-economic institutions such as property rights and the free exchange and barter of property. This included a treatise on the evolution of money and the foundation of the price mechanism (Aristotle 340 BCE, Book V).

The principle that economic activity is structured as a social division of labour was unquestioned through more than 2000 years of philosophical and social thought spanning Plato, Xenophon and Aristotle. Contributions were made in Islamic Scholastic and Latin Scholastic thought (Sun 2012, Chapter 2), but only during the period in the run-up to the industrial revolution in the seventeenth and eighteenth centuries was the idea significantly revived. The term "division of labour" was actually coined by Bernard Mandeville in an elaborate analysis of industrial shipbuilding and cloth-making in Volume 2 of his magnum opus, Mandeville (1714). In this work, the concept that economic wealth is generated through a social division of labour became absolute and indisputable. Mandeville also uses metaphors to promote this idea, in particular with his famous fable of the bees.

Mandeville brought the ideas of the ancient social philosophers into the world created by the industrial revolution. His contribution also included the introduction of the idea of the channelling of self-interest through the trade infrastructure of the economy. As Prendergast (2016) argues, this was not necessarily founded on an early understanding of "laissez-faire" economic policy by governments of nation-states—that unbridled self-interested decision-making leads to collectively optimal benefits under free trade—but rather a more sophisticated conception of the role of public government in the economy. In particular, Mandeville was hesitant about the potential for coercion in the labour markets in a modern industrial economy.

**Classical Political Economy** Although the roots of the emerging field of *political economy* were already laid prior to his contributions, Adam Smith (1759, 1776) firmly established this new science on the fundamental principle that economic wealth was generated through a social division of labour. This was set out in the first three chapters of Smith (1776), in which he famously expounded on the workings of the division of labour in a pin factory.

Smith also developed some theoretical consequences of the hypothesis of wealth generation through a division of labour. In particular, he linked the proper and efficient functioning of a social division of labour to the notion of competition, and developed the notion of the "extent of the market" to describe the limits of the wealth generation process in a social division of labour. This leads him on to an extensive debate about economic policy founding the development of the economy—embodied by the social division of labour—based on economic liberty and self-guidance. This was expressed most forcefully in Smith's concept of the "invisible hand": that selfishness and greed guide the social division of labour to its most optimal state.

After Smith, David Ricardo (1817) provided the next push in the development of the theory of wealth generation through a social division of labour. Based on the vision promoted by Malthus (1798), Ricardo was very concerned about the limits to economic growth. He introduced the theoretical notions of *marginal productivity* and an *equilibrium* as a state of the economy in which the rate of return on capital investments is negligible owing to the balance of the forces in the social division of labour.[1] Ricardo thus introduced two fundamental ideas into economics—marginalism and equilibration—changing economic thought forever.

Ricardo significantly changed the theory of wealth generation through a social division of labour, setting the scene for contributions that considered the incorporation of the division of labour into manufacturing organisations. The first main contribution to the understanding of manufacturing and its effects on the division of labour was made by Charles Babbage (1835). He formulated the "Babbage principle" that in an industrialised economy Increasing Returns to Specialisation are driven by advances in production technology and the organisation of work around mechanised production processes. This laid the foundations for modern economic growth theory.

The work of Babbage on manufacturing set the scene for the most comprehensive analysis of the industrial division of labour in the work by Karl Marx (1867, 1893, 1894). Marx fully incorporated the idea that tasks are organised hierarchically in social production organisations—through a *manufacturing* division of labour. His analysis considered the fact that produced commodities can obscure the way in which production is organised—referred to as "commodity fetishism" (Marx 1867, Chapter 1). For example, when buying a mobile phone, it is not clear how it was produced or where it originated; whether child or slave labour was used in its production; or whether its production process negatively impacted the natural environment.[2] Marx's theoretical framework attempted to reveal the workings and consequences of these obscured socio-economic mechanisms.

Marx set out to develop a complete theory of the capitalist economy. His perspective was very much a nineteenth-century one, centred on the notion of a commodity as a physical bearer of "use value". His theory distinguishes capitalism from other forms of socio-economic organisation through its focus on *capital accumulation*—generated surpluses are submitted to the social division of labour with the objective to generate further surpluses. This perspective was fully expounded in a mathematical theory by Sraffa (1960) and Roemer (1981).

---

[1] Ricardo's argument was innovative and revolutionary: Competition among capitalists will force the rate of return on investments to equalise in the economy. The sector with the lowest marginal productivity will thus determine the overall rate of return in the economy. Ricardo determined this resource to be arable land, the agricultural output of which will diminish with more intensive use. Diminishing returns on less productive land now drives the economy to an equilibrium in which the social division exactly generates enough resources to reproduce itself, thus enhancing the arguments seminally put forward by Malthus (1798). For a detailed discussion I refer to Foley (2006, Chapter 2).

[2] For a more complete treatment of Marx's theory of the social division of labour and the manufacture division of labour I refer to Sun (2012, Sections 5.2 and 5.3) and for Marx's general economic theory to Foley (2006) and Harvey (2017).

**The Social Division of Labour in the Marginalist Perspective**  After Marx, economics transformed itself radically from political economy into neo-classical economics based on marginalist reasoning in market environments. In some sense, neo-classicism gave in completely to commodity fetishism and focused solely on the trade of commodities as valued objects, neglecting the production processes through the social division of labour. Indeed, the idea that wealth is actually generated through a social division of labour does not play a significant part of economic theorising about the market: neo-classical economics focused completely on the description of the price mechanism and its power to guide the economy to an efficient state (Jevons 1871; Menger 1871; Walras 1926; Marshall 1890; Pareto 1906). Even though neo-classical economics is firmly founded on a mathematical approach to economic reasoning, there was no push to make progress on mathematical models of economic wealth generation through a social division of labour.

The development of neo-classical economic thought was further advanced by the contributions of Friedrich Hayek (1937, 1945, 1960), who considered the role of information and knowledge in a market economy. Hayek emphasised that knowledge plays a key role in the formation of the social division of labour. In particular, the availability of knowledge is localised and is critical for the assumption of socio-economic roles and specialisations by individual agents in the economy. The dispersed knowledge in the social division of labour is transformed into price information through the market mechanism, guiding individual agents in the processes to actually organise themselves into a social division of labour. As such, this knowledge transformation process is bottom up: dispersed knowledge in economic locations is transformed into central price information that guides all economic decisions.

Hayek viewed the market or price mechanism as the only socio-economic institution that can transform dispersed information in this fashion. He used it to promote the idea that any well-functioning economy should be founded on such a mechanism, making the market economy the only viable organisation form.

Hayek's view reverses the logic of Marxian commodity fetishism: economic decisions should be based solely on price information, which actually transforms and thus obscures the underlying localised knowledge that is present in the economy. Therefore, this form of commodity fetishism is a good thing rather than a bad one.[3] Hayek subsequently used his theory of the division of knowledge as the foundation of his theory of economic self-organisation and the rise of spontaneous economic order. These theories lie at the foundation for neo-liberalism that took hold of policy formation and corporate management from the 1980s.

---

[3] In Chap. 2 I discuss the idea that the 2007/2008 financial crisis was mainly caused by the fact that the prices of most financial derivatives did not reflect the true values and risks related to these products. Hayek's view does not consider seriously the effects of misinformation and unfounded beliefs in the assessment of the competitive market system as the main allocation mechanism.

**Market Economies with an Endogenous Social Division of Labour** Only rather recently has Xiaokai Yang (1988, 2001, 2003) revived an interest in the social division of labour as the main source of economic wealth, and developed a mathematical model that appropriately represents price-guided economic decision-making in the context of a social division of labour. Yang's main innovation was the introduction of the conceptual notion of a *consumer-producer*. This mathematical construct describes an economic decision-maker as one who embodies consumptive needs as well as productive abilities—extending the infamous notion of *Homo Economicus*.

Yang and Ng (1993) and Yang (2001, 2003) made the case that the consumer-producer approach can be used to describe wealth generation in an economy in which the competitive price mechanism guides the endogenous formation of a social division of labour.[4] Yang and Ng (1993) also argued that other questions about economic wealth generation can be addressed in this framework. As such, this theory is therefore a proper mathematical vehicle to represent Smithian and Ricardian ideas concerning the functioning of a social division of labour and its extent.

This mathematical framework has been developed further through contributions by Diamantaras and Gilles (2004), Sun et al. (2004), Gilles (2017a,b) and Gilles et al. (2017). These contributions show that a mathematical theory of the functioning of a social division of labour founded on price guided decision-making by consumer-producers leads to a general framework that can incorporate the ideas of Smith, Ricardo and Marx as well as Walras and Edgeworth. For more details I also refer to Gilles (2018).

**Toward a Comprehensive Framework** Despite these recent advances in the understanding of wealth generation through a social division of labour, some important questions remain unaddressed. The most important question is *why* the human economy has evolved to be organised through a social division of labour. Neo-classical economics is clearly founded on the principle that the economy is organised through a *competitive market system* and that the social division of labour is simply an outcome of the proper functioning of that market system. This was not the fundamental hypothesis on which classical political economy was based. Instead, in political economy the social division of labour itself has primacy, while the market system has essentially a supporting role.

Here, I set out to develop a comprehensive view to solve this fundamental question. Recent advances in anthropology and evolutionary biologyshow that the human species evolved as a thoroughly social, cooperative species. The unique feature that actually separates *Homo sapiens* from other hominid species is that humans evolved to solve problems cooperatively and flexibly.

---

[4] Only very recently in Gilles (2017b) I have formally shown this to be the case for a "large" economy in which individual productive abilities are subject to Increasing Returns to Specialisation. The theory requires a sophisticated mathematical treatment that goes beyond the scope of Yang's original framework.

This allowed the human species to embark on a trajectory of socio-economic development. In other words, *Homo sapiens* is characterised by its economy, organised through a social division of labour. This evolutionary characterisation of the human economy provides a foundation for a comprehensive understanding of how the economy functions and how economic wealth is generated.

My argument is that there is a unifying socio-economic view of the human species that explains the emergence of the social division of labour as the primal human generator of economic wealth: *Humanity evolved as a species of social networkers that through social organisation exploited their unique ability to learn and be more productive if focused on a limited set of tasks.* Thus *Homo sapiens* combines its ability to socially organise itself with its characteristic that labour is subject to Increasing Returns to Specialisation.

This comprehensive viewpoint allows for a proper understanding of how economic wealth is generated, the crucial role of socio-economic trust in the human social organisation and how an economy founded on a social division of labour functions. Central to this viewpoint is the role of institutions in the human economy. Indeed, socio-economic institutions guide human activity and allow human decision-makers to properly interact and cooperate. The competitive price mechanism is just one of these possible socio-economic institutions, but certainly not the only one.

From this thesis, a perspective emerges that the global economy is a huge cooperative human project instead of the neo-classical and neo-liberal view that economic interaction is based on competition rather than cooperation. Thus, it follows that economics should provide a better understanding about the wealth creation processes that occur in the global economy; economics should revert to being a "worldly philosophy"—as was indeed the perspective of many classical political economists, including Adam Smith, David Ricardo, John Stuart Mill and Karl Marx, but which has been lost since the third quarter of the nineteenth century with the rise and establishment of neo-classical economics.

Neo-classical economists considered—and still consider—themselves hard, high-brow scientists who use mathematical models to understand and especially measure economic behaviour and performance. This scientific project has turned out to be much less successful than as was set out at the introduction of the mathematical scientific method in the 1870s, in what is known as the *marginalist revolution*. In particular, after the financial crisis of 2007/2008 and the subsequent lasting sluggishness of the global economy, economics has been found wanting. Many voices are calling for a new form of economics; a theoretical, mathematical economics that is open to addressing the pressing questions of our times, without being methodologically constrained and restricted.[5]

---

[5] The current state of neo-classical economics is that it is held together and defined by its methodology. Indeed, its practice and theories have a common methodology based on the principles of methodological individualism, methodological instrumentalism, methodological equilibration and the axiomatic method (Arnsperger and Varoufakis 2006).

I will attempt to go back to the roots of our understanding of the generation of economic wealth and justify the concepts used here. This requires me to bring together a number of very old and new ideas to sketch a theoretical understanding of the foundations of wealth creation in our contemporary global economy that is rather different from the one communicated to us by neo-classical economists. Therefore, the perspective set out here has to be understood as an attempt to communicate that the established, neo-classical viewpoint is actually contrived in a political way, and has to be viewed as much more ideological than scientific (Backhouse 2010; Chang 2014). By presenting an alternative vision, I hope to communicate the importance of certain aspects of human socio-economic behaviour and organisation that seem to be neglected in the prevailing economic world view.

## 1.1    FORMULATING A THEORETICAL FRAMEWORK

In this chapter I develop a theoretical framework that is founded on a number of fundamental hypotheses about human economic wealth generation and the logical consequences of these hypotheses. This creates a well-defined and holistic view of economic wealth creation and, consequently, of an economy as a whole. This helps us to understand the processes that we discern in the past as well as the contemporary global economy, setting out a perspective that defines a well-constructed worldly philosophy of human economic interaction. Unfortunately, this does not mean that an all-inclusive and complete perspective on our contemporary global economy emerges; reality remains too complex to comprehend with any set of simple concepts and theories.

Most of contemporary economics is centred on the notion of a commodity and its generated values as the main subject of study.[6] In my conceptualisation, I start from the viewpoint that the infrastructure of socio-economic relationships founded on the social and hierarchical division of labour should be our prime focal point. Therefore, the commodities are only of secondary importance; they are the objects of economic transactions and conversion processes in the prevailing trade infrastructure, but by no means fully characterise that infrastructure. Indeed, many contemporary socio-economic transactions concern immaterial services. These are fully determined by the social relationship between procurer and provider, in which both procurer and provider are instrumental in the determination and resolution of that service transaction; the service transaction is completely social or "relational".

I consider a simple example of a contemporary service commodity to extend this discussion. If one procures a haircut, it is unusual that the stylist as the provider completely imposes the chosen cut; the selection of the hairstyle is based on the desires of the customer, and the hairstylist acts as a facilitator for

---

[6] As mentioned, Marx (1867, Chapter 1) already pointed out that the focus on the commodity as the main subject of study obscures a view of the underlying production and trade processes.

this. As such, the process is mutual and collaborative, rather than one size fits all. A proper interpretation of the haircut is that it is the immaterial bearer of the relational transaction between the procurer (customer) and the provider (hairstylist). Thus the production process is much less obscured than is the case for material commodities such as food stuffs and physical luxury goods.

I argue that *all* commodities should be interpreted in this fashion. So, commodities have to be understood as carriers of the underlying production processes and are recognised as such.[7]

This fits with the perception that, in our contemporary twenty-first-century economy, economic subjects are very concerned about the impact of their activities on their environment, social as well as natural: consumers care about where their consumed commodities originate; whether the production processes involve corrupt practices such as the use of child and/or slave labour; whether these production processes impose significant externalities on the global natural environment; and whether the label on the product actually represents accurately what substances are used in its production. Similarly, firms are much concerned about certain properties of their supply chains, especially their sustainability and resilience. These concerns, in some sense, characterise our contemporary global economy and its reliance on services and interconnections through complex socio-economic networks.

This leads to the conclusion that the main object of economic study should be the social organisation of all processes conducted through the social division of labour and the associated trade infrastructure. The networks that make up this trade infrastructure should be the subject of our investigation and the focus of our modelling, rather than only the outputs that materialise from these (hidden) processes. In that regard, the objective of economics should be to "de-fetishise" these commodities, to use an expression from the Marxian perspective.

The theories developed here are, therefore, *relational* in nature and concern the interaction between social collaborators. This relational perspective has an institutional foundation. The development of this is the main subject of this first volume, while in the second volume (Gilles, 2018) I turn to the development of more quantitative, mathematical approaches to modelling economic wealth creation through a social division of labour.

**Developing an Axiomatic Framework** In this chapter I set out the fundamental principles of my institutional approach. I develop this framework as a formal treatise. I state five fundamental hypotheses on which my approach is founded and derive lemmas from these hypotheses that address the posed questions about the human economy. This thought framework is further developed in subsequent chapters of this book. The second volume (Gilles, 2018) turns

---

[7] It is common in economic theory to view a commodity solely as a bearer of consumptive and productive properties. Commodities are not considered as carriers of socio-economic processes.

to mathematical models that develop the classical issues of economic wealth generation and its allocation through an evolving social division of labour.

Throughout, it becomes clear that this framework is general enough to capture the capstone ideas of classical political economy, Marxian economics, as well as neo-classical and neo-Walrasian economics. Therefore, this framework aims to provide a proper basis for the further fruitful development of theoretical economics.

Of course, any theory is limited and I do not claim that the theory developed in this book is able to do full justice to the complexities of our socio-economic interactions. However, the structure set out here is founded on hypotheses that are inspired by ancient ideas about economic wealth generation as well as recent findings in research in scientific fields such as anthropology and sociology.

I introduce and formulate five hypotheses that lay the foundation of a theoretical explanation of the process of human economic wealth creation:

**Hypothesis 1:**   The principal axiomatic representation of an economic decision-maker is that of an *economic agent* and that this agent is principally defined by two characteristics, the *social brain hypothesis* and the *bounded rationality hypothesis*;

**Hypothesis 2:**   The economic agent embodies productive abilities as well as consumptive needs and desires, being the conductor of all socio-economic wealth creation processes;

**Hypothesis 3:**   All productive abilities are subject to *Increasing Returns to Specialisation*;

**Hypothesis 4:**   Consumptive abilities are subject to consumptive smoothing, thus facilitation *gains from trade*;

**Hypothesis 5:**   Founded on (1) the ability to build social networks; (2) Increasing Returns to Specialisation; and (3) consumptive smoothing, economic agents are brought together through an appropriate social organisation to achieve economic wealth generation processes.

These five hypotheses support and explain the emergence of the social division of labour (Lemma 1.7) that functions as the engine for economic wealth creation. I point out that the social division of labour only functions in the context of an institutional framework that prescribes how economic decision-makers interact. Thus *wealth creation only emerges in an institutional economy*.[8]

**Introducing a Unifying Framework**   A framework for the analysis of the wealth generation processes in an institutional economy is a so-called *socio-economic space*. This represents economic decision-makers in the context of

---

[8] A *market economy* is one possible incarnation or example of such an institutional economy. However, the assumption that an institutional economy consists solely of market interactions is unrealistic, in particular since a deep social division of labour naturally results in supply chains and networks of socio-economic interactions. So, the most natural incarnation of the institutional economy is actually a *network economy*.

the common institutional framework that guides their decisions and inter-actions. Thus a socio-economic space consists of economic decision-makers who interact through institutional intermediation and build socio-economic networks—or a *trade infrastructure*. In such a socio-economic space, markets are explicitly seen as platforms that emerge in these networks. This framework is developed in full detail in Chap. 3.

The theoretical framework of a socio-economic space is represented as a mathematical model using the representation of economic decision-makers as Yangian *consumer-producers*. These consumer-producers can interact in a variety of institutional settings. Human history has explored many institutional organisation forms, and I explore some of these trade institutions in this chapter to further explain the main line of theoretical development. It should be emphasised that institutions are critical in understanding how economic wealth is actually created and allocated: different institutional settings might lead to rather different economic outcomes.

The five hypotheses stated here and the thought framework that these hypotheses underpin also provide a foundation for an institutional theory of trust and trusting behaviour that extends well beyond the individualistic per-spective that all trust is *interpersonal*. I argue that trust is fundamentally founded on our social brain and our blind faith in the socio-economic institutions that we abide by. This institutional trust extends to our fellow human neighbours as they are members of the same institutional socio-economic space. So our daily interactions become possible through our blind faith that the people we interact with will abide by the same set of socio-economic institutions that guide our lives. Thus, what is referred to in the literature as interpersonal trust is actually transferred institutional trust, which I refer here to as *operational confidence*. Further consequences of this theoretical construction are explored in Chap. 4.

**Wealth Creation and Economic Development**  The social division of labour that is embodied in a socio-economic space is the main generator of economic wealth. As such, the allocation of this wealth and its creation are closely linked. Inequalities in the allocation of the generated wealth might lead to lower wealth levels in general owing to the adverse incentives that are present in the system.

Changes in the social division of labour usually lead to changes in the level of wealth generated, or economic development. The most effective change that causes an increase in the wealth generated is the *deepening* of the social division of labour. Dividing the tasks executed in some production process into more specialised tasks results in higher output levels owing to the fundamental prop-erty of Increasing Returns to Specialisation in production. Thus, by separating hunting from gathering, and subsequently spear-making from hunting, a tribe can increase overall food production and individual productivity significantly. This implies that there emerges a social division of labour made up of specialised hunters, spear-makers and gatherers. It is the emergence of these innovative socio-economic roles that drives economic growth.

The deepening of the social division of labour—and economic growth—is, therefore, closely related to institutional innovation, in particular the emergence of new *socio-economic roles* and new commodities that embody the innovative production technologies that are used to allow the further division of labour. This innovation of socio-economic institutions and infrastructures is denoted as the *entrepreneurial function* in the socio-economic space. The strongest expression of the entrepreneurial function is that of "entrepreneurship", when an individual "entrepreneurial agent" transforms certain crucial aspects of the governance structure of socio-economic institutions to cause a punctuated change in the social division of labour and to trigger significant economic development as a consequence. The full investigation of entrepreneurship and the entrepreneurial function in the socio-economic space is more fully developed and explored in Chaps. 3 and 5.

## 1.2    FUNDAMENTAL PRINCIPLES OF ECONOMIC WEALTH CREATION

The most fundamental principle on which wealth creation rests is the understanding of humans as social networkers. It has been shown in anthropological research that the human species evolved as a species of social networkers. The large human brain combined with the human ability to walk upright, the voice box, and human dexterity serve the human ability to relate to other humans in an effective and cooperative fashion. Thus human evolution has to be viewed as representing a social developmental process as well as a process of physical adaptation. Our species evolved to deal with pressures on the species from its environment and we evolved specifically to be social networkers to deal effectively with these pressures. Ultimately, we evolved to organise our societies around social divisions of labour that guaranteed an effective use of these human abilities in the generation of economic wealth.

Dunbar (2014) and Harari (2014) discuss how human evolution went through a number of stages. Hominid species evolved into *hominins* and, ultimately, into modern humans, *Homo sapiens sapiens*. The main evolutionary theory concerning the species of *Homo sapiens* is centred around two hypotheses, namely the *social brain hypothesis* and the hypothesis regarding *time budgets*—or, using more economically familiar terminology, the hypothesis of *bounded rationality*. Both hypotheses concern the understanding of why humans have evolved such big brains. Both assert that human evolution is in essence *social* rather than purely physical. Indeed, both hypotheses concern how the evolution of the human brain is driven by responses to the social environment of hominid and hominin species.

**The Social Brain Hypothesis**  The social brain hypothesis states that the development of the human brain is directly related to the social organisation of the communities in which hominids and hominins evolved. The most primitive hominid stage of human evolution can be gleaned from the observation of the behaviour and social organisation of (modern) great primate species in their current habitat. Research has indicated that in these species (chimpanzees, bonobos, gorillas and orangutans) there is a clear correlation between brain size and the complexity of social organisation of their communities[9] and the ability to reason and relate to other animals in primate populations (Dunbar 2014, Chapter 2). The main conclusion is that a larger size of the community is correlated to a larger brain size of the primate species in question. It has been recognised that hominids developed large brains specifically to deal with the computational demands of their uniquely complex social systems that require some form of order and organisation (Whiten and Byrne 1988).

The social organisation of these hominid species concerns mainly the conduct of relationships with other members of one's community. The number and complexity of these relationships guides brain development. In many mammal species this mainly refers to mating behaviour, but in hominids this also refers to social relationship-building beyond sexual interaction. Indeed, large hominid communities impose the maintenance of many non-sexual, social relationships with other community members.

A large brain implies two important other factors for survival (Dunbar 2009). First, a large brain is very expensive to maintain; it requires a disproportionally large intake of calories to maintain functioning. This implies that a species with a large brain needs to find high-calorific food and requires techniques to make ingestion of these calories manageable.[10] Second, a large brain is very hard to grow. This refers mainly to the number of years that are required to grow the prefrontal cortex layers in the brain. This requires a long period of nurturing by parents and the social training of young adults.[11]

This has dramatic implications for social behaviour and the organisation of human communities. It actually requires a group of human beings to cooperate effectively in order to feed itself, to raise the next generation, and to survive— social organisation is required to provide for the collective. In fact, human social organisation centres around the collective generation of foodstuffs to maintain large brains and to allow the effective nurturing of young humans in their developmental stage. Thus, human sociality is deeply embedded in our species.

In particular, the standard prehistoric form of human organisation was a *tribe*, which was able to respond quickly to changing environmental conditions and to survive collectively in a hostile environment. It is likely that the

[9] Generally, brain size and the complexity of the social organisation of mammal populations are strongly correlated as research shows. Dunbar (2014, Figure 3.1) provides empirical evidence that there is a strong relationship between the size of frontal lobe and neo-cortex development and social group size for a variety of species. Social group size acts here as a proxy for the complexity of social organisation of the communities in which members of these species operate.

[10] For example, gorillas are known to eat bamboo shoots for eight hours a day to maintain their brain. To maintain this disproportionally large brain, humans invented cooking techniques to transform sufficient calorific intake from food into manageable proportions and speed up the digestion process. Without cooking, the human species would actually not have developed.

[11] In humans, brain development takes up the first 20–25 years of a lifespan.

emergence of *Homo sapiens* was caused by changes in the climatic conditions in the hominins' African homelands; in order to survive as a species these humans were required to venture out in the open and dangerous fields of the African savannah. Only effective cooperation could guarantee the survival of the species. This forced a further development of the human brain, resulting in the *Homo sapiens sapiens* subspecies (Harari 2014).

In order to develop such cooperation and social organisation within groups of human beings, complex fictional narratives were developed (Graeber 2011). It is the human ability to accept these complex fictional narratives and to learn to organise one's life around these narratives that is embodied by the social brain hypothesis. For example, in order to hunt large animals a human tribe needs to set out a plan of capturing and killing the animal, requiring all members of the hunting party to be able to comprehend and accept such a scheme. This requires abstract planning through a collective narrative, embodying a production technology of hunting large game by a collective of trained hunters.

**Bounded Rationality** The social brain hypothesis asserts that the human brain has evolved for functioning in social situations and for survival in hostile environments. Furthermore, the human brain does not have infinite abilities to reason and to deduce meaning from observations. Indeed, as stated, the human species interacts through fictional narratives such as heuristics and behavioural rules that explicitly signify that the human brain is limited; indeed, in some sense, these fictional narratives make it possible to extend the brain of an individual member of the tribe into a collective, "tribal", brain. Thus, these fictional narratives not only provide a social environment in which the individual members can bond and develop collective actions, but also give meaning to human life, enhancing even further the social function of the tribe.

This implies in particular that individual members of the species *Homo sapiens* should be viewed as boundedly rational. It is their use of fictional narratives that are successful in many of the environments in which the human species evolved (Tversky and Kahneman 1974). Such a perception that our rationality is inherently bounded with respect to the information we have regarding our environment and of ourselves, the cognitive limitations of our minds and the time available to make the decision fits with findings from a variety of different disciplines that have investigated the human mind. This leads to the acceptance of the hypothesis that our cognitive and computational abilities are fundamentally bounded.

This is formalised through the introduction of the first fundamental hypothesis of our framework for modelling human economic collaboration.

**Hypothesis 1** *An economic agent is an economic decision-maker who satisfies the following fundamental hypotheses:*

*Social Brain hypothesis:* *Economic agents interact in large and complex social groups that embody flexible cooperative societies through which they collectively solve complex problems of survival. This ability is based on the genetic willingness to accept and adhere to collective fictional narratives to guide one's decisions and participation in the social group.*

**Bounded Rationality hypothesis:**    *Every economic agent has limited cognitive abilities to compute the consequences of their own and others' actions.*

The two hypotheses brought together in the notion of an economic agent appear to stand diametrically opposed to each other. Indeed, the social brain is a positive force that allows humans to cooperate and to overcome adverse situations in a collective fashion. It is a *building force*. It can also be understood as a *centripetal force* that binds humans into a social infrastructure.

As discussed above, the Social Brain hypothesis originates from Dunbar's proposition that the human brain evolved to allow humans to cooperate in larger social entities that collectively solve problems in their natural environment and habitat (Dunbar 2009). Here I state the hypothesis in a different form, to facilitate a purely economic interpretation and to build upon it to explain the emergence of the social division of labour as the main driver for creating economic wealth.

On the other hand, bounded rationality implies that these assumed human abilities are actually restrained and as such can be interpreted as a limiting force. This can also be understood as a *centrifugal force*: Bounded rationality is limiting human abilities, and it pushes individuals away from each other by limiting common understanding and potential collaboration. This contrasts significantly to the social brain as a centripetal or binding force.

There are two natural consequences to bounded rationality that can be formulated as two lemmas to the bounded rationality hypothesis. First, a direct expression of bounded rationality is Dunbar's number, which describes the upper limit to the human ability to retain information about other humans:

**Lemma 1.1 (Dunbar's Number)** *Every human being has on average the ability to remember the names and faces of approximately 150 other humans (Dunbar 1992).*

The second consequence of bounded rationality is that humans fundamentally cannot predict the consequences of their actions. In economics, this is known as Knightian uncertainty (Knight 1921).[12] An alternative formulation would be to state that we are unable to forecast the future in any significant detail.

---

[12] In the context of the Knightian uncertainty concept, I point out the difference between risk and uncertainty. *Risk* refers to measurable probabilities attached to future events. Risk is as a consequence computable and we can make assessments of risky situations using statistical tools and methods. *Uncertainty*, however, refers to unmeasurable events. Hence, if a situation is uncertain we cannot attach objective probabilities to the related events. Uncertain outcomes are consequentially uncomputable.

**Lemma 1.2 (Knightian Uncertainty)** *Economic agents are unable to predict and assess the full consequences of their collective and individual actions and interactions.*

Knightian uncertainty affects our daily economic affairs directly. Some direct consequences of it are captured in the notion of *transaction costs*, which refer to the costs related to conducting socio-economic interactions. Most of these costs directly emanate from the fundamental inability to predict the consequences of doing these economic transactions; this includes the correct price of the commodities traded as well as the assessment of the quality of those goods.

Second, Knightian uncertainty implies the fundamental unpredictability of the macro-economy. We are confronted with this regularly, in particular during the institutional trust crisis in the contemporary global economy after the Great Panic of 2008 (see Chap. 2 of this book). Of course, econometric techniques are used to generate approximations to trends in the global economy, but when unpredicted events hit the global economy these approximations do not forecast these trends very well.

There is another viewpoint of the fundamental hypotheses of the social brain and bounded rationality and how they relate. Indeed, the one cannot exist without the other. Since humans are boundedly rational, they have to overcome this deficiency by extending their abilities. This is done through social interaction and cooperation. It is in this regard that the boundedness of human abilities drives human cooperation. Thus the boundedness of the human brain facing survival in a hostile environment relates directly to the human social brain.

As such, these defining properties of the human condition are inseparable but opposite. They are at the foundation of many of the arising conflicts in human societies. Another interpretation would be to identify these two properties as being "dual" in nature.

### 1.2.1    Human Sociality and Organisation

The evolution of *Homo sapiens* resulted in the interplay between the human brain and his social environment. Prehistoric humans typically operated in tribes and these tribes form the social platform on which economic activities develop. Thus humans hunt in parties and can capture and kill much larger and more dangerous animals than a single human can. A single human is actually completely insignificant in the face of a mammoth or a lion, but collectively humans can set up hunting parties and overcome these odds.

The main human ability is that of *flexible* social organisation. Unlike other animal and hominin species, *Homo sapiens* has been able to organise cooperation flexibly and effectively. The ability to do so emerged 70,000 years ago and has been called the *cognitive revolution* (Harari 2014, Part One). Since then the human species has changed the face of the earth and affected all parts of the world that it inhabits. For example, as Harari describes, after settling in the Australian subcontinent 45,000 years ago, humans have hunted many abundant animal species there into extinction. This changed the Australian subcontinent forever; no other animal or hominin species has had such a profound effect on its environment and the natural habitat in general.

The biological evolution of the human brain, therefore, goes hand in hand with our ability to socially interact and, particularly, to empathise with others. Our brain holds information about others so that we are able to recognise them and are able to identify the social signals they communicate to us. These social signals can be very subtle compared with those used by other species. Here I refer to the subtle difference between smiling and laughter, which are unique human traits, and the human ability to recognise very subtle facial expressions.

As mentioned, this empathy is exemplified by the unique human ability to accept and adhere to collective fictional narratives. These narratives guide the actions and decisions of the individual members of the tribe and allow the emerging social organisation of such a tribe to be extremely flexible and effective. Ultimately these collective fictional narratives are transformed into social *institutions* such as the acceptance of leadership and a social hierarchy; of tribal rituals that bond the members; of specific practices; and also of guidelines in the social organisation of economic production, such as hunting. The emergence of institutions that guide an individual's behaviour is a quintessential human trait that allows the emergence of a flexible human social organisation of activities.

**Governance: The Role of Institutions**   As discussed, the human social brain facilitates the formulation and acceptance of common fictional narratives that guide human behaviour and interaction (Beaudreau 2004; Harari 2014; Haegens 2015). Indeed, by building on such common narratives, a *commons* was created around which all members of a tribe could come together and assume a collective identity (Beaudreau 2004, Chapter 2). Not only did these narratives explain observed phenomena, they made it possible to accept a tribal identity and even hierarchical authority emanating from tribal and religious practices.

Harari (2014) points out that human social organisation evolved in uncountably many forms. There were organisation structures founded on patriarchal, matriarchal, dictatorial and purely communal or even Marxian principles.[13] From this myriad of socio-economic organisation forms there emerges a common understanding about human sociality: the organisation of economic wealth creation is always driven by a set of commonly accepted socio-economic institutions.

The common fictional narratives on which human social organisation has been and still is founded are referred to as socio-economic *institutions*. As

---

[13] I explore some of these organisation forms in the model of wealth creation in Sect. 1.4 of this chapter.

pointed out, the emergence of these institutions is a direct consequence of the interplay of the social brain and the boundedness of human social abilities. In human evolution there emerged a variety of such institutions. The most basic are the media that conduct our direct interactions such as language, hand gestures and facial expressions. The difference between laughing and smiling is one of these human institutions that is unique: a smile builds confidence and understanding, while laughter might be condescending and undermine confidence (Seabright 2010).

More advanced institutions are the rules of human organisation. These include the practices and consequences of the social hierarchy that is adopted in the human community or society. This is closely followed by religious beliefs and practices. Human religious practices result usually in a hierarchical authority structure, which affects the overall social organisation of the society. Central authority is actually essential for all human socio-economic activities and endeavours. Gilles et al. (2015) show that stable economic environments are only possible in the context of hierarchically structured socio-economic organisations.

With the establishment of a central authority in a human community, more commonly accepted behavioural rules and heuristic guides to human interaction can be introduced. This forms the foundation to what I can denote as "governance" of human socio-economic interaction. The next lemma is a formal statement of this; its validity follows from the two fundamental hypotheses formulated in the definition of an economic agent.

**Lemma 1.3 (Governance)** *From the interplay of the social brain and its inherent boundedness, there emerges a system of institutions that governs the socio-economic interactions in a human community. All human socio-economic interaction is conducted through the intermediation of institutions that make up our common accepted governance system.*

The human social brain affords the development of common fictional narratives within a human community, society and even a nation, which translates into a *governance system* of institutions that guide human behaviour. Once established, this governance system expands to include numerous alternative advanced instruments, heuristics and tools. It allows the individual human brain to expand beyond its inherent limitations. Indeed, the individual human brain even lifts to a certain extent the fundamental uncertainty that surrounds us and makes behaviour by other humans more predictable.

**Socio-Economic Embeddedness** The existence of a governance system of institutions and social heuristics is a hypothesis that is shared with a substantial economic literature, including institutional economics and "new" institutional economics. When discussing the nature of economic action, Torsten Veblen (1898, pp. 188–193) remarked that "man mentally digests the content of habits under whose guidance he acts, and appreciates the trend of these habits and propensities. [···] By selective necessity he is endowed with a proclivity for purposeful action. [···] He acts under the guidance of propensities which have been imposed upon him by the process of selection to which he owes his differentiation from other species." To Veblen, habits—which evolved from a process of natural selection—guide economic action and decision-making. These ways of doing things become embedded within the economic decision-maker herself.

The discussion of habits proposed by Veblen propagated a discussion of more external forces that guide decision-making; namely formal and informal institutions. The economic historian Douglass North provides a general definition of institutions, stating that institutions are the "humanly devised constraints that structure political, economic and social interaction" (North 1991, p. 4). Here, institutions are viewed as rules that provide the relative payoffs to the actions and strategies of individual humans. We follow these rules blindly in order to form economic interactions and realise gains from trade.

These perceptions regarding the nature of economic decision-making suggest that on the one hand human decision-makers are embedded in institutions, but on the other hand institutions are also embedded within these humans. Thus, one can view the governance system as an extension of the individual human brain: it is the social brain on communal steroids. As a consequence, we can no longer distinguish the individual from the social or the communal.[14] I refer to this fundamental property as socio-economic embeddedness: humans can no longer distinguish their individual characteristics and beliefs from the beliefs and heuristics in the collective institutional governance system.

**Lemma 1.4 (Embeddedness Hypothesis)** *Individual humans completely accept and identify with the prevailing institutional governance system in their social environment. Consequently, their socio-economic interactions are guided through the institutions that form this governance system.*

We can conclude that humans are not purely individualistic, but have to be assessed and viewed within the context of their commonly accepted governance system of socio-economic institutions; humans "embody" the socio-economic institutions that govern their behaviour and decision-making. Of course, unique individualistic abilities and characteristics make many humans more or less accepting of certain aspects of the prevailing governance system, but only through the intermediation of institutions that make up the common governance system can these individuals interact in a meaningful way with other humans.

It is actually rather difficult for humans in the twenty-first century to accept that they are not completely individualistic. In fact, our secular or humanistic

---

[14] This is completely antithetical to the argument that we are purely individualistic and that all our economic decisions are guided and driven by purely individualistic characteristics. This argument is known in economics as the hypothesis of *methodological individualism*.

individualism is just another fictional narrative that is promoted by neo-liberal politicians and marketing campaigns. We are actually much less individualistic than we pretend: our preferences are mostly socially induced and our productive abilities result from training in an educational system that operates under commonly accepted standards of knowledge and vocational abilities.[15]

The human condition that emerges from the embeddedness hypothesis is one that human nature embodies social being as well as individual being. Our individualism only exists in the social context of other humans; if one found oneself alone in the Sahara desert, one would have ultimate freedom from collective institutions, but one would be completely lost and without existential basis. Humans are no monads; they are interacting through the matrix that is provided in their society, in particular through the intermediation of the prevailing governance system (Simon 1991).

One of the major fallacies of our contemporary economic beliefs is that individualism and individual freedom are considered to be absolute. This is founded on Humean traditions that originated in the Enlightenment period in the eighteenth century (Hume 1740, 1748). Nevertheless, our human condition is one of permanent conflict of the individual in his or her social environment. *Individual* freedom is a social construct; on the other hand, *social* freedom is essential for building society and a functional and productive economy.[16]

I also remark here that socio-economic embeddedness is a *centripetal social force*, akin to how I categorised the social brain and its socio-economic effects. Indeed, embeddedness immediately follows from the social brain hypothesis and in this regard translates the social brain into an effective instrument of economic activity. Through the adoption of the various socio-economic institutions, humans are able to collaborate effectively, which is an expression of the socio-economic embeddedness described here.

**The Entrepreneurial Function** The opposite force to socio-economic embeddedness is the human ability to develop and innovate the institutions that guide their socio-economic actions. This refers to the ability to introduce new institutional instruments in society to change the economic wealth creation processes. I link this ability directly to the well-known concept of "entrepreneurship". Clearly, entrepreneurship in this context is a much broader

---

[15] That modern humans have social preferences is commonly observed in economic experiments that have been conducted during the past decades. Under methodological individualism, this has been explained as "altruism" or "inequality aversion", but I would like to categorise these explanations as just more fictional narratives. I refer to Bowles and Gintis (2011) and Gintis (2017) for an extensive overview of experimental evidence for this and a comprehensive discussion of the resulting insights.

[16] Social freedom refers to the ability to build relationships with other individuals, thereby giving up parts of one's individual freedom. The assumption of a role in the governance system of socio-economic institutions is part of this social freedom as well. I refer to Chap. 3 for a detailed discussion of this aspect of the theory set out here.

descriptor than the usual one, which is limited to initiating and managing incorporated capitalist production organisations. In the theoretical framework developed here, I refer to entrepreneurship as a human activity that leads to any modification of an existing socio-economic institution or the development and introduction of new socio-economic institutions that affect economic wealth creation processes in society.

As a consequence, entrepreneurship is a term that is too narrow for the functional role it has in the context of human economic agency. Instead, I will use the notion of the *entrepreneurial function* in a human economy. It refers to the broad category of human socio-economic activities that affect the functioning of the institutional governance system that guides economic agents in their economic wealth creation processes.

**Lemma 1.5 (The Entrepreneurial Function)** *Institutional change in the human economy is driven by the entrepreneurial function that represents how economic agents change the prevailing socio-economic institutions through their actions and behaviours.*

The entrepreneurial function acts in two different forms. The first, most prevalent, form is the evolutionary process of change in an institutional economy. Over time habits and expectations change, which induces changes in the governance system that guides the social division of labour. This is very much a collective process and, as such, is a form of collective entrepreneurship. It can be referred to as the *weak* entrepreneurial function.

The second, more direct, form of the entrepreneurial function is *entrepreneurship* in its regular and narrower interpretation. This refers to a revolutionary or punctuated change induced by the actions of a limited number of economic agents—usually a single person, the "entrepreneur". I will be discussing these different forms of entrepreneurship as expressions of the more general force denoted as the entrepreneurial function throughout this book.

I interpret the entrepreneurial function as a general socio-economic force that acts in the context of a human economy. It embodies the human ability to develop more complex and effective socio-economic agents to further human collaboration and to advance the wealth creation processes in the economy. It embodies fundamental socio-economic processes that extend the human social brain and overcome the limitations imposed on it through human bounded rationality. In that regard it is directly linked to the boundedness of human socio-economic abilities and, as such, has to be recognised as a centrifugal force: Entrepreneurial activity expands the bounds of human socio-economic ability and furthers the wealth creation processes that economic agents can collectively enact.

**The Two Forces in a Balanced Human Economy**  Socio-economic embeddedness (Lemma 1.4) and the entrepreneurial function (Lemma 1.5) form two opposite forces in a human economy that affect its performance and its ability to generate collective wealth. In a balanced economy, these forces interact productively. Economic agents would be sufficiently embedded to have the full benefits of the institutions that guide the collective wealth creation processes. On the other hand, the entrepreneurial function should be developed sufficiently to allow for sufficient institutional development to enhance these wealth creation processes.

However, in many historical episodes these two fundamental forces are insufficiently balanced and the economy will enter a severe institutional crisis. Most recently this has been the case in the Great Financial Panic of 2008, which I will discuss in detail in Chap. 2. In the run-up to that crisis, the entrepreneurial drive to innovate in the financial sector of the global economy resulted in the development of toxic financial instruments that could not be sustained in the prevailing institutional environment. This caused a disruption of the balance in the financial sector of the global economy, causing the banking trust crisis at the heart of the financial panic that swept the global economy.

There have also been historical periods in which economic progress was strong and steady, founded on a balanced functioning of effective socio-economic embeddedness in combination with appropriate socio-economic institutional development to allow for a strong economic performance. I refer to the "Global Plan" period from 1945 to the late 1960s, during which the global capitalist economy grew strongly through steady development of innovative and productive socio-economic institutions.

As history indicates, the two fundamental forces in the human economy have a tendency to become unbalanced on a regular basis. The periods of balanced socio-economic development are interrupted owing to growing instabilities and institutional drift. This results in the crises mentioned here.

### 1.2.2    The Nature of Socio-Economic Trust

The introduction of a governance system of human institutions and heuristics that guides human behaviour to allow members of a human society to cooperate and leads to the embeddedness hypothesis has a further consequence. Indeed, if these institutions form an extension of the individual human brain through the embeddedness hypothesis as argued, then humans are able to interact through the bond that we know as trust or trusting behaviour. It refers to the human ability to blindly assume that fellow humans are fully embedded in the same governance system of institutions and heuristics as they themselves are. Hence we do not question the assumption that other members of our socio-economic environment follow and apply the same institutions and adhere to the same behavioural rules and heuristics as we do; we assume that we share a common institutional matrix in which we operate and build cooperative collaborations with other humans.

Hardin (2006) emphasises that trust is truly blind and unquestioned. Only if it is proven that another human is untrustworthy would we deviate from this fundamental assumption and ostracise this person from our circle. In this regard, trust has to be distinguished from trustworthiness. Indeed, trustworthiness refers to a much more rational process; it only comes into the picture if we suspect a violation of our trust. Trustworthiness is founded on observed behaviour of the other person, while trust is more fundamental and refers to our institutional embeddedness.

In the framework set out here, I base the theoretical foundation of such trusting behaviour on the definition that trust actually refers to the *dual* of embeddedness. This implies that trust is simply the other side of the embeddedness relationship between humans and the governance system of institutions and heuristics that guide our social behaviour. In all our social actions we blindly follow these institutions and unquestionably assume that our fellow tribal members are similarly embedded. In other words, trust is a phenomenon that is a manifestation of the embeddedness of our social behaviour in a well-defined and commonly accepted set of institutions, behavioural rules and heuristics. As such, the presence of trust is simply an expression of socio-economic embeddedness in a system of socio-economic institutions that guide our behavioural choices.

Only if other humans do not adhere to these institutional principles of social conduct do we question their embeddedness in the same governance system. This might be the case if the other person is corrupt—that is, the other person is a member of the same tribe, but deliberately undermines the common behavioural principles to become individually better off. Or it is the case if the other person is a member of a different tribe that is founded on a different governance system. The latter might be the case if different tribes interact in friendship or in strife; Graeber (2011) refers to anthropological rituals of gift exchange between neighbouring tribes to establish a common ground and to build trustworthiness.[17]

In conclusion, the trust hypothesis is a direct consequence of the embeddedness hypothesis and, as a consequence, has to be stated as a lemma that follows from it.

**Lemma 1.6 (Trust Hypothesis)** *The socio-economic embeddedness of economic interaction and socio-economic trust embody a duality.*

The consequences of the embeddedness hypothesis and its dual, the trust hypothesis, are that human society truly can take shape to facilitate social

---

[17] I emphasise here that true trust can only be established if this common ground expands to a governance system in which both tribes accept the same social institutions and heuristics in their acceptable social conduct. Such institutional expansion is at the foundation of globalisation.

behaviour. Hence human society provides a matrix in which humans can develop, be supported and be protected:

> Each human being depends for survival on the immediate and broader surrounding society. Human beings are not the independent windowless Leibnitzian monads sometimes conjured up by libertarian theory. Society is not imposed on humans; rather, it provides the matrix in which we survive and mature and act on the environment. Families and the rest of society provide nutrition, shelter and safety during childhood and youth, and then the knowledge and skills for adult performance. Moreover, society can react to a person's activities at every stage of life, either facilitating them or severely impeding them. Society has enormous powers, enduring through a person's lifetime, to enhance and reduce evolutionary fitness.
>
> Herbert Simon (1991, p. 35)

The interplay of the embeddedness and trust hypotheses facilitates the emergence of a human society in which our social brains can reach out to each other. The next step is to facilitate the creation of human wealth through this web of social interaction. This leads us to accept that economic wealth is created through a social division of labour and that this is an expression and a consequence of the human social brain, in particular our embeddedness and our trusting behaviour. This is the subject of the next stage in the development of our theoretical framework.

## 1.3    THE SOCIAL ORGANISATION OF ECONOMIC WEALTH CREATION

Any theory of economic development and the emergence of a process of economic wealth creation should first address the economic nature of the human individual decision-maker. This should encompass the individual's productive abilities as well as her consumptive desires or needs. Extending our axiomatic framework, I arrive at a further characterisation of an economic agent as a bearer of productive abilities as well as consumptive needs.[18] This is laid down in Hypothesis 2:

**Hypothesis 2 (Embodiment of Production and Consumption)** *Economic agents are the principal bearers of consumptive needs as well as productive abilities.*

---

[18] The concept of an economic agent as the embodiment of an economic decision-maker was seminally proposed by Yang (1988) and further developed in Yang and Ng (1993), Yang (2001, 2003) and Gilles (2017b). This embodiment is also referred to as a *consumer-producer*. This notion stands in contrast to the standard neo-classical hypothesis that consumption and production are socially separated: Neo-classical economics is firmly founded on the social dichotomy of consumption and production. See the discussion below.

This embodiment hypothesis introduces a unified view of two fundamental economic forces. Indeed, an economic agent is the ultimate and unique source of the two fundamental forces of production and consumption in a human economy. This source is human in nature; not technical. However, the unification of production and consumption that is introduced through Hypothesis 2 allows us nevertheless to inspect these two fundamental sources separately.

It should be emphasised that the two economic abilities of consumption and production that are embodied in the economic agent only come to full fruition through social interaction. Indeed, it is through the social brain that economic agents tap into their economic abilities to engage in a wealth-creating interaction. So, if a tribe of humans hunts a large animal, individuals use their specific productive abilities to generate economic wealth, which is subsequently realised through the consumptive abilities of these same individuals.

The embodiment hypothesis also introduces the notion that production and consumption could be considered separately. This is traditionally referred to as the *dichotomy* of production and consumption. It depends on the social arrangements whether that is actually the case. Hence the institutions in the governance system determine whether the dichotomy between production and consumption is socially expressed. For example, hunting and foraging of food can be fully separated from the consumption of this food in the activities of the tribe. In more advanced economies founded on the use of a price mechanism to guide economic decisions, consumption and production are strictly separated. This is discussed in subsequent chapters.

I emphasise that the embodiment hypothesis only addresses the potential dichotomy of production and consumption decisions solely at the *individual* level. It does not concern the social dichotomy of production and consumption at the *social* or *collective* level discussed above. Later I will point out that this social dichotomy—which is at the foundation of standard neo-classical growth theory—results quite naturally in an incorporated economy; however, it does not emerge within the human relational economy developed here.

I have now set out the social model of an economic decision-maker: an economic agent is an embodiment of productive and consumptive abilities, who can engage with other economic agents in a cooperative activity in a well-structured society guided by a defined set of institutions, behavioural rules and heuristics. This sets us up for the next step in our theory, the foundations of a social process of economic wealth creation.

**Methodological Individualism**  One of the neo-classical founding axioms of scientific methodology is the one that prescribes that the unit of theorising is that of the individual economic decision-maker (Arnsperger and Varoufakis 2006). This is referred to as *methodological individualism* in the literature on economic scientific methodology. It reduces all socio-economic processes to interactions between individual decision-makers. Individual decision-makers are endowed with opportunities and abilities as well as an objective that they try to optimise. The outcomes of all socio-economic processes in this reductionist approach are therefore states in which none of these individual decision-makers have an incentive to deviate from that equilibrium state. In principle, this methodology effectively denies the existence of any social forces, unless reducible to the equilibrium outcomes purely resulting from individual decision-making.

The vision of a socio-economic actor postulated in the embodiment Hypothesis 2 in combination with its definition postulated as Hypothesis 1 introduces a different, enhanced methodology. Indeed, economic decisions are made by individual economic agents, but they operate in an environment that is more structured and in which collective decisions are possible that are individually suboptimal for the decision-makers considered. So economic actors would be willing to sacrifice individual well-being for the "greater" or "public" good, which trait is observed throughout the history of the human economy. This can be referred to as *social decision-making* in comparison with self-motivated individual decision-making.

It is clear that methodological individualism is a further specification of the framework postulated through Hypotheses 1 and 2 postulating the nature of human economic actors. Indeed, methodological individualism excludes the possibility of social decision-making and introduces a view of the economy as a social organisation that only regulates itself through balancing the individualistic incentives of all decision-makers: the system thus reaches an equilibrium state in which all decision-makers have no incentive to deviate from the prescribed actions.

The exclusion of social motives in decision-making and the true ability of altruism and self-sacrifice by decision-makers only can be introduced through the appropriate adjustment of the objectives of these individual decision-makers. Thus altruism becomes an individual trait rather than a social norm that more subtly directs tribal members to share outputs with other members under different circumstances. Here, on the other hand, I argue the viewpoint that this targeted form of altruism is not an individual trait, but rather a socio-economic behavioural norm that is part of the governance system.

**Reflecting on the Economic Nature of Consumption and Production** The embodiment Hypothesis 2 allows us to inspect further the nature of economic consumption and production. Here, *production* is the ability to convert certain inputs into certain other outputs. In more economic terms, we view production as the ability to convert certain economic goods into other economic goods. The notion of an economic good is used very abstractly here: it could mean any form of human labour or knowledge, but it could also represent physical goods such as food stuff or timber to build shelter.

If the outputs of a production process are processed through an agent's consumptive abilities, they generate *economic value*.[19] The economic goods

---

[19] I refer to the Oxford English Dictionary's definition of the term "value" as *The importance or preciousness of something*. What I refer here to as "economic value" is referred to as "use value" by

that are processed in this fashion are denoted as *consumption goods*, which, through the agents' consumptive abilities, are then converted into economic value. Here I use the term "economic value" quite loosely and without any theoretical context. Rather the term just expresses that the consumption goods resulting from a production process add to our existence in the community that we live in. Throughout I assume that the only relevant form of economic value is that of consumptive value, the satisfaction that is derived from the act of consumption.

As pointed out above in the discussion of the embodiment Hypothesis 2, productive activities are in the human context very closely intertwined with consumptive activities. Indeed, "consumption" as such is also a production process; it converts consumption goods as a specific category of economic goods into (consumptive) economic values. For example, the act of preparing and cooking a meal is a necessary act of conversion required before the actual consumption of most food stuffs. Thus, even though a head of lettuce is principally a consumption good, it has to be prepared—washed, sliced and tossed into a salad—before its consumption properties can be accessed. In this regard, for all practical reasons the act of *consumption* itself could even be seen as an act of *production of consumption values*. So, in many respects, all of human economic activity is actually purely productive in nature.

However, it would be unwise to not separate the ultimate attainment of consumptive value through the acquisition of consumptive properties of the generated consumption goods from the act of producing these. So two intertwined concepts, namely the agent's individualistic productive abilities and the agent's consumptive function—described by the resulting consumption values generated from consuming the generated consumption goods—have to be introduced at the foundation of the description of an economic agent, introduced in the embodiment Hypothesis 2.

### 1.3.1   Increasing Returns to Specialisation in Production

The nature of human productive abilities is unique in the sense that it is subject to a fundamental property, namely that repeating the same task makes a person more proficient at executing that task. In other words, human productive activity is subject to *learning*. This implies that if individuals concentrate on the repetitive execution of certain tasks, their productivity increases: more units of output are generated within the same time span and using lower required levels of inputs.[20]

---

Marx (1867, Chapter 1). The term "use" seems more appropriate for physical goods, but less so for service goods. This justifies the term used here.

[20] This exactly refers to what is meant with the word "productive" as it actually refers to increased ability. Indeed, the Oxford English Dictionary gives as one of the accepted definitions that productive means "achieving a significant amount or result".

We express this by saying that human productive activity is subject to Increasing Returns to Specialisation.[21] Here I define Increasing Returns to Specialisation as the property that specialising in the production of a single output results in a higher productivity, meaning that with the same amount of inputs a larger number of outputs can be generated.

**Hypothesis 3 (Increasing Returns to Specialisation, or IRSpec)** *Human productive abilities are subject to the property that specialising in the production of any single input is maximally efficient.*

As pointed out by Seabright (2010) and Ridley (2010), the self-conscious acceptance of this IRSpec property is uniquely human. Hominid species other than *Homo sapiens* have not consciously recognised their ability to use the property of increased returns to specialisation to build a social system of production based on a division of labour that collectively is subject to IRS. *Homo sapiens* has been the only species that has accomplished this society-building task and has engaged in the great human economic experiment of founding its existence on this social ability of accumulating collective wealth (Seabright 2010, Chapter 18). Our close hominin cousins, the Neanderthals, seem not to have been consciously aware of this property (Horan et al. 2005; Kuhn and Stiner 2006).

### 1.3.2    Gains from Trade

From the previous discussion, IRSpec addresses the properties describing the productive abilities of individual economic agents. However, this is only one side of the possibility to fruitfully generate economic wealth. As discussed in relation to the embodiment Hypothesis 2, economic wealth is ultimately expressed in the values generated through the consumption of the produced consumption goods. What are the properties that are descriptive of the consumptive abilities of these economic agents?

The main assumption about consumption that has been developed in economics is that consumers prefer mixed bundles of consumption goods over bundles consisting of very few goods. This is also known as *consumptive smoothing*. The happiness from consumption is increased by making more consumption goods available. Throughout economic history the economy has been able to generate more and more consumption goods.[22]

---

[21] This compares to the neo-classical notion of increasing returns to scale (IRS). The latter refers to the ability to have increasing output per unit of input if the production process is enlarged in total. This mainly refers to industrial or societal production processes, rather than the ability of a single individual.

[22] As an illustration for the principle that mixed consumption bundles are preferred, I refer to the symbol of ultimate consumptive sumptuousness, the Dutch-Indian *Rijsttafel*. After the Dutch East-Indian Company (VOC) established itself in the Dutch Indies—Indonesia, as it is known

Most peasants—from prehistoric tribal times through medieval times into the twentieth century—have lived in mud huts and only consumed simple foodstuffs; clearly these peasants needed both categories of fundamental consumption goods to survive. Only through the rise of economic wealth after the industrial revolution did large classes of humans gain access to a wide variety of consumption goods that went beyond basic foodstuffs and shelter. In our modern affluent global economy, we have access to a wide variety of foodstuffs, furnishings to make our dwellings pleasant family homes, a variety of goods to support different transportation modes and a wide variety of luxury goods that are not directly required for basic human survival. This latter category includes, for example, electronic consumables and entertainment outside the home.

The fundamental principle that humans "want it all" is embodied by the mathematical property that humans have *convex consumptive preferences*: Mixed consumption bundles are preferred over bundles of just a few different goods.[23] The convexity of human consumptive preferences is as fundamental as the hypothesis of increasing returns to specialisation 3. I refer to this convexity hypothesis as the principle of "gains from trade".

**Hypothesis 4 (Gains from Trade)** *Economic agents prefer to consume mixed bundles of consumption goods over bundles that contain only a limited set of such consumption goods.*

The gains from trade hypothesis results in the fundamental potential to generate significant economic wealth through a social organisation of production and trade. Indeed, specialised individual economic agents delve into their abilities of increasing returns to specialisation in production to produce large quantities of a single output. This results into a social division of labour that delivers a high level of output of consumption goods. Through the process of trade between these specialised individuals these outputs are mixed into consumption bundles.

Therefore, the convexity of human consumptive preferences implies that there are indeed gains from trade of consumption goods produced by fully specialised economic agents. As pointed out in our discussion, human behaviour is guided through a common governance system of behavioural rules and heuristics—referring to the embeddedness hypothesis. Therefore, the trade of goods between specialised individuals occurs in a common infrastructure. This common infrastructure evolves from the embeddedness of the economic agents in the governance system and, thus, is guided by the institutions and heuristics that are embodied in the governance system.

---

today—they found a rich cooking culture. The Dutch colonists brought their own interpretation to this and started to mix the diverse meals into a single sumptuous meal.

[23] Formally, preferences are *convex* if for any two commodity bundles $x$ and $y$ such that if $x$ and $y$ are equally good ($x \sim y$), it holds that any mixed bundle of $x$ and $y$ is strictly better than both $x$ and $y$—that is, $tx + (1 - t)y \succ x$ as well as $tx + (1 - t)y \succ y$ for any $0 < t < 1$. This principle and its mathematical representation are further discussed in Gilles (2018).

The hypotheses of IRSpec and gains from trade provide a foundation for the emergence of the social organisation of economic activities in a human society. This foundation for the social division of labour is pursued in the next section.

### 1.3.3    The Social Organisation of Economic Wealth Creation

Humans recognised early on that individuals with the ability to specialise in a variety of productive tasks can be organised socially to achieve a collective state that generates collective economic wealth that is subject to *IRS*—if all inputs, including population, increase, then the total collective output increases more than proportionally. This means that if all used resources in the economy grow with a certain percentage $x\%$, then the generated collective output increases with *more than $x\%$*.

Human societies recognised that the appropriate social organisation of production allowed that society to use the IRSpec of individual productive abilities to coalesce in overall societal productivity that is subject to IRS. This social organisation is usually called the "social division of labour", and it forms the foundation of any human society since the emergence of the species *Homo sapiens* in the African continent.

On the other hand, *Homo neanderthalis* was a very successful hominin species that never seems to have established a social organisation founded on communities achieving collectively IRS. Indeed, the Neanderthals apparently never discovered the most rudimental social division of labour based on a division of tasks between the sexes. In primitive human hunter-gatherer societies, males usually hunted and females usually gathered. Cave paintings left by Neanderthals indicate that Neanderthal females hunted as well, reducing the likelihood that there was a functional social division of labour based on specialisation in production in Neanderthal societies. This indicates that such a gender-based social division of labour is uniquely human (Horan et al. 2005; Kuhn and Stiner 2006).

From a theoretical perspective, the step to a fully developed social division of labour requires an additional hypothesis that is as fundamental as the embodiment hypothesis, IRspec, and the gains from trade hypothesis. This hypothesis essentially formulates the realisation that a social organisation is more than just the sum of the individual abilities present in the human society; a social organisation frees up synergetic forces.

**Hypothesis 5 (The Effective Social Organisation of Production)** *Production in a human economy is based on the idea that through an appropriate social organisation individual human productive abilities—being subject to IRSpec— can be employed to achieve a social economy that generates collective economic wealth, which is subject to IRS.*

The organisation of the social economy introduced in the social organisation Hypothesis 5 refers to the division of specialised tasks among individuals within a human community. It refers to the social organisation of a community or society to achieve a collective social economy that is subject to IRS in its productive abilities. This is achieved through a *social division of labour*, which nature is subject of a further exposition.

Within a social division of labour, individual economic agents assume specialised productive tasks. This requires that individuals perform tasks that are recognisable by all members of the society as socially acceptable and economically viable. This social recognition involves two elements:

- First, the social recognition of an economic, productive task requires that the task is performed with socially recognised inputs and outputs. Thus, each task within a social division of labour concerns the conversion of socially recognised and measurable inputs into socially identifiable and measurable outputs.

- Second, the social division of labour is only functional as a social organisation—as called for in the social organisation Hypothesis 5—if the generated socially recognised consumption goods can be distributed among the members of the society in a socially recognised fashion. In economic terms, the generated outputs are *publicly exchangeable* with outputs generated by other specialised individuals. Such a public exchange can only occur through socially recognised exchange mechanisms.

This implicitly leads to the conclusion that such a social division of labour can only be established through the guidance of a set of effective socio-economic institutions and behavioural norms. Hence the implementation of a social division of labour requires a supportive social system of institutions and mechanisms. This system has previously been introduced as the *governance system* in which all economic agents are embedded.

This governance system has to encompass multiple economic elements: a set of socially recognised economic goods acting as inputs and outputs in the social division of labour; a set of socially accepted productive tasks, usually denoted as "professions" or "socio-economic roles"; a common language and cultural system that guides communication among individuals within the social economy; and, finally, a set of socially recognised exchange mechanisms founded on behavioural rules and supportive socio-economic institutions.[24]

---

[24] When tribal human societies coalesced in large empires—such as the Sumerian and the Egyptian empires—human economic development was accelerated through the creation of a large society around a common public project, the *res publica*. This particularly took the form of a religious project, exemplified by the temple economy of Sumer. A governance system can be viewed as an extension of this *res publica* in the sense that the common public project results and transforms itself into derivative socio-economic behavioural rules, socio-economic roles and other supportive economic institutions.

The embeddedness of economic interaction within a governance system is fundamental to our understanding of the social economy. This refers back to the interpretation and clarification of the social division of labour as a system in which individual production tasks are combined with economic exchange. This is summarised in the following specification, which is founded on the embeddedness hypothesis (Lemma 1.4) and the social organisation hypothesis (Hypothesis 5).

**Lemma 1.7 (The Social Division of Labour)** *The organisation of a social economy is formed as a social division of labour in which individuals execute specialised productive tasks and exchange the resulting outputs from these tasks through socially recognised exchange mechanisms. This social division of labour and exchange mechanism are guided through institutions in the governance system.*

We have now arrived at the point where we recognise that the fundamental organisation of a human society are centred around the social division of labour. A set of mechanisms and heuristics in the governance system allocates individuals to specialised tasks—or socio-economic roles—that are resolved through a trade mechanism in which these specialised individuals trade the produced goods, including intermediary inputs as well as consumption goods.

**A Numerical Illustration: A Simple Tribal Economy** To illustrate the concepts developed thus far, consider a tribal society in which unskilled labour time is converted into a skilled labour force that produces foodstuffs and basic shelter.

*Example 1.1* We assume that there are two economic goods, foodstuffs ($X$) and shelter ($Y$). Here, we think of foodstuffs as simple staples such as root vegetables, fruits, fish and meat and of shelter as simple huts made of straw and mud.

All tribe members desire foodstuffs and shelter in equal measure. We assume that the tribal leadership aims to deliver both goods $X$ and $Y$ in equal quantities to the individual tribe members. Therefore, the social division of labour is directed to generate equal total amounts of each good.

Unskilled labour providers can be trained as skilled hunter-gatherers, producing $X$ only, or as builders, producing $Y$ only. The social division of labour is founded on the following three roles:

(i) **Hunter-gatherer:** A tribe member can use all available labour time to hunt and gather foodstuffs such as meat, fruits and roots. This results in the production of four units of foodstuffs, represented by the basic production plan $P_H = (4, 0)$.[25]

---

[25] I emphasise here that a "unit" is a completely fictional and arbitrary enumerator of output. The indicator $P$ represents the output bundle of an individual for the two critical goods, foodstuffs and shelter.

(ii) **Builder:** A tribe member can also become a full-time provider of shelter, using wood and mud to build huts for other tribe members. This results in the production of four units of shelter, represented by the basic production plan $P_B = (0, 4)$.

(iii) **Unskilled tribe member:** A tribe member can remain unskilled and be engaged with providing both foodstuffs as well as shelter, represented by the production plan $P_U = (1, 1)$.

Furthermore, we allow for social learning in the resulting social division of labour.[26] Hence the size of the two main professional classes determines the synergies and social learning that occur in each of them. We let $\lambda \colon \mathbb{N} \to \mathbb{R}_{++}$ be a function that describes these synergies. Here $\lambda(k) > 0$ determines the resulting increases of labour productivity due to social learning. We impose that $\lambda(1) = 1$ and that $\lambda$ is strictly increasing: $\lambda(k) > \lambda(k')$ for all $k > k'$.

In particular, a hunter-gatherer, respectively a builder, in a professional class of size $k \in \mathbb{N}$ now generates an output represented by

$$P_H(k) = \lambda(k)\, p_H = (4\lambda(k),\, 0), \quad \text{respectively,} \quad P_B(k) = \lambda(k)\, p_B = (0,\, 4\lambda(k)). \tag{1.1}$$

We can now explore how the tribe should organise its production if the objective is to maximise the total collective output subject to having equal amounts of foodstuffs and shelter. We denote by $F \colon \mathbb{N} \to \mathbb{R}_+^2$ the function that gives the total collective output $F(n)$ resulting from an *optimal* social division of labour in a tribe of $n$ members. In particular, if $n$ is even, then the tribe is optimally organised by making half of the population hunter-gatherers and half of the population builders. If $n$ is odd, then a similar social division of labour is imposed, provided that exactly one tribe member is non-specialised.

For every $k \in \mathbb{N}$ we identify the resulting total collective output levels from the corresponding optimal social divisions of labour:

$$F(2k) = \qquad k \times P_H(k) + k \times P_B(k) \qquad = (4k\lambda(k),\, 4k\lambda(k)) \tag{1.2}$$

$$F(2k+1) = k \times P_H(k) + k \times P_B(k) + 1 \times P_U = (4k\lambda(k) + 1,\, 4k\lambda(k) + 1) \tag{1.3}$$

We use the standard definition that a collective output function *exhibits IRS* if for every $n \in \mathbb{N}$ and every $\mu > 1$ it holds that $F(\mu n) > \mu F(n)$.

Let $k, k' \in \mathbb{N}$ with $k > k'$. Then from $\lambda(k) > \lambda(k')$:

$$F(2k) = 4k\lambda(k)\,(1,\, 1) = \frac{k\lambda(k)}{k'\,\lambda(k')} F(2k') > \frac{k}{k'} F(2k') \tag{1.4}$$

---

[26] Here, *social learning* refers to the sharing of experiences and best practices among equally specialised tribe members. The size of the professional group is critical for social learning, since the more widespread and established a specialisation is, the higher the individual productivity of such a specialist. This strengthens the IRSpec property of the productive output of a single tribe member.

Hence IRS is confirmed for even population sizes, since

$$F(2k) > \frac{2k}{2k'} \, F(2k') \qquad (1.5)$$

These inequalities show that IRS emerges principally because of the effects of social learning in the social division of labour. ◆

A more complete implementation of IRS in the collective output function is possible for more complex production situations where synergies are more social and less individualistic, or where there are a larger number of goods produced through the social division of labour.

**Advanced Social Divisions of Labour** The nature of the social division of labour is that tasks are performed through a deliberate sequence. This allows the production of relatively complex consumption goods through multiple intermediary production stages, each performed by distinct specialised individuals. For example, in a relatively simple but moderately advanced "urban" economy, bread is produced through a number of distinct stages connected through the exchange of intermediate goods. A farmer grows wheat outside the town; the wheat is transported to a mill, where a miller grinds it into flour; and, finally, the flour is used by the town's baker to produce the final consumption good, bread. Only the final consumption good is allocated to the town's inhabitants.[27]

The social division of labour results in well-structured social production chains, naturally resulting with the conclusion that the trade infrastructure in the economy is organised in a complex network structure. Again, I generalise this insight beyond the constrained view of the social division of labour and apply this to any human economic interaction.[28]

**Lemma 1.8 (Relational Nature of Economic Interaction)** *Most forms of economic interaction are principally relational; economic interaction has mainly to be understood as being between economic agents that generate economic values that satisfy certain consumptive and/or productive needs.*

From the above, I conclude that the nature of the human economy has brought us to a view based on a socio-economic organisation with a social division of labour consisting of economic relationships that are embedded within a socially recognised governance system of social media, socio-economic roles (or professions), behavioural rules and related socio-economic institutions. This

---

[27] In a more primitive peasant economy, all production stages are executed by a single non-specialised individual, namely the peasant herself. The home-produced bread is consumed by the peasant as well. In this economy there is only a rudimentary social division of labour and no exchange of intermediate goods. In Chap. 2 of Gilles (2018) this type of society is called an *autarkic* economy.

[28] Exceptions are trade relationships within superstructure organisations such as centrally controlled and guided markets.

structural organisation is only functional and sustainable, though, if it is held together by a binding force. This fundamental bond is that of *trust*.

The introduction of our notion of an economic agent—as the embodiment of the human social brain subject to the bounded rationality hypothesis—implies that these economic agents are social networkers, or *Homo dictyous* (Christakis and Fowler 2009). The formation of networks of social and economic relationships depends on a set of rules and norms that guide society, forming the governance system. As economic interactions become more sprawling, there can emerge problems of opportunism and information asymmetries which naturally derive from the division of labour (Jackson et al. 2012). This is further exacerbated by the boundedness of human intelligence and cognition. This is supported by the following quote:

> [I]ncreasing specialization and division of labor necessitate the development of institutional structures that permit individuals to take actions that involve complex relationships with other individuals both in terms of personal knowledge and over time. The evolution of more complex social frameworks will not occur if such institutional structures cannot reduce the uncertainties associated with such situations. So, institutional reliability is essential, because it means that even as the network of interdependence caused by the growth of specialization widens we can have confidence in outcomes that are necessarily increasingly remote from our personal knowledge.
>
> Douglass North (1989, p. 1322)

In other words, the governance system needs to be developed sufficiently to allow for more involved socio-economic infrastructures to emerge.

**The Reproduction of Positions in the Social Division of Labour**   In classical political economy—through contributions by Adam Smith, David Ricardo and Karl Marx—it was assumed that labour in the social organisation of production has to be *reproduced*. This means that it is assumed that individuals who provide labour to the production processes require certain goods and services to sustain that provided labour force. This includes sufficient calorific intake from foodstuffs to maintain it, the availability of shelter, and the existence of supporting services such as health and social care.

Labour force reproduction is a natural concept if one considers the production of commodities through a social division of labour. The elements that form the inputs for the production of these commodities includes the labour force that is required in the production process. In turn, that labour force requires its own commodity inputs to be created, delivered and sustained. Therefore the commodity bundles that represent this labour reproduction should be included in the description of the social division of labour.[29]

---

[29] Classical political economists considered reproduction to be a completely natural element in their considerations of the capitalist economy. Marx (1867) developed his theory of capitalist exploitation on this feature of the social division of labour. This construct has been pursued further

This logic can naturally be extended to more abstract positions in the social division of labour. Indeed, in a capitalist economy the social division of labour is made up of human labour force providers as well as incorporated social production organisations, or "firms". If human labour providers require reproduction, it is natural to extend this logic to firms as well. To sustain itself, a firm requires the use of an elaborate set of commodities and services. Usually these required reproduction inputs are simply incorporated into the inputs of the firm's production process. Hence the reproductive inputs are inseparable from the direct inputs required in the production process. In cost terms, these are usually denoted as *fixed* versus *variable* production costs.

It is crucial for the assessment of the effectiveness of the social division of labour to distinguish reproduction explicitly in the production processes. Only if the collective output of the social division of labour exceeds the reproduction of all positions in that social division of labour can one talk about true economic wealth creation. The generated economic wealth is, therefore, defined as the *surplus* beyond this reproduction.

*Example 1.2* To illustrate this notion, I refer to the example of the simple tribal economy with hunter-gatherers and builders considered in Example 1.1. If each tribe member requires a reproduction of its labour of $R = (1, 1)$, then the economic wealth created through a social division of labour is computed as the surplus given by $S(n) = F(n) - nR$. For even population sizes $n = 2k$ we explicitly compute from the data given in Example 1.1 that

$$S(2k) = (4k\lambda(k), 4k\lambda(k)) - 2k(1, 1) = 2k[2\lambda(k) - 1](1, 1) \gg (2k, 2k) \tag{1.6}$$

This computation illustrates the generative power of a social division of labour, even constituted on a few simple socio-economic roles and professions.    ◆

This logic of surplus generation applies also to the model of an economy with a social division of labour formulated by Roemer (1980, 1981).

## 1.4    THE FUNCTIONING OF THE SOCIAL DIVISION OF LABOUR

Our axiomatic theory of human wealth creation has been founded on five fundamental hypotheses. These have guided us to the conclusion that wealth creation in a human economy is organised socially through a division of labour. This social organisation encompasses a relational trade infrastructure through

by Sraffa (1960) and Roemer (1981), who have both introduced mathematical representations of social division of labour that included descriptors of labour reproduction. I refer to Gilles (2018, Chapter 6) for more details of my discussion of production networks.

which specialised individuals interact and trade, achieving a higher standard of living than could be accomplished through autarky.

Next I investigate some consequences of this form of social organisation in a human economy. Before discussing these properties and consequences, I emphasise that my focus remains the human economy, rather than the capitalist, incorporated economy. I avoid discussing the complex organisational forms that arise in an economy that is centred around hierarchical social production organisations that incorporate a vertical division of labour, guided through the exercise of authority. Thus, we remain in the realm of a horizontal social division of labour that is centred on fully specialised and engaged individuals.

The conclusions that we draw in the context of a horizontal division of labour remain valid in a capitalist economy, which also encompasses incorporated, hierarchically structured social production organisations. I can even argue that all of these properties remain valid in the more complex organisational structure that is at the foundation of the contemporary capitalist global economy.

The main properties that are absent from our discussion here include mainly the Marxian discussion points, such as the systemic exploitation of certain classes of individuals in the social division of labour. This is much less pronounced in an economy that is founded on a horizontal division of labour even though it is possible, as currently shown in the form of the "gig economy" that has emerged in contemporary capitalism.[30]

Here, I limit myself to the discussion of four important aspects of the functioning of an economy in which wealth creation is conducted through a social division of labour.

- First, I debate the foundational logic that supports wealth creation through a social division of labour. One can identify two fundamentally different logics that are founded on opposite ideals of human productivity.
- Second, I discuss the fundamental relational nature of socio-economic interaction in an economy that is founded on a social division of labour. This includes the markets through which we trade the generated outputs from our production processes.
- Third, the relational trade infrastructure naturally imposes transaction costs on all interactions that are conducted through it. The resulting transaction efficiency is a core property that determines how advanced the social division of labour is that can be supported in the prevailing trade infrastructure and the institutions that govern it.
- Fourth, I consider the role of entrepreneurship and socio-economic innovation in an economy with a social division of labour. This role is fundamental and forms an essential aspect of conducting production

---

[30] I refer to the discussion of some important properties of advanced capitalist economies founded on a mixed social division of labour in Gilles (2018). There I will consider network models of the social division of labour that explicitly address the consequences of the absence of mobility and the existence of competitive barriers in the social division of labour.

processes. Therefore I refer to this as the "entrepreneurial function" in the social division of labour. It is the main source of institutional renewal and innovation and, as such, the main source of economic development and growth.

I do not claim that these four aspects are the only important emerging features of wealth creation through a social division of labour. In the literature, other aspects that are also rather fundamental have been identified. Some of these other aspects will be discussed later, in particular in the context of mathematical models of wealth creation and of the endogenous emergence of a social division of labour.

### 1.4.1    Two Views on Economic Wealth Creation

Economic wealth creation through a social division of labour is founded on three essential elements: (1) all human productive activity is subject to *IRSpec*, which is the main source of the created wealth; (2) there is a trade infrastructure through which specialised individuals interact and achieve *gains from trade*; and, (3) the emerging social organisation is guided through a system of *socio-economic institutions* that is founded on human institutional trust.

All three elements are essential in the economic wealth creation process, and as such form its *logic*—its *"raison d'être"*. All three elements need to be present to create conditions for the emergence of a social division of labour, which was the situation under which *Homo sapiens* developed in the African savannahs.

The main economic question is *how* these three elements come together and how a social division of labour emerges and functions. The theoretical explanation of the functioning of the social division of labour is that individual productive abilities are subject to IRSpec, causing the total output generated through the social division of labour to exhibit IRS. Therefore the fundamental source of economic wealth generation has been identified as the increasing efficiency of individual human productive abilities due to specialisation (IRSpec). Economists and social philosophers have focused on this source in their investigations, and there have emerged two different fundamental views to which we can attach the names of the two classical political economists Adam Smith and David Ricardo.[31]

Plato (380 BCE) and Aristotle (340 BCE, 350 BCE) already reflected on the IRSpec property as the fundamental source of economic wealth (Silvermintz 2010). Plato, Aristotle and many Enlightenment thinkers considered these increasing returns to originate from the talents of a specific individual: an

---

[31] I have adopted the terminology introduced by Buchanan and Yoon (2002) to delineate these two different viewpoints. Buchanan and Yoon refer to these viewpoints as "logics", which term I avoid. The logic of the social division of labour or of trade—as referred to by Buchanan and Yoon—is actually founded on the tripolar interaction between IRSpec, gains from trade and institutions in the social division of labour and its accompanying trade infrastructure.

economic agent specialises in those tasks in which he is particularly able to achieve IRSpec. Therefore these early thinkers did not recognise IRSpec to be a *universal* human trait, but rather an *individualistic* trait.

The work of Adam Smith changed this perspective. He proposed that IRSpec is very much a universal human trait: there is no requirement that individuals are required to tap into specific talents to achieve these increasing returns. Instead, every individual is in principle able to increase his or her output if specialised in certain specific tasks (Buchanan and Yoon 2002; Buchanan 2008). Indeed, most people are quite talentless, but still fully participate in economies that are founded on specialisation in the generation of economic wealth. As such, most people participate fully in the global division of labour that generates our collective economic wealth.

The two resulting views can now be summarised as follows:

**The Platonian or Ricardian view:**   The fundamental source of IRSpec is individualistic human talent. The source of economic wealth generation, therefore, has an individualistic logic. Individual differences guide the individual to assume the socio-economic role that is most suited to them and in which they are most productive. David Ricardo (1817) elevated this principle to its full logical conclusion and identified subjective differences of individual human talents and abilities as the principal sources of economic wealth creation. In this Ricardian view, individuals are guided to their chosen specialisations by their talents and abilities and, therefore, interpersonal differences are the fundamental source of economic wealth. Wealth creation itself is founded on *comparative advantages* between the members of the social division of labour.

**The Smithian view:**   Adam Smith (1776) describes an economy in which there emerges a social division of labour among *intrinsically identical* individuals. Essentially these individuals are guided by a system of governing institutions, inducing appropriate incentives, to some specialisation. Individual talents and abilities are fundamentally secondary in the production processes conducted among these individuals. Their interpersonal differences emanate from their specialisations rather than the other way around. Thus, the socio-economic roles in the division of labour are the fundamental source of interpersonal differences of individuals in the economy that is founded on this social division of labour.

The Smithian and Ricardian views are diametrically opposed. The differences between these two viewpoints are much more profound than one would initially suspect (Sun 2012, pp. 13–14). I discuss the main consequences from these two viewpoints in some detail.

First, I emphasise that contemporary neo-classical economic theory is firmly founded on the Ricardian view of the functioning of the wealth generation process. This is a natural consequence of the adoption of *methodological individualism* as the main principle of economic modelling: since all sources of economic wealth creation are theoretically placed with these individuals, the sources of this wealth obviously have to be attributed to that individual as well. The Smithian view is diametrically opposed to this, which by itself creates a rift between contemporary economic theorising and the principles emanating from the Smithian view that I discuss below.[32]

**Ricardo's Principle of Trade**  Ricardo (1817) seminally discussed the principles for mutually beneficial trade. He pointed out that the fundamental source of mutual gains from trade is the differences between the productivity rates between the trading parties. There are no *absolute* differences required, but rather *relative* differences in productivity. Even though one trade partner can have lower absolute output levels in all goods under complete specialisation than the other trade partner, mutually beneficial gains from trade can still arise if the less productive party specialises in the product that she is relatively most productive in. Hence it is the relative productivity that guides the specialisation decision, rather than the absolute productivity. This is referred to as the theory of *comparative advantage* in trade under endogenous specialisation, and it forms the major part of the foundation for the theory of international trade.

The source of the ability to trade and to create economic wealth is therefore the intrinsic, interpersonal differences between the parties in a trade relationship. Within a social division of labour the creation of economic wealth is founded on the intrinsic difference between the productivities of the individuals that make up that social division of labour. All these individuals are guided to that specialisation in which they are comparatively most productive; the social division of labour is firmly grounded in and founded on the interpersonal differences between individual talents and abilities.

There emerge two main consequences to this viewpoint. First, there might arise a problem in the absence of individual talent or ability concerning the production of certain goods. Indeed, if there is an absence of talent to produce a certain good, there might naturally result underprovision of that good. Therefore, economic development and the deepening of the social division of labour is accidental and completely guided by the presence and absence of individual talent.

Second, individual talents and abilities are the fundamental cause of the (relative) economic well-being of these individuals. Indeed, individual talents that apparently lead to high gains from trade in the social division of labour would cause an individual to become relatively rich, while a poor person apparently lacks the talents to assume a highly profitable position in the prevailing social division of labour. This leads to the conclusion that poverty is based on the lack of individual abilities, and in particular moral failings.

---

[32] I emphasise that the Smithian viewpoint is at the foundation of the approach developed here. I believe that the Smithian viewpoint is more natural in view of what we know of human evolution based on the social brain hypothesis. In this regard, the theoretical framework set out in this book and its companion volume are Smithian in principle. Similarly, the work of Yang (1988, 2001) and Yang and Ng (1993) can be interpreted as fundamentally Smithian in nature as well.

This viewpoint was promoted during the era of nineteenth-century Victorian capitalism and has recently made a come-back under neo-liberal ideology.

In this regard, the Ricardian viewpoint is a regression from Smith's position, since Ricardo's theory of comparative advantage harked back to Plato's original standpoint that talent drives IRSpec. As Yang and Ng (1993, Introduction) point out, the Ricardian frame of thought was the first step to abandon the study of economic wealth creation and to focus economics solely on the question of the allocation of generated wealth. This development ultimately resulted in neo-classical economics, which indeed focuses mostly on issues of allocation and redistribution of economic wealth. It even resulted in the abandonment of the study of the social division of labour.

**The Smithian View and Economic Competition**  If the source of economic wealth is founded on the intrinsic interpersonal differences among diversely specialised individuals, rather than their talents and abilities, there emerges a rather different view of the functioning of the human economy. Indeed, individuals are not guided by their individual talents, but rather by the social matrix provided in the human society in which they operate. Ultimately, it is the social system of training and education that determines the abilities of individuals to produce goods and determines the output of the production processes conducted through the social division of labour. The Smithian view is therefore more inclusive and socially comprehensive than the Ricardian view.

The differences between individuals are not driven by interpersonal differences of ability, but rather by the functioning of the social matrix that is provided in that society. Therefore, individual economic well-being is determined by whether individuals have equal access to the various roles in the social division of labour. Equality is therefore mainly a result of the *equality of opportunity* (Roemer 1998), or the equal access to education that facilitates a role or specialisation in the social division of labour.

The Smithian view thus reflects directly on an institutional approach to competition. The main form of competition is institutional, and is founded on the equal access to roles and positions in the matrix that makes up the social division of labour. Barriers to the free assumption of roles in the social division of labour are the main causes for imperfect competition and the resulting inequality.

I show in Gilles (2018, Chapters 3 and 4) that free mobility and open access to positions in the social division of labour results in a truly equal society in which market prices reflect the social cost of producing the good. In other words, in an open Smithian framework with free mobility between specialisations, there is no conflict between the labour value of the traded goods and their market value. It shows that Smith was fundamentally correct in his assessment that such free mobility—also referred to as "natural freedom"—leads to an equal and just economy in which the labour values of the traded goods are properly reflected in the market prices. It is clear that Smithian natural freedom is a form of social freedom, as discussed earlier.

Finally, Smith's ideal of natural freedom and equality of opportunity would be facilitated through an open and public system of education and training. Many education systems in our contemporary global economy meet these requirements. Indeed, these systems are founded on the principle that any student can master the required knowledge for any specialisation in our advanced global division of labour. This knowledge is a product of accomplishments, learning and scientific research conducted in the prevailing infrastructures of past generations. This established knowledge is so vast that individual talent and abilities are relatively unimportant in the assumption of a role in the social division of labour that is founded on it. That there are major inequalities in the contemporary global economy is a result of artificial barriers that restrict Smithian natural freedom and opportunity equality.

**The Smithian View and Socio-Economic Embeddedness** The Smithian point of view, that an individual's specialisation and role in the trade infrastructure in which the social division of labour is embedded, determines that individual's productive attributes can be extended to *all* attributes of that individual, productive as well as consumptive. The arguments for this are based on the following observations:

- First, the assumption of some socio-economic role in the social division of labour fully determines the reproduction bundle of commodities for that individual economic agent in that particular role. This differs for different roles and specialisations; the position in the social division of labour that the role prescribes also determines the reproduction requirements for that role.
- Second, the assumption of a socio-economic role in the production processes that are conducted through the prevailing division of labour demands a significant effort by the individual to acquire the required knowledge and adopt the prevailing institutional features of that role. This implies that the individual truly becomes embedded in that role and the institutional features that accompany it.

These arguments imply that the Smithian view fully supports the conclusion that all specialised economic agents are socio-economically embedded in the prevailing institutional governance system. Each individual agent is embedded in her assumed socio-economic role and adopts the particular institutions that determine that role and its immediate socio-economic environment. This also implies that the agent is embedded from the perspective of her consumptive activities, not only from the corresponding productive activities: this embeddedness is complete.

We conclude that the Smithian view conforms fully with the fundamental hypothesis of socio-economic embeddedness, and therefore fits with the axiomatic theory proposed in this chapter. This contrasts with the Ricardian view, which seems far less in line with the framework proposed here.

### 1.4.2    The Relational Nature of Economic Interaction

The theoretical framework set out here also implies that the nature of any socio-economic interaction has to be viewed as relational. Indeed, humans are social networkers and create socio-economic networks through their interactions. It is through these networks that we are able to cooperate with each other and that we are able to accomplish complex tasks.

The most pronounced of these network structures is the social division of labour itself. It has formed the foundation of human society since the cognitive revolution and as such provides a relational matrix into which humans can develop and prosper. It has been recognised that from the social division of labour there emanates a *trade infrastructure* that is essentially relational in nature. It is through this infrastructure that we conduct our economic wealth creation. This trade infrastructure is founded on the fundamental relationships between specialised individuals and firms in the prevailing social division of labour as well as the networking skills of these parties. Thus, the trade infrastructure is a network of complex relationships in different strengths and intensities.

**Markets in the Contemporary Global Economy**   Markets are an essential part of the trade infrastructure. At first it seems there is a contradiction between the relational nature of the networks that make up our trade infrastructure and the nature of a market in which demand and supply meet and establish trade contracts. However, there is actually no contradiction at all: markets are networks as well. Here I consider a number of empirical studies of markets rather than purely theoretical studies as pursued in neo-classical economics.[33] Interestingly, the main conclusion of this research confirms the hypothesis set out here: that *markets are networks.*

Geertz (1979) studied the organisation of and the transactions in a Moroccan bazaar, also known as a *suq*. Geertz observed that reciprocity played a central role in the functioning of the *suq*. Reciprocal relations in the *suq* are not fixed, but rather fluid. This leaves open the possibility for personal bargains and nepotism. Moreover, this reflects the tenuousness of the trust that is present in this bazaar; it is not founded on a determined reputation of the trader, based on a straightforward idea of reciprocity. Rather, it is founded on more long-term trade relationships that function under constraints informed by other trade options open in the *suq*. Thus, a picture of the *suq* emerges that is rather different from the neo-classical idea of a market. Trade relations are not anonymous, but rather flexible, although not completely static either.

---

[33] Amazingly, mainstream economics has never properly defined the market concept. Theoretical and philosophical discussions about the conception of the market notion can be found in, for example, Swedberg (1994), Ménard (1995), and Rosenbaum (2000). Unfortunately, this discussion just shows that the notion of a market is very hard to grasp and define, in particular if one intends to include the underlying institutional foundations such as the issue of the definition and implementation of property rights.

Haegens (2015) investigates several contemporary trade systems as well and concludes that most of these have the form of networks in which controlling middlemen play an important role. In particular, he looks at financial markets (Chapter 5) and the market for sweet peppers or "paprika" (Chapter 6). For both he concludes that these trade systems are highly networked. Trade contracts are made between parties that are tied together in ongoing relationships. Haegens, therefore, concludes as well that trade is conducted in systems that are very different from the idealistic demand–supply settings considered in neo-classical economics.

**The Marseille Fish Market** Vignes (1993), Kirman and Vriend (2001) and Vignes and Etienne (2011) investigate economic behaviour in the Marseille fish market. They report that the market has 40 registered sellers and accommodates 400 buyers. Note that this market is not "open"; sellers are required to be members. This in itself is already a significant deviation from neo-classical market theory. The buyers represent retail sellers and restaurants.

In this market, prices are not posted publicly. This allows them to be set in a maximally flexible fashion: each seller decides her own prices; different buyers might set different prices; and prices can vary over time. Most importantly, there is no bargaining between buyers and sellers: prices are communicated privately, but have a clear take-it-or-leave-it nature.

The trade patterns that emerge in the Marseille fish market exhibit some interesting properties. First, there is widespread loyalty among buyers and sellers. In that regard the market exhibits a network structure and trade relationships are clearly founded on reciprocity and trust. Second, there is persistent price dispersion that fits well with the perceived network nature of this market. Of course, the presence of price dispersion in the Marseille fish market confirms the perception that market prices are far from unique; the "law of one price" is not an empirical fact.

The traditional view of a market is that the laws of demand and supply result in an *unique* "equilibrium" price. However, viewing a market as a collection of trade relations introduces multiple prices emerging within the trading patterns in this market. Indeed, trade relationships are flexible and allow for the flexible application of the price mechanism; both trading parties are willing to accept a range of prices or exchange rates to support the desired trade. This introduces flexibility in these relationships, resulting in more stable price patterns over time, even though traders charge multiple prices for the same commodity.[34]

Vignes and Etienne (2011) applied network analysis to understand the functioning of the Marseille fish market. The conclusion from their analysis

---

[34] It seems paradoxical that flexibility implies stability, but in this case it allows sellers to hold the asking price at a constant level even though market circumstances change. It avoids the large costs of price adaptation as is expected in theoretical markets founded on the application of the laws of demand and supply, in which prices are continuously fluctuating with every change in circumstances in which trade occurs.

is most clearly depicted graphically as Figure 3 in Vignes and Etienne (2011, p. 57). From this analysis it is clear that the Marseille fish market does not exhibit the classical pattern of a competitive market based on a demand–supply analysis. This is confirmed by the price data, reported in Vignes and Etienne (2011).

The most important conclusion from these empirical investigations is therefore that the investigated markets are relational in nature rather than anonymous, as assumed in mainstream economic market theory. This should be combined with other aspects of our contemporary global economy—such as the prevalence of services (Fuchs 1968)—that are not part of the theories developed in mainstream neo-classical economics (Leijonhufvud 2007).

**Some Theoretical Relational Perspectives**    If one accepts that markets are not anonymous, but relational in nature, then this opens the possibility to further theorise about how these structures should be understood.

Herbert Simon was one of the first to point out the relational perspective on the economy in Simon (1991), based on his seminal work on employment relations (Simon 1951). He points out that if a Martian landed in our contemporary global economy, this alien would not observe consumers, producers and markets, but rather relational structures between individuals. These relational structures represent trading patterns, authority structures and collaborative networks. The result would be a view of the economy that is indeed very alien from the neo-classical perspective. Simon also points out that the relational structure of the economy provides a *matrix* in which individuals can develop and position themselves to achieve higher living standards. The image of the relational structure of our economy as a matrix is a useful metaphor.

A first attempt at developing a mathematical network model of a market was made by Fourie (1991) and Snehota (1993). These contributions introduce the view of a market as a network of stable trade relationships. As such this view is incomplete, but allows practical and mathematical modelling. The main deficiency of this theory is the omission of any governing institutions that support and determine the functioning of these relational trade structures.

On the other hand, governance is central in the approach suggested by Pieter Ruys. His perspective is informed through the introspection of the service sector of the contemporary globalised economy, in particular issues related to the health care sector. Starting from a general equilibrium perspective (Ruys 2002), he developed a purely relational approach in Ruys (2006, 2008, 2009). This theory imposes a categorical approach to economic activities and considers a hierarchical model of this categorisation. His theory captures many of the different aspects of an institutional network economy that are also developed and presented throughout this book.

My own perspective on the relational nature of human socio-economic interaction is set out here and is inspired by these alternative perspectives, in particular the Ruysian perspective of the service economy. On the other hand, I contend that a relational view emerges naturally when one's starting point is that of the social division of labour as the main generator and allocator of human economic wealth. The social division of labour imposes a network structure on any economic interaction, which is more natural than the market view adopted in neo-classical economics. It forms the theme of this book.

### 1.4.3    Transaction Efficiency and the Extent of the Market

Yang and Ng (1993) point out that the hypotheses set out here naturally imply the presence of *transaction costs* in the common infrastructure at the foundation of the economy. Indeed, instead of all production occurring in a closed household, it is brought out into the open and conducted through a social organisation. This social organisation has two elements, closely related to the two hypotheses underlying it: (1) specialised production in organisations that facilitate this specialisation and (2) a trade infrastructure that accommodates the exchange of specialised commodities resulting in gains from trade.

This implies that an external organisation form supersedes an internal form of organisation. The original production costs are therefore extended into two cost categories: the direct costs related to the production of commodities in a specialised social organisation (*Direct Production Costs*) and, second, the costs related to the transaction mechanism used to realise gains from trading the generated commodities in the collectively recognised exchange or trade mechanism (*Transaction Costs*). Direct production costs are fully determined by the production technologies that are used in the production processes in the economy. Transaction costs, on the other hand, are completely determined by the effectiveness and efficiency of the institutions and heuristics in the governance system that govern the trade of commodities in the prevailing trade infrastructures.[35]

Throughout history there has been a tendency to create better trade technologies and to build more effective trade infrastructures. In the feudal era, trade was conducted along treacherous road systems on which the transportation of goods was done at very high costs owing to imposed tariffs by land owners and municipalities as well as robbery and fraud. As a consequence trade was extremely costly, and this hampered the development of a well-functioning social division of labour.

**Markets and Transaction Efficiency** Important elements of the trade infrastructure have always been *markets*. Historically, a market refers to a location—such as a town square—in which traders came, and still come, together to buy

---

[35] The concept of transaction costs has a long history in economic thought. Viewed as one of the most difficult concepts to theorise about, it is generally recognised as being critically important to understand our contemporary economy, but remains unclear owing to the difficulties of giving it the correct expression in economic theories. The understanding of transaction costs has been pursued in general equilibrium theory (Hahn 1971, 1973; Hahn and Starr 1976; Ulph and Ulph 1975; Sun et al. 2004) as well as new institutional economics (Williamson 1979, 2000; North 1990). I also refer to Klaes (2000) for an exposition.

and sell their wares. These traders usually travelled to these market locations, also known as *market towns*, inducing significant transportation costs. To minimise costs, these market towns emerged at intersection points of the main transportation lines, such as where two or more roads intersect or at the location of a bridge across a major river. The implementation of such markets results in a significant reduction of transaction costs, if compared with a system of dispersed trades.

We can compare these historical descriptions to trade infrastructural elements in our contemporary global economy, in which trade is conducted at much lower costs. Trade is now conducted over much longer distances with the use of modern technology such as aeroplanes, mega-freighter ships, rail systems and highly efficient road systems. The result is a trade infrastructure that generates a rather low transaction cost level from which we reap significant gains.

Transaction costs are an expression of *transaction efficiency* of the underlying institutions and heuristics in the governance system as well as the trade infrastructure in the economy through which trade is conducted. It is the transaction efficiency that determines whether production occurs in a social division of labour or internally in the household.[36]

**Lemma 1.9 (Transaction Efficiency)** *The extent of the social division of labour is determined by the transaction efficiency embodied in the trade infrastructure in the economy as well as the effectiveness of the institutions and heuristics in the prevailing governance system that guide trade in these infrastructures.*

This implies that if the social division of labour deepens through the introduction of new economic goods and new specialisations, the transaction efficiency is directly affected. On the other hand, the transaction efficiency determines the extent to which the social division of labour can deepen. This is the subject of my next discussion.

**The Smith-Young Theorem on the Extent of the Market** The notion of transaction efficiency can also be interpreted in a completely different fashion. Indeed, the transaction efficiency of a trade infrastructure in combination with the potential demand for consumption goods that is present in the economy determines Adam Smith's notion of the *extent of the market* (Smith 1776, Book I, Chapter 3). This refers to the bounds from the available production and transaction technologies as well as the demand side in the economy. It refers essentially to what the total economy can bear and what limits there are to the total trade volume that an economy can generate. Smith's notion of the extent

---

[36] For example, throughout most of the twentieth century there was no day care for babies and toddlers, which consequently implied that child rearing was a full-time service provided within the household. It prevented many women from joining the labour force and fully participating in the social division of labour.

of the market and its effects on the social division of labour is formulated as the first statement of Corollary 1.10.

Smith (1776) formulated this famous proposition as the title of Chapter 3 in Book I that stated "the social division of labour is limited by the extent of the market". This refers to the principle that the social division of labour is fully determined by the factors embodied in the economic system, particularly the production and transaction technologies as well as the overall potential demand for goods. This seems rather straightforward, but this principle has been neglected in neo-classical economics after a short, but fierce, discussion in the 1920s (Blitch 1983).

Smith's principle has been extended by Allyn Young (1928) in a major contribution to the economics of wealth creation through a social division of labour. Young expounded that the extent of the market is actually driven by the social division of labour. The more advanced and sophisticated the social division of labour, the more the economy develops and grows, the higher the potential demand for goods will be and, consequently, the broader the extent of the market is; it forms the foundation for meaningful economic progress and development. It reintroduced *Say's Law*—that demand is determined by supply in the economy—in economic discourse (Say 1826; Sowell 1972). Young's vision was that Say's Law requires that increased supply is produced under IRS—resulting from IRSpec—and can be absorbed through elastic demand, stated as the second assertion in the Corollary 1.10.

We can now extend this debate by adding transaction efficiency as a determining factor to this mix (Lemma 1.9). The social division of labour is actually driven by transaction efficiency as well as the factors Young put forward. These factors clearly interact. Furthermore, transaction efficiency is largely determined by the advances in production technology as well as the depth of the social division of labour (Corollary 1.10).

**Corollary 1.10** The Smith–Young Theorem.

*Smith (1776):*    *The social division of labour is limited by the extent of the market.*
*Young (1928):*    *The social division of labour, the extent of the IRSpec and the extent of the market are interdependent.*
*Our conclusion:*    *The social division of labour, the extent of the IRSpec, transaction efficiency and the extent of the market are interdependent.*

### 1.4.4    Economic Development and the Entrepreneurial Function

The vision put forward by Young (1928) clearly links economic progress and development to the social division of labour. As in any process, development is defined and determined by *changes* in that process (Hidalgo 2015). In an economy founded on a social division of labour, enhancement of economic wealth relates directly to the deepening of that social division of labour. This refers to the introduction of new production technologies, new goods and new socio-economic roles embodied as socially recognised professions.

In Example 1.1 I have already considered a simple tribal economy in which economic development was sketched in relation to the emergence of IRS from individual IRSpec. It was pointed out there that the creation of surplus in an economy that organises its production through a social division of labour is closely related to the scope of that division of labour and the quality of the governance system that guides the production and trade processes in the economy. Here I consider the different sources of economic wealth creation separately.

**Population growth:**    The most mundane source of the development is simple population growth. The more economic agents participate in the social division of labour, the larger the total economic wealth that is generated. This mostly refers to the widening of the social division of labour, rather than its deepening. For a deepening of the social division of labour, there is needed more than simply an increase in the number of its participants (Example 1.1).

**Deepening of the division of labour:**    Enhancements in the production technologies translate to higher output levels of fully specialised economic agents. This refers to Schumpeterian innovation of production in the economy, which contributes directly to a higher economic output (Schumpeter 1926). This usually refers to a normal process of economic growth based on a low level of economic progress through the enhancement of prevailing production technologies. This process of economic development affects the outputs achieved through the principle of IRSpec. Clearly, new goods are tied in with new socio-economic roles and professions, which embody new production plans that can be assumed by economic agents in a social division of labour.

As an illustration, one might consider the introduction of a bow and arrow, besides the spear, in the hunt. With a bow and arrow it was possible to hunt fowl and other fast-moving animal species in an effective way. This resulted in higher output levels and a wider variety of foodstuffs available to the hunter-gatherer tribe.

It can also be illustrated by thinking of the introduction of the socio-economic role of a miller. Before millers emerged in the social division of labour, farmed grain and wheat was milled at home or at a bakery and used for baking bread. The introduction of innovative production technologies in medieval times meant that wind and water energy were used to grind grain and wheat into flour on a much larger scale. Productivity increased tremendously through the introduction of specialised millers who operated these large-scale grinders. As a consequence, flour became an intermediate product in the social division of the labour process to produce bread (Gimpel 1976).

**Institutional innovation:**    Economic development is advanced by the introduction of innovative heuristics and conventions in the governance system. This refers to the possibility of lowering transaction costs and enhancing economic interaction directly through governance. This is known as institutional innovation and is effected by (political) leaders as well as entrepreneurs.

An example of such institutional innovation is the reintroduction of coin money, the *Denier*, by Pepin III "the Short" in 754 in the Frankish empire, followed by monetary reforms by Charlemagne in the second half of the eighth century. At the time, money was limited by the ancient and dwindling supply of remaining Roman coins. By issuing their own coins, the Carolingian kings stimulated trade, resulting in enhanced economic development in the ninth century, although there is only mixed evidence for this (Verhulst 2002).

The force that effectuates change in the social division of labour—resulting from innovations in production technologies, new goods and socio-economic roles as well as institutional innovation—can be summarised as the entrepreneurial function in the economy, as already introduced in Lemma 1.5. The next corollary is a direct consequence of that fundamental force of institutional change in a developed economy, which is founded on a social division of labour.

**Corollary 1.11 (The Entrepreneurial Function in the Social Division of Labour)** *Institutional innovation and change in an economy founded on a social division of labour are driven by the entrepreneurial function in that economy.*

It has already been mentioned that the entrepreneurial function has two fundamental forms: individual entrepreneurship leading to revolutionary change and collective entrepreneurial activity resulting in evolutionary institutional change. Both of these forms of the entrepreneurial function fulfil important roles in the development of the social division of labour that drives wealth creation in human economy. They directly affect the institutions that provide the foundation for wealth creation processes in such an economy. This includes the deepening of the social division of labour as well as technological development in the social division of labour.

**Entrepreneurial Incentives and Theories of Value** What drives economic development and the entrepreneurial function? Why would individuals seek to find technological innovations or to introduce new goods or socio-economic roles? These fundamental changes require incentives for their creation and implementation.

The obvious answer to this question is that individuals or groups of economic agents expect to benefit from these changes; they are incentivised to pursue these innovations. This has to do with the evaluation of the goods that are generated and traded in the trade infrastructure of the economy as well as the institutional environment in which these agents interact. To understand this fundamental economic concept, we have to delve a bit deeper into the theories that describe the fundamental value of a commodity in an economic trade system.

Classical economists, from Adam Smith, David Ricardo and John Stuart Mill to Karl Marx, proposed a *labour theory of value*: the true value of a good is the amount of labour time past and present that has been used to produce it. This includes the amount of time it took to develop and build the capital assets that are used in its production process. This also includes the human labour time to create the knowledge to design these assets and the production processes themselves.

This notion of labour value is based on the fundamental theory put forward by Marx (1867, 1893).[37] For example, the labour value of bread includes the direct labour used to grow the wheat, to mill it, and to bake the bread, but also the past labour time to develop the farming technologies used to grow the wheat; to design and build the windmill for grinding the wheat; to create the recipe to bake bread, including finding out about the role of yeast in this process; as well as to build the oven in which the bread is baked.

There is a strong logic behind the evaluation of an economic good using its labour value. It is still relevant in our contemporary global economy, since many commodity prices charged have a cost basis, which is in spirit similar to the labour value of that commodity.

A completely alternative approach to value was developed in the marginalist revolution in economics. This *market theory of value* founds the value of a commodity on the equilibrium between demand and supply forces in a market. In this perspective, the value of an economic commodity is based on the balance between quantities demanded and supplied in the market for that commodity. The interplay of demand and supply is set out in models of market economies originating from the contributions of the seminal "marginalists", Jevons (1871), Menger (1871) and Walras (1926). The market theory of value states that the true value of a good is represented by its *competitive market price*—or its *market value*.

**Equivalence Between Different Theories of Value**  In Gilles (2017b), I show in a mathematical model that there is fundamentally no difference between these two theoretical approaches if an appropriate institutional framework is used to express the fundamental forces in an economy with an endogenous social division of labour: *the labour value and the market value of a good are fundamentally the same in a competitive economy founded on a functioning social division of labour.* This conclusion is confirmed by the insight that from a long-term historical perspective the social division of labour is infinitely flexible and adaptable to the developments in the economy, so that any demand can be met

---

[37] A modern treatment is given in Harvey (2017), while a mathematical theory of a Marxian economy based on a social division of labour has been developed by Roemer (1980, 1981).

by an appropriate supply through the rearrangement of the social division of labour. The resulting market value is therefore determined fully by the supply side in the economy and can be shown to be exactly equal to the labour value of a good.[38]

Additionally, using the flexibility of the social division of labour, other exchange processes and mechanisms result in exactly the same outcomes. These alternative trade mechanisms are also known as Edgeworthian barter processes (Edgeworth 1881)—and are also represented as the "core" of the economy. If the social division of labour is sufficiently flexible, there holds *core equivalence*: The Edgeworthian barter processes result in exactly the same outcomes as a social division of labour that is guided through the identified market and labour values. So we conclude that in an ideal competitive economy founded on a flexible social division of labour every good has a unique *economic value*, which is equal to its labour as well as its market value. The theories that support this insight are fully developed in Gilles (2017a,b) and are founded on advanced mathematical models of an ideal, competitive economy with an endogenous, perfectly flexible and adaptive social division of labour.

There is, however, a third, fundamentally different, approach to understanding and determining the value of a good. Indeed, in a (non-competitive) institutional economy with a trade infrastructure that is founded on a social division of labour, the main characteristic is that of *trade networks* that are governed through the prevailing socio-economic institutions. In such an institutional network economy, a commodity can have many different exchange values—or "prices"—depending on the *local* circumstances in the trade network for that commodity. Thus, a commodity can have many *network values* in such an institutional network economy founded on a social division of labour. These network values stand in contrast to the unique economic value that the commodity has, which is based on the underlying fundamentals of the economy. The differences between these network values and the fundamental labour value drives economic change and institutional innovation. This is stated in the final lemma of our axiomatic framework:

**Lemma 1.12 (Fundamental Theorem of Economic Development)** *The entrepreneurial function is driven by the difference between the network values of the traded commodities and the fundamental underlying economic value of these commodities.*

---

[38] A similar conclusion is reached in a perfectly flexible economy in which production is founded on constant returns to scale or "linear" production technologies. These are known as *Leontief economies* after the seminal contribution by Leontief (1936). In Gilles (2017b) I show that in the long term an economy with an endogenously adapting social division of labour functions in the same fashion as a Leontief economy, thus establishing the equivalence between market values and labour values for all produced commodities. For details I refer to Chapter 4 in Gilles (2018).

To illustrate this lemma, consider a specific good—a loaf of bread. Suppose that the economic value of this bread is equivalent to £1, which is based on the labour time invested in its production—directly as well as historically through the employed capital assets in the production process.[39] If the bread trades at £2 per loaf in a certain location on the trade network in an imperfectly competitive institutional economy, then there are clear indications that the producers sell this bread at a premium profit. This opens the door for classical Marshallian competition and incentivises competitors to move into this location to take a share of the profit (Marshall 1890). On the other hand, if bread trades at £0.50 per loaf, these producers trade at a loss and in the long run have an unsustainable operation. There is again room for modification of the competitive structure in the network economy, to allow these producers to increase their prices.

There are many reasons why there emerge in a network economy differences between the network values of a good and its underlying economic value. The main causes for discrepancies are actually imperfections in the network structure of the economy, in particular the emergence of middleman positions in trade networks and supply chains, as well as imperfect governance through imperfect institutions. These network positions induce power that is akin to monopolistic control by such a middleman, allowing the generation of excess windfall profits by trading goods and services at prices that are higher than their labour values. I debate in Chap. 2 the middleman positions occupied by transnational banks in various financial provision networks, which caused the financial collapse of 2007/2008. I refer to Chap. 2 for an elaborate discussion.

The second fundamental source of discrepancies is institutional. Indeed, institutional imperfections might insufficiently support the production networks in the economy, leading to their collapse and disintegration. It also might disincentivise individual economic agents to take the correct economic decisions. In particular, corruption and bureaucracy can hamper proper economic development and guide the economy to unstable states. Again, I refer to the Great Panic of 2008 as a prime example of institutional collapse; as pointed out in Chap. 2, the prevailing institutions in the run-up to the crisis resulted in significant corruption in the financial sector, thereby undermining trust and the functioning of the social division of labour in that sector. The collapse of production networks in the financial sector in 2008 triggered a global panic.

**Contestation** If imperfections in the trade infrastructure (Kets et al. 2011) and the institutional governance of the economy (Cervellati et al. 2008) lead to exploitation of certain categories of economic agents, there might emerge resistance from these economic agents.[40] As stated, such exploitation can be

---

[39] Of course, labour values should be expressed in units of (unskilled) labour time. However, using the prevailing monetary price of such a unit of labour time, we can convert it to a pound sterling or US dollar price.

[40] Exploitation results in unnatural inequality in the economy, which can lead to unexpected outcomes. The events of 2016—mainly the Brexit vote in the UK, the election of Trump in the

identified if the economic value of the goods and services provided is lower than the network price charged by the provider. Efforts to abate these exploitations can be referred to as *contestation* of these exploitative situations.

This contestation can assume several effective forms in the institutional economy. First, it can simply refer to the avoidance of such exploitative situations by offering alternative service provision. This can take the form of market competition or the provision of an alternative platform. This form of contestation is based on the direct enhancement of the trade infrastructure itself. Second, contestation can take the form of innovation in the social division of labour through the introduction of new goods and/or socio-economic roles. This takes the contestation into a different dimension by innovation away from the exploitative situation, making the goods and services subject to this exploitation (partially) obsolete. Third, the contestation can take the form of innovation in the institutions and heuristics of the governance system itself.

In all cases, contestation is a driver for innovation in the network economy and can overcome imperfections present in the prevailing trade infrastructure and its institutional governance system. Such contestation can be prevented and obstructed by defensive strategies from the parties in the economy that occupy the exploitative positions in the trade infrastructure. For example, Google and Facebook have presently an effective strategy of buying out and procuring potentially competitive corporations. Not only do these procurements enhance the services provided by these corporations, but they also prevent the potential emergence of alternative platforms. Many of the innovative start-up companies procured are simply shut down and their innovative products patented out of existence.

To summarise, imperfections in the institutional network economy—owing to structural or institutional features as well as temporary modifications created by the introduction of innovations—result in the extraction of excess rents. This refers to the fact that goods and services have a network price that exceeds their underlying economic value. Contestation of these extractions, positional as well as institutional, drives further innovations, and causes economic progress as well as economic development and growth through modification of the social division of labour.

## 1.5    BRINGING IT TOGETHER: A FIRST, SIMPLE MODEL OF WEALTH CREATION

In this section I bring together the elements that generate economic wealth and build two simple models to illustrate the most pertinent issues concerning wealth generation through a social division of labour. These models are founded

---

USA and the rise of so-called "post-fact" social and political discourse—can be understood from that perspective. This seems to be a natural consequence of the network imperfections and the institutional failure in the global neo-liberal economy laid bare by the Great Panic of 2008 (Duménil and Lévy 2011).

on the representation of an economic decision-maker through the embodiment Hypothesis 2. Indeed, we represent economic decision-makers as *consumer-producers* to reflect this embodiment. These economic agents make decisions about production as well as consumption. Consequently, they are endowed with productive abilities as well as preferences over consumption plans. Therefore I explicitly introduce appropriate mathematical concepts that represent consumptive and productive abilities of these tribe members as consumer-producers.

In the first model, I focus mainly on different institutional foundations of trade and economic decision-making. Different organisational structures and institutional designs result in different outcomes for the decision-making processes in the tribe. This shows in a very simple setting that institutions and organisational forms really affect economic wealth generation and allocation.

In this first model I also study the consequences of a simple process of economic development, in the form of how an increase in one tribe member's productivity affects collective wealth generation for the different institutional and organisational settings. It shows how different organisational structures lead to rather different effects in the generation and allocation of wealth.

In the second model, I consider how different processes affect economic wealth generation in a fixed institutional environment. I look at the simple rule of egalitarian division of collectively generated wealth in a hunter-gatherer tribe closely related to the first model. In this setting I investigate (1) how population growth leads to increased wealth; (2) how technological progress results in increased wealth generation; and (3) how the fundamental deepening of the social division of labour affects wealth generation. I show that all three developments result in increased wealth generation, but that the deepening of the social division of labour should be recognised as the main source of economic development and growth. This is akin to the seminal assessments of Smith (1776) and Schumpeter (1934), who phrased this as a form of creative destruction through entrepreneurial activity.

**Setting Up the Basic Elements in the Model** We focus only on the production and allocation of foodstuffs in this economy. We assume that in a simple hunter-gatherer society there are in principle two distinct economic goods: meat and vegetables. We denote meat by $X$ and vegetables by $Y$. Obviously, meat $X$ is acquired through the hunt and vegetables $Y$ are foraged from around the tribe's dwellings. This provides a commodity foundation to a social division of labour through two socio-economic roles, those of hunters and gatherers.

As usual, quantities of these two consumables, meat $X$ and vegetables $Y$, are represented through vectors of non-negative real numbers: $(x, y) \in \mathbb{R}^2_+$ represents a quantity $x \geqslant 0$ of meat as well as a quantity $y \geqslant 0$ of vegetables. It should be pointed out here that a bundle $(x, y)$ can represent a consumption bundle as well as a production plan.

### 1.5.1    Institutions and Wealth Generation in a Hunter-Gatherer Economy

We first consider a hunter-gatherer society in which there are four individuals. These tribal members are numbered 1, 2, 3 and 4, endowed with consumptive as well as productive abilities. It is assumed here that individuals 1 and 2 are male and individuals 3 and 4 are female. We use the anthropological findings that males specialised as hunters and females as gatherers in such tribal societies to assign productive abilities to these four individuals.

Using standard techniques from economic theory, consumptive preferences or "needs" are modelled through utility functions. A utility function $u \colon \mathbb{R}^2_+ \to \mathbb{R}$ assigns to every consumption bundle $(x, y)$ a utility level $u(x, y)$. A utility function represents a subjective preference that *ordinally* ranks the various consumption bundles of meat and vegetables.[41] Throughout, we assume that all individuals have exactly the same preferences, represented by the Stone-Geary utility function (Geary 1950–1951; Stone 1954), which is a modification of the standard Cobb-Douglas utility function so commonly used in microeconomics:

$$u(x, y) = (x + 1)(y + 2) \tag{1.7}$$

for all $(x, y) \in \mathbb{R}^2_+$.

The given Stone-Geary utility function indeed reflects a preference of tribe members for meat over vegetables, since the marginal utilities for $x = y$ reflect this:

$$MU_X = \partial U / \partial x = y + 2 > MU_Y = \partial U / \partial y = x + 1.$$

The productive abilities of the individuals in this tribal hunter-gatherer society are based on their abilities to generate output when fully specialised in two distinct socio-economic roles. We assume that each individual can be either a hunter or a gatherer, but not both.

A *hunter* uses his innate human labour time to acquire meat $X$ through hunting large animals with a spear. A hunter is fully specialised and does not generate any foraged vegetables, since he will not have labour time remaining for such activity. Since a hunter is fully specialised, we apply the property of IRSpec in our model and reflect increased hunting skills in higher output levels of meat $X$.

A *gatherer* uses her labour time to forage the forest, savannah and swamps for edible fruits, berries, roots, plants and mushrooms, collectively represented by the foodstuff category $Y$. A gatherer is fully specialised and the hypothesis of IRSpec applies. This is expressed in higher output levels of vegetable foodstuffs $Y$.

---

[41] It should be pointed out that ordinal ranking is different from cardinal ranking. In the first methodology, only the rank of the item in question is important and the utility level merely expresses this ranking. In the second methodology, the utility function assigns a meaningful quantity to the consumption bundle that has relevance by itself. Thus, in that case, the difference between two assigned utility levels expresses how much one bundle is better than the other.

We can now summarise the resulting productive output levels for fully specialised individuals in the following table. In this table, for each individual the resulting production plan in the two specialisations is reported. Clearly, each individual only produces positive quantities of the good that he or she is specialised in. From these output levels, it is clear that individual 1 is considered as an alpha male who is able to do both tasks well. Individuals 2 and 3 are average citizens with gender-based differences in their abilities. Individual 4 is a female with high foraging abilities.[42]

| Individual | Hunter | Gatherer |
| --- | --- | --- |
| 1 | (5,0) | (0,4) |
| 2 | (4,0) | (0,2) |
| 3 | (2,0) | (0,4) |
| 4 | (3,0) | (0,5) |

There is no third socio-economic role. For completeness we can introduce the assumption that all individuals can withdraw from society and produce a zero-vector $(0,0)$. This, however, is just a theoretical possibility, since for survival all individuals are required to be productive.

To complete our model, we need to introduce a framework of how behaviour in this society is regulated. Indeed, as indicated in archaeological and anthropological research, it has been established that foraging tribes of hunter-gatherers were extremely diverse. Each tribe could have different social conventions, religious practices and economic governance systems (Harari 2014, Chapters 1 and 2). We reflect this here by adopting different economic governance systems represented by three different exchange mechanisms to allocate the food to the members of the tribe. We discuss joint consumption, a bilateral matching mechanism of household formation and a tribal marketplace.

**Collective consumption:** One of the most common tribal organisation forms is based on collective production and consumption of the economic wealth that the tribe generates. This represents a natural state of collectivism and egalitarianism. Irrespective of an individual's contribution, the allocated consumption of food is simply an equal share of the total granary.

This organisation form assumes an authoritarian leadership—like a *matriarchy*—or a collective decision-making process resulting in a collective preparation of a joint meal and equal participation in that meal.

Assuming that the assignment of productive tasks focuses on collective maximisation of the total output—or *Pareto efficiency*—it is easily established that a gender-based social division of labour results in a maximal collective

---

[42] In fact individual 1 has an absolute productive advantage over individuals 2 and 3, while individual 4 has an absolute advantage over individual 3.

output. Indeed, if individuals 1 and 2 are hunters and individuals 3 and 4 are gatherers, the total output is $(5, 0)+(4, 0)+(0, 4)+(0, 5) = (9, 9)$. Collective egalitarian consumption results in an individual's consumption bundle as $\left(2\frac{1}{4}, 2\frac{1}{4}\right)$ resulting in uniform utility level of $U_J = \left(2\frac{1}{4} + 1\right) \times \left(2\frac{1}{4} + 2\right) = 13\frac{13}{16} \approx 13.81.$[43]

**Household formation:**   A second, commonly adopted form of socio-economic governance is based on individual property rights and the formation of households.

Under this institutional framework, the tribe settles in a pattern of optimally formed two-person households, based on the productivity of the two members of each household. The following table summarises the potential household combinations. If individuals $i$ and $j$ form a household, the household's output is based on an optimal division of labour between the two household members. This output is consumed collectively and each individual household member is assigned an equal share.

| Household | Joint output | Individual consumption | Utility | |
|---|---|---|---|---|
| 1–2 | (4, 4) | (2, 2) | $U_{12} = 12$ | |
| 1–3 | (5, 4) | $\left(2\frac{1}{2}, 2\right)$ | $U_{13} = 14$ | |
| 1–4 | (5, 5) | $\left(2\frac{1}{2}, 2\frac{1}{2}\right)$ | $U_{14} = 15\frac{3}{4}$ | ⋆ |
| 2–3 | (4, 4) | (2, 2) | $U_{23} = 12$ | ⋆ |
| 2–4 | (4, 5) | $\left(2, 2\frac{1}{2}\right)$ | $U_{24} = 13\frac{1}{2}$ | |
| 3–4 | (3, 4) | $\left(1\frac{1}{2}, 2\right)$ | $U_{34} = 10$ | |

In an individually free tribe, the resulting equilibrium household pattern ⋆ emerges in which individuals 1 and 4 form a household to achieve the maximal utility level of $U_{14} = 15\frac{3}{4}$. This leaves individuals 2 and 3 to form the remaining household, resulting in utility level $U_{23} = 12$.

In this equilibrium the collective output is again $(5, 5) + (4, 4) = (9, 9)$, but the allocation of these resources is no longer egalitarian or "fair". Individualism and selfishness result in the exploitation of opportunities of the individuals rather than complete reference to the collective tribal wealth level: we get a rich household and a poor household.[44]

**A tribal market:**   Finally, I consider a fully developed tribal marketplace in which both food types are traded at competitive market prices. We assume

---

[43] It can easily be checked that indeed any other specialisation pattern among the four individuals in this economy results in a lower common utility level under egalitarian division.

[44] It should be remarked that owing to their natural productive proclivities that we assumed here, the resulting households in this equilibrium are of mixed gender. It is therefore correct to think of these households as "families", which also function for procreation.

that meat $X$ acts as a *numeraire* and that the price of foraged vegetables $Y$ is expressed in $X$-terms. Let $p \geqslant 0$ be the price of one unit of $Y$ in terms of units of $X$.

At market price $p$, every individual now maximises his or her income by selection of an optimal production plan. Then the common utility function results in demand functions that are given by

$$d(p) = \left( \frac{I + 2p - 1}{2}, \frac{I - 2p + 1}{2p} \right), \qquad (1.8)$$

where $I \geqslant 0$ is the earned income from selling the produced outputs on the market.

To compute the equilibrium, we can now express incomes as functions of the price $p$ for the different individuals in the tribe. We can do this for each potential production plan of each individual in the tribe. This is summarised in the next table:

| # | Plan 1 | Income 1 | Consumption 1 | Plan 2 | Income 2 | Consumption 2 |
|---|--------|----------|---------------|--------|----------|---------------|
| 1 | $(5,0)$ | 5 | $\left(2 + p, \frac{3}{p} - 1\right)$ | $(0,4)$ | $4p$ | $\left(\frac{6p-1}{2}, \frac{1}{2p} + 1\right)$ |
| 2 | $(4,0)$ | 4 | $\left(\frac{3+2p}{2}, \frac{5}{2p} - 1\right)$ | $(0,2)$ | $2p$ | $\left(\frac{4p-1}{2}, \frac{1}{2p}\right)$ |
| 3 | $(2,0)$ | 2 | $\left(\frac{1+2p}{2}, \frac{3}{2p} - 1\right)$ | $(0,4)$ | $4p$ | $\left(\frac{6p-1}{2}, \frac{1}{2p} + 1\right)$ |
| 4 | $(3,0)$ | 3 | $\left(1 + p, \frac{2}{p} - 1\right)$ | $(0,5)$ | $5p$ | $\left(\frac{7p-1}{2}, \frac{3p+1}{2p}\right)$ |

An assignment of roles ("hunter" or "gatherer") of the four individuals in this economy now establishes a social division of labour. An assignment, representing such a social division of labour, is *stable* if no individual would be willing to switch roles given the market price for good $Y$. The latter means that all individuals maximise their income, given their productive abilities and the prevailing market price for $Y$.

We now claim that the natural role assignment—where individuals 1 and 2 are hunters and individuals 3 and 4 are gatherers—is indeed stable. Given the natural role assignment, we compute that $p^* = \frac{13}{17}$ is the equilibrium market price of $Y$. The resulting equilibrium production–consumption allocation is represented in the next table:

| Individual | Production | Income | Consumption | Utility |
|------------|-----------|--------|-------------|---------|
| 1 | $(5,0)$ | 5 | $(2.76, 2.92)$ | $U = 18.5$ |
| 2 | $(4,0)$ | 4 | $(2.26, 2.27)$ | $U = 13.9$ |
| 3 | $(0,4)$ | 3.06 | $(1.79, 1.65)$ | $U = 10.2$ |
| 4 | $(0,5)$ | 3.82 | $(2.18, 2.15)$ | $U = 13.2$ |

In this fully individualised economy, the market price guides the individual tribesmen to select optimal production plans and to achieve optimal consumption plans. Indeed, again the two males are specialised as hunters and the two females as foragers. The resulting equilibrium utility levels are actually the same as resulting from household formation.

The most interesting aspect of the price mechanism is that there emerges a *dichotomy of production and consumption* at the level of the individual decision-maker (Gilles 2017b, Theorem 2.6). The prices quoted for the two goods guide an individual to maximise income independently of the consumption decision: if income is maximised, consumption will be optimal as well. This dichotomy is purely the consequence of the introduction of the price mechanism in the society; it is an unintended consequence.

These three quite common governance systems in a tribe of hunter-gatherers have no clear comparative advantages, as is shown above. All three of these institutional frameworks are legitimate and have clear advantages and disadvantages.

The joint decision-making process that results in the egalitarian allocation of resources to the members of the tribe has some clear advantages: it instils communal spirit and collectivism; it minimises the allocative differences among the tribesmen; and it requires few formal structures and organisational forms. The disadvantages are also obvious: it only works in relatively small communities of equally minded individuals; it requires the absence of a selfish leadership; and it can easily result in inefficiencies in the collective production decisions.

The household formation process results in much larger inequalities: we get rich and poor households. It also results in a fragmented society in which different households operate independently and can lose fruitful contact with other tribesmen. On the other hand, incentives within the households and through the household formation process guarantee that reasonably efficient production decisions are made.

The competitive market binds the tribe into a common process of trade and interaction. However, individualism in the decision-making processes underlying the market might undermine the social fabric of the tribe as a whole. Moreover, the market results in sizeable inequalities in the emerging economy. This might further undermine the social, interpersonal trust on which the market trading process rests. On the other hand, the first fundamental theorem of welfare economics guarantees that competitive pricing results in optimal usage of all physical resources in the economy (Gilles 2017b, Theorem 3.3).

### 1.5.2    *The Consequences of Ricardian Development*

A simple modification of the example discussed above can make clear how economic development and growth might affect the resulting allocations and production decisions under the three different governance systems that we discussed. We apply the *Ricardian view* of the functioning of the social division of labour. This is rooted in the productive abilities of individual tribesmen. The resulting growth of the total economic output of the tribe is firmly founded on the individual talents of the tribesmen.

Returning to the simple example, we now assume that individual 3 becomes more effective as a gatherer and is able to increase the amount of foraged vegetables $Y$ that she is able to generate from 4 units to 5 units. The modified output levels are now described by

| Individual | Hunter | Gatherer |
|---|---|---|
| 1 | (5,0) | (0,4) |
| 2 | (4,0) | (0,2) |
| 3 | (2,0) | (0,5) |
| 4 | (3,0) | (0,5) |

Again we investigate the three organisational forms of trade and exchange in this simple tribal economy based on the same Stone-Geary utility function. In particular, we can investigate the changes that this simple modification of 3's output level has on the overall wealth in the economy. Clearly, the consequences of this individual development reverberate across the tribal economy and affect all members' happiness and well-being.

**Collective consumption:** As before, the tribal leadership or the collective will instruct the tribesmen to specialise in their most efficient profession. This results now in a total Pareto optimal output level of $(5, 0) + (4, 0) + (0, 5) + (0, 5) = (9, 10)$. Collective egalitarian consumption results in each individual's consumption bundle as $\left(2\frac{1}{4}, 2\frac{1}{2}\right)$ resulting in uniform utility level of $\overline{U}_J = \left(2\frac{1}{4} + 1\right) \times \left(2\frac{1}{2} + 2\right) = 14\frac{5}{8} \approx 14.63 > U_J = 13.81$.

**Household formation:** As before, we assume that households are formed by two individuals, who then subsequently coordinate their productive specialisation to generate a maximal utility for the members of the household. We compute for each potential household the following characteristics:

| Household | Joint output | Individual consumption | Utility | |
|---|---|---|---|---|
| 1–2 | (4, 4) | (2, 2) | $\overline{U}_{12} = 12$ | |
| 1–3 | (5, 5) | $\left(2\frac{1}{2}, 2\frac{1}{2}\right)$ | $\overline{U}_{13} = 15\frac{3}{4}$ | ★ |
| 1–4 | (5, 5) | $\left(2\frac{1}{2}, 2\frac{1}{2}\right)$ | $\overline{U}_{14} = 15\frac{3}{4}$ | • |
| 2–3 | (4, 5) | $\left(2, 2\frac{1}{2}\right)$ | $\overline{U}_{23} = 13\frac{1}{2}$ | • |
| 2–4 | (4, 5) | $\left(2, 2\frac{1}{2}\right)$ | $\overline{U}_{24} = 13\frac{1}{2}$ | ★ |
| 3–4 | (3, 5) | $\left(1\frac{1}{2}, 2\frac{1}{2}\right)$ | $\overline{U}_{34} = 11\frac{1}{4}$ | |

From this there result two equilibrium patterns: ($\star$) Households 1–3 and 2–4 are formed, resulting in an equilibrium utility level of $\overline{U}_{13} = 15\frac{3}{4}$ for individuals 1 and 3 and an equilibrium utility level of $\overline{U}_{24} = 13\frac{1}{2}$ for individuals 2 and 4; ($\bullet$) Households 1–4 and 2–3 form, resulting in an equilibrium utility level of $\overline{U}_{14} = 15\frac{3}{4}$ for individuals 1 and 4 and an equilibrium utility level of $\overline{U}_{23} = 13\frac{1}{2}$ for individuals 2 and 3.

In either equilibrium, there is a significant increase in the utility levels for the poor household, lifting the well-being of individuals 2 and 3 significantly. In that regard, individual 2 as the partner of individual 3 benefits from the increased productivity of individual 3 more than any other individual. This seems natural under the institutional setting of a household economy.

**A tribal market:**    Again consider a competitive market mechanism in which the price of foraged vegetables is $p \geqslant 0$ per unit $Y$ in terms of units of $X$. Again we can describe all potential production plans and resulting incomes for all four tribesmen as we have done in the previous analysis. Again we can identify the stable role assignments in this case and compute the resulting equilibrium market price for foraged vegetables $Y$.

As before, the natural role assignment in which individuals 1 and 2 are hunters and individuals 3 and 4 are gatherers is stable. Indeed, the total market supply of foraged vegetables $Y$ increases owing to the production change for individual 3. This is reflected in a lower equilibrium price of $Y$ computed as $\hat{p} = \frac{13}{18}$. The resulting equilibrium is as before represented as

| Individual | Production | Income | Consumption | Utility |
|---|---|---|---|---|
| 1 | $(5, 0)$ | 5 | $(2.72, 3.15)$ | $\overline{U} = 19.2$ |
| 2 | $(4, 0)$ | 4 | $(2.22, 2.46)$ | $\overline{U} = 14.4$ |
| 3 | $(0, 5)$ | 3.61 | $(2.03, 2.19)$ | $\overline{U} = 12.7$ |
| 4 | $(0, 5)$ | 3.61 | $(2.03, 2.19)$ | $\overline{U} = 12.7$ |

From the analysis it is immediately clear that the utility level of individuals 1, 2 and 3 has increased when compared with the previous case. However, individual 4 has lost her privileged position as the most effective gatherer and this is reflected in a lower utility level.

Second, comparing the household formation process with the tribal market, there again emerges a clear distinction in the outcomes. In the market, the hunters clearly benefit from the increased productivity of individual 3 as a gatherer. This is much more pronounced than under the institutional structure of a household economy. There only the assigned partner to individual 3 benefited from the increased productivity of that individual.

From the discussion of the simple example of a hunter-gatherer tribe, it becomes clear that growth has very different effects under different systems of governance and institutional configurations. The enormous importance of the governance system and the tribal organisation is reflected in the contemporary debates about economic performance in our global economy. How should we organise our economy? Which institutions are most effective and result in the highest levels of wealth? *There are no clear answers to these important questions*, owing to the complexity of the governance system in combination with the economic characteristics of the members of the economy. This important conclusion very much sets the tone of this book.

There is a second important point made in this simple example. The productivity increase is founded on the individual ability of a single individual in the tribe. However, in more developed economies productivity is a function of the institutional organisation of the economy directly. Indeed, in a well-developed economy, individuals are trained in a collective education system. Therefore, advances in productive abilities are not individualistic, but public or collective. Innovative production technologies and practices are disseminated through the institutions that govern the economy.

A more advanced, institutional economy like this can enhance wealth creation in multiple fundamental ways. This is the subject of the following discussion of a larger tribe in which individual tribesmen are less important and have less impact. In that environment, the economy can develop through population growth and technological progress as well as through structural enhancements of production networks in the social division of labour.

### 1.5.3 Smithian Development in a Social Division of Labour

In the previous discussion, I considered a simple tribal economy with just four productive individuals, in which one tribe member increased her individual ability to forage. In this section, I develop a second model of a hunter-gatherer tribe and investigate different Smithian mechanisms of change, representing the considerations following from the Smithian view of the functioning of the social division of labour. This Smithian form of change is social and institutional rather than individualistic, as considered in the previous example. Increased productivity is therefore not due to an individual economic agent accidentally acquiring more productive abilities to forage—as considered for individual 3 in the preceding discussion—but rather it is a consequence of collective institutions and actions.

I assume throughout that there are resources available and socio-economic institutions in place to provide all tribesmen with equal abilities to hunt and to gather. Therefore there are no longer any individualistic differences between the tribe's members. In other words, all tribe members have similar education or training and are equally productive in the hunt and in the foraging of vegetables. This takes us, in principle, away from a gender based social division of labour and allows us to address whether a social division of labour is optimal.

**Model Fundamentals** Again we denote by $X$ the meat that is provided by the hunting activities in the tribe and by $Y$ the vegetables that are gathered by tribe members. We assume now that the tribe is made up of 16 members and that all of them are completely equal in consumptive preferences as well as productive abilities. Furthermore, we assume that the preferences of all members are given by the same Stone-Geary utility function, expressing a slight preference for meat over vegetables, which is expressed in (1.7): $U(x, y) = (x + 1)(y + 2)$.

Finally, we change the production plans for this tribe in comparison with our previous model. In particular, we assume that all tribe members can produce three basic production plans represented as output vectors: fully specialised hunters produce $(10, 0)$; fully specialised gatherers produce $(0, 10)$; and non-specialised individuals produce an output of $(4, 4)$.[45] This reflects the increasing returns to specialisation that are present in the human ability: specialised individuals produce a relatively higher output level than non-specialised individuals.

This construction introduces the fundamental hypothesis that all tribesmen are now educated through a collective education system that provides them with similar abilities. Of course, in reality individuals are slightly different in their productive abilities, even when educated in exactly the same system and undergoing exactly the same training. However, these interindividual differences are negligible in the totality of the economy, if it is sufficiently large. Therefore, we follow the Smithian logic that all economic agents are essentially identical in their productive abilities and have equal access to the means of production (Smith 1776; Buchanan and Yoon 2002).

In this basic setting we consider some simple questions. We consider an optimal organisation of the tribe through a well-chosen social division of labour; we consider the expansion of the tribe's population and how it affects total well-being for tribe members; we study the impact of technological progress or development on tribal well-being; and finally we look at the deepening of the social division of labour through entrepreneurial activity and the introduction of new goods and productive activities.

Throughout the discussion we assume that the tribe uses the exchange rule of *egalitarian division* of the total tribal output to arrive at consumption bundles for all its members. This hypothesis is limiting, but it makes comparisons and computations more straightforward. The mathematical calculus, therefore, remains accessible and the analysis transparent.

### 1.5.3.1    Introducing a Social Division of Labour

As a theoretical benchmark, we note that if all members of the tribe do not specialise and there is no tribal institutional structure to guide it to a social division of labour, every member would produce and consume the bundle $(4, 4)$ resulting in a benchmark utility level of $\underline{U} = 5 \times 6 = 30$.

A major improvement is already possible if the tribe organises itself into a social division of labour founded on the collective access to the returns to

---

[45] Technically, this is the same as requiring that every tribe member can select exactly one production plan from an objectively given set $\mathcal{P} = \{(10, 0), (4, 4), (0, 10)\}$.

specialisation. Indeed, if the tribe organises itself as eight hunters and eight gatherers, the total collective output would be $8 \times (10, 0) + 8 \times (0, 10) = (80, 80)$ resulting through the egalitarian division rule in a consumption bundle of $\frac{1}{16}(80, 80) = (5, 5)$. The well-being of the members would increase to $U(5, 5) = 42 > \underline{U}$.

However, this social division of labour is not *optimal* and does not maximise the total collective output and per capita consumption. This is achieved through the maximisation of the utility of an arbitrary tribe member as a function of the social division itself. This is explored next.

**The Optimal Social Division of Labour**  We show here that further improvement in the well-being of the tribe members is possible through the organisation of the tribe in an optimal social division of labour. We compute this optimal configuration of productive specialisations through the use of some variables.

Suppose that there are $k \in \{0, 1, \ldots, 16\}$ fully specialised hunters in the social division of labour. Then there are $16 - k$ fully specialised gatherers. The total generated output through this social division of labour can now be computed as

$$O_1(k) = k \times (10, 0) + (16 - k) \times (0, 10) = (10k, 160 - 10k). \tag{1.9}$$

The consumption bundle for each member under the egalitarian division rule is therefore

$$C_1(k) = \frac{O_1(k)}{16} = \left( \tfrac{5}{8}k, 10 - \tfrac{5}{8}k \right)$$

and the resulting individual utility of each tribe member is now computed as

$$U_1(k) = \left( \tfrac{5}{8}k + 1 \right) \left( 12 - \tfrac{5}{8}k \right) = 12 + 6\tfrac{7}{8}k - \tfrac{25}{64}k^2 \tag{1.10}$$

The *optimal* social division is now determined by solving the optimisation problem $\max_k U_1(k)$, which solves to $k = 8.8$. Therefore, the feasible optimal social division of labour in this tribe is determined by $k_1 = 9$ with a total output of $O_1(9) = (90, 70)$, an individual consumption bundle of $C_1(9) = \left( 5\tfrac{5}{8}, 4\tfrac{3}{8} \right)$ and an individual utility level of $\overline{U}_1 = U_1(9) = 42.23$.

Although the improvement of moving from a balanced social division of eight hunters and eight gatherers to the optimal social division of labour with nine hunters and seven gatherers is modest, it is clear that optimality of the social division of labour is a desirable property. In this case, such optimality is achieved rather easily, since all tribe members are assumed to be completely equal in their abilities. In general situations where individuals are differentiated in their productive abilities and consumptive preferences, such optimisation might be harder to establish.

In the subsequent discussion I turn to various developments that affect the optimal social division of labour and the resulting well-being of the tribe members. In particular, I consider (1) population growth, (2) technological progress and (3) fundamental Schumpeterian entrepreneurial innovation resulting in the deepening of the social division of labour. In each of these cases I will recompute the optimal social division of labour and show that significant improvements in tribal well-being are possible.

### 1.5.3.2    Tribal Expansion: The Consequences of Population Growth

First, I consider the growth of the population in the tribe from a total size of 16 to a total size of 20. Throughout, I assume that all tribe members have exactly the same productive abilities as well as identical preferences, as assumed thus far. The only change considered is, therefore, that the population increases. Analysis shows that such a population increase has a positive effect on the total tribal well-being without any modification of the productive abilities of the tribe's members. This is owing to the ability of a larger tribe to achieve a more optimal social division of labour.

As before, we compute the optimal social division of labour, now given the total population size of 20. For that purpose let $k \in \{0, 1, \ldots, 20\}$ be the total number of fully specialised hunters in the social division of labour. Then there are $20 - k$ fully specialised gatherers. The total generated output through this social division of labour can now be computed as

$$O_2(k) = k \times (10, 0) + (20 - k) \times (0, 10) = (10k, 200 - 10k). \tag{1.11}$$

The consumption bundle for each member under the egalitarian division rule therefore is

$$C_2(k) = \frac{O_2(k)}{20} = \left( \tfrac{1}{2}k, 10 - \tfrac{1}{2}k \right)$$

and the resulting individual utility of each member is now determined as

$$U_2(k) = \left( \tfrac{1}{2}k + 1 \right) \left( 12 - \tfrac{1}{2}k \right) = 12 + 5\tfrac{1}{2}k - \tfrac{1}{4}k^2 \tag{1.12}$$

The optimal social division is again determined through the solution of the maximisation problem $\max_k U_2(k)$, which solves to $k_2 = 11$. Therefore, the optimal social division of labour in this expanded tribe results in a collective output of $O_2(11) = (110, 90)$, an individual consumption bundle of $C_2(11) = \left( 5\tfrac{1}{2}, 4\tfrac{1}{2} \right)$ and an optimal utility level of $\overline{U}_2 = U_2(11) = 42.25 > \overline{U}_1 = 42.23$. This shows indeed that population growth results in slightly higher levels of well-being, although these gains are very modest. This corresponds to an increase in tribal well-being, computed as

$$\Delta_2 = \frac{\overline{U}_2 - \overline{U}_1}{\overline{U}_1} = 0.00037 \tag{1.13}$$

This corresponds to a very modest 0.037% increase in tribal well-being owing to the assumed population growth of 25%. It should be clear that population growth is only a rather minor factor in economic growth, as shown in this simple example.

Indeed, the growth of the population by itself only affects the well-being that is achieved through the social division of labour as far as the optimal social division is imperfectly executed, owing to population size restrictions. Larger populations simply achieve an optimal social division of labour more perfectly than smaller populations of similar agents. Such an optimal social division of labour is only perfectly achieved in an economy with an infinitely large population—modelled as a *continuum economy* (Aumann 1964; Hildenbrand 1974; Gilles 2017b).

### 1.5.3.3 *Technological Progress*
In economics, technological progress has been recognised as the main source for economic growth. This refers to the introduction of more efficient ways to produce commodities and to accomplish higher returns per unit of input. In our simple tribal model this refers to the ability of tribe members to hunt more and/or larger animals with the same input of labour time or to dig up more roots using more human ingenuity. In either case, there are no major changes made to the fundamentals of the model other than that the productive abilities of the specialised individuals that make up the social division of labour increase. This change is usually gradual, and changes in the output levels increase modestly with a few percentage points every year.

**Regular Technological Progress** First we consider the type of technological progress that corresponds to the modest technological progress that is observed throughout history. Here we assume that the gathering techniques develop to allow a 10% increase in output per unit of labour time invested. So a specialised gatherer is able to generate an output of $(0, 11)$ rather than $(0, 10)$. This change should still lead to an increase in well-being in the tribe of at least 5%.

One can compute[46] that the optimal social division of labour does not change. Hence, given a discrete number of gatherers, the optimal number of hunters remains $k' = 11 \equiv k_2$ and the optimal number of gatherers remains $20 - k' = 9$. Under increased productivity of these gatherers, the total tribal output becomes

$$O' = 11 \times (10, 0) + 9 \times (0, 11) = (110, 99)$$

and consumption can be computed as $C' = \frac{O'}{20} = \left(5\frac{1}{2}, 4\frac{19}{20}\right)$. This results in a utility level of $U' = 45.175$. Therefore, a 10% increase in the productivity of a

---

[46] I leave the details of this computation to the interested reader.

gatherer leads to an increase in tribal well-being computed as

$$\Delta' = \frac{U' - \overline{U}_2}{\overline{U}_2} = 0.069 \tag{1.14}$$

Thus the 10% increase in the productivity of a gatherer results in a 6.9% increase in tribal well-being.

**Technological Innovation** Next, in this example, I focus on the impact of a major technological development in gathering techniques that significantly increases the output of edible roots and berries per unit of labour time. In particular, I increase the output of a specialised gatherer from $(0, 10)$ to $(0, 20)$, representing a doubling of the productivity of a gatherer. In this case the optimal social division of labour is affected significantly.

As before, we consider a tribe of 20 members in which each can either specialise as a hunter and produce $(10, 0)$ or as a gatherer and generate $(0, 20)$. Again we compute the optimal social division of labour under these modified circumstances. As before let $k \in \{0, 1, \ldots, 20\}$ be the total number of fully specialised hunters in the social division of labour. Then there are $20 - k$ fully specialised gatherers. The total generated output through this social division of labour can now be computed as

$$O_3(k) = k \times (10, 0) + (20 - k) \times (0, 20) = (10k, 400 - 20k). \tag{1.15}$$

The consumption bundle for each member under the egalitarian division rule is therefore
$$C_3(k) = \frac{O_3(k)}{20} = \left( \tfrac{1}{2}k, 20 - k \right)$$

and the resulting individual utility of each member is now computed as

$$U_3(k) = \left( \tfrac{1}{2}k + 1 \right)(22 - k) = 22 + 10k - \tfrac{1}{2}k^2 \tag{1.16}$$

The *optimal* social division is now determined by $\max_k U_3(k)$, which solves exactly to $k = 10$. Therefore, $k_3 = 10$ and the optimal social division of labour in this expanded tribe results in an output of $O_3(10) = (100, 200)$, an individual consumption bundle of $C_3(10) = (5, 10)$ and an optimal utility level of $\overline{U}_3 = U_3(10) = 72 > \overline{U}_2 = 42.25$.[47]

Again we can now compute the increase in tribal well-being brought about by the doubling in productivity of its gatherers:

$$\Delta_3 = \frac{\overline{U}_3 - \overline{U}_2}{\overline{U}_2} = 0.704. \tag{1.17}$$

---

[47] We compare this optimal social division of labour with the case where we do not change the social division of labour and impose that there remain $k_2 = 11 > k_3 = 10$ hunters. In that non-optimal case, $O_3(11) = (110, 180)$, $C_3(11) = \left(5\tfrac{1}{2}, 9\right)$ and $U_3(11) = 71\tfrac{1}{2} < \overline{U}_3 = 72$.

This corresponds to an 70.4% increase in tribal well-being if the productivity of its gatherers doubles. This large effect is owing to the combined effects of technological progress as well as the adaptation of the social division of labour in response to these changes.

Obviously, technological progress is a major source of economic growth, expressed here as an increase in the utilitarian well-being of the tribe's members—referred to as the "tribal well-being". This explains the fixation of economic policy debates in our global economy on the promotion of technological progress and enhancing the education levels of a nation's population.

### 1.5.3.4    The Deepening of the Social Division of Labour

The most important source of increased well-being is *not* the technological progress discussed in the previous section, but a much more disruptive force in the social division of labour. This refers to the fundamental *deepening* of the social division through the introduction of new specialisations and new commodities that are attached to these new specialisations. Such deepening of the social division of labour concerns the fundamental enhancement of the institutional foundations of productive processes in the economy. By introducing new specialisations and new commodities that are attached to these new specialisations, we fundamentally enhance the resulting social division of labour. This also requires the introduction of other institutions to guarantee the proper functioning of this more complex social division of labour. We illustrate this with the introduction of a new production technology to hunt animals.

In our simple tribal setting, consider the introduction of hunting tools such as sophisticated, properly balanced spears. These spears need to be produced by fully specialised *tool-makers*. As before, we denote by $X$ the meat acquired through the hunt; $Y$ the vegetables foraged through the tribal gathering; and $Z$ as the spears used in the hunt.

The introduction of spear-makers in the social division of labour requires higher levels of tribal *trust*. Indeed, these spear-makers rely for their livelihood completely on the foodstuffs provided by the hunters and gatherers in the tribe. Such spear-makers can thus only be introduced in the tribal division of labour if the leadership of the tribe supports the provision of goods to these members. This might require a stronger leadership model, based on enhanced political and socio-economic institutions.

The deepening of the social division of labour clearly corresponds to disruptive innovation. In fact, Schumpeter (1934, 1935) referred to these fundamental changes as *creative destruction*. Indeed, the introduction of new specialisations and new commodities fundamentally affects the social division of labour, and thus this creation destroys the old social division of labour. This might even cause anxiety and social unrest. Only after settling into the new social division of labour can trust levels return to normal and the full benefits of this fundamental change be reaped.

**Model Implications** Returning to our model, in the case of this fundamental innovation a tribe member can now select from three specialisms or "professions":

(i) *Hunting:* A hunter uses his or her own labour time and one spear to generate 30 units of meat. This is represented by the production plan $(30, 0, -1)$.

(ii) *Foraging:* As before, a gatherer produces an output of 20 units of vegetables, represented by the production plan $(0, 20, 0)$.

(iii) *Tool-making:* A spear-maker produces one spear, represented by a production plan $(0, 0, 1)$.

Note here that spears now become necessary inputs to the production of meat. Therefore, under the described production technologies 30 units of meat are essentially produced by two fully specialised individuals in the tribal division of labour: one hunter and one spear-maker.

Again we compute the optimal social division of labour under these modified circumstances. As before let $k \in \{0, 1, \ldots, 20\}$ be the total number of fully specialised hunters in the social division of labour. Each hunter is necessarily supported by one spear-maker, as pointed out above. Therefore, there are $k$ spear-makers in the social division of labour as well. Consequently, there are exactly $20-2k$ fully specialised gatherers in the resulting social division of labour. The total generated output through this social division of labour can now be computed as

$$O_4(k) = k \times (30, 0, -1) + (20-2k) \times (0, 20, 0) + k \times (0, 0, 1) = (30k, 400-40k, 0). \tag{1.18}$$

The consumption bundle for each member under the egalitarian division rule is now computed as

$$C_4(k) = \frac{O_4(k)}{20} = \left( 1\tfrac{1}{2}k, 20 - 2k, 0 \right)$$

and the resulting individual utility of each member is now determined as

$$U_4(k) = \left( 1\tfrac{1}{2}k + 1 \right) \left( 22 - 2k \right) = 22 + 31k - 3k^2 \tag{1.19}$$

The *optimal* social division is now determined by solving the maximisation of this utility: $\max_k U_4(k)$, which solves to $k = 5\tfrac{1}{6}$. Therefore, the feasible optimal social division of labour in this tribe is determined as $k_4 = 5$ and results in a social division of labour made up of five hunters, ten gatherers and five spear-makers. This tribal division of labour results in a total tribal output of $O_4(5) = (150, 200, 0)$, an individual consumption bundle of $C_4(5) = \left( 7\tfrac{1}{2}, 10, 0 \right)$ and an optimal utility level of $\overline{U}_4 = U_4(5) = 102 > \overline{U}_3 = 72$.

Again we compute the increase in tribal well-being due to this particular deepening of the social division of labour in the tribe:

$$\Delta_4 = \frac{\overline{U}_4 - \overline{U}_3}{\overline{U}_3} = 0.417. \tag{1.20}$$

This implies that the deepening of the tribal division of labour results in an increase in tribal well-being of 41.7%. This indicates the order of development and wealth creation that can be accomplished through disruptive change, such as this deepening of the social division of labour.

## 1.6   Some Further Considerations

In this discussion of the example of a hunter-gatherer economy that creates wealth through a primitive social division of labour, I have brought together the main elements that have to be considered:

(a) The economy is made up of agents that have consumptive as well as productive abilities. This is fully expressed in the notion of a "consumer-producer".

(b) These productive abilities are subject to *increasing returns to specialisation, or IRSpec*, which is at the foundation of any social wealth generation process. This refers to human ability to achieve higher levels of output when specialising in specific productive tasks.

(c) The social division of labour itself is mainly built around an infrastructure in which specialised individual agents are embedded in production and trade networks. Hence the economy has a distinct network structure, rather than a market structure. The chains of specialised agents form *production networks*—also known as "supply chains" in our contemporary capitalist global economy—founded on mutually beneficial trade relationships in which specialised goods and services are exchanged or traded.

(d) The social division of labour itself is only possible through the human ability to act cooperatively and rely on others. This sociality provides the glue that holds the production and trade networks in the social division of labour together.

(e) This human sociality finds its effective expression in socio-economic institutions in which the social division of labour is *embedded*. These institutions guide all activities in the social division of labour—and thus in the economy. The trade mechanisms as well as the socio-economic roles in the social division of labour form part of the institutional governance structure that guides the economy.

I emphasise that without institutional governance there is no social division of labour and that, consequently, economic performance is tied closely together with the effectiveness of these institutions. In this regard, the social division of labour is organised through the intermediation of institutional guidance.

These institutions include the trade mechanisms that guide our economic decisions. In particular, the price mechanism is an explicit institution that can guide all actions in the production and trade networks. Therefore the "competitive market" is an institution that guides such decisions, but can by itself not be all encompassing. Different network structures lead to possibly different outcomes under the same competitive price mechanism.

This fundamental model of wealth creation leads naturally to a theory of economic growth and development that is fully in line with Smith's and Ricardo's theories. The sources of economic development and enhanced wealth creation can be categorised in two distinct groups:

**Basic development:**    These sources for economic growth refer to processes that modify the building blocks of the social division of labour, but do not affect the architecture of that social division directly. Hence this refers to changes in descriptors of consumer-producers such as production technologies and preferences. We distinguish here the following elements:

- **Population growth:** This refers to the number of available consumer-producers in the economy. As pointed out, an enhanced population makes it possible to establish a more perfect approximation of an optimal social division of labour, leading to modest increases in the level of the generated wealth.
- **Technological progress:** Production technologies can develop in two forms. *Incremental progress* refers to gradual change of productive abilities of the individuals in the social division of labour to produce goods. This is the change that drives most of a steady growth in the economy.
  *Significant innovation:* This refers to the implementation of inventions that significantly push forward the productivity of individuals. This leads to more radical adaptation of the social division of labour, substantially altering the structure of the economy.

**Institutional development:**    This refers to the fundamental *deepening* of the social division of labour through the introduction of new economic goods, new socio-economic roles and new trade institutions. This represents the most disruptive change in the social division of labour. This disruptive change leads to significant changes in the level of economic wealth that is generated. *Entrepreneurship* is closely related to institutional change, as we will see in the subsequent chapters.

As shown in the simple example, introducing new intermediary inputs and socio-economic roles significantly changes the social division of labour. This might result in very significant economic growth. The deepening of the social division of labour results in longer chains in the production networks in the economy, which require strong guidance of socio-economic institutions to maintain stability. Thus, the deepening of these chains is tied in with significant institutional innovation at all levels. Without such institutional innovation and strengthened governance, these chains might collapse.

Indeed, I emphasise that institutional change might lead to significant growth in economic wealth, but also to catastrophic economic collapse as shown in the Great Panics of 1873 and 2008. In Chap. 2, I will develop a comprehensive analysis that shows that the deepening of the mortgage supply chains in the financial sector of the global economy led to economic catastrophe. In both cases, the socio-economic institutions in the economy were insufficiently well developed and provided ineffective guidance in the economy, allowing these deeper chains to collapse. Indeed, if the institutional foundation of the economy is unable to support the deepening of the social division of labour, major economic crises might result. This is debated in depth in Chap. 2.

In our contemporary global economy, all of these identified sources are simultaneously at work and affect the processes of economic growth. It is recognised in the political debates about immigration that population growth is a necessity in the creation of more economic wealth in the global economy—not only to make a more perfect approximation of the ideal social division of labour possible, but also to allow technological progress and institutional change to take hold in the economy.

Similarly, technological progress through improved education of the labour force is considered vital in the search for higher economic growth. In the debates on immigration and education in our contemporary western capitalist economies, the emphasis lies mainly on these sources for economic growth.

On the other hand, in our political discourse about economic policy, the deepening of the social division of labour through institutional innovation is far less recognised as a fundamental source of economic growth. This is an important omission. As the example and the accompanying discussions show, the deepening of the social division of labour is a fundamental source for increasing economic wealth generation and economic growth. Such deepening is closely tied in with a much broader form of institutional innovation. And, as pointed out, such institutional innovation might result in major economic advances, but also in major economic collapse. The innovation process itself induces major uncertainties that accompany the deepening of the social division of labour. This is further explored in Chap. 2, where I look at the history of economic wealth generation through the lens of the development of the social division of labour and its institutional governance.

## Appendix: The Nature of Markets

In our daily lives the words "market" and "market economy" are used in many different contexts and with various meanings. Remarkably, we mean rather diverse things with the same word, and these meanings do not correspond in general to the meaning given to markets in economic theory such as presented in the standard microeconomics text books. In this appendix I hope to clarify some misunderstandings about the usage of these terms.

I emphasise that the usage of the term "market" and "price" is central to a contemporary perspective on our society and especially our globalised economy. For a large part it defines how politicians view the world and it characterises how economics has influenced our perception of the world around us in a profound way. Sadly, this perception is biased and incomplete at best. Misunderstandings about markets are plentiful and strongly affect economic policies, thus resulting in misguided efforts by national and local governments and authorities. It is within this context that I provide an incomplete typology of the usage of the market concept as it appears in our daily discourse.

**Markets as cost pricing:**    A price is often interpreted as a measurement of the production cost of a certain commodity. This reflects a pure supply-side reasoning as underlying a commodity's market price; prices are defended based on a distinctive cost basis rather than on a demand–supply reasoning. Particularly, increases in prices of essentials such as food, energy and housing are defended and analysed on these grounds.

This reasoning about commodity prices is deeply rooted in the *labour theory of value* (Ricardo 1817; Mill 1848; Marx 1893). The main reason for invoking such labour theoretical foundations for the pricing of a commodity is that this reasoning is usually rather intuitive and that indeed in many instances prices do not reflect social scarcity of the commodity, but rather a cost price. Monopolistic producers, such as energy companies, justify price changes purely on a cost basis. Examples are the pricing of petrol, which is depicted as being driven by the price on the world market for oil, and natural gas, which price in Europe is linked to the price of oil rather than being determined in its own market.

Can we dismiss the invoking of cost pricing in the context of our contemporary global economy? I do not think that this is easily done. There are simply too many practical instances of the use of cost pricing in our contemporary global economy to dismiss such reasonings out of hand.

Since its inception in the 1870s, market theory has promoted the fundamental hypothesis that the pricing of traded commodities is fully determined by demand as well as supply. As discussed, neo-classical market theory embraced a market theory of value, which replaced the labour theory of value. It is interesting to see that after nearly 150 years of promoting this market theory of value, these ideas have not settled in society.

**Markets as notional demand:**    Politicians and business leaders might also discuss and use the term "market" to represent a demand-side perspective only. This is when one says that "one's market is determined by the local conditions under which one operates". It is intended that the word "market" here describes the potential demand for a product. The supply of this product is not subject to this consideration.

For example, Queen's University is the largest provider of higher education in Northern Ireland. One can describe this as being that the "market" for Queen's University is determined by the demand for higher education in Northern Ireland. In other words, "Queen's market" is equated with the region of Northern Ireland.

A superior terminology of such a consideration is to refer to the *notional* demand or the demand potential for a good. Here the notion of notional demand incorporates a more complex perspective than only the potential demand for a product; it also refers to the totality of conditions under which trade occurs. This includes the very basic ability of the economic subjects involved to be able to communicate with each other and to formulate their desires and abilities. Economic subjects therefore need to accept the same economic institutions to be able to properly interact. For example, these economic subjects need to recognise the same monetary system as a precondition for trade (Mitchell 1944).

Again the use of the terminology of a market as notional demand is rather unsatisfactory from the point of view of neo-classical economic theory. Indeed, demand and supply are principally separated and only meet in the setting of a market. A market cannot describe only one of its two essential components.

In Chap. 3 I give a more precise definition of notional demand through the broader notion of a *socio-economic space*. Such a space is a construct that incorporates notional demand as well as notional supply in an institutional framework. Therefore a socio-economic space introduces a context in which markets and other trade networks can emerge. It brings together all pre-conditions that make trade possible, including the economic institutions that facilitate such trade. These institutions include, but are not limited to, monetary systems, pricing conventions and the market institutions themselves.

**Markets as political abstractions:**    If politicians debate economic policy, they usually invoke the abstraction of a "market" to promote their favourite economic policy. Here, the notion of a market simply refers to the ideal of a capitalistic economic system. It usually includes the ideological logo that voluntary decisions by "free" individuals determine the outcome of these economic process and, therefore, can be deemed to be "good". In the decades since the 1980s this ideal of private decision-making has infiltrated economic policy in a fundamental fashion throughout the western advanced economies. A wave of privatisation of publicly owned and operated enterprises was the result. This included the privatisation of health care facilities such as hospitals and insurance providers, of energy providers, in particular government-controlled electricity companies, and even of postal services in the European Union.

Public considerations were reduced and replaced by private solutions supported by the idealised view that privately informed decisions are superior to public or political decisions. Indeed, market theory promotes the idea that private actions within the context of a competitive market result in an efficient or socially optimal state.

Here the reference to the "market" actually points to private decision-making rather than collective decision-making through a political process. There is usually no regard for the conditions that are required to be implemented to make such private decision-making processes result in a socially optimal state. As such, the use of the notion of "market" is very misleading in this context, which is shown by considering the actual outcomes of such privatisation processes. An excellent example is the failure of health care systems founded on private ownership of health care providers and privately provided health insurance in the USA as well as several countries in the European Union.

**Markets as actual market places:**   Traditionally, markets were viewed as localities or physical spaces in which trade takes place. I refer to the seminal marginalists Jevons (1871) and Menger (1871) for the invocation of such a definition. The usage of the concept of a market in this context actually refers to trade taking place on market squares in cities; in buildings such as stock exchanges and shopping malls; in auction houses; and on websites such as eBay and other online trading companies.

Clearly, in this context the notion of a market indeed refers to the purest form of what actually is represented by a theoretical market: a place at which demand and supply meet and are resolved through a process of price adjustment.

However, in reality such marketplaces usually do not conform with theoretical conditions as assumed in economic models. Indeed, commodities are never truly transparent; transaction costs are rarely absent; and information about the trades that occur is hard to come by. All in all, practical markets are rather problematic examples of the theoretical constructions considered by neo-classical economists.

On the other hand, I believe that markets as invoked above come closest to the ideal advocated in economic theory. Instead, the question has to be asked whether the theory cannot be improved to reflect the actual dealings that occur in these market places. Geertz (1979) and Kirman and Vriend (2001) imply that practical market places can much better be understood as networks. Influences such as customer loyalty and long-run relationships lead me to believe that these markets are indeed networks rather than a system in which demand and supply interact totally to establish a unique market price for every commodity traded.

**Markets as trade networks:**   Finally, I come to the usage of the notion of the concept of a "market" that comes closest to my understanding of how a market actually should be perceived and approached: as a social trade network rather than a place in which demand and supply are resolved.

The neo-classical market theory assumes that all executed trades are guided by a unique market price for each a commodity and that information about these prices and the trades performed is freely available. This free information exchange in turn makes the formation of such a unique market price possible through the competitive forces in the market that in turn are founded on the private, selfish motives of the traders.

However, in a trade network such considerations are far less obvious. It is not clear why the same, unique price can be sustained in different parts of the network, even if all information is freely available to the traders. Only if sufficient competition can be generated that actually makes the network obsolete or trivial can prices be corrected through the threat of trades at other prices with remote traders in the network. This is usually not the case. Instead, prices are not unique and are locally determined through the trades that occur in a certain part of the network and the abilities of the traders to generate competing trades.

Furthermore, information travels very awkwardly within a social network and can be distorted.[48] This, in turn, affects trade decisions. Therefore it can be expected that trade networks are particularly vulnerable to information problems.

I refer here to my discussion of the main mortgage-provision chain in Fig. 2.2, which is subject to agency problems based on ex-post information deficiencies. In practice the agency problems were compounded by the presence of misinformation, in particular the high ratings put on the mortgage-backed securities as traded in the financial markets.

From a theoretical point of view, there emerge two important conceptions from this discussion. First, the network trade processes can be captured as it were in an envelope formulation through the notion of Edgeworthian barter processes (Edgeworth 1881) and the *core* of the economy as a consequence captures the possible outcomes. Second, the prices of goods that emerge in these trade networks can be denoted as the *network prices* of a good. Therefore, one good can obviously have many network prices depending on the local conditions under which trade in the network is executed. This refers to the theoretical modelling of "product differentiation" through the diversification present in the trade network. Instead of using a contingent commodity concept to express this differentiation or diversity, it is expressed through the local conditions and the diversity in the trade network.

I do not claim to be complete in my typology of the usage of the notion of the market; far from it. Rather, I hope to capture the main meanings that prevail around us when people and decision-makers use the word "market" in their justifications. For a more elaborate discussion I also refer to Rosenbaum (2000).

---

[48] This again refers to one of the animal spirits considered by Akerlof and Shiller (2009), namely the effect that stories have on economic decision-making. Gossip is particularly distorting within a sparse social network: Stories might morph into different forms and misinformation can abound. This is even the case in such highly developed networks as facilitated by the internet; in many cases blogging has increased the amount of misinformation rather than facilitated the improvement of the quality of the information shared.

# REFERENCES

Akerlof, G.A., and R.J. Shiller. 2009. *Animal Spirits: How Human Psychology Drives the Economy and Why it Matters for Global Capitalism.* Princeton, NJ: Princeton University Press.

Aristotle (340 BCE). *Ethica Nicomachea.* 2009 ed. Oxford: Oxford University Press.

Aristotle (350 BCE). *The Politics: A Treatise on Government.* 1995 ed. Oxford: Oxford University Press.

Arnsperger, C., and Y. Varoufakis. 2006. What Is Neoclassical Economics? The Three Axioms Responsible for Its Theoretical Oeuvre, Practical Irrelevance and, Thus, Discursive Power. *Post-Autistic Economics Review* 38: 1–12.

Aumann, R.J. 1964. Markets with a Continuum of Traders. *Econometrica* 32: 39–50.

Babbage, C. 1835. *On the Economy of Machinery and Manufacturers.* 4th enlarged ed. London: Augustus M. Kelley Publishers.

Backhouse, R. 2010. *The Puzzle of Modern Economics: Science or Ideology?* Cambridge: Cambridge University Press.

Beaudreau, B.C. 2004. *World Trade: A Network Approach.* New York, NY: iUniverse.

Blitch, C.P. 1983. Allyn Young on Increasing Returns. *Journal of Post Keynesian Economics* 5: 359–371.

Bowles, S., and H. Gintis. 2011. *A Cooperative Species: Human Reciprocity and Its Evolution.* Princeton, NJ: Princeton University Press.

Buchanan, J.M. 2008. Let Us Understand Adam Smith. *Journal of the History of Economic Thought* 30: 19–28.

Buchanan, J.M., and Y.J. Yoon. 2002. Globalization as Framed by the Two Logics of Trade. *Independent Review* 6(3): 399–405.

Cervellati, M., P. Fortunato, and U. Sunde. 2008. Hobbes to Rousseau: Inequality, Institutions and Development. *Economic Journal* 118: 1354–1384.

Chang, H.J. 2014. *Economics: The User's Guide.* Gretna, LA: Pelican.

Christakis, N.A., and J.H. Fowler. 2009. *Connected: The Surprising Power of Our Social Networks and How They Shape Our Lives.* London: Harper Press.

Diamantaras, D., and R.P. Gilles. 2004. On the Microeconomics of Specialization. *Journal of Economic Behavior and Organization* 55: 223–236.

Duménil, G., and D. Lévy. 2011. *The Crisis of Neoliberalism.* Cambridge, MA: Harvard University Press.

Dunbar, R.I.M. 1992. Neocortex Size as a Constraint on Group Size in Primates. *Journal of Human Evolution* 22: 469–493.

Dunbar, R.I.M. 2003. Evolution of the Social Brain. *Science* 302: 1160–1161.

Dunbar, R.I.M. 2009. The Social Brain Hypothesis and Its Implications for Social Evolution. *Annals of Human Biology* 36(5): 562–572.

Dunbar, R.I.M. 2014. *Human Evolution: A Pelican Introduction.* Gretna, LA: Pelican.

Edgeworth, F.Y. 1881. *Mathematical Psychics: An Essay on the Application of Mathematics to the Moral Sciences.* London: C. Kegan Paul & Co.

Foley, D.K. 2006. *Adam's Fallacy: A Guide to Economic Theology.* Cambridge, MA: Belknap Press.

Fourie, F.C.V.N. 1991. The Nature of the Market: A Structural Analysis. In *Rethinking Economics: Markets, Technology and Economic Evolution,* ed. G.M. Hodgson and E. Screpanti, 40–57. Aldershot: Edward Elgar Publishing.

Fuchs, V. 1968. *The Service Economy.* National Bureau of Economic Research, New York, NY, General Series No. 87.

Geary, R.C. 1950–1951. A Note on "A Constant Utility Index of the Cost of Living". *Review of Economic Studies* 18(1): 65–66.

Geertz, C. 1979. Suq: The Bazaar Economy in Sefrou. In *Meaning and Order in Moroccan Society: Three Essays in Cultural Analysis*, ed. C. Geertz, H. Geertz, and L. Rosen, 123–313. Cambridge, MA: Cambridge University Press.

Gilles, R.P. 2017a. The Core of an Economy with an Endogenous Social Division of Labour. Working Paper, Management School, Queen's University Belfast, Belfast, UK.

Gilles, R.P. 2017b. Market Economies with an Endogenous Social Division of Labour. Working paper, Queen's University Management School, Belfast, UK.

Gilles, R.P. 2018. *Economic Wealth Creation and the Social Division of Labour Volume II: Network Economies*. London: Palgrave Macmillan.

Gilles, R.P., E.A. Lazarova, and P.H.M. Ruys. 2015. Stability in a Network Economy: The Role of Institutions. *Journal of Economic Behavior and Organization* 119: 375–399.

Gilles, R.P., M. Pesce, and D. Diamantaras. 2017. The Provision of Collective Goods through a Social Division of Labour. Working Paper #369, CSEF—Centre for Studies in Economics and Finance, Department of Economics, University of Naples Frederico II, Naples, Italy.

Gimpel, J. 1976. *The Medieval Machine: The Industrial Revolution of the Middle Ages*. London: Penguin.

Gintis, H. 2017. *Individuality and Entanglement: The Moral and Material Bases of Social Life*. Princeton, NJ: Princeton University Press.

Graeber, D. 2011. *Debt: The First 5,000 Years*. Brooklyn, NY: Melville House Publishing.

Haegens, K. 2015. *De grootste show op aarde: De mythe van de markteconomie*. Amsterdam: AmboAnthos.

Hahn, F.H. 1971. Equilibrium with Transaction Costs. *Econometrica* 39: 417–439.

Hahn, F.H. 1973. On Transaction Costs, Inessential Sequence Economies and Money. *Review of Economic Studies* 40: 449–461.

Hahn, F.H., and R.M. Starr. 1976. Equilibrium with Non-Convex Transaction Costs: Monetary and Non-Monetary Economies. *Review of Economic Studies* 43: 195–215.

Harari, Y.N. 2014. *Sapiens: A Brief History of Humankind*. London: Vintage Books.

Hardin, R. 2006. *Trust*. Cambridge: Polity Press.

Harvey, D. 2017. *Marx, Capital and the Madness of Economic Reason*. London: Profile Books.

Hayek, F.A. 1937. Economics and Knowledge. *Economica* 4: 33–54.

Hayek, F.A. 1945. The Use of Knowledge in Society. *American Economic Review* 35: 519–530.

Hayek, F.A. 1960. *The Constitution of Liberty*. Chicago, IL: University of Chicago Press.

Hidalgo, C. 2015. *Why Information Grows: The Evolution of Order, from Atoms to Economies*. London: Allen Lane (Penguin).

Hildenbrand, W. 1974. *Core and Equilibria of a Large Economy*. Princeton, NJ: Princeton University Press.

Horan, R., E. Bulte, and J. Shogren. 2005. How Trade Saved Humanity from Biological Exclusion: An Economic Theory of Neanderthal Extinction. *Journal of Economic Behavior and Organization* 58(1): 1–29.

Hume, D. 1740. *A Treatise of Human Nature*. Oxford Philosophical Texts. Oxford: Oxford University Press. Reprint 2002, ed. David Fate Norton and Mary J. Norton.

Hume, D. 1748. *An Enquiry Concerning Human Understanding.* Oxford Philosophical Texts. Reprint 1999, ed. Tom L. Beauchamp. Oxford: Oxford University Press.

Jackson, M.O., T.R. Barraquer, and X. Tan. 2012. Social Capital and Social Quilts: Network Patterns of Favor Exchange. *American Economic Review* 102(5): 1857–1897.

Jevons, W.S. 1871. *The Theory of Political Economy.* 1970 ed. London: Penguin.

Kets, W., G. Iyengar, R. Sethi, and S. Bowles. 2011. Inequality and Network Structure. *Games and Economic Behavior* 73: 215–226.

Kirman, A.P., and N.J. Vriend. 2001. Evolving Market Structure: An ACE Model of Price Dispersion and Loyalty. *Journal of Economic Dynamics and Control* 25: 459–502.

Klaes, M. 2000. The History of the Concept of Transaction Costs: Neglected Aspects. *Journal of the History of Economic Thought* 22(2): 191–216.

Knight, F.H. 1921. *Risk, Uncertainty and Profit.* Boston, MA: Houghton Mifflin.

Kuhn, S.L., and M.C. Stiner. 2006. What's a Mother to Do? The Division of Labor among Neandertals and Modern Humans in Eurasia. *Current Anthropology* 47: 953–980.

Leijonhufvud, A. 2007. The Individual, the Market and the Division of Labor in Society. *Capitalism and Society* 2(2): Article 3.

Leontief, W. 1936. Quantitative Input and Output Relations in the Economic Systems of the United States. *Review of Economics and Statistics* 18(3): 105–125.

Malthus, T.R. 1798. *An Essay on the Principle of Population, as it Affects the Future Improvement of Society.* London: J. Johnson.

Mandeville, B. 1714. *The Fable of the Bees; Or, Private Vices, Publick Benefits.* 1924 ed. London: J. Tonson.

Marshall, A. 1890. *Principles of Economics.* 8th ed. London: Macmillan Press.

Marx, K. 1867. *Capital: A Critique of Political Economy — Volume I: The Process of Production of Capital.* 1967 ed. New York, NY: International Publishers.

Marx, K. 1893. *Capital: A Critique of Political Economy — Volume II: The Process of Circulation of Capital.* 1967 ed. New York, NY: International Publishers.

Marx, K. 1894. *Capital: A Critique of Political Economy — Volume III: The Process of Capitalist Production as a Whole.* 1967 ed. New York, NY: International Publishers.

Ménard, C. 1995. Markets as Institutions Versus Organizations as Markets? Disentangling Some Fundamental Concepts. *Journal of Economic Behavior and Organization* 28: 161–182.

Menger, C. 1871. *Grundsätze der Volkswirtschaftslehre.* 1976 ed. New York, NY: New York University Press.

Mill, J.S. 1848. *Principles of Political Economy.* London: John W. Parker.

Mitchell, W.C. 1944. The Role of Money in Economic History. *Journal of Economic History* 4(Supplement: The Tasks of Economic History): 61–67.

North, D.C. 1989. Institutions and Economic Growth: A Historical Introduction. *World Development* 17(9): 1319–1332.

North, D.C. 1990. *Institutions, Institutional Change and Economic Performance.* Cambridge: Cambridge University Press.

North, D.C. 1991. Institutions. *Journal of Economic Perspectives* 5(1): 97–112.

Pareto, V. 1906. *Manual of Political Economy.* 1972 reprint ed. London: Macmillan Press.

Plato (380 BCE). *Republic.* 2007 ed. London: Penguin Classics.

Prendergast, R. 2016. Bernard Mandeville and the Doctrine of Laissez-faire. *Erasmus Journal for Philosophy and Economics* 9(1): 101–123.

Ricardo, D. 1817. *On the Principles of Political Economy and Taxation*. London: John Murray.

Ridley, M. 2010. *The Rational Optimist: How Prosperity Evolves*. London: Fourth Estate.

Roemer, J.E. 1980. A General Equilibrium Approach to Marxian Economics. *Econometrica* 48(2): 505–530.

Roemer, J.E. 1981. *Analytical Foundations of Marxian Economic Theory*. Cambridge: Cambridge University Press.

Roemer, J.E. 1998. *Equality of Opportunity*. Cambridge, MA: Harvard University Press.

Rosenbaum, E.F. 2000. What Is a Market? On the Methodology of a Contested Concept. *Review of Social Economy* 58(4): 455–482.

Ruys, P.H.M. 2002. A General Equilibrium of Managed Services. In *Equilibrium, Markets and Dynamics: Essays in the Honour of Claus Weddepohl*, ed. C. Hommes, R. Ramer, and C. Withagen, 117–139. Berlin: Springer.

Ruys, P.H.M. 2006. The Governance of Services. TILEC Discussion Paper Series, Tilburg University, Netherlands.

Ruys, P.H.M. 2008. A Constructive Theory of Representation. CentER Discussion Paper Series, Tilburg University, Tilburg, The Netherlands.

Ruys, P.H.M. 2009. The Nature of a Social Enterprise. Working Paper, CentER for Economic Research, Tilburg University, Tilburg.

Say, J.B. 1826. *Traité d'Économie Politique*. Paris: Chez Rapille.

Schumpeter, J. 1926. *Theorie der wirtschaftlichen Entwicklung: Eine Untersuchung über Unternehmergewinn, Kapital, Kredit, Zins und den Konjunkturzyklus*. 2nd ed. Berlin: Duncker und Humblot.

Schumpeter, J. 1934. *The Theory of Economic Development: An Inquiry into Profits, Capital, Credit, Interest and the Business Cycle*. Cambridge, MA: Harvard University Press.

Schumpeter, J. 1935. The Analysis of Economic Change. *Review of Economic Statistics* 17: 2–10.

Seabright, P. 2010. *The Company of Strangers: A Natural History of Economic Life*. Revised and enlarged edn. Princeton, NJ: Princeton University Press.

Silvermintz, D. 2010. Plato's Supposed Defense of the Division of Labor: A Reexamination of the Role of Job Specialization in the Republic. *History of Political Economy* 42(4): 747–772.

Simon, H.A. 1951. A Formal Theory of the Employment Relationship. *Econometrica* 19(3): 293–305.

Simon, H.A. 1991. Organizations and Markets. *Journal of Economic Perspectives* 5(2): 25–44.

Smith, A. 1759. *The Theory of Moral Sentiments*, Cambridge Texts in the History of Philosophy. Reprint 2002, ed. Knud Haakonssen. Cambridge, MA: Cambridge University Press.

Smith, A. 1776. *An Inquiry into the Nature and Causes of the Wealth of Nations*. Reprint 1976. Chicago, IL: University of Chicago Press.

Snehota, I. 1993. Market as Network and the Nature of the Market Process. In *Advances in International Marketing*, ed. D. Deo, 31–41. Greenwich, CT: JAI Press.

Sowell, T. 1972. *Say's Law: An Historical Analysis*. Princeton, NJ: Princeton University Press, Third printing, 1989.

Sraffa, P. 1960. *Production of Commodities by Means of Commodities: Prelude to a Critique of Economic Theory.* Cambridge, MA: Cambridge University Press.

Stone, R. 1954. Linear Expenditure Systems and Demand Analysis: An Application to the Pattern of British Demand. *Economic Journal* 64: 511–527.

Sun, G. 2012. *The Division of Labor in Economics: A History.* Routledge Studies in the History of Economics. London: Routledge.

Sun, G., X. Yang, and L. Zhou. 2004. General Equilibria in Large Economies with Endogenous Structure of Division of Labor. *Journal of Economic Behavior and Organization* 55: 237–256.

Swedberg, R. 1994. Markets as Social Structures. In *The Handbook of Economic Sociology*, ed. N.J. Smelser and R. Swedberg, 255–282. Princeton, NJ: Princeton University Press.

Tversky, A., and D. Kahneman. 1974. Judgment Under Uncertainty: Heuristics and Biases. *Science* 185(4157): 1124–1131.

Ulph, A.M., and D.T. Ulph. 1975. Transaction Costs in General Equilibrium Theory: A Survey. *Economica* 42: 355–372.

Veblen, T.B. 1898. The Instinct of Workmanship and the Irksomeness of Labor. *American Journal of Sociology* 4(2): 187–201.

Verhulst, A. 2002. *The Carolingian Economy.* Cambridge Medieval Textbooks. Cambridge, MA: Cambridge University Press.

Vignes, A. 1993. Dispersion de prix et marchés décentralisés: le cas du marché au poisson de Marseille. Ph.D. thesis, European University Institute, Florence, Italy.

Vignes, A., and J.-M. Etienne. 2011. Price Formation on the Marseille Fish Market: Evidence from a Network Analysis. *Journal of Economic Behavior and Organization* 80: 50–67.

Walras, L. 1926. *Eléments d'économie politique pure, ou théorie de la richesse sociale (Elements of Pure Economics, or the Theory of Social Wealth).* 4th ed. Paris: Richard D. Irwin Inc. Translation by William Jaffe, 1954.

Whiten, A., and R.W. Byrne. 1988. Tactical Deception in Primates. *Behavioral and Brain Sciences* 11: 233–273.

Williamson, O.E. 1979. Transaction-Cost Economics: The Governance of Contractual Relations. *Journal of Law and Economics* 22: 233–261.

Williamson, O.E. 2000. The New Institutional Economics: Taking Stock, Looking Ahead. *Journal of Economic Literature* 38(3): 595–613.

Xenophon (362 BCE). *Œconomicus.* 1994 ed. vol. Translated by Sarah B. Pomeroy. Oxford: Clarendon Press.

Xenophon (370 BCE). *Cyropædia: The Education of Cyrus.* 1914 ed. London: Pantianos Classics.

Yang, X. 1988. A Microeconomic Approach to Modeling the Division of Labor Based on Increasing Returns to Specialization. Ph.D. thesis, Princeton University, Princeton, NJ.

Yang, X. 2001. *Economics: New Classical Versus Neoclassical Frameworks.* Malden, MA: Blackwell Publishing.

Yang, X. 2003. *Economic Development and the Division of Labor.* Malden, MA: Blackwell Publishing.

Yang, X., and Y.-K. Ng. 1993. *Specialization and Economic Organization: A New Classical Microeconomic Framework.* Amsterdam: North-Holland.

Young, A.A. 1928. Increasing Returns and Economic Progress. *Economic Journal* 38: 527–542.

# CHAPTER 2

# Of Bubbles and Crises: A History of Wealth Creation

As I write these lines, our global economy seems to have embarked on a prolonged journey of continuing crisis and depression. In 2007 a bubble in the housing market morphed into a disruptive bank crisis, which in turn resulted in a governmental budgetary crisis around the world—also known as the *sovereign debt crisis* of 2010–2011. Currently, the global economy has entered a phase of relatively low productivity growth that can be interpreted as the third stage of the ongoing trust crisis. This is compounded by general unrest in large parts of the world, causing political volatility and the rebirth of nationalism.

In this chapter I sketch how the global economy has got into this bind, and infer lessons about the global economy from the perspective set out in Chap. 1. For alternative accounts and perspectives, I also refer to Morris (2008), Phillips (2008), Stiglitz (2010), Johnson and Kwak (2010), Varoufakis (2011), Mirowski (2013), Mason (2015), Roberts (2016) and Harvey (2017). For my own analysis and historical perspective, I am drawing partially on these sources as well as numerous other accounts.

I will present here a historical perspective on wealth creation and link the current predicament of the global economy to the historical development of the social division of labour and of wealth creation. There are two main lessons to be taken from this analysis. First, these crises are quite normal in the history of wealth creation; there are inevitable failures of wealth creation processes through the deepening of the production chains that make up the social division of labour. The lengthening of these chains weakens them, and without strong institutional embedding of these chains failure is actually inevitable. Thus, wealth creation processes as conducted through a social division of labour are inherently unstable.

Second, the current crisis seems in many respects unique. New production technologies require extreme institutional innovation and the development of alternative arrangements of the global production processes. However,

© The Author(s) 2018                                              83
R. P. Gilles, *Economic Wealth Creation and the Social Division of Labour*,
https://doi.org/10.1007/978-3-319-76397-2_2

entrenched capitalist structures block the inevitable innovation required. Our global social division of labour has regressed rather than progressed during the past decades, and consequently this has resulted in a *platform economy*— based on the extraction of value from middleman positions in the networks that make up the global trade infrastructure. Instead, the economy should move to a network-based form in which zero marginal cost production technologies can be liberated in the social division of labour and separated from the allocation of the generated collective wealth from these networks. This *network economy* remains a dream, however, and it is unclear whether it will ever be realised (Mason 2015).

**Outline of This Chapter**  I divide this chapter into three parts. First I develop a dynamic theoretical framework of how to perceive the historical institutional innovation processes. This is done through the concept of an "institutional wave". Next, I apply this theoretical framework to understand the history of wealth creation. This takes us from feudalism to the precapitalist economy and contemporary global capitalism. I provide a detailed analysis of the Great Panic of 2008 by investigating the division of the labour chain to produce financial products, in particular mortgages in the US economy. I conclude by speculating about the next stages in the development of wealth creation and its institutional setting.

## 2.1    INSTITUTIONAL WAVES

A number of general access books have been written in the aftermath of the financial crisis of 2007/2008 and the subsequent sovereign debt crisis and secular stagnation, reflecting on "how we got here".[1] A historical perspective is very useful to see whether a certain theoretical framework clarifies and explains the observed phenomena in world economic history.

Here I set out to investigate historical human development and the history of human wealth creation from the relational–institutional perspective developed in the previous chapter. I restrict myself to tracking the historical development of the institutions at the foundation of the governance system in the global economy. Such development clearly comes in leaps and bounds. Periods of evolutionary change and modest institutional change are punctuated by periods of significant institutional development and revolution. These revolutionary periods of renewal and restructuring can be viewed as periods of extreme

---

[1] Here I refer to Phillips (2008), Akerlof and Shiller (2009), Stiglitz (2010), Johnson and Kwak (2010), Varoufakis (2011), Harari (2014), Haegens (2015), Mason (2015), Roberts (2016) and Harvey (2017). Many of these books put the financial crash of 2007/2008 in a historical perspective and some of them are completely focused on human history and development. Many of these authors propose a historical view that is *not* founded on a neo-classical economic perspective. The reason is that this perspective actually does not make a lot of sense when it comes to explaining human (economic) history in general and the crisis of 2007/2008 in particular.

entrepreneurial activity. These periods come about owing to the underlying evolutionary forces in the economy in which extractive structures are contested through the introduction of innovative institutions, goods and networks. Therefore, there emerges a perspective in which institutional development is expressed through waves or cycles.

An *institutional wave* can be described as developing through four stages. Each stage corresponds to the effects that an institutional framework has on human interaction and development. I distinguish these stages roughly as follows:

**Innovation:**    After the institutions on which the previous wave has been based have matured, there emerge innovative alternative institutions, goods and trade infrastructural elements. These innovations affect the governance system and the economic wealth creation process is stimulated by the rise of these new institutional instruments of wealth creation.

Initially, the economy will be affected only marginally by the emergence of these innovative elements and institutions. They will allow the economy to expand and develop into areas and networks that were unexplored previously.[2]

Only in the second development stage will innovative developments start to affect the larger economy and established economic wealth creation processes. This second stage can be denoted as the stage of "contestation".

**Contestation:**    After innovative institutions emerge and establish themselves, the resulting economic opportunities are identified more widely and, consequently, are exploited more widely as well. This process leads naturally to the contestation of established institutions and trade infrastructures. The alternative ways to generate economic wealth—through innovations in the social division of labour, new goods and specialisations as well as innovative trade infrastructures—will encroach on the established but declining institutions. This causes friction and conflict.

The first consequence of such contestation might be recessions and financial panics. The emergence of the internet in the 1990s resulted in a tremendous overvaluation of the emerging web-based business opportunities. This resulted in the 2000 dot-com financial crisis and the subsequent recession. This episode is very minor compared with the serious consequences of the railway mania of the 1840s in response to the newly emerged rail transportation industry, which was a very similar process of financial overvaluation of innovation in the processes of economic wealth creation.

---

[2] The most contemporary example of such institutional innovation is the emergence of the *internet* and its usage since the early 1990s. Initially the internet only had a marginal effect on economic performance, but more recently its use has expanded into a more developed source of economic wealth creation through information gathering, cloud computing and the *Internet of Things*. Information technology is now clearly causing fundamental changes in the governance system of our contemporary global economy.

The second consequence is a further resettlement of the institutions and rules that govern these economic processes—as embodied in the governance system. This may cause significant social and political upheaval. The conflict between established political forces and new political movements founded on these innovative ideas can even spill into political and military conflict. For example, the First World War (1914–1918) can be viewed as a part and an expression of the resettlement of the political system after the emergence of the institutions that govern consumer capitalism in the late nineteenth century. The war was the last stand of the imperial powers that controlled classical capitalist societies in the nineteenth century.

Third, at the level of the social division of labour and the prevailing industries that embody it, there emerges a direct contestation of middleman positions occupied by established industrial powers in the networks that make up our trade infrastructure. Alternative trade infrastructures are built to circumvent these middleman positions. This might be accompanied by increased or decreased regulation by governments and other public bodies. A prime example is the breakdown of monopolistic corporations that controlled markets at the beginning of the twentieth century and stood in the way of the liberation of working classes to emerge as consumers. At that time, market regulation by governments through the enforcement of newly created anti-trust laws diminished the monopolistic tendencies in many consumption goods markets.

**Maturity:**    After the stage of contestation, the old institutions and infrastructural elements are marginalised and a new system based on the innovative institutions comes to fruition. A period of building and creation will enhance productivity in the social division of labour and there results a period of significant economic growth and development. In this stage these institutions and infrastructures mature, resulting in their full exploitation. The two most recent periods of such maturation are the Victorian age, between 1848 and 1873, and the consumer capitalist global plan era, between 1945 and 1971 (see below for further discussion).

The stage of institutional maturity is relatively short lived. It is a period in which the forces that emanate from the innovative institutions are uncontested and during which economic development is driven by the full use of these new instruments in all economic processes. Indeed, the Victorian age was driven by major innovations in mechanised production technology and transportation, while the global plan era is founded on the exploitation of the new consumption good markets created by innovative nineteenth-century technologies, such as the combustion engine and the use of electricity.

**Extraction:**    After the maturation of institutional innovation in the governance system, there follows a period of decline. The wave of innovations have mostly been exploited and the rate of return on them reduces, resulting in two accompanying effects.

First, the main mode of economic conduct becomes to extract as much value from middleman positions in the trade infrastructure as possible. This refers to the political and economic ability of individuals, government agencies and corporations that occupy middleman positions in these networks to exploit their position. They extract rents from their positions, rather than from innovation; gains are made from established assets—whether regular capital or social capital—instead of innovation in production technology, network building and/or institutional innovation. This refers to a period in which returns from capital outstrip the returns from true innovation, which is recognised in the classical Marxian analysis of capitalism (Marx 1867, 1893, 1894) and, more recently, in empirical research into neo-liberal capitalism (Piketty 2014).

Second, this stage of consolidation is accompanied by extreme financialisation. Innovative uses of monetary instruments and financial products such as options and derivatives drive the process of further exploitation of existing technologies and infrastructures rather than proper innovation. This refers to the ability to create rents through financialisation. As a consequence, the financial sector of the economy booms and involves itself in highly uncertain activities. This increased uncertainty opens the door to busts from financial crises. This can take the form of stock market panics (1929, most famously), banking crises or "panics" (1873 and 2008) and generally increased uncertainty in our daily lives.

This stage results in a period in the institutional wave that is based on exploitation, increased uncertainty and diminishing returns. The declining economic performance in turn provides incentives for innovation that will trigger the next institutional wave.

The institutional wave introduced here is akin to the "long waves" identified by other economists in the process of economic development. The long wave was seminally described by Kondratief (1979), which originally appeared in 1926 in the *Archiv für Sozialwissenschaft und Sozialpolitik*. The Kondratief wave is approximately 50 years in length and is identified through the trend of many economic indicators such as employment rates, prices of major commodities and financial indicators. Kondratief himself identifies three of these waves: 1790–1845, 1845–1895 and from 1895. When he published his paper, Kondratief had already identified the decline of the third wave.

Mason (2015, Chapter 2) uses Kondratief wave theory to explain developments in capitalism since the industrial revolution. He identified the third wave as lasting until 1945 and introduced the idea that the fourth Kondratief wave in contemporary capitalism, starting in 1945, has actually not ended yet. The reason for the unending nature of the fourth wave is proposed as being that capitalism itself ran into difficulties with the introduction of information technologies, which introduced truly increasing returns to scale in the global economy. This is owing to the very nature of information and related innovative technologies as having non-rivalrous characteristics, causing its repeated usage at no additional cost (Romer 1990). This is discussed further in the section on neo-liberalism and the global platform economy.

An institutional wave is in principle longer than a Kondratief long wave. Indeed, an institutional wave is identified by the institutional cycle of innovation, maturation and decline of institutions and heuristics that guide the generation of related trade infrastructures. The Kondratief wave is instead identified by the cycle of commodity prices, interest rates, wage rates and investment levels. This was investigated as empirical evidence of these waves in the seminal contribution Kondratief (1979) itself.

In fact, an institutional wave should be viewed as approximately *double* the Kondratief long wave. As such, since the industrial revolution I only identify two complete institutional waves and the initialisation of a third one: the classical capitalist institutional wave based on the incorporated economy between the 1770s and the 1870s and the consumer capitalist institutional wave from the 1870s until the 1980s. A third institutional wave is founded on the emerging platform economy founded on innovative information technologies, which emerged during the 1980s and 1990s. This wave has had a particularly ominous start and has not yet reached the stage of contestation owing to a combination of factors as described by Mason (2015).

The first half of an institutional wave corresponds to a Kondratief wave, which is driven by its innovation and contestation stages. This implies that it describes an extended period of restlessness and uncertainty. Historically this seems a better institutional fit than the Kondratief long wave. For example, the third Kondratief wave since the industrial revolution started in the 1890s, but had severe institutional problems until its conclusion in 1945. This included multiple financial panics in the growth period between 1895 and 1914. These problems ultimately resulted in the devastation of the First World War and the subsequent financial collapse in the 1920s and 1930s, followed by the even more profound devastation of the Second World War.

Only after the old institutional framework was removed thoroughly through direct contestation did a prosperous, tranquil period emerge as the upward, first half of the fourth Kondratief wave took hold and the consumer capitalist institutions matured. This fourth Kondratief wave concluded with a period of extraction and decline in the institutional framework. This corresponded to the period of prosperity between 1945 and 1973 and the subsequent collapse in the Keynesian recessions of the 1970s and 1980s.

I debate the history of wealth creation in more detail in the next section. This analysis is based on one of the main consequences of the social division of labour as the driver of economic wealth creation: that all economic interaction is *relational* and that, consequently, our global economy is organised through a trade infrastructure that is made up of *networks*.

## 2.2   A Very Short History of Economic Wealth Creation

Human economic history started around 70,000 years ago when the human species acquired the ability to cooperate and socially organise on a tribal scale.[3] This *cognitive revolution* set in motion the processes that led humans to dominate the earth. Instead of being a marginal species, humans were able to fundamentally alter their natural environments and to make the world function for their benefit (Bulte et al. 2006; Harari 2014). What exactly triggered the cognitive revolution is not clear, but it has to do with the human social brain and its development. Horan et al. (2005) argue that after the cognitive revolution humans were able to consummate the fundamental process of economic wealth creation through the implementation of a social division of labour—founded on increasing returns to specialisation in combination with the principle of gains from trade.

After the cognitive revolution, humanity became the global dominant force and was able to command global resources. Other species—including all other hominin species as well as numerous animal species—suffered and even became extinct owing to this human dominance. The dominance of the human species has been recognised as an epoch-changing force in geological terms as well denoting the current geological epoch as the *Holocene*, starting 11,700 years ago with the onset of the agricultural revolution. Recently, it has been proposed to recognise human impact even further by declaring the current geological epoch as the *Anthropocene*, setting its date of inception on 16 July 1945, the day that the first atomic bomb was detonated.

**The Agricultural (R)evolution**   The tribal organisation of human economic wealth creation processes was replaced by permanent settlement in agricultural communities after the so-called *agricultural revolution* about 12,000 years ago. Around the same time, agriculture was discovered at multiple locations simultaneously. Subsequently, in the "Fertile Crescent" (Sumeria), the Yangtze and Yellow river basins (China), Central Mexico and north-west South America, there emerged agricultural societies.

Over the past decades, archaeological research has shown that the "revolution" to agriculture was actually evolutionary. Tribes initiated the cultivation of plant species and the domestication of animal species slowly by controlling their direct environment. This is akin to gardening and environmental control.

---

[3] From a biological point of view, human evolution originated earlier than 70,000 years ago; approximately 100,000–280,000 years ago. Initially, DNA analysis by paleoanthropologists confirmed that there was a common human ancestor, who originated from Africa. Through DNA this human was identified as a female, "Mitochondrial Eve" (Cann et al. 1987). Later, Tishkoff et al. (2009) used data from alternative sources—not just mitochondrial DNA—to conclude that the Angola–Namibia border region near the Atlantic Ocean is likely to be near the geographical point of origin of modern human genetic diversity. This origin was founded in an ancestral tribe, rather than a single ancestor.

Slowly there emerged an agricultural economy. Humans found by accident that cultivating crops such as wheat and rice as well as domesticating certain animals increased the output level of foodstuffs (Diamond 1997). It turned out to be a two-edged sword, since humans now had lives that depended completely on the success of their cultivated crops.

The emergence of agricultural economies also fundamentally shifted human existence from a nomadic existence to a settled life. There emerged urban centres that were supported by the output generated by the agricultural economy (Lawrence and Wilkinson 2015). It has been pointed out that at this time there emerged institutions such as private property rights in these primitive societies (Bowles and Choi 2013, 2016; Bowles 2015). This clearly points to the institutional innovation that coevolved with the introduction of agricultural production technologies: the emergence of the agricultural economy incorporated an institutional revolution rather than just being a period of technological change.[4]

However, the agricultural revolution also introduced a problem of basic survival and wealth distribution. Work became harder and life was in a permanent state of subsistence owing to the Malthusian nature of the economy (Malthus 1798). This was driven by a combination of a limited availability of arable land—for the given agricultural production technologies—and insufficient institutional innovation to enhance and deepen the social division of labour (Ricardo 1817). In particular, the *Malthusian state* of the economy refers to the problem that increased output and larger crops result in the survival of more children, thus increasing the total population. This population dynamics, the limited quantity of arable land and the lack of sufficient institutional innovation balance individual consumption bundles at the same subsistence level. The Malthusian state of low individual economic wealth levels became normal after the agricultural revolution and largely lasted until the industrial revolution (Clark 2007).

In some sense, the human species became a victim of its own economic success after the agricultural revolution. Most people lived their lives in small communities made up of extended families. Nearly all humans could be considered to be peasants, toiling for a meagre marginal existence by working the land and keeping animals. These societies were rather egalitarian and only modest surpluses above and beyond economic subsistence were generated. This modest surplus nevertheless allowed these agricultural societies to develop further and to coalesce into larger empires with a significant public sector. This

---

[4] Bowles and Choi (2013) point out that the agricultural revolution seems to a chicken-and-egg problem; technology and institutions evolved in tandem. Most problematic here is that agriculture was initially *not* more productive than traditional foraging (Bowles 2011). The emergence of property rights therefore cannot be explained as an institutional response to promote and protect these more productive activities. Rather, Bowles and Choi (2013) point to a coevolution of property rights and farming: farming requires a system of property rights, which is not viable in a foraging economy; property rights required farming and farming required property rights.

was extensively studied by Hudson (1994, 2002) for the ancient agricultural empires, also known as the "Temple" economy.

In the following historical perspective I distinguish significant features of economic wealth creation before the emergence of capitalism as well as five different institutional waves in the history of capitalism. This implies that I put the beginning of the capitalist system in institutional terms in the fourteenth century, triggered by the implications of the fourteenth-century anomalies (Campbell 2010, 2016). This was followed by four further development stages of the institutional foundations of capitalism. The most recent innovative wave was initiated in the 1980s with the emergence of the internet and information technology. There is, however, a problem with this institutional wave that I discuss in more depth later.

### 2.2.1    Development Before Capitalism

The introduction of agriculture and the domestication of animals allowed humans to coalesce into larger societies than was feasible under the hunter-gatherer social division of labour. Humans settled and entered into long-standing relationships with their local habitat. Limited mobility in an agricultural economy resulted in a rather different division of labour.

As stated above, the main state of existence for humans in these agricultural economies became that of an extended *peasant* family. The returns from their agricultural operations barely sufficed for their survival. Thus, the peasant economy returned a level of "reproduction" of their labour and only a small surplus. The peasant lifestyle was complemented by a culture of cooperation and mutual dependency in the frequent times of agricultural and economic crisis.

The modest economic surplus in the peasant economy supported the emergence of the first cities in human history—such as the city of Ur with its Great Ziggurat at the centre of the temple complex. These cities functioned as trade centres: peasants transported their surpluses to the city to trade for advanced goods such as pottery, cloth and tools (capital assets), and foodstuffs that they were not able to grow. In these economies, trades were conducted through the temple at the heart of the city. The resulting *temple economy* was managed by the religious public servants of the temple. They developed a system of bookkeeping in which traders were assigned recorded debits and credits, which were subject to interest if they were held as debts (Hudson 2002). These trades were recorded on cuneiform clay tablets. These financial instruments created the first monetary system in history, which implies that money really started out as debt registration.

The role of religious centres in the peasant economy is critical. It reflects a physical implementation of authority and the enforcement of norms, heuristics and written laws. A fine example of this was the *Code of Hammurabi* from 1750 BCE, which reflects a complex set of laws and rules guiding many aspects of human life in the empire. It is the first implementation of a governance system that involved a significant population that was much larger than the average tribal hunter-gatherer economy. The development of governance and its most important incarnation of government has been the subject of recent studies by Weatherford (1997), Acemoglu et al. (2005), Greif (2006), Ogilvie (2007), Baker et al. (2010) and Acemoglu and Robinson (2012).

**The Res Publica** In the social division of labour of these ancient agricultural economies, the peasant agricultural class was complemented with otherwise specialised individuals in the cities. This included in particular the necessary class of religious servants ("priests") that supported the religious and governmental functions that emerged in the economy. The priest class embodied the governance system itself at the heart of the empire and formed its bureaucratic heart. It is through this governance system that the empire and its economy functioned.

An embodiment of the governance system—which included a strong religious component in combination with an elaborate system of norms, heuristics and written laws as well as a physical embodiment such as a temple complex or a palace in the capital city—can be called the *Res Publica*.[5] The meaning of this term reflects well the implementation of a governance system in these ancient empires that was based on a social division of labour with a very large class of peasants that generated the required economic wealth at its foundation. It also reflects that the governance system ties together with political and religious authority in these ancient economies.

During Roman times, the phrase *Res Publica* referred even to the governmental system of Rome itself, of divided rule by an aristocratic class of wealthy Roman citizens. This became known as the Roman "Republic" and forms the foundation for republican governmental systems in our contemporary global economy.

**The Roman Economy** The final stage of ancient economic development and the deepening of the agrarian social division of labour was reached in the era of the Roman Empire. This emerged from the fourth until the first century BCE and was centred on the city of Rome. Historians have considered the second century CE as its apogee, although recently there has been some divergence from this (Beard 2015).

The Roman empire embodied a very well-developed social division of labour in which an agricultural peasantry supported the emergence of market towns and a well-developed trade network throughout the Mediterranean. Wallerstein (2011b) refers to the Roman economy as a *world empire*; a system that is founded on a complete social division of labour and functions in a self-contained fashion.

The road infrastructure that supported this empire was very advanced and its quality was only matched by modern road systems in the twentieth century.

---

[5] "Res Publica" translates from Latin to the "public thing" or "public cause".

This is illustrated with findings after excavations in the buried Roman city of Pompeii. While visiting the city, one can still see remnants of its fast food outlets, its brothels, the basilica (market hall) and the bath houses; all signs of an economy that functioned at a very advanced level of sophistication and diversity in its social division of labour.

The Roman social division of labour was relatively advanced and in the cities there emerged numerous artisan professions. These workers were organised in *collegia*, each representing a group of workers of the same profession and in a certain location.[6] These *collegia* were expressions of a deep embeddedness of these workers in their socio-economic role. As such, the Roman Empire gave rise to a well-functioning horizontal division of labour—with a limited proportion of vertical or hierarchical structures such as firms—that generated an economic wealth level that was unmatched for nearly two millennia. As such it is proper to describe the advanced imperial economy as a *Platonian economy*—with reference to Plato (380 BCE), who described the functioning of economies founded on a well-developed horizontal social division of labour.

Economists have considered the Roman economy as a well-functioning "market" economy (Temin 2006, 2012). However, this seems too simplistic. It can be argued that the Roman economy was driven by very advanced economic development through a well-functioning social division of labour and was organised through trade networks, rather than markets. The imperial government played a crucial role and provided advanced infrastructure, particularly sophisticated road systems, and advanced law systems to regulate economic interaction. In particular, there seems to have been a well-developed system of propagating and educating people throughout the Roman provinces about Roman norms and law systems. This is attested to by the many inscribed monuments that have been found throughout Europe and the Middle East.

Membership of the Roman Empire was desirable because of its well-functioning economy and its relative peaceful society. Instead of being conquered, many people voluntarily joined the Empire in the pursuit of economic wealth and general well-being.

The Roman imperial economy, however, became stagnant and calcified over the centuries. The level of technological innovation was insufficient to maintain the required level of economic productivity. Furthermore, the Roman socio-economic institutions failed to bind the empire into a coalesced structure. This was signified by the political unrest after the second century CE. The collapse of the western Roman Empire in the fifth century CE was a major economic event, expressed by lost knowledge of productive technologies and inventions.

---

[6] Compared with the medieval guild system, a *collegium* was a much more open and localised association. It did not regulate the entry of new workers into the profession, in this regard being more akin to a (local) union or representative association. I refer to Epstein (1991) and Beard (2015) for more details.

The western European economy regressed into a feudal state, returning it to a form similar to the earlier peasant economies.

### 2.2.2    The Institutional Development Leading to Capitalism

From an institutional perspective on the social division of labour, we can categorise four different economic systems that have prevailed throughout human history. Each of these four systems is founded on different sets of socio-economic institutions. The next characterisations are set out in order of complexity of the economic system. We subsequently discuss the feudal economy, the Platonian economy, the capitalist economy and the platform economy. The future might, however, be for a new form of economic system based on networks supported by a socialist system that allocates the generated economic wealth.

#### 2.2.2.1    The Feudal Economy

The Roman Empire declined and collapsed throughout the fourth and fifth centuries CE. In its place there emerged a volatile system of limited and confused governance. The European economy settled after 350 years of sporadic and brutal government into a system that is known as *feudalism*. Feudalism is based on a peasant economy with a strong religious as well as a secular hierarchy. Surpluses generated by peasants on their homesteads were transferred to the clerical as well as to the secular authorities. Consequently, the feudal economy consisted of three classes: essentially autarkic peasants, the clergy (subordinate to the ultimate authority of the pope) and the nobility (subordinate to a king or emperor). In feudalism the pope and the kings represented God's authority on Earth and, as such, were His caretakers (Cantor 1993). All other humans were principally subjected to this divine authority.

The economy was initially founded on a pure system of peasantry working the land within small communities. As a consequence, trade was minimal and there was no need for money, as attested by the continued use of Roman coins without significant money creation until the eighth century. Through slow technological development, peasants were able to generate a more significant surplus that supported significant classes of clergy and nobles. In the twelfth century, this resulted in the *medieval Renaissance*, a period during which elaborate cathedrals were erected and monastic orders proliferated. Similarly, the aristocracy was able to build strongholds, castles and walled cities in a display of secular power (Postan 1972; Verhulst 2002).

The generated surpluses in the feudal economy in the twelfth and thirteenth centuries also allowed a return to increased trade and the rise of artisan professions (Wallerstein 2011a; Gimpel 1976). Cities and towns gained more relevance as centres of developed social divisions of labour, contributing to a higher economic wealth. Universities arose as centres of learning, and were established seminally in Bologna, Italy, and Paris, France.

The feudal economy collapsed during a sequence of destructive natural anomalies during the fourteenth century (Campbell 2016). This period set the stage for the next step in the development of the human economy. I note, however, that evolutionary institutional developments and the growth of agricultural output would have pushed the economy to inevitable reform if the fourteenth-century anomalies had not happened.

To summarise, the feudal economy is characterised by the essentially autarkic existence of its members in a permanent Malthusian state of subsistence. The social division of labour was minimal and only modest surpluses generated commercial trade networks. Most of the generated surpluses were appropriated by clerical and aristocratic elites, exploiting their self-proclaimed divine authority.

**Prelude to the Precapitalist Economy: "The Great Mortality"** The feudal economy was confronted with a series of three natural calamities in the fourteenth century. An unprecedented change in climatic conditions resulted in back-to-back harvest failures in 1316–1317, which resulted in a serious famine. As Campbell (2010, p. 288) writes, "After a three-year respite, the harvest failed again in 1321 with a one-third reduction in net yield with, this time, the barley and oats sown in spring 1321 faring worse than the wheat and rye sown in autumn 1320."

At the same time, a second calamity hit, in the form of a highly contagious bovine pestilence that wiped out European cattle herds. Quoting again from Campbell (2010, p. 289): "Yet the epidemic's effects upon agricultural producers were profound: Reproductive capacity was undermined, the output of milk and dairy produce greatly diminished, vital manure supplies reduced, and, most seriously of all, draught-power resources curtailed wherever oxen were used for ploughing and carting. Capital-rich great estates purchased replacement draught animals as soon as it was prudent to do so but relied much more upon natural replacement to rebuild their dairy and breeding herds, which never recovered to their pre-plague strength."

These two calamities resulted in a protracted socio-economic crisis during 1315–1322. This period is also known as the *Great European Famine*. This and the bovine pestilence were followed by a human epidemic of unprecedented proportions, known as the Black Death—or by fourteenth-century contemporaries as the Great Mortality. It was caused by a bacillus that originated in the south of present-day Russia and spread through Europe between 1346 and 1353 (Kelly 2005).[7] The disease followed the main trading routes and was spread by sailors on infected ships.

---

[7] There are some doubts about whether the *Yersinia pestis* bacillus was indeed solely responsible for the epidemic. Descriptions of contemporaries do not fully conform with the known disease patterns that it causes. Since the epidemic occurred nearly 700 years ago, we might never know what the exact cause was.

The cost to human life was massive: between 30 and 50% of the population perished, depending on the location one considers. The disease was indiscriminate and affected peasants as well as kings and archbishops. In particular, the clergy were hit badly owing to their obligation to care for the sick and the dead. This resulted in a major reformation of the socio-economic fabric of fourteenth-century Europe. In fact, the effects were revolutionary, ultimately paving the way for the establishment of a new world order—one that we know now as *capitalism*.

The direct effects of the Great Mortality on economic indicators are discussed in detail in Campbell (2010, 2016). Campbell's analysis shows the effects of the reduction of the population on grain prices as well as wage rates. Clearly, labour became extremely scarce, even in the feudal system of serfdom, resulting in a permanent doubling of real wages. Furthermore, the demand and supply for food collapsed owing to the extreme reduction of the population (as a workforce and as consumers), resulting in a much lower yield for grain. This had an effect on grain prices as well, although this was much less pronounced.

**The Long-Term Effects of the Fourteenth-Century Anomalies** Campbell also reports the long-term effects of the fourteenth-century anomalies on socio-economic indicators, in particular estimated wage rates. This is particularly shown in Figure 2 in Campbell (2010, pp. 286–287), where it is shown that real wages remained high throughout the fourteenth century into the fifteenth century. Thus, the effects of the Great Mortality on wage rates commanded by the working population were lasting. Clearly this is owing to the permanent reduction of the total population in Europe and its effects on the relative scarcity of labour in medieval Europe.

Herlihy (1997) argues that the long-term effects of the Black Death were not only quantitative, but also qualitative; it changed the European societies and economies institutionally and paved the way for the emergence of capitalism. Indeed, basic labour became much more valued and appreciated, resulting in two phenomena that are closely related.

First, labourers—in particular the peasants who were tied to their land under the feudal system of serfdom—themselves became self-conscious and revolted on multiple occasions throughout Europe.[8] This increased the drive of these people to seek self-determination in their lives and to seek opportunities beyond peasantry and serfdom.

Second, the peasants themselves became more wealthy—creating a class of well-to-do *yeomen* in the fifteenth century. Their lives changed, their household goods improved and this gave rise to new industries. Money and trade became more important, which resulted in the rise of urban economies in which rich social divisions of labour could flourish. Thus, peasants flocked to urban centres

---

[8] The 1381 Peasants' Revolt in England is well known and acts as a prime example of this new-found awareness among peasants.

and transformed themselves into representatives of these new professions. For details of this I refer to Herlihy (1997), Huppert (1998) and Cantor (2001).

Cantor (2001) also points out that the dominant place of the Church changed and that Christianity became more private in nature. At least 40% of clerics died during the Black Death, and this resulted in a fundamental change as the Church allowed more inexperienced and younger priests to take charge. Reactions to this—such as the rise of the reformist *Lollards* with superior qualifications—laid the groundwork for the period of reformation and the rise of Protestantism in the sixteenth century.

These developments resulted in increased wealth from the urban, diversified social division of labour and an increased secularism in the urban population, which provided a foundation for the rise of the *Renaissance*. Combined with the much higher labour costs to maintain an army, this resulted in a decline in the power of the nobility, in particular as related to kingship. The rise of urban centres and the decline of the feudal hierarchy went hand in hand. This gave rise to the rebirth of the Platonian economy.

### 2.2.3    The Rebirth of the Platonian Economy

From feudalism—owing to the revolutionary interruption by the fourteenth-century anomalies—there now emerged an economic system founded on a deeper and more extended social division of labour, which formed the foundation of urban economies. The deepening of the social division of labour was based on the emergence of more socio-economic roles. However, the social division of labour remained essentially *horizontal*: goods were produced through chains of independent specialised individuals who passed intermediary products to the next economic agent in the chain—so-called *production networks*. The nature of the socio-economic roles that emerged was in principle that of artisans, independent economic agents who used production technologies that were slowly developing and rather static in nature.[9]

Furthermore, the horizontal social division of labour acted as an *allocation mechanism* for the distribution of the generated wealth in the economy. Through the production of intermediary goods, the economic agents generated an income from selling these goods to the next specialised agents in the chain. This allocation mechanism has been one of the main features of any economic system since the advent of more complex and developed social divisions of labour after the agricultural revolution.

---

[9] For example, bread was produced through a chain of a farmer producing wheat; a miller grinding the wheat into flour; and a baker converting the flour into a loaf of bread. Of course, bread requires more intermediary inputs, such as yeast and butter, and capital assets such as a mill and an oven. This shows that a chain in the social division of labour has a tree-like structure with multiple product chains leading to the producer of the final consumption good. This example also reflects the fundamentally urban nature of a horizontal social division of labour.

I refer to this economic system as *Platonian* in reference to Plato (380 BCE), who seminally described this economic system in detail. As mentioned above, the Platonian economy not only emerged from feudalism, but also characterises the ancient, classical era in human history. The horizontal division of labour was prevalent in the empires from antiquity. The Platonian economy is clearly "precapitalist", since it essentially omits vertically structured elements of the social division of labour, such as firms, bureaucracies and public production organisations.

**The Long Sixteenth Century** We can now set out a theoretical perspective on the emergence of the modern "world-system" through its initialisation during the "long sixteenth century", the period of 1450–1640, which saw major institutional developments that allowed the Platonian economy to (re)emerge from feudalism.[10] During this period, the forces that were unleashed in the fourteenth century came to fruition and there emerged a Platonian social division of labour.

Wallerstein (2011a, p. 67) already denotes this economic system as "capitalist", since it is founded on separating political and economic decisions so they are made by two distinct social classes—aristocratic politicians and merchants. I would rather denote this era as *precapitalist*, since production is organised through a (Platonian) horizontal social division of labour rather than a system founded on (capitalist) vertically structured social production organisations. Furthermore, the assets required for production in the Platonian economy demand less capital investment and the production technologies are not owned explicitly by individual capitalists, but are shared among groups of professionals. This was also evident through the emergence of guilds in urban production centres; these provided training of apprentices to uniform standards and regulated admission of new members to the profession (Epstein 1991; Ogilvie 2004, 2014).

During the long sixteenth century the European economy boomed and developed in urban centres. Significant surpluses were generated and cities were able to develop major social and artistic projects. We can still admire the results in cities dating from the Italian Renaissance (such as Florence, Genoa and Naples) and the economic centres in the Low Countries (such as Amsterdam, Utrecht and Antwerp). These economic centres were founded on their commercial success. Amsterdam was at the centre of the emerging Dutch economy, which success was based on the commercial trade routes that it controlled. These included the fish trade, the cloth trade and the Baltic wheat trade.

---

[10] The notion of the world-system in the social theory set out by Immanuel Wallerstein (2011a,b,c,d) has similarities to the notion of a socio-economic space as a theoretical construct to address questions concerning and developing models of economic wealth creation processes. Wallerstein's notion of the world-system is less institutional in nature and incorporates more political elements into its construction.

The socio-economic institutions in Europe also changed fundamentally through the advent of individualism and geographic discoveries in the fifteenth century (Mortimer 2014). Individualism brought about a new perspective that supported secularism and economic independence. The desirability of spices from the East Indies and the discovery of the American continent in 1492 by Christopher Columbus set off a race around the globe for new trade opportunities and riches. A gold rush ensued, for example, resulting in the destruction of the Aztec and Inca empires by a few zealous conquistadors.

The financial system supporting these economic developments was founded on innovative practices in banking and financial accounting. I refer to Chapter 5 for an in-depth description of the banking empire set up by the Medici house in Florence. New monetary instruments (Mitchell 1944) paved the way for further economic development and the financing of major collaborative undertakings, such as the ventures to the east Indian archipelago by the *Dutch East Indian Company* (VOC). The Dutch Republic became the first hegemonic power in the global economy at the end of the sixteenth century, which was completely based on its prowess as a middleman in the trade networks spanning the global economy (Israel 1995). This is illustrated by the founding of the first stock capital market in human history in Amsterdam and the fact that the VOC was the first incorporated company, a harbinger for the capitalist economy to come.

**Decline of the Precapitalist Economy**  By 1650 the new institutional foundations of the precapitalist Platonian economy had lost their innovative effects. There followed a period of consolidation and retreat, exemplifying the maturity and extraction stages of an institutional wave. Recessions followed and the premodern economy went into a period of decline. Major social unrest was unleashed in the form of the Thirty Years War (1618–1648). Furthermore, economic strictures owing to the monetary standards being based on two metals, silver and gold (Sargent and Velde 1999), resulted in further economic decline. In the period 1650–1750 the economy reversed itself and developed into a more rural system, based on a restructuring of the social division of labour into a shallower form (Wallerstein 2011b).

The decline of the precapitalist economic institutions may also be expressed by three observations. First is the decline of the Dutch republic as a hegemonic economic power after 1650. The Dutch economy quickly lost its middleman position in the major global trade networks, mainly submitting to the British efforts to establish colonies by force throughout the world.

Second, the decline of the French empire after 1720 is illustrative of the reduced ability of the old institutions to deliver the economic wealth required. Financialisation and increased debt plagued the French monarchy until the situation got out of control in 1789 and the French Revolution ensued. It was part of the painful process of removing the old premodern institutions and structures to pave the way for the next stage of institutional economic development: *capitalism.*

Third, the precapitalist economy was firmly founded on the monetary institution of *commodity money*. The purchasing power of money was based on the market value of the gold and silver that were incorporated in coins. Money coins had already emerged in the Lydian empire in ancient times and commodity money was used as a means of exchange in most ancient empires, including the Roman economy (Weatherford 1997). As such, commodity money is an important institutional cornerstone of any Platonian economy. In the precapitalist Platonian economy it developed into a sophisticated institutional system that supported European trade networks through advanced credit systems that were based on extended trust relationships between traders.

Commodity money as used in precapitalist economies was based on the dualism of gold and silver: both metals were used in monetary coins. This system functioned reasonably well as long as the trade volume in the economy was limited. However, the emergence of international trade routes beyond Europe induced a revolution in financial instruments through the introduction of bills of exchange and promissory notes in the fifteenth century. These notes promised the payment of commodity money at an unspecified future date to the bearer. This set in motion a monetary revolution that supported international trade and was at the foundation of the Italian Renaissance, as exemplified in the discussion of the Medici banking system (Chapter 5).

Despite these monetary and financial innovations, the duality of gold and silver resulted in frictions between the two metals through *Gresham's Law*: "bad money drives out good money." Regular debasements and (re)adjustments between the two metals had to be applied by local authorities (Velde et al. 1999). There also resulted regular economic crises owing to coin and metal shortages. As a consequence the precapitalist Platonian economy was severely restricted in its development (Sargent and Velde 2002), which was particularly prevalent after 1650.

### 2.2.4   The Capitalist Economy

By 1650 the next institutional wave had already entered its innovation stage and an array of new institutions were emerging. These laid the foundation for the rise of the capitalist economy and society after 1750. Capitalism was founded on many new institutions that took hold over the long sixteenth century and matured in the seventeenth and eighteenth centuries. It would be too cumbersome to list all of them; instead, I limit myself to the most important innovative institutions that took hold in this period and provide a foundation for the capitalist economy[11]:

**Enlightenment philosophy and secularisation:**   In   western   European thought and philosophy a revolutionary wave was unleashed after 1650.

---

[11] Again I emphasise that this list is far from a complete typology. For a more comprehensive view of institutional change after 1650, I refer to Allen (2011), who includes discussion of unexpected institutional change during the industrial revolution.

Central in this Enlightenment philosophy was the justification of a more secular and individualistic view of the human condition. This has formed the foundation for our capitalist society ever since.

Israel (2001) argues that the Enlightenment philosophical movement was remarkably homogeneous throughout Europe. It formed around a number of central ideas, including a core of strict logical reasoning founded on an axiomatic methodology. These core ideas were developed by René Descartes (1596–1650), Baruch de Spinoza (1632–1677) and Gottfried Leibniz (1646–1712), amongst others.[12] This new philosophy was innovative, even controversial, and opened the door to a completely new, more scientific outlook on human existence and the physical world in which we are embedded.

Enlightenment philosophy justified broadly the liberalisation of humans, who in general had rather subservient lives. People had their assigned positions in the feudal hierarchy, and also (in the Platonian economy) little freedom to determine the path taken in their lives, in most cases. This new form of liberal philosophy instilled a spirit of entrepreneurship and innovation that was at the foundation of many aspects of life, particularly in western Europe, in the century before the industrial revolution. This affected a multitude of socio-economic institutions.

First, it promoted a secular vision of the human condition based on liberty and equality. This provided a foundation for the open and equal societies that political thinkers strived for after the enlightenment period. It no longer became necessary to submit one's life and livelihood to clerical and secular authorities and aristocrats. There was no justification under Enlightenment thought to deny an individual his or her fundamental liberty.

Second, individual human beings were now infused with the ability of making their own lives and livelihoods. It was no longer impossible to deny the self-determination of individual merchants to build economic enterprises and acquire socio-economic positions of power and control in these secular societies. This was a major step away from the normal position of limited self-determination in the Platonian economy that preceded the capitalist era.

**The emergence of the nation-state:**    During the seventeenth century, there emerged a brand-new platform for socio-economic development, the *nation-state*. The modern nation-state was formed by two major events, the Treaty of Münster of 1648 and the Glorious Revolution of 1688.

The *Treaty of Münster* concluded the Thirty Years War that ravaged central Europe between 1618 and 1648. The signatories to this treaty recognised

---

[12] The cultural historian Jonathan Israel has promoted forcefully the viewpoint that Spinoza put forward the most comprehensive and logically sound philosophy of all these early thinkers (Israel 2001). From this viewpoint, Spinoza should therefore be recognised as the most influential of the Enlightenment thinkers, and his ethical philosophy founded the framework for thought that is still dominant in our secular societies. I also refer to Nadler (2011) for an elaborate discussion of the impact of Spinoza's work on European society.

nation-states as political sovereign entities, thereby providing an international legal recognition for their existence. These nation-states represented a collective of people who identified themselves around the same "nationality" and governed themselves. This nationality was tied to language, culture and behavioural norms as well as wide recognition of the sovereignty of the nation-state's government.[13]

The *Glorious Revolution* of 1688 put the people of England in control of their own government. This formed a model for the development of modern democratic government in Europe through the French Revolution of 1789 and the revolutionary year of 1848.

After their formation, nation-states established themselves firmly as the main platforms for capitalist economic development. The people in a nation-state quickly assimilated into their assigned nationality. From an economic point of view, this nationality should be interpreted as an artificial conception that provided a common narrative supporting the acceptance of the authority of the government of the nation-state to make and enforce laws. This allowed the increased uniformity of the members of a nation-state and the subordination of local authorities to the central government of that nation-state.

The centralisation of authority in a nation-state and the identification of its people as a "nation" resulted in major possibilities for socio-economic reform. Quickly the government of nation-states became controlled by the economically powerful classes, rather than the inherited aristocratic classes.[14] This was epitomised by the development of democratic government, which combined Enlightenment ideas of secularisation and the empowered economic classes in the nation-state (Israel 2010).

The nation-state quickly evolved as a platform which facilitated institutional socio-economic development. Through legalisation processes and the authority to enforce laws by force, nation-states imposed major institutional innovation on the economies they embodied.

**Financial and monetary reform:**    The    newly    emerged    nation-states provided strong institutional support for the rise of the capitalist economy. In this regard, the industrial revolution was as much institutional as it was technological (Allen 2011). As pointed out, a major issue was that

---

[13] For a complete discussion of the rise of the sovereign nation-state as the main platform in the capitalist economy, I refer to Spruyt (1994). He explores the feudal roots of the state and the concept of sovereignty.

[14] Remarkably enough, the exception to this is the UK, which developed a form of government that for a long time was still founded on control by landed aristocratic families. This evolved over time into a system that gives peerages to economically successful business leaders and capitalists. In the USA and continental Europe, however, the landed aristocracy was simply abolished in the nineteenth century and an open government of direct democracy was implemented.

the Platonian economy suffered from monetary problems owing to the fundamental shortages of the two main monetary metals, silver and gold. The persistent discrepancies between the value of these two metals caused regular economic crises (Sargent and Velde 2002).

This fundamental monetary problem was resolved by the European nation-states with the introduction of true *fiat money* in the form of coins made from inferior metals that replaced the commodity coins in circulation. Thus, silver and gold coins were replaced by copper and coins of mixed metals, in particular coins with reduced silver and gold content. These new monetary instruments were founded fully on the trust of economic agents in their ability to exchange these coins for economic goods in transactions. As such, the trust and authority of the nation-state were transferred to these new monetary instruments. The acceptance of such fiat money over time resolved the economic crises that were caused by monetary shortages.

The range of fiat money was expanded over time through the introduction of a fully fledged state-backed monetary system. Governments issued monetary bills and notes in different denominations with which they paid the state expenses and salaries to government employees. Moreover, taxes, tariffs and other dues could be paid to state authorities with these government-issued notes. Thus, paper money as we still know it was introduced. Nation-states also introduced central banks to support the regulation of the banking and financial systems. These took over the issuance of government-backed notes. The creation of the fiat monetary system provided an effective foundation for advanced economic development and growth, which picked up measurably over the following century. This allowed economies to take full advantage of the technological innovations that were created on the back of the scientific revolution that followed the period of Enlightenment.

A downside of this monetary development has been that instead of monetary shortages, the capitalist economies have been plagued with monetary gluts. These gluts—which took the form of a wide range of monetary and financial instruments—resulted in unsuspected events, in particular in bubbles in the trade networks for certain specific goods. I should also mention the episodes of hyperinflation caused by the excessive printing of paper money by the government that regularly plagued capitalist economies, an example being Germany in 1923 (Fergusson 1975). These inflationary episodes were at the foundation of several of the many panics and crises that have made up the history of capitalism since the rise of the nation-state.

**The inception of the firm:**    One of the main institutional innovations that founded capitalism was the introduction of legal institutional structures that allowed the rise of hierarchical social production organisations—-or *firms*. Formally, this innovation was founded on the concept of (private) ownership of non-physical goods such as production technologies and the design of products in the form of patents and blueprints. This allowed the emergence of vertical divisions of labour, in which subordinates execute productive tasks on behalf of the owner of the technology that is employed in the production process.

This major innovation allowed the deepening of the social division of labour, and as such is at the foundation of the success of the capitalist economy in generating economic wealth. It should be clear that the emergence of the nation-state is a necessary requirement for such a major advance: without the authority of the nation-state, the private ownership of ideas and production technologies is very hard to enforce. The emergence of firms introduced a new way to deepen social division further and to divide productive tasks into smaller and smaller units.[15]

Coase (1937, 1992) provides a theory of why the social division of labour went vertical rather than deepening through extending horizontal production chains. This is related to the notion of transaction costs in the trade networks that support these production chains to operate in the social division of labour. Indeed, independent operators have to manage their trade relationships in the production chains, the costs of which are very substantial. Contracts have to be negotiated; products have to be "marketed"; and shipments have be guaranteed through appropriate financial hedging and insurance.[16] By organising the various production tasks in a vertical organisation based on authority relationships these burdens are reduced considerably. Instead of formal contracts, vertical agency relationships are much more flexible and controllable through internal regulation and monitoring.

The existence of corporations is, therefore, firmly founded on the *transaction efficiency* in the trade infrastructures that accompany the social division of labour. If transaction efficiency is very low, there will be little division of labour and economic development suffers—as was the case in the feudal economy. As transaction efficiency improves, longer horizontal production chains emerge and a Platonian economy is established. Further transaction efficiency improvement allows the emergence of larger operations and, under the right institutional framing, the introduction of vertical social production organisations in these production chains (Yang and Ng 1993).[17]

---

[15] Ultimately, throughout the second half of the nineteenth century and the twentieth century this had a negative impact owing to the *alienation* that accompanied this vertical deepening of the social division of labour. This alienation gave rise to worker dissatisfaction.

[16] This neglects the costs of other aspects of the daily operations of an economic agent in a production chain. In particular, one's operations have to be financed, thus calling for the accessing of means of finance. Large corporations can command access to the capital and financial markets much easier than small operators. One of the accompanying institutional innovations of industrialisation was the introduction of corporate shares and bonds to finance large industrial enterprises.

[17] A further increase in transaction efficiency will diminish the reason for larger operations and reduce the need for vertically structured social divisions of labour. This is the case in the contemporary global economy—based on information technology and highly efficient logistic systems—in which the self-employed individual is on the rise. This is the essence of the network economy as discussed above.

The rise of the incorporated firm was accompanied by a variety of institutional changes. The main one was the emergence of a financial system that gave its name to the form of economic society that emerged: the capital market. Corporations acquired access to finance and the purchasing power to acquire capital assets through the raising of finance in the capital markets that proliferated in the western economies during the nineteenth century. This introduced new derivative activities, such as the trade of corporate stocks and bonds and the speculation that accompanies that trade. It was the gluts in the financial instruments of this system that have been a cause for concern in the capitalist economy over the past 250 years.

**Capital accumulation:**    Production can only be organised effectively within social production organisations if the formation of corporations is supported through capital provision. In a Platonian economy, founded on a horizontal social division of labour, productive activities are financially supported by savings from past activities and by relatively small loans provided by financiers.

On the other hand, incorporating production processes in a hierarchically structured division of labour requires significant capital provision to lay the foundations. This includes the financing of outlays for infrastructure, buildings, machinery and administrative services. Thus, the rise of capitalist organisation forms of production requires large financial support.

In the seventeenth century there had already emerged capital markets as main institutional organisations for the provision of financial means for capitalist production. They were complemented by elaborate banking systems in the nineteenth century. Capital provision systems thus provide firm foundations for the rise of the capitalist economy.

As Marx (1867) points out in his fundamental analysis of capitalism, the accumulation of capital is one of its defining features. Based on the availability of money, "capitalists" aim to follow the so-called $M$–$C$–$M$ conversion process: financial means $M$ are converted into commodities $C$, to be converted back into money $M$. Through this conversion process, capitalists aim to increase their financial holdings. Marx argues that this capital accumulation process sets capitalism apart from the preceding agricultural and Platonian economies.

The previous list of institutional innovations is far from complete. Many institutional reforms accompanied these major changes, including religious and political reform. For example, the economic policies of the governments of these new-fangled nation-states were deliberately developed, allowing the regulation of economic processes, for the first time in history. A truly new age was born.

**The Classical Capitalist Institutional Wave: 1750s–1870s** The capitalist institutional governance system that emerged from the developments in the seventeenth and eighteenth centuries resulted in the classical capitalist economy. The institutions that were adopted triggered a scientific revolution, in particular in Great Britain.[18] The period of intense scientific inquiry was accompanied by very significant technological innovations. The most prominent of these was the steam engine. In 1712 Thomas Newcomen developed the first commercially successful piston steam engine of 5 horsepower, and in 1781 the basic design was improved significantly by James Watt to double its output. This paved the way for large-scale application of steam engines in agriculture and industry.

This caused in turn the British industrial revolution, which was based on the burning of coal and steam engine technology. Economically, the industrial revolution expressed itself mainly as a transportation revolution. Steam engines made it possible to haul bulk goods over water and revolutionised land transportation through the development of railway systems. This supported the rise of heavy industry in Great Britain and the generation of significant wealth for the owners of these new coal-based production technologies.

I emphasise here that the industrial revolution was only feasible because of the application of these new technologies in the context of large-scale hierarchically structured social production organisations. It is not practical to have a steam-powered loom in a cottage; its application is only viable through significant capital investment, requiring a large-scale production organisation to maximise the output of such mechanised production processes. This was only made possible by capital provision through the innovative financial systems discussed above.

Until the political revolutions in 1848, the new capitalist institutional framework was contesting the old Platonian economic institutions. Only with the establishment of a democratic political system did there emerge a period of capitalist institutional dominance and of high wealth generation, relative stability and prosperity—between 1848 and 1873. This came to an end in the Great Panic of 1873, during which the American and European financial systems collapsed and a period known as the Long Depression began, lasting until the end of the nineteenth century.

The institutional changes that were brought about by the rise of the capitalist economy were permanent and irreversible. During the nineteenth century many socio-economic practices and traits vanished and were replaced by new arrangements. Cities rose in prominence and large-scale, dirty, coal-based industries dominated the cityscape, causing significant pollution, this being illustrated by the permanent smog in Victorian London.

**The Consumer Capitalist Institutional Wave: 1870s–1980s** The classical capitalist institutional framework declined after the Great Panic of 1873. New institutions were already forming and over the next 70 years they took hold. The rise of the consumer capitalist institutional system accommodated the expansion

---

[18] A very important branch of Enlightenment philosophy was cultivated through the work of a number of Scottish philosophers, including David Hume, Adam Ferguson and Adam Smith. This period of *Scottish Enlightenment* was rooted in the relative well-developed economy in Scotland in the second half of the eighteenth century.

of the social division of labour into new categories of economic goods, in particular consumption goods. Therefore, I view the institutional changes that underpin the consumer capitalist economy from this perspective.

The consumer capitalist institutional framework and the social division of labour are founded on one encompassing modification: the empowerment of the working class to become consumers. This was accomplished through a number of institutional innovations during the period between the 1870s and the 1940s[19]:

- The industrial base of the economy fundamentally shifted from the production of bulk goods to the production of diversified final consumption goods. This included the incorporation of marketing strategies that were founded on brand, quality and consumption properties.
- Workers were empowered to earn significantly higher wages to support a deepening of the social division of labour, which was founded on the production of final consumption goods. Workers needed to earn sufficient income to be able to participate in the emerging consumption society.
- A new ethos in the economy emerged: "consumerism". This new phenomenon was supported by innovative trade infrastructural elements such as shopping streets and malls; road systems to allow easy access of shoppers to marketplaces and shops; and the creation of larger home in suburbs to stimulate and facilitate enhanced consumption. The main driving force behind economic growth and development became the demand for consumption goods.
- This is closely related to the emergence of economic interventionist policies by the governments of nation-states. These policies coalesced into an economic policy vision known as *Keynesianism*. The core of this view was particularly founded on the macro-economic theories put forward by Keynes (1936). Economic recession was now directly linked to a lack of demand. This called for the increase in purchasing power of the working classes and an increase in government spending at times of economic recession. As a consequence, economic policy transformed into the active regulation of total demand in the economy.
- Workers organised themselves into *trade unions*, which represented them in dealings with employers and government. This was a major part of the empowerment of this class of economic agents in their transition to consumers. The unionised working classes commanded increasing purchasing power, thus further supporting the Keynesian view of the economy.
- The emergence of consumer capitalism required the reform of trade infrastructures as well. The prices that were charged needed to be seen as "fair" and "just". This became known as *competitive*, being supported

---

[19] For lucid descriptions of the consumer capitalist systems or "global plan" era I refer to Varoufakis (2011) and Chang (2014).

through the market theory of value. Government assumed a new role as the main protector of such competitive pricing and imposed anti-trust regulation on corporations in these trade networks. A major test case of this new political philosophy was the breakup in 1911 of Standard Oil, owned by John D. Rockefeller, to accommodate competition in the US refined oil sector.

- Government and its agents assumed the role of *pater familias* of its citizens. It actively and directly involved itself in the economy through such acts as market regulation, social policies, monetary policies and budgetary policies. The goal of the nation-state's government was to optimise living conditions for its citizens. This expressed itself further in three complementary developments:

  (i) Through several stages, democracy was extended to all adult individuals in the nation-state. This emancipated the working classes as well as women, making them fully engaged citizens and participants in the consumer capitalist economy.

  (ii) To guarantee the quality of the consumption goods traded, the government assumed the role of consumer watchdog. Business practices were subjected to rigorous standards and businesses were regularly inspected. Laws were written to impose sanctions and fines on firms that acted in bad faith and sold inferior products.

  (iii) The active socio-economic role of the nation-state's government extended later to support unemployed and disabled workers and to provide non-participants in the social division of labour with a basic income. Welfare programmes were created that allowed nearly all people to participate in the consumer capitalist economy.

- To accommodate enhanced international trade, nation-states coalesced into international bodies such as the *European Economic Community* and trade organisations such as the ones founded on the *General Agreement on Tariffs and Trade*, a precursor of the *World Trade Organisation* (WTO). Common product standards were imposed to support and to ease trade of goods across borders. These international trade treaties reduced tariffs and allowed a much larger catchment area in which the social division of labour could emerge. This also included the mutual recognition of regulations across nation-states, such as copyrights and measurement systems.

- International trade was particularly supported through the creation of an international currency system that resulted in stable exchange rates. The Bretton-Woods system was created in 1944 and as such supported the rise of multinational corporations. Money became more divorced from commodities than ever: government-issued notes were now linked to US dollars that were ultimately convertible into gold.

From these institutional developments there emerged three additional aspects that further characterise the consumer capitalist economy:

(i) The main platforms through which this economy developed were those of international treaties between nation-states. They included the development of common product standards, common property right systems and international regulatory bodies, in particular the International Monetary Fund (IMF) and the World Bank, which were created within the Bretton-Woods monetary system.

(ii) Consumer capitalism was based on oil as a main energy source as well as a principal input to many new products, including plastics. New technologies that developed in the second half of the nineteenth century shifted the focus from coal to oil as the main energy source and driver of economic growth. Only after the waning of consumer capitalism does it seem that oil is reducing as the principal commodity, being replaced by green energy technologies.

(iii) The USA became the dominant nation-state in the global consumer capitalist economy through military supremacy in the two world wars. It used its significant surpluses and political power to steer the world economy in the direction that was beneficial for US business and the US consumer.

The consumer capitalist economy had a very difficult and painful initial development. The contestation phase was set apart by the many very serious global conflicts, including two world wars, and two serious and deep economic depressions. The emancipation of the working classes through the social division of labour brought about major strife and destructive political ideologies such as fascism and communism. The situation only settled at the end of the Second World War into an era of stable international development and growth.

These conflicts emanated from tensions that the emancipation of working-class citizens imposed on the classical capitalist political structures in industrial economies. These tensions were mainly expressed through the rise of communism and fascism, both of which directly concern the position of working-class citizenry.

Already by the 1970s the institutional framework of consumer capitalism was faltering. The Keynesian policies that supported the international global plan were no longer effective and a serious crisis was triggered through the collapse of the Bretton-Woods system in 1971 and the First Oil Crisis of 1973–1974. A period of "stagflation"—stagnant economic growth combined with very significant inflation—followed, changing the outlook of government policies substantially. Since 1973 the average real US household income has been declining and governments have retreated from fully supporting the empowerment of the working classes. A new stage of institutional economic development has been initiated. This can be characterised as the platform economy. The next discussion tries to make sense of this new institutional framework and its viability.

**The Rise of the Platform Economy** In the 1970s, a period of stagflation in the western capitalist economies resulted in the undermining of the consumer capitalist framework. From the 1980s, through the implementation of neo-liberal economic policies, there emerged an institutional framework that I will refer to as the *platform economy*. This framework is clearly capitalist in nature, but has serious shortcomings that have been addressed in, for example, Lazzarato (2012), Zizek (2014), Mason (2015) and Harvey (2017).

The failure of the consumer capitalist institutions in the 1970s resulted in the abandonment of the "global plan" and Keynesianism in favour of the "Global Minotaur" (Varoufakis 2011) and *monetarism*, based on a return to classical capitalist perspectives. As such the neo-liberal monetarist policies on which the platform economy is founded have regressed from the Keynesian policies of the consumer capitalist era and are harking back to the neo-classical market theories of the 1870s. This viewpoint was founded on the philosophy put forward in Hayek (1944) and Friedman (1962), the fundamental position being that state government is a bad force in the economy and should retreat from the activist interventionist policies adopted since the Great Depression.

Reforms in the 1980s restored economic growth, and the 1990s are perceived as the boom era for the platform economy. Nevertheless, in the twenty-first century the performance of neo-liberal policies has strongly diminished. Growth in western economies has been lacklustre since the dot-com crisis of 2000–2001, resulting in the Great Panic of 2008 and the following depression. In 2015–2016 this malaise spread to the global economy as a whole. Only in 2017 did the global economy partially restore itself to a modest level of economic growth. In traditional western capitalist economies, the growth rate has not restored itself to reproductive levels, it seems.

Next, I argue that the institutional foundations of the platform economy are unsound and that the decline in economic wealth generation is directly linked to the neo-liberal policies supporting it.

**The Role of Transnational Corporations** Institutionally, the platform economy is characterised by the rise of transnational corporations (TNCs) as developmental platforms in the global economy, and the retreat of governments to such an extent that the nation-states have become irrelevant as developmental platforms. TNCs now exercise such influence and control over governments that socio-economic policies are global rather than local, and these policies benefit these TNCs rather than the citizens of individual nation-states. This is expressed by the benefits granted to TNCs through neo-liberal international trade treaties such as the Trans-Pacific Partnership (TPP), between the US and its Pacific partners, and the Transatlantic Trade and Investment Partnership (TTIP), between the European Union (EU) and the USA. Both treaties have been undermined significantly owing to resistance from voters in participating countries, in particular through lobbying of the EU regarding the TTIP and the election of Donald Trump as president of the USA in 2016.

Most TNCs occupy middleman positions in the global economy trade infrastructures and are designed to extract maximally from these positions. In this regard, the platform economy is clearly an expression of the extraction stage of the consumer capitalist institutional wave. The institutional arrangement of the platform economy complies with the extreme financialisation that is observed at this stage. Vitali et al. (2011) and Vitali and Battiston (2013) identify financial TNCs as the most powerful middlemen in our contemporary global trade and financial networks.

Nation-states are no longer supportive of their citizens and the working classes have lost their nationalist empowerment. Democratic government is retreating rapidly and the political class has become despised and distrusted. This is coupled with the decline in purchasing power for the working classes: average real household incomes have steadily declined since the 1970s. This has driven many people into private debt. Since the 1980s the indebtedness of nation-states—private as well as public—has risen sharply.[20] This is a direct consequence of the rise of the TNCs in controlling middleman positions in the trade networks and provision chains that make up the social division of labour.

The decline in the democratic control of the nation-state has been coupled with the wholesale disposal of national assets. State-owned corporations have been privatised, from postal services to prison systems. Most of these schemes have been considered wealth transfers from the state to private capitalists. This has supported the acquisition of more middleman positions by TNCs in many provision chains in the social division of labour, which were considered to be vulnerable by previous generations.

The platform economy has to be understood as founded on the exploitation of middleman power and the maximal extraction of income from these positions. This is further supported by the control of subordinates and the promotion of the "entrepreneurial self" as the model of *Homo economicus* (Zizek 2014). In the neo-liberal platform economy, the social division of labour is dysfunctional and breaking down. Economic growth is only caused by the growth of the financial services sector, which is founded on financial product innovation and exploitation, rather than through the normal extension and deepening of the social division of labour.[21]

---

[20] Keen (2011, 2017) presents an explanation of the Great Panic of 2008 based on the theories put forward by Minsky (1986); that indebtedness is single most important factor to determine the stability of an economy. This is clearly a non-institutional viewpoint that does not incorporate the health of the social division of labour. I recognise that indebtedness is a measure that indicates the healthy functioning of the social division of labour. However, indebtedness should be assessed as a consequence of the institutional dysfunction of the economy rather than its cause.

[21] This is illustrated by the fact that since the prolonged recession after 2008, the UK economy has grown only through the expansion of this sector and that the manufacturing sector of the UK economy has actually declined during this period.

The exploitation of middleman positions in the social division of labour has resulted in growing inequality in wealth and income distribution (Stiglitz 2013; Piketty 2014). This extreme inequality has resulted in an increased distrust of the economy in general.

The platform economy seems to be a response to the emergence of new institutions that should build the next phase in the history of human wealth creation. These new institutions are founded on the emergence of a truly global economy, which is based on innovative information technologies, green energy and the rise of fully automated production on demand. These new technologies are accompanied by the rise of extreme individualism and the possibility of true global citizenship. This supports the emergence of a global economy and the exploitation of zero-marginal cost production technologies. The latter calls for a fundamental separation of the allocation of economic wealth from the social division of labour. This requires the emergence of a global network economy in which wealth is allocated through different means than the social division of labour. I refer to Sect. 2.4 for a more elaborate discussion of the network economy as a natural successor to the consumer capitalist economy.

The platform economy is an expression of the contestation of these new institutional developments by the vested interests that embody the consumer capitalist economy. This is most clearly expressed by the abolition of the interventionist economic policies of nation-states in favour of supporting the exploitation of middleman positions by the TNCs in our global trade networks. This blatant exploitation has not occurred since the collapse of the feudal economy in the fourteenth-century anomalies.

It is difficult to assess the nature of the platform economy. Is it a transitionary institutional form or is it an expression of the terminal decline of capitalism? If it is the former, then we have to view the contemporary economy as an intermediary stage in the emergence of the network economy that represents the underlying institutional developments that were stopped by neo-liberalism from taking hold in the economy. In this respect, the current neo-liberal platform economy is an expression of turbulent transition, as was the case in the transition from classical to consumer capitalism between the 1870s and the 1940s.

If it is the latter, then a new institutional framework might be prevented from emerging at all. In that case we are looking at a state of permanent decline and developmental stagnation, signified by the viewpoint promoted by some contemporary economists (Cowen 2012, 2013; Baldwin and Teulings 2014), who coined the term *secular stagnation* for this state of affairs. This is founded on the fact that exploitation can never result in higher levels of economic wealth. The history of the social division of labour clearly shows that economic wealth is enhanced through its deepening, supported by a governance system of strong, productive institutions—referring, therefore, to a positive, building perspective rather than an exploitative view of wealth creation processes. I explain in the next section that the Great Panic of 2008 was exactly based on the exploitative design of certain chains in the social division of labour.

## 2.3    BUBBLES AND CRISES IN THE PLATFORM ECONOMY

The emergence of the neo-liberal platform economy has led us onto a path of major financial bubbles and busts. After the dot-com crisis of 2000, which was caused by the implosion of the bubble on the NASDAQ market for internet-based corporations, we headed straight for the *Great Panic of 2008* and the subsequent depression.[22] This crisis was a direct result of a major bubble in the mortgage provision system, as part of our global social division of labour. An analysis of the collapse of this system shows that the deepening of the social division of labour founded on financial innovation carries a fundamentally high risk of implosion. In this section I present a careful analysis of the mortgage provision network to illuminate the fundamental weaknesses that are embedded in financial networks.

Before I debate the causes of the mortgage provision failure and the Great Panic of 2008 in detail, I reflect a little on the history of financial crises in the global capitalist economy. This is structured around regular cycles of economic boom resulting in some financial market bubble followed by collapse or "bust" triggered by the bursting of that bubble.[23] Thus, a pattern of economic crises emerges that is very regular and directly tied to the financialisation that occurs in the declining phase of an institutional wave. It is a dynamic phenomenon of the capitalist economy that still has no proper explanation, although some features of economic behaviour have been pointed out as potential causes (Akerlof and Shiller 2009).

As I have already mentioned, the presence of institutional cycles in the capitalist economy implies that financial crises are caused by the decline of the institutional framework and the contestation of these old institutions by new ones. Financialisation extends the life-span of the old and inefficient institutions and allows the established elites to extract as much value from their middleman positions in the networks founded on these old institutions as possible. In a nutshell, financialisation is the direct cause of the Great Panic of 2008.

---

[22] A standard nineteenth-century term for a banking or financial crisis is that of a "panic". Two severe historical downturns stand out in a long list of financial panics and recessions. The first one is the *Great Panic of 1873*, which caused a sequence of three severe economic depressions. An economic depression from 1873 to 1878 was followed by an economic recession from 1882 to 1885 and a severe economic depression from 1893 to 1899. This extraordinarily recessionary period is also known as the *Long Depression*. The second one is actually the financial crisis of 2008: our current economic predicament is very similar to the Long Depression.

[23] This sequence of boom–bubble–bust cycles should not be confused with what is known as a *business cycle*. A business cycle is a much more mild and regular feature of the capitalist market economy, expressing the normal pattern of business. Business cycles are recognised as regular features of a normally developing economy. The boom–bubble–bust cycles I refer to are much more severe in nature and result in strong downturns of the economy.

**Table 2.1**  History of financial panics

| Crisis | Description |
| --- | --- |
| Crisis of 1772/1773 | Banking crisis in Amsterdam and London |
| Panic of 1792 | The first bailout of the banking sector by A. Hamilton |
| Panic of 1819 | First classical financial bubble-bust cycle |
| Panic of 1825 | British recession with near-failure of the Bank of England |
| Panic of 1837 | Initiates a five-year depression |
| Panic of 1847 | Financial crisis related to Railway bubble of the 1840s |
| Panic of 1857 | Recession induced stock market collapse |
| Great Panic of 1873 | Followed by a four-year depression |
| Paris Bourse crash | 19 January 1882 |
| Recession of 1882–1885 | Centred around the Panic of 1884 |
| Panic of 1890–1893 | Introduction to severe depression until 1899 |
| Panic of 1901–1904 | Recession following McKinley assassination |
| 1907 Bankers' Panic | Markets' collapse of 50% before intervention by J.P. Morgan |
| Great depression 1929–1939 | Stock market crash of 1929 |
| Oil crisis 1973–1975 | Stock market crash and economic recession |
| Black Monday 1987 | Freak stock market crash on 19 October 1987 |
| Asian Financial Crisis of 1997 | Capital flows abandon Asian economies |
| Dot-com crisis of 2000 | Recession following NASDAQ bust in March 2000 |
| Great Panic of 2008 | Financial panic and major trust crisis |
| Sovereign Debt Crisis 2010–2011 | Freezing of markets for sovereign debt of Eurozone countries |
| Secular Stagnation 2014–?? | General slowdown of global economic development |

A list of historical financial panics and crises is given in Table 2.1.[24] The regularity of these banking panics and financial busts is remarkable. As remarkable is the absence of such crises in the decades following the Second World War. Indeed, from the Great Depression until the Oil Crisis of 1973–1974 there was neither major crisis nor recession. In fact, given the relatively mild effects of the Oil Crisis, the Asian Financial Crisis, and the Dot-Com Bust, the Great Trust Crisis of 2007–2009 is the first financial panic since 1929.[25] Why is that the case?

---

[24] These list are available from Wikipedia, in particular at "http://en.wikipedia.org/wiki/List of economic crises" and "http://en.wikipedia.org/wiki/List of banking crises".

[25] A major anomaly in the given list is the event listed as the stock market collapse on Monday, 19 October 1987, also known as *Black Monday in 1987*. This compares with Black Monday in 1929, and it stands out as the most singular stock market crash in the history of the New York Stock Exchange (NYSE): the Dow-Jones industrial average plunged more than 22% in that single day. Uncharacteristically, this single-day collapse was not followed by an economic downturn. Instead, it fizzled out and had no lasting effects on the real economy, unlike the similar scenario in 1929.

### 2.3.1   Setting the Scene: Two Major Crises of Capitalism Before 2008

The ongoing economic crisis in our contemporary global economy is an example of a major *institutional trust crisis*. Very few economists have reflected on trust and the effects of the loss of trust in the governing institutions of the globalised economy. For the exceptions, I refer to Nooteboom (2002), Seabright (2010) and Akerlof and Shiller (2009). All these sources consider a loss of trust or confidence as the fundamental cause of any economic crisis.

In general, the mechanism works as follows: if economic agents lose confidence in the good outcomes to their economic actions, it undermines the very reason why these agents would act. The natural response to a loss of confidence is to forgo the riskiest actions, naturally leading to a reduction in the overall level of economic activity. In other words, it immediately causes a negative growth in economic activity, also defined as an *economic recession*. The Great Panic of 2008 is confirmed as a pure trust crisis by Caballero (2009). He points out that there were no other causes of the collapse; the trust foundation was pulled out from under the financial sector without much warning.

The loss of confidence can have devastating effects on the economy. This has occurred twice before in recent economic history, during the Long Depression of the 1880s and the 1890s and the Great Depression of the 1930s. Before I analyse the causes of the Great Panic of 2008, I will therefore reflect briefly on the causes of these two major trust crises.

**The Great Panic of 1873 and the Long Depression**   The Great Panic of 1873 should be interpreted as the financial crisis that is closest in nature to the Great Panic of 2008. The Great Panic of 1873 started in May 1873 with the collapse of the Vienna Stock Exchange. This was in nature a trust crisis that was caused by dishonest and fraudulent practices there combined with the failure of a number of European banks caused by overexuberance after the Franco-Prussian war of 1870–1871, the resulting unification of Germany and the payment of French war reparations.

The crisis of 1873 was triggered in New York by the failure of Jay Cooke & Co.,[26] a major New York financial institution, in September 1873, which caused a collapse of the stock market in New York (Lubetkin 2006). The sequence of events in Vienna and New York was followed by a chain reaction of bank failures and the temporary closure of the NYSE. This in turn caused economic collapse in both Europe and the USA. This depression lasted well into 1879, and was followed by a sequence of recessionary periods until 1899.

The Great Panic of 1873 is one of the purest examples in the history of the modern capitalist economy of a global trust crisis resulting from a financial panic and its devastating effects. Dishonest and fraudulent behaviour in the financial sector of the economy caused a collapse of trust between financial

---

[26] The bankruptcy of Jay Cooke & Co. was caused by a failure to sell $300 million in bonds to finance the expansion of the US railway system by the Northern Pacific Railway company.

institutions and among traders in the various stock markets. Indeed, the collapse of the Vienna Stock Exchange and the NYSE in 1873 shows the precarious foundations of the wealth creation processes in our global economy.[27]

The consequences of the Great Panic of 1873 were quite devastating. As Romer (1986) reports, after the stock market collapse in 1893 and during the Long Depression economic growth collapsed. US unemployment rose to 12.3% in 1893 and peaked at 18.4% in 1894. Unemployment did not fall back under 10% until 1899, at which point the Long Depression finally came to an end.

**The Crash of 1929 and the Great Depression**  As discussed above, the Great Panic of 1873 is only one in a rather long sequence of major financial trust crises throughout the nineteenth and early twentieth centuries. It has been recognised that such crises are symptomatic of an unregulated capitalist economy and show that market systems are actually prone to failure without proper oversight and regulation.

The last major economic crisis in this sequence is the "Great Depression" that lasted from the NYSE crash of 1929 until 1939.[28] The Great Depression and the economic policy recommendations by John Maynard Keynes changed the perspective of economic policy at a very fundamental level (Keynes 1936). Market regulation combined with monetary and fiscal policy became corner-stones of the prevailing view during the second half of the twentieth century. Indeed, this was rather successful, and major panics and crises were avoided until the Great Panic of 2008.

The *Stock Market Crash of 1929* has been debated extensively (Galbraith 1955; Bernanke 2000) and even considered to be a similar event to the Great Panic of 2008 (Ahamed 2009). I argue that there is actually a major difference between these two panics: in 1929 the stock market bubble burst, while in 2008 the banking lending networks froze.

Considering the Stock Market Crash of 1929, we observe that the collapse followed a long period of economic boom, known as the "Roaring '20s". The crash of 1929 occurred during three devastating trading days: Black Thursday (24 October), Black Monday (28 October) and Black Tuesday (29 October). On each of those days the stock prices on the NYSE fell on average by more than 10%. The NYSE continued its decline until 1934, when it had lost 90% of its value in comparison with 1929 levels. The Dow Jones Industrial Average index only regained its 1929 level of 380 in 1954, some 25 years later. The detailed account given by Galbraith (1955) in his celebrated work is very insightful.

---

[27] Dishonesty and fraud are very strong triggers for the loss of trust in a society's economic institutions. In general, (Akerlof and Shiller 2009, Chapter 3) refer to corruption as one of the animal spirits that guide economic decisions. Later in this book I will show that corruption is indeed directly related to institutional trust; as such it strongly undermines its formation and sustenance in economic institutions. For further details see the detailed account in Johnson and Kwak (2010).

[28] The Great Depression has much less in common with the current ongoing Great Trust Crisis than the Great Panic of 1873. Indeed, at its foundation there was a collapse of the NYSE, but not a major financial trust crisis as was the case in 1873 as well as in 2008.

The Stock Market Crash of 1929 triggered the *Great Depression*, a period of severe economic decline that was only halted definitively by the outbreak of the Second World War in 1939. The Great Depression resulted in massive unemployment and economic contraction. In the USA, unemployment rates peaked at 25.6% in 1933; in the UK a level of 26.6% was reached in 1931; and in Germany unemployment reached a staggering 33.7% in 1930 (Akerlof and Shiller 2009, p. 67). It is almost incomprehensible that economies can be this dysfunctional. Indeed, at such massive levels of unemployment one would expect that human ingenuity would find ways to induce the unemployed to be productive, subsuming them into the social division of labour and thereby reaching a better economic state. However, during these economic crises this did not occur. Instead, it took many years to get out of the slump and to reach reasonable unemployment rates.[29]

Economic policies introduced by the Roosevelt administration—also known as the "New Deal"—were far less effective than usually thought. In particular, a major recession was triggered by the reduction in government expenditure in 1937 after a period of apparent recovery. The main reason for this ineffectiveness is that once an economy is in a downward spiral, that dynamic is very hard to halt. The financial injections introduced through the New Deal were not large enough to permanently push the economy to recovery; only a world war generated enough spending to do so.[30]

### 2.3.2    *The Run-Up to the Great Panic of 2008*

I will now discuss my view of the causes of the financial trust crisis of 2007–2008 and the following global depression, which I refer to as the Great Panic of 2008. I particularly focus on the financial trust crisis rather than on the following governmental sovereign debt crisis in 2010–2011 and the slowdown in the BRIC economies (Brazil, Russia, India and China) during 2015–2016. The crisis clearly has the features of a spreading and ongoing fundamental institutional trust crisis, of which the Eurozone sovereign debt problems were just one incarnation.

I believe that the main cause of the Great Panic of 2008 was simply the failure of the fundamental relational or network structure of the economy in which our contemporary financial markets are embedded. This relational structure emerged in the three decades prior to the financial crisis—and, as such, were part of the financialisation processes in the failing institutional framework on

---

[29] Concerning unsustainable unemployment rates, I also refer here to the situation in Spain and Greece in which more than 25% of the labour force has been unemployed during the ongoing Eurozone depression since the sovereign debt crisis of 2010–2011.

[30] For more analysis of the Great Depression I refer to Galbraith (1955) and Chapter 6 in Akerlof and Shiller (2009) for an economic analysis and to Ahamed (2009) for an account of the particular role of bankers in the crisis.

which the consumer capitalist global economy was founded.

The Great Panic of 2008 in the USA happened in the context of a decade-long lacklustre economic performance (Johnson and Kwak 2010, Chapters 3–4). The economic boom of the 1990s had been followed by a major collapse of the stock market in 2000–2001 owing to the bursting of the so-called dot-com bubble in the NASDAQ stock market. Very high expectations for the future profitability of internet-based retail companies such as Amazon.com and Pet.com drove the price of the stock of these companies well beyond their true market value.

Financial policy and the adjustment of certain socio-economic institutions to facilitate the rise of the platform economy were causes of this crisis. Indeed, the bubble in the NASDAQ market was facilitated directly by a favourable US tax policy (Janszen 2008). This bubble had already been building up for a decade when it finally burst in 2000. This in turn resulted in the collapse of most US-based stock markets, followed by a downturn in the stock markets in Europe and a recession of the main western economies, including the US economy and the economies of the EU. The financial losses emanating from the NASDAQ collapse were in the neighbourhood of $7 trillion, which had to be absorbed by the global economy.

Partly, this tremendous financial loss was offset by the ensuing financial bubble in the housing market. The financial sector was able to write many high risk securities based on these inflated housing prices. These securities were in the form of complex financial assets based on a variety of mortgages and other real estate loans. I refer to Johnson and Kwak (2010) for further details.

Between the dot-com bust of 2000–2001 and the financial trust crisis of 2008 lies the Bush era of reduced market regulation, increased corruption (Enron and other fraudulent business practices), growing economic inequalities, unsustainable current account deficits, major government deficits owing to flawed tax policies, the execution of multiple wars and soaring entitlements, in particular related to health care provision (Medicare) and social security claims. These problems did not boost the rather dismal performance of the economy for the average citizen; there was little growth in average household income and commodity prices went up sharply owing to speculation by financial institutions in the various commodity markets.

The Bush policies can therefore be blamed directly for the resulting financial collapse in 2008. These neo-liberal policies were founded on the flawed principles of simple neo-classical calculus of the market as promoted by economic libertarians. Deregulation of the financial industry resulted in a climate of irrational exuberance of endless financial product innovation and the hedging of market positions by major financial institutions. Phillips (2008) points to the special position that the financial sector obtained in the USA, UK and Eurozone economies in comparison with traditional manufacturing industry during this time.[31] The financial institutions obtained unhealthy economic control over government policies, through the placement of their leaders in government—led by top bankers who acted as treasury secretaries: Robert Rubin, Henry Paulson and Timothy Geitner (Johnson and Kwak 2010).

**Increasing Inequality and Decreasing Trust**  The tax policies of the Bush government deepened the already existing income inequalities in the US economy.[32] Emulation of these libertarian policies in the UK and the EU resulted in increasing income inequalities in the European economies. In Asia the differences between people who were able to ride the waves of the booming economy and those who could not became increasingly stark. In 2008 the state of the global economy was, therefore, characterised by very significant economic inequalities, reminding us of the good old capitalist era of laissez-faire in the nineteenth century.

It is a well-known fact that significant income inequalities result in a less happy and functional society. Life expectancy drops and the overall happiness of the population declines. This is currently symptomatic of the western capitalist economies. I add to these well-accepted effects of inequality that it undermines trust and the foundations of the functioning of the economy. Indeed, economic inequality results in less willingness to accept one's position and station in society. Failure to correct this can result in general dissatisfaction with and distrust of the socio-economic and institutional structure of the economy. This undermines institutional trust as well as notional trust and eventually operational confidence in the economy. (See the detailed account on the nature of socio-economic trust in Chap. 4.)

Throughout the 1990s and the period up to 2005, the financial policies of the Federal Reserve System chairman Alan Greenspan resulted in unsustainably low interest rates. This brought about a huge inflationary boom in certain markets, in particular in housing prices, which soared worldwide. Housing mortgages and consumer credit resulted in a spending boom in the US, UK and EU economies. This spending was financed through the international markets in particular through financial recycling of surpluses from the Asian economies. The "globalised" world economy became de facto a huge monetary machine of capital flows between the US and the Asian economies (Varoufakis 2011).

This financial house of cards was essentially brought down by a crisis in the world food and oil markets in 2007–2008. More precisely, in late 2007

---

[31] This special position is also expressed in the fact that (investment) banks paid out and continue to pay out very large bonuses to their employees. This bonus craze further deepens existing income inequalities and shows the supremacy of the financial sector in comparison with manufacturing sectors. This in turn feeds the deterioration of economic trust in the economy as a whole.

[32] These income inequalities have been increasing since the Carter era in the late 1970s. Real income for working-class families have not increased and have even decreased over this period. As a consequence, working-class families have financed their expenditures more and more through credit in the form of home mortgages, consumer loans and credit cards (Piketty 2014).

and early 2008 a perfect storm brewed in the global economy. The first signs were increasing commodity prices—mainly energy and food prices—followed by major deflation in the housing markets worldwide. As the main culprit, pundits identified a "bubble" in the American housing market. Properties were seen as "overpriced" compared with their "true" value. Here the notion of a "true" underlying value seems misleading, even though it is used frequently in economic policy making.[33]

Subsequently, the collapse of the mortgage market resulted in a complete deterioration of trust in the world financial system, in particular a significantly reduced trust in the financial sector in the USA. In the media, pundits as well as the major economists immediately referred to this phase as the most major economic crisis since the depression of the 1930s, further undermining the trust of regular people in the financial system and the economy. The deflation of the housing bubble triggered a collapse of the markets for mortgage-backed securities, which in turn triggered the aforementioned complete deterioration of trust in the world financial system.

Subsequently, a major trust crisis in the financial sector ensued and a deep and prolonged global recession resulted. In many ways the mechanism of the collapse is an exact copy of the financial panics of the nineteenth century, in particular the Great Panic of 1873. This mechanism is identified as that of *a pure institutional trust crisis in the social division of labour itself.*

Next I discuss the fundamental cause of this institutional trust crisis in the mortgage provision system as part of the financial system that was constituted relatively recently in the 1990s. It is important here to recognise that this mortgage provision system is a network in which the provision of mortgage-backed securities is embedded. As such, this network is part of the global division of labour. Its failure triggered the trust crisis in the financial sector. Furthermore, this failure was perfectly predictable from the viewpoint of the functioning of the social division of labour.

### 2.3.3    The Subprime Mortgage Provision System

Throughout most of economic history, mortgages were provided directly by a bank, the *mortgagee*, to its client, the *mortgagor*. The bank secured the mortgage loan directly from its own reserves—based on deposits in its bank accounts of its depositors—and put very high standards on the solvency of the client before writing the mortgage contract. Thus, mortgage provision was part of regular retail banking business.

---

[33] It mainly refers to the static market price of a commodity. Usually this is a purely theoretical notion that cannot truly be measured and does not exist in neo-classical market theory. However, in terms of the institutional-network economic perspective developed in Chap. 1, the "true" value could be interpreted as the labour value of these commodities, while the network prices of these commodities far exceeded those labour values.

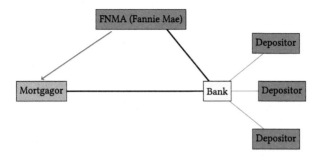

**Fig. 2.1**   Schematic of the network of US mortgage provision (1950s)

The schematic of this traditional mortgage provision network is depicted in Fig. 2.1. Clearly, the bank has a middleman position in this network, but the relative short supply chain from mortgagor to depositor makes the relationships transparent and trust-based. There is little opportunity for the bank to make significant gains—or "rents"—from its middleman position in this network, since the bank has to guarantee the satisfaction of its depositors. The bank operated in a relatively competitive environment and had to guarantee its depositors a decent return on their deposits. The operating margins were therefore rather modest.

In the traditional provision of mortgages in the USA, they were backed by the US federal government through several social financial corporations. Indeed, regulation of mortgage provision in the 1930s—following the Great Depression—resulted in the creation of multiple government-supported enterprises to secure the provision of sufficient number of mortgages to potential home owners. The best well-known agencies are the Federal Home Loan Mortgage Corporation (FHLMC)—better known as *Freddie Mac*—and the Federal National Mortgage Association (FNMA)—better known as *Fannie Mae*.[34] These government-owned enterprises support the issuance of mortgages through the provision of a sufficient number of guarantees. This government guarantee is depicted in Fig. 2.1 through a red arrow from the FNMA to the mortgagor.

This traditional form of mortgage provision was modified in several steps. This process can be identified as a normal deepening of the social division of labour: innovative financial products and new socio-economic roles were introduced to enhance the performance of the provision network for mortgages in the global economy. Mainly, the role of the bank as mortgagee was diversified

---

[34] There is also a third government-supported enterprise, the *Government National Mortgage Association* (Ginnie Mae), that is involved in the support of mortgage provision in the USA. Fannie Mae was founded in 1938. The original Fannie Mae corporation was partitioned into a new Fannie Mae and Ginnie Mae in 1968. Freddie Mac was created in 1970 to support the secondary mortgage market.

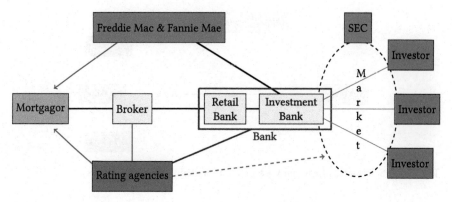

**Fig. 2.2**    Schematic of the network of US mortgage provision (2007)

to brokers and investment banks through the deepening and extending of the product chain in the social division of labour. This was a source of higher efficiency and enhanced wealth creation to all parties in the chain, in particular the retail and investment banks. A stylistic and simplified schematic of the enhanced mortgage provision network is depicted in Fig. 2.2.

In this representation, the main mortgage provision mechanism is depicted as a chain from the client, still the mortgagor, who wants to obtain a mortgage, to the mortgage broker to the mortgage providing bank to the market for mortgage-backed securities to the investors, who purchase these securities. But who the mortgagee is is no longer clear in such a complex system.

The main difference is immediately clear: the bank is now composed of a retail branch and an investment branch. Both these branches have a critical role in the mortgage provision network. The retail bank branch manages the relationship with the mortgagee and the mortgage brokers, while the investment bank branch manages the relationship with institutional investors on the capital market where mortgage-backed securities are traded.[35]

The main provision chain is supplemented by three main regulatory agencies. The institutions depicted in the light red box are the privately owned and managed rating agencies. The institutions represented by the blue boxes are government-controlled regulatory bodies. First, this comprises the social financial corporations, Freddie Mac and Fannie Mae, depicted in the same fashion as in Fig. 2.1. Second, the governmental *Securities and Exchange Commission*

---

[35] During the Great Depression the Glass-Steagall act legally required the separation of retailing and investment in US financial institutions. The bank in the 1950s mortgage provision network is, therefore, purely a retail bank. It had no relationship with any investment bank and therefore had no access to capital markets. During the 1990s the Glass-Steagall legislation was revoked and banks were allowed to merge. This was pursued vigorously, resulting in banking institutions that consisted of both retail and investment branches.

(SEC) oversees and regulates the functioning of financial markets. In this case, the SEC has a role in the regulation of the trade in mortgage-backed securities.

**Regarding the Mortgagor** The primary value-generating relation is now between the client (mortgagor) and the mortgage broker, who places the mortgage loan with the retail branch of a bank. In many cases the broker is an employee of a bank, but one of the innovations over the past decades is the rise of the independent broker. Even bank-employed brokers have to be formally independent and are forced to investigate competitive offers from other mortgage-providing organisations or banks. The broker only obtains an income from the brokerage of the mortgage itself. A commission is charged for the brokerage and the ties between the client and the broker are severed as soon as the mortgage is underwritten.

The proper securitisation of the mortgage loan is thus based on the ability of the broker to assess the creditworthiness of the client as well as her honesty in refusing brokerage if the client is insufficiently creditworthy. The support of the role of the broker in replacing the retail function of the banker herself is based on increased efficiency and lower transaction costs owing to specialisation.[36]

The assessment of the creditworthiness of the mortgagor by the broker is supported by privately operated consumer credit agencies, the main ones being Experian, Equifax and TransUnion.[37] A system of consumer credit ratings was designed to efficiently and effectively assess the risks of providing any credit to a private person or a family. The role of the consumer credit rating agency can be judged to be incentive compatible and has been functioning rather well from a systems perspective.[38]

On the other hand, the usage of this rating information by the broker has not been *incentive compatible*. The main incentive of the broker is to write as many mortgage contracts as possible. Since the broker has no responsibility of contract enforcement, there is no incentive for a long-term assessment of the contract structure. This has resulted in the writing of mortgage contracts with high-risk clients. In many cases the creditworthiness of these clients was overstated through inflated income numbers on the paperwork. The broker only has to satisfy himself with guaranteeing the payment of the loan in the first

---

[36] This is a standard effect of the introduction of specialisation into the economy, as first discussed in length by Smith (1776). Specialisation taps into increasing productivity owing to more advanced knowledge and productive ability. This in turns allows production activities to be decomposed into specialised tasks, resulting in much higher output level. Thus, an increasing return to specialisation results in overall increasing returns to scale for the economy as a whole (Buchanan 2008).

[37] These major consumer credit agencies operate internationally. Consumer credit ratings are assigned on a global basis using identical indicators of financial health of the potential debtor.

[38] It should be emphasised that the credit agencies discussed here are only the ones that assess the risk of providing credit to an individual person or a family. These agencies are not the ones that assess the risk of investment objects traded to investors operating on the financial asset markets. These credit agencies are subject to discussion in the following pages.

few months of the payment schedule, and the implementation of teaser rates assures that this is indeed the case. Such high-risk mortgage contracts are also known as *subprime mortgages*.

The process of issuing a mortgage is further supported through loan guarantees from the US federal enterprises Freddie Mac and Fannie Mae. It is remarkable how many mortgage guarantees are issued by these enterprises, even for low-risk mortgages for high-rated mortgagors. As a result of the overissuing of high-risk subprime mortgages, both Freddie Mac and Fannie Mae were put into receivership by the Bush administration in 2008. This implied that the mortgage guarantees issued by these enterprises were and still are backed by the lender of last resort, the US federal government.

**The Role of the Banks**  The second step in the mortgage provision chain is the broker's placement of the mortgage contract with the retail branch of a bank. As such the broker has a double agency relationship with the client as well as the bank.[39] In that respect the broker has a perfect middleman position which can be exploited, as happened throughout the system during the two decades leading up to the crash of the system in 2007. Such middleman positions are very problematic, since they combine positions of control, that is, power, with agency issues, usually resulting in severe problems that easily result in corruption. The subprime mortgage failure is a prime example of corrupting failure owing to middleman exploitation.

The retail branch of the bank manages the relationship with the mortgagor and the mortgage broker. After initialisation of the contract, the broker transfers the management of the mortgage to the retail branch of the bank. The bank schedules payments and pursues any outstanding payments due. The income of the retail branch is based on a substantial management fee.

The single most profitable innovation in the mortgage provision system has been the introduction of mortgage-backed securities and the placement of these securities with investors through market contracts, departing from the traditional deposit-backed finance model for mortgage loans. This is depicted in Fig. 2.2 as the last part in the chain, where investment branches of the banks intermediate the placement of these mortgage-backed securities with investors through their networks.

**Mortgage-Backed Securities**  Initially, the retail branch of the bank transfers the mortgage loan itself to its investment branch. The investment bankers

---

[39] An *agency relationship* is the relationship between two parties—a so-called *principal* and an *agent*—in which one party (the principal) has a goal that can be achieved by the execution of a task or service by a specialist (the agent). In this case the client has the goal of obtaining a mortgage that can be achieved through the services of a licensed broker, who can place the mortgage contract with a bank. Obviously, the client is the principal and the broker is the agent in this agency relationship. Similarly, the bank has the goal of obtaining good mortgage contracts, which can be identified by the broker assessing the various prospects before him. In this case the bank is the principal and the broker is again the agent.

allocate parts of the loan into portfolios with parts of other mortgage loans. This creates *mortgage-backed securities*. Portfolio theory asserts that a diversified portfolio consisting of multiple investments with a variety of riskiness has a reduced risk profile. Thus, reduction of risk through diversification is at the foundation of these mortgage-backed securities.

Even though they are founded on portfolio theory, these mortgage-backed securities are very complex contracts in which low- and high-risk mortgage contracts are spliced. Such securities are in principle too difficult to assess by an individual investor (Johnson and Kwak 2010). This was remedied through three different product innovations.

First, each mortgage-backed security was backed by a so-called credit default swap (CDS). A CDS is essentially an insurance policy that covers the potentiality of a failure of the security, and they were issued by large investment banks and insurers such as AIG.

Second, the mortgage-backed securities were rated by privately operated financial rating agencies, mainly Moody's, Standard & Poor's (S&P), and Fitch. Here again there was a major incentive failure: these rating agencies are closely tied to the investment banks that issue these securities. (This is depicted in the schematic in Fig. 2.2.) Hence, these agencies did not have any incentive to properly assess the risk of these securities. Hall (2009) describes the operation at Moody's, one of the main asset rating agencies operating at Wall Street. These operations can only be described as utterly untrustworthy and as undermining the functioning of these asset markets. Instead of acting on behalf of investors, Moody's was "incentivised" to act on behalf of its owners, the major US investment banks.[40] This resulted in the near fraudulent overrating of mortgage-backed securities as traded in the capital market.

Third, since these securities are traded on a regulated financial market, the SEC in principle had oversight of this market and could have stepped in to regulate these trades. However, in view of the neo-liberal hands-off policies of the Clinton and Bush administrations such measures were never even considered; the investment banks were allowed to freely push their tainted products.

Overall, the effect was that banks and rating agencies played a con game with the mortgagors and the investors. This was exacerbated by the problem that investors usually have a religious belief in the perfect efficiency of the market. Thus, these investors believed that the market price of the security in question will, of course, reflect its true value, and as such one does not have to know

---

[40] In the past, credit agencies were publicly owned, mainly by the investors themselves. Under that ownership structure, the credit agencies operated under correct incentives and provided correct assessments of investments traded on financial assets markets. Indeed, these agencies are more profitable if their paying clients, the investors, are happy with their performance. Recently, however, these agencies were acquired by the major investment banks. Hall (2009) describes that this changed the incentives drastically; Moody's now operated on behalf of its owners rather than the investors.

the exact properties of the mortgage-backed security under consideration; the market price would exactly reflect its value. Thus, investors had a low incentive to scrutinise the traded securities and instead relied on the judgments of other market participants. The result was a collective delusion based on blind faith in the efficiency of competitive financial markets as well as the illusion of the efficiency and effectiveness of the regulatory system of private financial rating agencies and government agencies.

In conclusion, this mortgage provision system is a perfect example of a network in which all relationships are riddled with major incentive problems and in which failure was actually imminent. The main mistake has been that such a system was actually designed and implemented at all. Its failure had immense consequences in the form of a complete collapse of trust in the banks that peddled their poisonous securities. Even trust among banks evaporated at the height of the crisis in 2008, and they were unwilling to provide each other with short-term loans on overnight money markets. Only at the end of 2008 did this ease somewhat, although it was too late to save the economy from a major recession, owing to the spreading of the distrust among other economic constituents. As such the failure of the mortgage provision network is a perfect example of a trust crisis, so aptly described by Seabright (2010, pp. 1–3).

Furthermore, I emphasise that neo-classical economics cannot contribute to the understanding of the causes and effects of this failure. In this case the securities market is fully embedded within a network of agency relations, and it is mainly the failure of the network rather than the market itself that is at issue here. Economics requires new theories to assess such complex networks and the institutional arrangements in which they function. In this text it is my aim to present a number of tools, old as well as new, that might help us to understand our network economy. These insights and tools have an emphasis away from markets and are more focused on the economic relationships themselves.

### 2.3.4    Some Direct Causes of the Great Panic of 2008

Next I discuss some direct causes of the subprime mortgage crisis, the subsequent financial trust crisis and the ultimate collapse of the globalised economy into a deep recession. Again I refer to recent overviews such as Morris (2008), Phillips (2008), Johnson and Kwak (2010) and Stiglitz (2010) for detailed accounts of many of these causes from alternative perspectives.

Some of the causes discussed in this section were already introduced in my discussion of the mortgage provision network—represented by Fig. 2.2. The focus of the discussion that follows is on the more abstract reasons behind these failures from a more general perspective.

**Financial Innovation and Financialisation**  Financial markets have become the prime focal point of economic market theorising over the past decades. Many neo-classical economists have realised that market theory has no direct applicability in the real world of daily life; rather the theory should be primarily applicable to the world of artificial financial markets in which financial institutions and investors trade designed financial products such as securities rather than actual real, physical commodities. These markets were also assigned a vital role in the neo-classical market theory, in the sense that the development of new financial instruments could "complete" an otherwise incomplete market system.

*Market incompleteness* refers here to the fact that there are an infinite number of circumstances in which commodities can be traded and that in principle there should be different markets for trading these commodities under these different circumstances. For example, consider the simple commodity of an umbrella. Trading umbrellas when it is sunny is very different from trading them if it rains heavily. Ideally there should be two separate future markets for umbrellas under these two different circumstances. In fact, umbrellas under these different circumstances are two different economic commodities. This refers to the so-called "contingent" commodity concept of Debreu (1959), who proposed that place, time and circumstances determine a commodity as much as its intrinsic consumption properties.

Now, there could be introduced two instrumental commodities, namely an option for buying an umbrella when it is sunny and an option for buying an umbrella when it rains. Two new financial markets are now introduced to properly evaluate the value differentials of an umbrella when it is sunny and when it rains. Thus, according to standard market theory, the allocation of umbrellas improves, since trade of these options is efficient and the market prices of these options exactly evaluate these differentials in values.

This could be done for all commodities in an infinite number of ways. Consequently, economic market theory promotes a perspective of (extreme) financial product innovation; and indeed this has taken hold of Wall Street, with new financial instruments being developed in rapid order. The innovation of the mortgage provision network in this fashion thus fits very well with the theory of market incompleteness.

The downside of all this is that such contingent financial instruments are very complex in nature. The case in point is that of mortgage-backed securities discussed above. This complexity obscures the true value of these financial products, which opens the door to some unwanted consequences. First, it makes it very easy to manipulate buyers of these securities, in particular if even rating agencies are not able to properly assess the true value of these securities. Second, the non-transparency of these securities allows fraudulent behaviour. It is possible to exploit the willingness of investors to buy by subsuming extremely bad assets into these securities, as was the case with subprime mortgages.

It is interesting to note that market incompleteness and the related innovation of financial instruments are expressions of a dogmatic belief in the competitive market. Indeed, the central tenet of this theory is that any commodity traded on a competitive market is subject to extreme scrutiny and its market price therefore fully reveals the true value of that commodity. This is known as the *efficient market hypothesis*.

Here it is conveniently forgotten that market efficiency is only true if these commodities are perfectly transparent and can be traded properly in markets with a large number of highly mobile buyers and sellers. Of course, most commodities are not perfectly transparent and markets are rarely large enough. And, as pointed out, any financial security is in nature highly non-transparent, and theoretically it cannot be expected that its market price reflects its true economic value. This makes the belief in efficient markets truly a case of dogma rather than science.

**Exploitation of Positional Power by Banking Institutions as Middlemen**
Central to the issue of the failure of the financial sector and the collapse of trust among financial and banking institutions is that middleman positions in the financial networks were exploited for gain—or economic "rents"—in a totally unscrupulous fashion. I refer to this phenomenon as the absence of *middleman contestability*. This is closely related to the well-known notion of *rent seeking*, in particular focused on network positions.

Owing to the impossibility of accessing the financial markets directly, the financial sector has become a complex of networks that connect various interested parties through chains of intermediaries with traders operating on these financial markets.[41] Many of these intermediaries or middlemen in these networks have considerable power to exploit their positions. This power is the other side of the non-contestability of the middleman's network position; usually there are no alternative networks that one can access to achieve the same goal without significant switching costs. As long as the middlemen levy fees that are below these considerable switching costs it is economically justified to satisfy their demands.

This was illustrated most recently by the London Interbank Offered Rate (LIBOR) crisis in 2014. It was revealed that the LIBOR rate at which banks lend money to each other was set by a small and select group of bankers. They exploited their controlling influence by manipulating the LIBOR rate in favour of other bankers who sought to further their personal career and realise large financial gains (Haegens 2015). Of course, this has had major implications for financial trades throughout the global economy, affecting the profitability of corporations and the well-being of individuals.

In Fig. 2.2, middleman contestability refers to the challenging of the positions of the mortgage broker and the bank in these mortgage provision chains. In many cases these positions are not contested: there are few alternative ways

---

[41] It is illustrative to consider what intermediaries are required to make a trade on the NYSE or the NASDAQ market. Normally, one has to think of a chain of three or four intermediaries: one's financial adviser, her brokerage firm, a related brokerage firm at Wall Street and finally the actual corner trader on the floor of the NYSE. All these intermediaries levy fees on the trade of the stock on the NYSE. This constitutes a very significant portion of the possible gains one tries to make from the trade. This results in very high returns to the financial brokers and small gains for the investors.

to obtain a mortgage without dealing with these middlemen. This feature is further enhanced by the agency problems that make these chains even more problematic. It is clear that brokers as well as banks can extract considerable rents from their respective middleman positions in these chains.

In the case of the provision of subprime mortgages this was particularly the case. Brokers took full account of their middleman position and manipulated their clients as well as the banks that they dealt with to obtain large rents without significant risks of financial failure if the client defaulted on the written mortgage.

**Failure of the Institutional Regulatory System**  Over time, financial markets have been embedded in a regulatory system set up by Wall Street itself. This system is essentially based on the elimination of problems that obscure the transparency of the instruments traded in the financial markets. These problems mainly concern informational aspects such as the sharing of estimated probabilities of failure. Crucial in the assessment of these aspects are the privately owned and operated financial asset rating agencies such as S & P, Fitch and Moody's. These companies sell risk assessments of securities and the financial corporations backing these securities. As such these agencies are responsible for the proper assessment of risky investments.

These asset rating corporations are, however, owned by large investors and banks; in particular, they were acquired by the major banking institutions in the run-up to the Great Panic of 2008. This implies that these entities are subject to incentives emanating from the agency relationship with their owners, which are also their main beneficiaries—the banks. It has now become apparent that this institutional framework of risk assessment is as much prone to failure as the market itself. The system has significant design flaws that could have been revealed and assessed properly by looking at the incentive structure of the relational framework in which these agencies are embedded. It would be very hard to adjust the system without replacing these rating corporations with independent rating agencies. In practice, this would only be achieved through the introduction and incorporation of public rating agencies, the ownership of which is not in the hands of large institutional investors and banks, but rather in those of third parties or the government.

This is debated by Hall (2009) for the particular case of the rating agency Moody's. Moody's introduced a fundamentally flawed methodology to rate securities to boost its profitability, thereby deliberately losing sight of the interests of the investors. This resulted from a change in regulatory rules in the 1970s: the investors no longer paid for these ratings, rather the issuers of the assets under consideration did. This in turn translated into wrong incentives to please the issuers of debt, rather than its procurers, the investors. Hall (2009) reports that this policy change was supported with very strong incentives within the internal organisation of Moody's.

The case of Moody's is just an example of the extreme incentives driven by greed in these financial markets. Economists do not yet understand very well the consequences of (extreme) greed; their understanding is limited to the classical assertion that Adam Smith's invisible hand will guide greedy motives to an efficient state in the economy.[42] The self-organisation of the competitive market economy was also promoted in Hayek (1937, 1945, 1960), providing a foundation for the neo-liberal socio-economic policies that essentially caused the Great Panic of 2008.

**Decreased Governmental Oversight and Regulation of the Financial Sector** The second half of the regulatory institutional framework in which financial networks are embedded is the system of government oversight and regulation of the financial sector of the economy. This includes numerous federal as well as New York state government agencies that regulate the financial markets themselves. The main one is that of the SEC, which has the authority to directly interfere and intervene into the financial networks. This includes the regulation of trade of financial securities and the regulation of major investors and brokerage firms.

A second group of government regulatory agencies concern themselves with the regulation of the banking sector. The main government institutions that regulate banking are the treasury department itself, the Federal Reserve System and the Federal Deposit Insurance Corporation (FDIC). These institutions may impose solvability and liquidity constraints on retail banks and can also operate on money markets by trading government papers.

Over the past decades these institutions have mainly retreated from a strict regulation of the financial sector. Instead, they have assumed a more and more passive role in a sector that has grown more complex and essentially more in need of regulation than ever before in history. The retreat of these institutions from regulatory oversight was based on the philosophy that government is limited in its abilities to make society and that government might well be a problem itself. This has emanated from the neo-liberal economic policies of all governments since the 1980s. These policies were even more strongly enforced during the Bush era (2001–2009) during which these institutions were practically banned from regulating Wall Street. This paved the way for increased financial exuberance and the drifting of the financial and banking systems into uncharted territory of extreme financial innovation.

The previous point focuses on the systematic decrease in oversight of especially the US federal government regarding the financial sector of the US economy. EU oversight of the European financial sector was similarly reduced, although not as severely as in the USA. Furthermore, the Eurozone was designed around an ineffectual central banking system, the European Central

---

[42] I emphasise here that the invisible hand metaphor only played a very minor role in Adam Smith's work; it mainly featured in his "Moral Sentiments" (Smith 1759). However, the misunderstanding about what the invisible hand notion exactly entailed in his philosophy spread throughout twentieth-century neo-classical economics and, in fact, became one of its cornerstones (Ingrao and Israel 1990; Grampp 2000).

Bank (ECB). Only recently has the ECB assumed more control and even initiated quantitative easing operations in the Eurozone money markets.

**Failure of a Proper Government Response** Concerning the response of governments and their agencies after the financial panic started in September 2008, a campaign was launched in the US media for a bailout package of $700 billion to relieve US financial institutions from the subprime mortgage-backed securities that it had created itself. The promoted philosophy behind this measure was to liberate banks from high-risk assets to free up resources for restarting the credit markets, as these had dried up after the collapse of trust among financial institutions. The US Congress gave complete control of the bailout to the US Treasury Department.

Next, in view of a British proposal to inject resources directly into failing financial institutions—mainly commercial investment banks—the US Treasury Department decided to pursue a similar strategy. Large capital injections were given to banking institutions and several banks were merged, with the backing of the US Treasury Department's resources.

Instead of unlocking the frozen credit markets, these capital injections were mainly used for long-run purposes such as shoring up solvency and capital positions of the banks and the purchase of assets in competing banks. Thus, a further consolidation of the financial sector resulted, which led to rather unhealthily sized banking corporations that are essentially "too large to fail", and certainly would extract excess rents from their monopolistic positions in financial networks under these circumstances of reduced contestability. Unfortunately, this is as expected. Indeed, economic confidence in general and trust among economic subjects in particular has to be rebuilt differently, using regulatory instruments and strong socio-economic institutions.

The irony is that the financial bailout plan countered the creative destructionism at the centre of the free capitalist system. Indeed, according to Schumpeter's view, failing institutions need to be removed from the system through bankruptcy in order to make way for innovative initiatives that generate renewed economic development and growth (Schumpeter 1927, 1928, 1934).[43] So, from a purely capitalist market perspective it would be better to let these banks fail and to replace them with new financial institutions that develop new financial instruments to counter the effects of financial toxins such as subprime mortgage-backed securities and the accompanying credit default swaps. This natural process, however, did not get a chance to play out, for fear that it would lead to significant economic upheaval and possibly collapse.

As it happened, banks survived, but still a major trust crisis emanated and a severe recession resulted. This was followed by a budgetary crisis in the Eurozone and the UK. The actions of the Treasury Department—and Treasury Secretary Henry Paulson in particular—did not build any trust. Paulson's

---

[43] For a good account of Schumpeter's theory I refer to the excellent biography of Schumpeter, McGraw (2007), that centres on this issue.

flipflopping among various policy tracks was too obvious, resulting in further unrest in the financial sector and the wider economy, and the US government in general became untrustworthy (Johnson and Kwak 2010).

Unfortunately, the policy followed by the Obama administration was not very convincing either. It has been widely argued that Treasury Secretary Timothy Geitner and the president's main economic advisor, Lawrence Summers, were too much insiders of the tainted financial industry on Wall Street. Reregulation of the financial sector has not been very strong and very large financial institutions have not been dismantled to prevent future relapses.

The lack of financial and economic intervention by nation-states in the global economy is a natural consequence of the current relative insignificance of the nation-state as a socio-economic platform. Clearly, the future is to evolve into a fully connected global economy, in which nation-states have rather subordinate roles. Any regulation should emanate from global initiatives. Given the insignificance of global treaties in various areas, this is a very hard goal to achieve.

**Significant Socio-Economic Inequalities** My two final points concern the general and abstract conditions of the socio-economic environment in which the global economy is currently embedded. The most recognised deficiency of the global economy at the beginning of the twenty-first century is the presence of significant inequalities (Stiglitz 2013; Piketty 2014). These inequalities form a basis for distrust among actors in the economy.

Large economic inequalities were present throughout the nineteenth century and were a major cause for the panics and crises throughout that period, including the Long and Great Depressions. Economic inequalities are a violation of perceived fairness in a society. This in turn undermines the functionality of the economy directly, in particular through the reduction of trust or confidence in economic institutions (Akerlof and Shiller 2009, Chapters 2 and 6).

First, I would like to point out the significant economic inequalities that are present in the US and Asian economies and to a lesser extent in the Eurozone economies. This does not only refer to income inequalities as discussed above, but also to unequal access to health care and education; it refers to *opportunity inequality*.

Second, large inequalities not only bring down the overall state of mind of people, but also undermine the economy from the point of view of a trusting society. As pointed out above, inequalities result in distrust among various groups of people. In the USA, the UK and Eurozone countries one observes high levels of distrust among various race groups, immigrants versus citizens, and economic elites versus poor population groups. Such distrust results in an overall reduced state of trust in economic institutions as well as governmental agencies.

Most recently these inequalities—mainly expressed as inequality of opportunities—have morphed into populist democratic dissent. In particular, nationalist views have been propelled forward in response to the inequalities emanating from the globalisation of the economy. In Europe this has resulted in the election of several nationalist political leaders as well as xenophobic policies, such as those related to the admission of refugees from the wars in the Middle East and the UK leaving the EU ("Brexit"). In the USA this has been expressed through the election of Donald Trump as president in 2016.

**A Global Culture of Fear**    Finally, the Great Panic of 2008 exploded into a general culture of fear that was instigated in the media and through government policies and actions. Fear in general undermines trust in a significant way. Throughout the past two decades the level of general fear has increased significantly through reports about terrorism in the media as well as through the security policies of various governments. This has been a problem in particular in the USA, the EU and the UK.

This culture of fear has been building up for the last 40 years, essentially since the Oil Crisis of 1973–1974; it did not necessarily emerge in a vacuum after security policies were formalised and wars were initiated after the attacks on 11 September 2001. The first primary source of fear is reporting in the commercial media, in particular in the USA and the UK. The purpose of these media is not to undertake investigative reporting, but to attract sufficiently high ratings and large audiences. Broadcast news programs have turned into full entertainment shows that report the most grisly news to attract more viewers. This has become particularly the case since these media are now part of large corporations. The result is an onslaught of negative reports and warnings, especially concerning crime and terrorist threats. Although crime rates have dropped, many Americans believe that they live in a very violent society in which at any moment they could become a victim of crime. In reality, however, compared with other societies, the overwhelming majority of Americans live in very safe circumstances.

The second primary source of fear is the policies implemented by government agencies. These agencies have generated a tremendous overuse of warnings and alarms for the most trivial of things. Nearly every day Americans are confronted with weather warnings and traffic alarms. Air travel has become a huge burden, especially since the terrorist attack on 11 September 2001. Every traveller is treated as a potential terrorist and is subjected to extreme scrutiny. After 2001, the level of fear has risen tremendously for political purposes. Elections have been won by emphasising and propagating the fear of crime, immigrants and terrorists.

The result of these two prime sources is that Americans and Britons essentially live in a fearful society. This fear undermines the required trust necessary to fulfil our daily economic transactions.[44]

---

[44] For example, when Hurricane Ike approached the Texas coast in 2008, many people in the south-east USA were panicked into expecting severe gas shortages. The result was a run on gas stations on the day before the hurricane made landfall. Reserves were depleted and a true panic

## 2.4    LOOKING TO A POSSIBLE FUTURE: THE NETWORK ECONOMY

Looking at the situation that the rise of the platform economy has created during the past 40 years, it is clear that we have come to an important junction. Either the decline initiated by the Great Panic of 2008 continues—which seems the case after the sovereign debt crisis of 2010–2011 and the subsequent global secular stagnation—or we collectively overcome this difficult period and a new institutional wave takes hold. The jury is out on what will occur.

There are already glimpses of a new institutional framework that should replace the failing neo-liberal capitalist system. This indicates a very different type of economy in which the creation of economic wealth through the social division of labour is divorced from the allocation of the generated wealth. I would like to refer to this arrangement as the *network economy*. The following institutions and trends have emerged during the past decades to provide a foundation for such a framework:

**Globalisation and individualism:**    The only way forward for our global social division of labour is to truly encompass all people in the world. Institutions need to support this. International treaties do not suffice; world-governing bodies and agencies—including the IMF, WTO and the United Nations—need to be strengthened and innovated to support the proper implementation of a global division of labour. This is extremely hard, since the rather obsolete nation-states are obstructing the way forward. They have handed control and power to TNCs, which exploit the institutional vacuum in the global economy.

However, there are clear trends contrary to these old institutional structures. Their principal proponent is true individualism through virtual social networks such as Facebook and Twitter. Individualism refers here to a personal, secular state that is truly equal to all individuals in the global economy, regardless of background and perceived nationality. Individualism supports the building of true global networks and the organisation of groups into productive coalitions. This is already the case for online information systems such as Facebook, Wikipedia, Twitter, Google, Snapchat and Flickr. These information systems are created collectively through the input of a disparate group of individuals around the globe.

**Green technologies:**    TNCs in the platform economy are reluctant to embrace green energy and production technologies, since they would make the extraction of wealth from oil and other natural resources less viable.

---

emanated; that day gas prices rose significantly and stayed much higher than the trend, which was downward in the rest of the country. This (small) gas panic was the result of negative reporting in the media to which people responded strongly, even though there has been no historical precedent for such gas shortages in the recent past. Even when in 2005 hurricanes Katrina and Rita brought major destruction to the oil industry in Louisiana and Texas, such shortages did not result. This local gas panic in the fall of 2008 can therefore be categorised as "fully irrational".

However, renewable energy and green production technologies have arrived and will take hold in the global social division of labour. These renewable sources will expand in unforeseen ways. The global economy is currently undergoing a technological revolution in which information technologies and advanced engineering are driving extreme change. These innovations will support the rise of a complete alternative economy.

**Zero-marginal cost production:**    In particular, these renewable and green technologies are driving down the marginal costs of production. A remarkable trend since the Great Panic of 2008 is that commodity prices have declined and inflation has come to a halt, even though extreme financialisation has driven up the total quantity of monetary instruments in the global economy.[45]

Meanwhile, 3D printers and other technological innovations indicate that the lack of inflation is really driven by the downward trend in marginal production costs. This implies that the competitive market price and labour value of most commodities will be negligible, which is clearly the case for many commodities. Only the middleman positions of many TNCs prevents a total price collapse, implying the extreme profitability of these TNCs in the current platform economy.

When the hold of TNCs over these middleman positions is broken, there is likely a move to a complete collapse of the prices in the trade infrastructure of the global economy. This will then induce a separation of the global social division of labour and the allocation of the generated economic wealth. This should take the form of an allocation of wealth through a global mechanism rather than through the social division of labour, as has been the case since the collapse of the feudal economy. Experimentation with a *universal basic income* indicates that nation-states are already searching for alternative mechanisms for the allocation of generated economic wealth. Innovative information technology will likely play a major role in the ultimate design of such a global allocation mechanism.

**A networked global society:**    As indicated in my discussion above, networks play a principal role in the reform of the neo-liberal platform economy. Global networks should replace the obsolete nation-states as entities through which individuals coalesce, and eventually should replace TNCs as the main developmental platforms in the global economy. This is already clear from the functioning of Facebook and Twitter as platforms in information exchange and of Wikipedia as a platform for knowledge exchange.

---

[45] Fischer's *quantity theory of money*—expressed through the famous equality $MV = PQ$ (Fischer 1930)—predicts that if money reserves $M$ increase, the overall price level $P$ will increase as well. However, in the platform economy that does not seem to be the case. Inflation is minimal, and without extreme quantitative easing by western central banks it might well be deflation that will mark this economic era.

The nature of these social networks as the principal developmental platforms provides the impetus for me to denote the emerging institutional framework as the *network* economy.

**E-money:**   Money has undergone a complete transformation during the rise of the neo-liberal platform economy. It has transformed from fiat money—based on a remote gold standard under the Bretton-Woods system—into a privately managed system of debt registration. Money is no longer in your pocket as coins and bank notes, but as an electronically accessible bank account, which represents all the debts that one is owed in the global economy at large. This form of financial instrument can best be referred to as *e-money*.

This is rather remote from the principles of a government-controlled form of fiat money; government policies have allowed financial TNCs, in particular global banks, to emerge as providers and regulators of e-money. This is expressed through the use of quantitative easing in money creation rather than using the government printing presses, such as was the case throughout traditional consumer capitalism.[46] Under quantitative easing policies, central banks transfer monetary reserves onto the books of the banks through money market operations. This in turn gives the banks a higher capacity to issue loans to its customers, thus generating more reserves in the bank accounts of the account holders. This procedure cannot effectively be controlled by a financial authority such as a central bank and has largely failed during the past decade, necessitating the continued execution of quantitative easing operations.

E-money is completely based on the trust of economic subjects in the banking system and, in particular, the banks with which they have relationships. It should be clear that this system transfers extraordinary power and control to the banking TNCs in the global economy. The abuse of this power was one of the underlying causes for the Great Panic of 2008 and the ongoing financial chaos in the global economy.

The next developmental stage of e-money should be to a mechanism that will restore trust in the financial system and to provide adequate means for global investment in the innovative green production technologies. A harbinger of the possibilities is the *Bitcoin* system and similar networked monetary systems, which provide e-currencies through the use of blockchain technologies of public debt registration. It is clear that the future will provide alternatives to this system, which could introduce a true global e-monetary system.

After 2008, few authors have dared to predict the changes in the global economy over the subsequent decade. Steve Keen (2011, 2017) is one of the

---

[46] The most extreme case of fiat money creation was the 1923 episode of hyperinflation in Germany. The German government saw itself forced to pay the mandated war reparations through the printing of Reichsmarks. The result was a complete collapse of the German monetary system and economy (Fergusson 1975).

few economists, who predicted a financial meltdown prior to the Great Panic of 2008. He founds his predictions on the theories put forward by Hyman Minsky (1986; Wray 2016). The Minskyan view focuses on the amount of private debt held in the economy and describes mechanisms that result in an economic crisis owing to high-level indebtedness and the cascading consequences of default on these debts. Keen (2017) points out that after the Great Panic of 2008 there have been no significant socio-economic policy changes to prevent another private debt build-up. Therefore, he forecasts a second crisis of similar magnitude if policy changes are not implemented.

Another exception is Mason (2015), who brings together a variety of economic theories and perspectives to sketch the possibilities of a global network economy. Mason's perspective is formulated through a Marxian analysis of the post-crisis economy, enhanced by the idea that the economy is dynamically driven by a Kondratief cycle. In his analysis, Mason also points to the institutional elements considered in my approach and develops a long-term view of a network economy that is founded on socio-economic collaboration in production networks.

It is clear from these discussions that the way forward is toward a post-capitalist network economy in which the allocation and the creation of economic wealth are separated. This path might be very long and clearly the process of contestation will be violent and riddled by economic and political upheaval, signified by the unexpected election of Donald Trump and the outcome of the Brexit referendum in 2016.

## REFERENCES

Acemoglu, D., and J.A. Robinson. 2012. *Why Nations Fail: The Origins of Power, Prosperity and Poverty*. London: Profile Books.

Acemoglu, D., S. Johnson, and J.A. Robinson. 2005. Institutions as the Fundamental Cause of Long-Run Growth. In *Handbook of Economic Growth*, ed. P. Aghion and S. Durlauf. North-Holland: Elsevier.

Ahamed, L. 2009. *Lords of Finance: The Bankers Who Broke the World*. London: Penguin.

Akerlof, G.A., and R.J. Shiller. 2009. *Animal Spirits: How Human Psychology Drives the Economy and Why it Matters for Global Capitalism*. Princeton, NJ: Princeton University Press.

Allen, D.W. 2011. *The Institutional Revolution: Measurement and the Economic Emergence of the Modern World*. Chicago, IL: University of Chicago Press.

Baker, M., E. Bulte, and J. Weisdorf. 2010. The Origins of Government: From Anarchy to Hierarchy. *Journal of Institutional Economics* 6: 215–242.

Baldwin, R., and C. Teulings, eds. 2014. *Secular Stagnation: Facts, Causes and Cures*. London: CEPR Press.

Beard, M. 2015. *SPQR: A History of Ancient Rome*. London: Profile Books.

Bernanke, B.S. 2000. *Essays on the Great Depression*. Princeton, NJ: Princeton University Press.

Bowles, S. 2011. Cultivation of Cereals by the First Farmers Was Not More Productive than Foraging. *Proceedings of the National Academy of Sciences* 108: 4760–4765.

Bowles, S. 2015. Political Hierarchy, Economic Inequality & the First Southwest Asian Farmers, SFI Working Paper 2015-06-015, Santa Fe Institute, USA.

Bowles, S., and J.-K. Choi. 2013. Coevolution of Farming and Private Property During the Early Holocene. *Proceedings of the National Academy of Sciences* 110: 8830–8835.

Bowles, S., and J.-K. Choi. 2016. The Neolithic Agricultural Revolution, SFI Working Paper 2016-09-016, Santa Fe Institute, USA.

Buchanan, J.M. 2008. Let Us Understand Adam Smith. *Journal of the History of Economic Thought* 30: 19–28.

Bulte, E., R.D. Horan, and J.F. Shogren. 2006. Megafauna Extinction: A Paleoeconomic Theory of Human Overkill in the Pleistocene. *Journal of Economic Behavior and Organization* 59: 297–323.

Caballero, R. 2009. The "Other" Imbalance and the Financial Crisis, Working Paper, MIT, Cambridge, MA.

Campbell, B.M.S. 2010. Nature as Historical Protagonist: Environment and Society in Pre-industrial England. *Economic History Review* 63: 281–314.

Campbell, B.M.S. 2016. *The Great Transition: Climate, Disease and Society in the Late-Medieval World.* Cambridge: Cambridge University Press.

Cann, R.L., M. Stoneking, and A.C. Wilson. 1987. Mitochondrial DNA and Human Evolution. *Nature*, 325: 31–36.

Cantor, N.F. 1993. *The Civilization of the Middle Ages.* New York, NY: Harper Collins.

Cantor, N.F. 2001. *In the Wake of the Plague: The Black Death & the World it Made.* New York, NY: Free Press.

Chang, H.J. 2014. *Economics: The User's Guide.* Gretna, LA: Pelican.

Clark, G. 2007. *A Farewell to Alms: A Brief Economic History of the World.* Princeton, NJ: Princeton University Press.

Coase, R.H. 1937. The Nature of the Firm. *Economica* 4: 386–405.

Coase, R.H. 1992. The Institutional Structure of Production. *The American Economic Review* 82: 713–719.

Cowen, T. 2012. *The Great Stagnation: How America Ate All the Low-Hanging Fruit of Modern History, Got Sick, and Will (Eventually) Feel Better.* London: Penguin.

Cowen, T. 2013. *Average Is Over: Powering America Beyond the Age of the Great Stagnation.* London: E P Dutton & Co Inc.

Debreu, G. 1959. *Theory of Value.* New York, NY: Wiley.

Diamond, J. 1997. *Guns, Germs, and Steel: The Fates of Human Societies.* New York, NY: W.W. Norton & Co.

Epstein, S.A. 1991. *Wage Labor and Guilds in Medieval Europe.* 2006 reissue ed. Raleigh, NC: University of North Carolina Press.

Fergusson, A. 1975. *When Money Dies: The Nightmare of the Weimar Hyperinflation.* New York, NY: William Kimber & Co.

Fischer, I. 1930. *The Theory of Interest: As Determined by Impatience to Spend Income and Opportunity To Invest It.* New York, NY: Macmillan Press.

Friedman, M. 1962. *Capitalism and Freedom.* 40th anniversary ed. Chicago, IL: University of Chicago Press.

Galbraith, J.K. 1955. *The Great Crash of 1929.* London: Hamish Hamilton.

Gimpel, J. 1976. *The Medieval Machine: The Industrial Revolution of the Middle Ages.* London: Penguin.

Grampp, W. 2000. What did Smith Mean by the Invisible Hand? *Journal of Political Economy* 108(3): 441–465.

Greif, A. 2006. *Institutions and the Path to the Modern Economy: Lessons from Medieval Trade, Political Economy of Institutions and Decisions*. Cambridge, MA: Cambridge University Press

Haegens, K. 2015. *De grootste show op aarde: De mythe van de markteconomie*. Amsterdam: AmboAnthos.

Hall, K.G. 2009. How Moody's Sold its Ratings-and Sold Out Investors. *McClatchy Newspapers*, http://www.mcclatchydc.com/227/v-print/story/77244.html.

Harari, Y.N. 2014. *Sapiens: A Brief History of Humankind*. London: Vintage Books.

Harvey, D. 2017. *Marx, Capital and the Madness of Economic Reason*. London: Profile Books.

Hayek, F.A. 1937. Economics and Knowledge. *Economica* 4: 33–54.

Hayek, F.A. 1944. *The Road to Serfdom*. Routledge Classics. reprint 2001 ed. London: Routledge.

Hayek, F.A. 1945. The Use of Knowledge in Society. *American Economic Review* 35: 519–530.

Hayek, F.A. 1960. *The Constitution of Liberty*. Chicago, IL: University of Chicago Press.

Herlihy, D. 1997. *The Black Death and the Transformation of the West*. Cambridge, MA: Harvard University Press.

Horan, R., E. Bulte, and J. Shogren. 2005. How Trade Saved Humanity from Biological Exclusion: An Economic Theory of Neanderthal Extinction. *Journal of Economic Behavior and Organization* 58(1): 1–29.

Hudson, M. 1994. Land Monopolization, Fiscal Crises and Clean Slate 'Jubilee' Proclamations in Antiquity. In *A Philosophy for a Fair Society*, ed. M. Hudson, G. J. Miller, and C. Feder, 33–79. London: Shepheard-Walwyn.

Hudson, M. 2002. Reconstructing the Origins of Interest-Bearing Debt and the Logic of Clean Slates. In *Debt and Economic Renewal in the Ancient Near East*, ed. M. Hudson and M. van de Mieroop. Bethesda, MD: CDL Press.

Huppert, G. 1998. *After the Black Death: A Social History of Early Modern Europe*. Bloomington, IN: Indiana University Press.

Ingrao, B., and G. Israel. 1990. *The Invisible Hand: Economic Equilibrium in the History of Science*. Cambridge, MA: MIT Press.

Israel, J.I. 1995. *The Dutch Republic: Its Rise, Greatness, and Fall*. London: Clarendon Press.

Israel, J.I. 2001. *Radical Enlightenment: Philosophy and the Making of Modernity 1650-1750*. Oxford: Oxford University Press.

Israel, J.I. 2010. *A Revolution of the Mind: Radical Enlightenment and the Intellectual Origins of Modern Democracy*. Princeton, NJ: Princeton University Press.

Janszen, E. 2008. The Next Bubble: Priming the Markets for Tomorrow's Big Crash. *Harper's Magazine* 316(2): 39–45.

Johnson, S., and J. Kwak. 2010. *13 Bankers: The Wall Street Takeover and the Next Financial Meltdown*. New York, NY: Pantheon.

Keen, S. 2011. *Debunking Economics: The Naked Emperor Dethroned?* revised and expanded ed. London: Zed Books.

Keen, S. 2017. *Can We Avoid Another Financial Crisis?* Cambridge: Polity Press.

Kelly, J. 2005. *The Great Mortality: An Intimate History of the Black Death, the Most Devastating Plague of all Time*. New York, NY: Harper Perennial.

Keynes, J.M. 1936. *The General Theory of Employment, Interest and Money*. London: Macmillan Press.

Kondratief, N.D. 1979. The Long Waves in Economic Life. *Review (Fernand Braudel Center)* 2: 519–562.

Lawrence, D., and T.J. Wilkinson. 2015. Hubs and Upstarts: Pathways to Urbanism in the Northern Fertile Crescent. *Antiquity* 89: 328–344.

Lazzarato, M. 2012. *The Making of the Indebted Man: An Essay on the Neoliberal Condition*. Los Angeles, CA: Semiotext(e) Intervention.

Lubetkin, M.J. 2006. *Jay Cooke's Gamble: The Northern Pacific Railroad, the Sioux, and the Panic of 1873*. Norman, OK: University of Oklahoma Press.

Malthus, T.R. 1798. *An Essay on the Principle of Population, As It Affects the Future Improvement of Society*. London: J. Johnson.

Marx, K. 1867. *Capital: A Critique of Political Economy - Volume I: The Process of Production of Capital*. 1967 ed. New York, NY: International Publishers.

Marx, K. 1893. *Capital: A Critique of Political Economy - Volume II: The Process of Circulation of Capital*. 1967 ed. New York, NY: International Publishers.

Marx, K. 1894. *Capital: A Critique of Political Economy - Volume III: The Process of Capitalist Production as a Whole*. 1967 ed. New York, NY: International Publishers.

Mason, P. 2015. *PostCapitalism: A Guide to Our Future*. London: Allen Lane.

McGraw, T.K. 2007. *Prophet of Innovation: Joseph Schumpeter and Creative Destruction*. Cambridge, MA: Harvard University Press.

Minsky, H.P. 1986. *Stabilizing an Unstable Economy*. New Haven, CT: Yale University Press.

Mirowski, P. 2013. *Never Let a Serious Crisis Go to Waste: How Neoliberalism Survived the Financial Meltdown*. London: Verso.

Mitchell, W.C. 1944. The Role of Money in Economic History. *Journal of Economic History* 4(Supplement: The Tasks of Economic History): 61–67.

Morris, C. 2008. *The Trillion Dollar Meltdown: Easy Money, High Rollers, and the Great Credit Crash*. New York, NY: PublicAffairs.

Mortimer, I. 2014. *Centuries of Change: Which Century Saw the Most Change and Why It Matters*. London: The Bodley Head (Random House).

Nadler, S. 2011. *A Book Forged in Hell: Spinoza's Scandalous Treatise and the Birth of the Secular Age*. Princeton, NJ: Princeton University Press.

Nooteboom, B. 2002. *Trust: Forms, Foundations, Functions, Failures and Figures*. Cheltenham: Edward Elgar Publishing.

Ogilvie, S. 2004. Guilds, Efficiency, and Social Capital: Evidence from German Proto-Industry. *Economic History Review* LVII: 286–333.

Ogilvie, S. 2007. 'Whatever right, is right?' Economic Institutions in Pre-Industrial Europe. *Economic History Review* 60: 649–684.

Ogilvie, S. 2014. The Economics of Guilds. *Journal of Economic Perspectives* 28: 169–192.

Phillips, K. 2008. *Bad Money: Reckless Finance, Failed Politics, and the Global Crisis of American Capitalism*. New York, NY: Viking.

Piketty, T. 2014. *Capital in the Twenty-First Century*. Boston, MA: Harvard University Press.

Plato. 380 BCE. *Republic*. 2007 ed. London: Penguin Classics

Postan, M.M. 1972. *The Medieval Economy and Society*. London: Penguin.

Ricardo, D. 1817. *On the Principles of Political Economy and Taxation*. London: John Murray.

Roberts, M. 2016. *The Long Depression: How It Happened, Why It Happened, and What Happens Next*. Chicago, IL: Haymarket Books.

Romer, C. 1986. Spurious Volatility in Historical Unemployment Data. *Journal of Political Economy*, 94: 1–37.

Romer, P.M. 1990. Endogenous Technical Change. *Journal of Political Economy* 98(5): S71–S102.

Sargent, T.J., and F.R. Velde. 1999. The Big Problem of Small Change. *Journal of Money, Credit and Banking* 31(2): 137–161.

Sargent, T.J., and F.R. Velde. 2002. *The Big Problem of Small Change*. Princeton, NJ: Princeton University Press.

Schumpeter, J. 1927. The Explanation of the Business Cycle. *Economica* 21: 286–311.

Schumpeter, J. 1928. The Instability of Capitalism. *The Economic Journal* 38: 361–386.

Schumpeter, J. 1934. *The Theory of Economic Development: An Inquiry into Profits, Capital, Credit, Interest and the Business Cycle*. Cambridge, MA: Harvard University Press.

Seabright, P. 2010. *The Company of Strangers: A Natural History of Economic Life*. revised and enlarged ed. Princeton, NJ: Princeton University Press.

Smith, A. 1759. *The Theory of Moral Sentiments*. Cambridge Texts in the History of Philosophy. Cambridge: Cambridge University Press, Reprint 2002, edited by Knud Haakonssen.

Smith, A. 1776. *An Inquiry into the Nature and Causes of the Wealth of Nations*. Chicago, IL: University of Chicago Press, Reprint 1976.

Spruyt, H. 1994. *The Sovereign State and Its Competitors: An Analysis of Systems Change*. Princeton, NJ: Princeton University Press.

Stiglitz, J.E. 2010. *Freefall: Free Markets and the Sinking of the World Economy*. London: Allen Lane.

Stiglitz, J.E. 2013. *The Price of Inequality*. London: Penguin.

Temin, P. 2006. The Economy of the Early Roman Empire. *Journal of Economic Perspectives* 20(1): 133–151.

Temin, P. 2012. *The Roman Market Economy*. Princeton, NJ: Princeton University Press.

Tishkoff, S.A., F.A. Reed, F.R. Friedlaender, C. Ehret, A. Ranciaro, A. Froment, J.B. Hirbo, A.A. Awomoyi, and J.-M. Bodo. 2009. The Genetic Structure and History of Africans and African Americans. *Science*, 324(5930): 1035–1044.

Varoufakis, Y. 2011. *The Global Minotaur: America, the True Origins of the Financial Crisis and the Future of the World Economy*. London: Zed Books.

Velde, F.R., W.E. Weber, and R. Wright. 1999. A Model of Commodity Money, with Applications to Gresham's Law and the Debasement Puzzle. *Review of Economic Dynamics* 2: 291–323.

Verhulst, A. 2002. *The Carolingian Economy*. Cambridge Medieval Textbooks. Cambridge: Cambridge University Press.

Vitali, S., and S. Battiston. 2013. The Community Structure of the Global Corporate Network. arXiv:1301.2363v1.

Vitali, S., J.B. Glattfelder, and S. Battiston. 2011. The Network of Global Corporate Control. *PLOS One* 6(10):e25995.

Wallerstein, I. 2011a. *The Modern World-System I: Capitalist Agriculture and the Origins of the European World-Economy in the Sixteenth Century*, vol. 1, reprint ed. Berkeley, CA: University of California Press.

Wallerstein, I. 2011b. *The Modern World-System II: Capitalism and the Consolidation of the European World-Economy, 1600-1750*, vol. 2, reprint ed. Berkeley, CA: University of California Press.

Wallerstein, I. 2011c. *The Modern World-System III: Second Era of Great Expansion of the Capitalist World-Economy, 1730s-1840s*, vol. 3, reprint ed. Berkeley, CA: University of California Press

Wallerstein, I. 2011d. *The Modern World-System IV: Centrist Liberalism Triumphant, 1789-1914*, vol. 4. Berkeley, CA: University of California Press.

Weatherford, J. 1997. *The History of Money: From Sandstone to Cyberspace*. New York, NY: Three River Press.

Wray, L.R. 2016. *Why Minsky Matters: An Introduction to the Work of a Maverick Economist*. Princeton, NJ: Princeton University Press.

Yang, X., and Y.-K. Ng. 1993. *Specialization and Economic Organization: A New Classical Microeconomic Framework*. Amsterdam: North-Holland.

Zizek, S. 2014. *Trouble in Paradise: From the End of History to the End of Capitalism*. London: Penguin.

# CHAPTER 3

# A Framework for Modelling Wealth Creation

The relational perspective on the functioning of the economy—axiomatically constituted in Chap. 1—is firmly founded on the embeddedness hypothesis (Lemma 1.4) as well as the hypothesis of the entrepreneurial function (Lemma 1.5). Both these fundamental hypotheses follow directly from the social brain hypothesis and the hypothesis of bounded rationality. These principles state that all economic interactions are embedded in a governance system of socio-economic institutions and that economic agents' actions change these socio-economic institutions to fit their objectives. Hence, economic interactions are not only governed by these socio-economic institutions, but also are facilitated by these institutions. Conversely, economic interactions might directly and indirectly affect and change the governing institutions.

This becomes clear through the study of some historical episodes in the global economy. I have already referred to the analysis of the Marseille fish market (Vignes 1993; Vignes and Etienne 2011) to illustrate that economic interactions indeed are relational and that they are guided as well as facilitated by the socio-economic institutions in place. In the previous chapter I also discussed cases of entrepreneurial activities that directly affected the socio-economic institutions that guide those interactions and economic behaviour.

In this chapter I delve deeper into the foundations of the embeddedness of socio-economic activities into a governance system of socio-economic institutions as a foundation for economic wealth creation. I bring this embeddedness together into a single framework with the entrepreneurial function to describe an institutional network economy. A full account of this framework is introduced through the notion of a *socio-economic space*. As such, this chapter is, therefore, a further development of the structural theory of a network-institutional economy introduced in Chap. 1.

A socio-economic space can be understood as a completely developed representation of the embeddedness and entrepreneurial function hypotheses. It brings together economic agents, socio-economic institutions as well as socio-economic interaction infrastructures in a single comprehensive framework.

© The Author(s) 2018

R. P. Gilles, *Economic Wealth Creation and the Social Division of Labour*,
https://doi.org/10.1007/978-3-319-76397-2_3

Socio-economic spaces could be interpreted as models or *platforms* in which we can describe how economic development and growth takes place.

As mentioned in the Appendix to Chap. 1, we refer to such platforms as "markets". Indeed, markets have to be assessed as places—physical, virtual or notional—in which economic agents interact and build a social division of labour embedded within a set of trade networks. This is exactly what is represented by our notion of a socio-economic space. This implies that networking is the main activity that takes place in these socio-economic spaces.

Similarly, we might refer to a nation-state as a socio-economic space, since it refers to a notional space that is structured through a certain set of socio-economic institutions in which citizens can build networks, build economic relationships and ultimately "do business". In short, a nation-state can be represented as a socio-economic space in which citizens can branch their economic endeavours.

**Structuring Economic Interaction** As stated, a socio-economic space has two constituting forces, namely the Embeddedness Hypothesis—which relates economic agents to socio-economic institutions—and the countervailing power of the Entrepreneurial Function—which relates the functionality and the design of these institutions to the activities enacted by the economic agents in the space. In particular, embeddedness refers to economic agents that are fully guided in their actions by the institutions; entrepreneurship on the other hand refers to the evolutionary and revolutionary processes in which economic agents affect socio-economic institutions through their actions.

It was already mentioned that these two forces have opposite directions. Embeddedness is a centripetal force; it pulls economic agents together and binds economic agents to act in the context of the socio-economic institutions in the space's governance system. On the other hand, entrepreneurship is a centrifugal force that disrupts the functioning of the prevailing system of socio-economic institutions. New institutions emerge and existing institutions might be changed; both affect the functioning of the institutional framing of all agents' interactions.

I remark that the socio-economic space embodies the framework developed in Chap. 1. It encapsulates the social division of labour and its embodiment, the networks that make up the trade infrastructure. This infrastructure emerges owing to the effects of the hypotheses stated in Chap. 1: the embodiment of productive and consumptive abilities in an economic agent (Hypothesis 2); increasing returns to specialisation (Hypothesis 3); gains from trade (Hypothesis 4); and the ability to effectively organise economic interaction (Hypothesis 5). However, the forces represented by embeddedness and entrepreneurship bind this structure together into a spatial environment for economic development.

**Structure of This Chapter** In subsequent sections of this chapter, I first develop a comprehensive vision of the concept of a socio-economic space (Sect. 3.1). Next, I carefully look at the role of institutions in the socio-economic space. First, I develop a typology of socio-economic institutions. Of course, any typology is incomplete and can be appended with different categories of institutions. However, the typology given in Sect. 3.2.1 can act as a guide for understanding socio-economic institutions in general.

In Sect. 3.2.2 I present an elaborate example in which we consider a simple socio-economic space, representing a straightforward market situation, in which different institutional frameworks result in different effective trade networks. The analysis of these trade networks results in the quantification of the performance of these different trade institutional frameworks. In the simple example considered, we see that different institutional configurations result in rather different allocations and outcomes. This signifies that outcomes are rather sensitive to institutional configurations and that socio-economic government policies can have significant intended or non-intended consequences for economic performance.

By further developing (mathematical) descriptions of socio-economic institutions, networks and socio-economic roles, we can even quantify the performance of institutions of a certain type through the measurement of the resulting trade networks. In particular, the rules that govern trade in a market allow us to measure the outcomes as well as the efficiency of these rules.

Section 3.3 is devoted to the discussion of the notion of networking as the act of building socio-economic relationships in a socio-economic space. This leads to the emergence and development of trade infrastructures. As already stated in Chap. 1, economic goods and services have to be considered as carriers of these networking activities. The resulting interaction structure is therefore a network of effective trade relationships that are centred on these commodities. Thus, it is easier to view markets simply as trade networks, which allows us to quantify these markets through the analysis of these networks. This is exactly the approach followed concerning the Marseille fish market discussed in Chap. 1. I provide examples of different types of trade networks, representing different market forms.

Finally, in Sect. 3.4 I discuss the role of the entrepreneurial function and entrepreneurship in the context of the socio-economic space. The entrepreneurial function refers to the permanent, continuous and ongoing process of institutional development and change in a socio-economic space. There are two forms of institutional change: evolutionary development and revolutionary change. Both are induced through actions and choices of economic agents in the socio-economic space.

Usually entrepreneurship is attached to the idea that it leads to revolutionary change, but I argue that evolutionary development is as important. It is more appropriate to think of the entrepreneurial function as an evolutionary process of institutional development interspersed with revolutionary episodes. The technical term for this is that of *punctuated evolution*.

Furthermore, when revolutionary change happens, there are two forms it can take. First, this revolutionary institutional change can be instigated by the actions of a single individual, the *entrepreneur*. On the other hand, such change can also be the outcome of the actions of a group of individuals, referred to as *collective entrepreneurship*. Both forms are discussed in some detail here.

## 3.1    THE STRUCTURE OF A SOCIO-ECONOMIC SPACE

As stated above, a socio-economic space has to be interpreted as an embodiment of the full framework developed in Chap. 1 of an economy that is centred around a social division of labour. A population of economic agents is embedded into a governance system of socio-economic institutions that guides the behaviour of these economic agents into specialisations that form the foundation of that social division of labour. This behaviour results in an interaction infrastructure that consists of a variety of socio-economic networks and incorporated production organisations.

The principal notion expressed through the formal concept of a socio-economic space is that it represents a population of economic decision-makers that operate under a well-defined, common set of socio-economic institutions—its *institutional governance system*—as well as the outcomes of their actions and choices. In this regard a socio-economic space is completely determined by the institutions that make up its governance system.

Therefore, the economic agents in the population of the socio-economic space and the set of governance institutions stand in a two-way relationship. First, agents are embedded within the governance system made up by these institutions. Economic agents use these socio-economic institutions to design roles in the social division of labour and to build networks with other agents. The richness of the system of governing socio-economic institutions determines how economic agents are able to function, thus determining their individual and social freedoms.

Second, these institutions are affected by the actions of these economic decision-makers. The creative process underlying the evolutionary development of the institutions in the governance system can be understood as the entrepreneurial function in that socio-economic space. This refers to a feedback between the subjects of the governance institutions—or "governed"—and the institutions themselves; it is the governed that determine largely the evolution of their governance.

A structural representation of the notion of a socio-economic space is depicted in Fig. 3.1. The space itself consists of a three-layered body, made up of economic agents, the governance institutions themselves and the generated infrastructure of networks and organisations that make up the social division of labour itself. Furthermore, there are two dynamic relational elements represented in this space, namely the embeddedness relationship of agents and the governance institutions, and the evolutionary process of institutional change in the governance system—represented by the entrepreneurial function.

To clarify the terminology introduced in Fig. 3.1, I note the following:

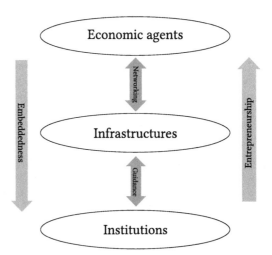

**Fig. 3.1** Stylistic representation of a socio-economic space

**Networking:**  We might denote the creation of organisational forms and socio-economic network relationships of interactions between economic agents as "networking". It refers mainly to the building and maintenance of relationships in the socio-economic space, which implicitly includes the setup of hierarchical production organisations—or "firms".

**Guidance:**  The institutions in the governance system "guide" how economic agents interact, and thereby determine the organisational forms and trade infrastructures that emerge in the socio-economic space.

**Embeddedness:**  This represents the centripetal force that binds economic agents in the system of governing socio-economic institutions. This acts as a form of "gravity" in the socio-economic space, providing a guide to networking and the participation in the trade infrastructure.

**Entrepreneurship:**  This represents the countervailing force of inducing change in the institutional governance system that anchors the socio-economic space. It indicates that the governing socio-economic institutions are affected and determined through the interaction and behaviour of the economic agents in the space.

I emphasise that the social division of labour emerges as a fundamental factor in the infrastructures generated in the socio-economic space. As noted in Chap. 1, the networks that are built by economic agents emerge through the acceptance of certain socio-economic roles adopted by the various economic agents, which naturally result in supply chains and socio-economic networks that form the constituting elements of the social division of labour. For a further elaboration I refer to Sect. 3.3.1.

## 3.2  GOVERNANCE: THE ROLE OF INSTITUTIONS

In Chap. 1 I have already elaborated on different types of socio-economic institutions that make up our contemporary governance system. I have already indicated that these institutions form a very diversified and differentiated spectrum, from the extremely primitive—such as social conventions concerning the use of smiling and laughter—to the extremely advanced—such as the role of financial derivatives in our contemporary globalised financial system.

Before categorising some aspects of our contemporary governance system more comprehensively, I would like to emphasise that socio-economic institutions are history or path dependent. Indeed, the entrepreneurial function in the socio-economic space follows a specific developmental path that depends on specific actions of certain individuals and historical events that trigger certain institutional responses. This means that the institutional governance at any historical stage of development depends on the past actions of the agents in that socio-economic space. These actions could have been influenced to make these institutions more efficient and effective, but also less effective or even inefficient.

For example, exceptional entrepreneurs such as the first Roman emperor Augustus, the Italian banking family dè Medici, the English politician Margaret Thatcher and the American entrepreneur Steve Jobs have singularly steered the development of our socio-economic institutions in certain specific directions. This is interspersed with epochs of extreme socio-economic development based on collective action, such as the agricultural (r)evolution in the Sumerian empire, the collapse of the feudal system after the fourteenth-century anomalies, the birth of liberalism and capitalism in the eighteenth-century Enlightenment movement and the rise of neo-liberalism since the 1980s.[1]

### 3.2.1  A Typology of Socio-Economic Institutions

I distinguish seven categories of socio-economic institutions in our contemporary global economy as a single, cohesive socio-economic space. I discuss these categories in more detail.

**1. Language and Heuristic Behavioural Rules ("Media")** The category of most primitive and embedded socio-economic institutions is that of our ability to communicate through social behaviour and language. Body language is already present in many animal species, and when hominid species evolved their abilities to communicate through facial expressions and body language this

---

[1] I emphasise here that institutional change is not necessarily "good". There have been voices that have argued that certain innovations are clear failures if viewed from the perspective of the functionality of the socio-economic space. Currently, the socio-economic consequences of inequality caused by the adoption of neo-liberal institutions comes to mind (Stiglitz 2011, 2013; Piketty 2014).

allowed for advanced interspecies cooperation. The larger brains of hominids allowed the emergence of complex social conventions of communication. This can still be studied in primate behaviour, which is guided very much by non-verbal language based on bodily expressions and facial expressions.

In humans the ability to use body language is multiplicative. We are able to detect very subtle difference in bodily stance and gestures to "read" intentions and conditions of another person. It is an ability that is innate to humans and as such is an important part of how we conduct our daily affairs, including making complex economic deals and the conduct of our business.

Hominin species developed the ability to use their voice box to communicate with other members of their tribe. There is evidence that language was rather common among the more advanced hominin species, including the Neanderthals (Albanese 2011; Dediu and Levinson 2013) and Homo sapiens. In this regard, language is not a uniquely human ability. However, we have taken this ability to very advanced usage in service of our functioning as a species. We are able to express very complex ideas and thoughts to other humans. This ability allows us to conduct very complex socio-economic interaction and ventures.

Ultimately in our twenty-first-century global economy, we conduct socio-economic interaction through the specific use of language, which we can call *Business English*. This encompasses advanced linguistic expressions of specific terms that allow us to interact and trade quickly and efficiently with each other on very complex economic contracts. This has now been taken into a virtual dimension through the introduction of automated trade and interaction through computerised automation and the internet, affecting the global financial markets in particular (Johnson et al. 2013). In this case, natural language has been replaced by a purely machine code through which trade is conducted, and algorithms compute best responses to the environment that these machines detect through observing the coded language used.

**2. Social Conventions** Behavioural rules and language are rather primitive and embedded socio-economic institutions, and form the most basic category of socio-economic institutions. With human development, there also emerged a secondary category of behaviour that we know as "social conventions". We use commonly accepted and understood conventions to communicate with each other and make economic deals. To illustrate the effectiveness of social conventions in the economy, I will discuss two very common examples, the use of a handshake and the recognition of property rights.

One of the most fundamental and important social convention is that of greeting as well as closing a deal or sealing a contract. For both we use in western capitalist societies the *handshake*.[2] The handshake reflects all the features of a social convention that is crucial to our daily interactions. Of course, the use of

---

[2] The handshake is a very ancient social convention that has been depicted throughout history in art and texts. Many ancient artworks show representations of a handshake used for greeting and confirmation of accepted contracts.

the handshake and its precise form differ over time and from community to community. However, in the contemporary global economy the handshake has the form as first adopted in Europe: the clasping of two right hands. This is summarised in two crucial properties of the handshake as a social convention.

First, the handshake is an expression of mutual equality and respect. In Europe it is and has been common to show respect to a social superior through bowing and symbolic submission. The handshake as such is a signal of equality, which has to advance any socio-economic interaction.

Second, over time the handshake became in the capitalist society a tool that embodied the sealing of a contract between traders. When a deal is reached to which both (equal) parties agree, there is a symbolic, but binding, acceptance of the contract through a handshake. In this respect the handshake is an embodiment of mutual trust and respect. Subsequently, the handshake has even received legal recognition as a form of unwritten contract.

Another important social convention is the recognition of *property rights* in human societies. Tribal life usually centred on the "commons", which refers to the common property of the tribe. It usually refers to land that is not owned individually, but by the community as a whole. That individual members of a community could own land was a significant development of the economic system under which people traded. Eventually individual property rights evolved as the founding feature of the capitalist system in which we now operate. Since the 1980s this has evolved to such an extent that common property and the related public goods have much less presence in our economic activities and interactions.

Bowles and Choi (2013, 2016) argue that property rights emerged *before* the agricultural (r)evolution. These authors present evidence that the institutions founding the agricultural economy emerged prior to its full implementation. In particular, property rights of individual tribe members of land were commonly accepted before such land was cultivated for agricultural crops. This shows the power of institutions to facilitate innovative productive practices and the fundamental deepening of the social division of labour through the introduction of new commodities, socio-economic roles and production technologies.

More generally, social conventions evolved naturally from language and commonly accepted behavioural rules. These conventions involved more complex behavioural forms and are used to support socio-economic interactions. However, social conventions remain generally unwritten and refer to commonly accepted practices and rights. Laying down these conventions in legal documents results in a higher form of socio-economic institution, which I discuss next.

**3. Legal Systems** As soon as humans developed writing, we started to write down social conventions and social behavioural rules as *laws*. Many of our social conventions can also be understood as "common" law, which refers to a system of unwritten rules that are recognised commonly in a society. These conventions quickly gave way in ancient times to law codes, mainly concerning civil and criminal law.

During the Roman era, very significant law codes were developed and adopted. One of the major law codes was the Justinian Code—or *Codex Justinianus*—, which was developed under the Byzantine emperor Justinian (issued 529–534 CE). This codex also incorporated religious law, regulating Christian religious practices in the Byzantine empire.

The Justinian Code forms the basis for all law systems in Europe that were developed later. In 1804, Napoleon Bonaparte issued the very influential Napoleonic Code, which is a main precursor to modern systems of law. Its Commercial Code (adopted 1807) regulated important aspects of civil law pertaining to property rights and contracting, which are essential for the development of nineteenth-century capitalist societies in Europe.

The successful implementation of these systems of commercial law was also based on the recognition of *nation-states* as regulators of capitalist socio-economic interaction. After the collapse of the feudal system, the nation-state acquired a monopoly on violence and the enforcement of laws over the subsequent centuries. This was formally recognised in the Treaty of Münster (1648) and the Glorious Revolution of 1688. This in turn was based on the recognition of and trust in the nation-state as the main platform for the development of the capitalist socio-economic space in Europe and North America. The emergence of the nation-state as a platform for capitalist socio-economic development is an expression of the entrepreneurial function in the main western socio-economic spaces at that time.

One of the main tools that nation-states introduced as a binding force for trust-building is that of a *constitution*. These constitutions bring together the basic rights and obligations of members of these nation-states and the constitutional rules that govern the nation-states. As such, constitutions provided a set of common rights in the emerging capitalist socio-economic space in the nineteenth century.

Modern law systems are not just founded on civil and criminal law codes, but also on international treaties between nation-states. These were based on the emergence of international organisations of nation-states in the early twentieth century as the main platforms for the further development and integration of the capitalist socio-economic space. The evolution of the *European Union* (EU) from several limited international treaties and less integrated economic communities is the prime example of this development.

Through neo-liberal policies of nation-states and the EU since the 1980s, the importance of nation-states and international organisations has diminished in the twenty-first century in favour of transnational corporations (TNCs) as the main development platforms in our global economy as socio-economic spaces. Indeed, TNCs impose their own set of rules on its suppliers and customers that are binding and go beyond any jurisdiction. As a principal example of this phenomenon, I refer to Facebook, Twitter and Google as enforcers of their own "laws" in the internet platforms that they provide. This form of platform enforcement can also be extended to the global banking system that enforces rules of conduct on account holders, threatening to take away access to e-money for violators of their policies of conduct.

In the twenty-first-century global economy, this has now evolved into the recognition of *platform operating systems* as legal and even constitutional frameworks in which we interact with each other. These operating systems include protocols for internet connectivity (TCP/IP), mobile telephony standards, operating software for mobile communication (e.g. iOS and Android) and rules and regulations imposed by platforms such as Google, Facebook, Twitter and Instagram on their users. These new *global platform constitutions* now replace largely the constitutions on which nation-states and international political bodies are established.

**4. Government**  Closely related to the institutional category of legal systems is the importance of government. "Government" should be distinguished here from the more general category of "governance". Government refers to the leadership of a tribe, community or society that through violence can enforce its will on the members. Modern government refers mainly to the leadership of a nation-state, although this is a rather narrow categorisation as well.[3]

Government arose as an important economic regulator from ancient times during the successful empires in the early agrarian age. The role of government as a regulator was initially based on the implementation of security and the rule of law. Both require elaborate systems of provision that are financed through taxation. Government played a very important role in the later empires as well. In particular, Roman government was prominent and supported a strong performing economy (Temin 2006, 2012). It supported a peaceful socio-economic space centred on the Mediterranean Sea that was very conducive for economic development and high wealth generation.

After the collapse of the Roman Empire, the Middle Ages were characterised by an absence of strong governmental regulation and support of the economy. Instead, the fragmented feudal organisation of medieval society resulted in the organised exploitation of a large underclass. This resulted in subsistence levels of economic wealth generation. Feudalism blossomed in the twelfth-century medieval Renaissance, which was rooted in the higher agricultural returns due to favourable climatic conditions during this time. Feudalism, therefore, depended existentially on climatic conditions, which is also shown in its collapse during the fourteenth-century anomalies as discussed in Chap. 2 (Campbell 2016).

Only after the collapse of the feudal system, there slowly emerged a basis for stronger government regulation. The rise of capitalism can be understood as

---

[3] On the other hand, governance in the broad sense refers to the regulation and conduct of socio-economic interaction through a system of commonly accepted institutions and rules. Government can be an important part of that, but governance can be strong even in the presence of a weak government. The main example is economies that are founded on a strong sense of morality and conduct following accepted social conventions.

the direct result of the emergence of strong government related to the rise of *nation-states*. The emergence of the democratic nation-state after the American and French revolutions stimulated the enforcement of strong property rights; the introduction of human rights, in particular individual liberty; the implementation of a fiat money system, followed by the further development of a national bank and protected banking system; the regulation of competition in the market economy through anti-trust legislature; direct intervention in the economy through monetary and fiscal policies; and the development of national services as public goods.

Recently, Mazzucato (2014) has argued that the nation-state has also played and still plays a crucial role in the entrepreneurial function of the socio-economic space. Government funding of research and development as well as a national educational system contributed significantly to the emergence of the consumption capitalist economy in the twentieth century. For example, the invention of the internet can be attributed directly to government-backed ventures.

As stated above, during the twentieth century nation-state governments initiated international treaties to open up their national socio-economic spaces to create the global socio-economic space that we know today. These treaties resulted not only in international collaborative economic organisations such as the EU and the Organisation for Economic Co-operation and Development, but also in global economic regulatory bodies such as the International Monetary Fund, the World Trade Organisation and the World Bank. This allowed in turn the emergence of TNCs as the new transnational platforms for global socio-economic development. However, there are significant concerns about whether this is a good development, since these policies also resulted in very significant inequalities in the prevailing global socio-economic space, denoted as the "second gilded age". This is predicted and assessed as to be unsustainable in the long run (Stiglitz 2013; Piketty 2014).

It has now been argued that there is again a significant role for nation-state governments to regulate the global economy. However, given their relative weakness and obvious obsolescence in the contemporary global economy, it is unclear that effective government regulation will be revived.

**5. Platform Architectures**  Economists consider platforms to be institutional arrangements that bring together multiple groups of economic agents and allow them to interact (Rochet and Tirole 2003; Evans 2003; Evans and Schmalensee 2013; Hagiu and Wright 2011). This could be as simple and broad as a common economic language, a common operating system to allow exchange of software, a common industrial standard or a commonly accepted measurement system. I categorise these broad platforms, however, as "media", as indicated in the discussion above.

Instead I restrict the definition of a platform to a less broad category of interaction structures. In this restricted sense, a platform is an institutional arrangement that facilitates economic agents to interact with each other under common conditions. In particular, platforms include physical marketplaces; shopping malls; chain stores; social networks such as Facebook, Instagram and Twitter; virtual marketplaces such Amazon.com and eBay[4]; brokerage systems that bring together different trade parties; and auction systems that facilitate trade for specific types of goods such as art and flowers.

The institutional category of platform *architectures* refers to the common rules and officers that support the formation of various types of such platforms. For example, there has emerged a set of rules concerning how websites are structured and presented. This is supported by employees ("officers") of the firms that run these platforms to enforce these rules and to police conduct on these platforms. This makes these websites more accessible to users. These website "architectures" are examples of institutions in the governance system that facilitate the bringing together of economic agents to generate socio-economic values or wealth. A good example of such regulatory systems is Wikipedia, which is regulated and policed by a large group of core users of the platform.

The oldest category of such platforms is that of common physical or geographical *marketplaces*. These marketplaces were developed according to a set of well-defined rules and features. The marketplace itself is usually a (market) square in an urban setting, which facilitates its protection. The protection of market participants is a principal feature that was provided by local urban authorities or the local noble ruler. It usually involved the policing of the marketplace and the trade routes leading to the market place. Protection was also guaranteed by physical walls around the city or market town.

The organisation of the market that took place on the marketplace or square also was structured and organised according to a set of accepted rules. There was a market master; stalls were allocated according to a pricing scheme and seniority; there was regulation of the type of goods that could be traded in the square; and amusement was offered to stimulate a positive trade environment.

Finally, trade itself was conducted according to certain rules and measurement systems that were enforced by the local authority. Bulk goods were usually weighted at a scale located in the marketplace prior to the completion of the transaction. The transport of goods was organised through local guilds. A historical example of such a market is the cheese market in Alkmaar, the Netherlands, which is still conducted according to traditional rules. The local guilds are distinguished by the colour of their hats and market masters, managing the bills of sale and the weighing of the cheeses, are clearly distinguished by their white outfits.

---

[4] It would be prudent to distinguish here the categories of media and platforms, even though they are closely related. The internet is clearly a medium, as is the mark-up language HTML and the programming language JAVA for building websites that allow platforms to develop. The platforms mentioned are built on top of these media. Indeed, Facebook uses the internet, HTML and JAVA to perform functions in its website design. Facebook itself, with its commonly accepted conventions, is however a platform that facilitates social interaction among its customers.

Platform architectures form an important category of socio-economic institutions that support trade and economic interaction. These architectures have been used since the dawn of humanity and have evolved in many forms in our contemporary global economy.

**6. Monetary Systems** Human economic activity is only possible if one can regulate the exchange of goods through a temporal system of wealth transfer. In particular, this takes the form of *debt*: debt is the transfer of surpluses in one part of the economy to shortages in another (Graeber 2011). Early monetary systems were simply recording systems of such transfers from one person to another. These debts were recorded and over time resolved through opposite transfers (Hudson 1994, 2002).

Debt became much easier to handle through the introduction of commodity money, usually a valuable metal such as silver and gold. Surplus was converted into these specific commodities, which essentially signified the debts that others in society had to the bearer of these commodities. Major advances were made with the introduction of coins of these valuable metals, making transfers easier and debt identification possible.

Coin-based or "commodity" money emerged in the large empires that arose after the agricultural (r)evolution. Graeber (2011) argues that commodity money explicitly evolved from a need to maintain large armies to fight the wars in which these empires were engaged. Soldiers had to be paid and commodity money was the most obvious and efficient way to do so. Without the emergence of large empires that based their existence on military might, there probably would not have evolved a coin-based form of money.

From coin-based commodity money systems there emerged an international system of banking based on deposits into personal accounts. Banking was founded firmly on the development of bills of exchange, which replaced large quantities of commodity money. The institution of banking made it possible to hedge debts into larger volumes of bank loans. This multiplier effect on the quantity of money made significant wealth generation possible.

Banking also opened the door to monetary speculation and monetary policy. This was seized by the governments of the nation-states in the nineteenth century through the introduction of fiat money and central banks. Fiat money refers to the use of trust in the nation-state to issue worthless paper that replaces commodity money. Thus, governments were able to introduce low-value metal coins and bank notes to replace silver and gold coins.

Fiat money introduced a period of monetary stability in the global economy, preventing recurring monetary crises due to devaluation of the various metals used in the commodity money systems. These crises stinted economic development during the premodern era and should be understood as at least as important as the introduction of social production organisations in capitalism (Sargent and Velde 2002).

Central banking guaranteed the appropriate control of the fiat money system introduced by the nation bank and the regulation of the banking systems in the evolving capitalist economy. Through a central bank, government acted as a lender of last resort for private banks, thus stabilising the solvency of these banks. Moreover, a central bank regulated the money quantity in the economy by setting interest rates on loans to private banks and the actual printing of paper money.

The system based on state-sanctioned fiat money was very successful until the 1980s, when under neo-liberal ideology it was converted into the next stage of the monetary system: *e-money*. Control of the supply of money was de facto transferred to private banks through the replacement of paper and coin money with virtual currency in a checking or credit account. Money thus became a number on a computer screen at the ATM or on one's home computer.

Under the e-money system we have reverted to the earliest monetary system: private banks essentially register the debts one owns and is owed. One's solvency or creditworthiness is reduced to a single measure based on these registered debts and payment habits.

Consequently, the government of the nation-state has forfeited its control of the money supply to private banks, leaving the central bank with only marginal control through setting the interest rate charged for loans to private banks. The attempts to increase money supply are now referred to as "quantitative easing", although private banks can just absorb these additional tranches of credit from the central bank in their asset balance.

The Great Panic of 2008 can also be understood as the first serious crisis of the e-monetary system. Through the privatisation of public money and its derivatives, there is a significant possibility that monetary and financial crises will return with much higher frequency than under the fiat monetary system.

**7. Objective Socio-Economic Roles** When multiple trade relationships morph into subjectively specialised interactions there will emerge a social recognition of these specialisations. The root diggers might be named "gatherers" and the meat-gathering specialists be known as "hunters". The introduction of this terminology comes with clear expectations of the abilities and skills of the individuals who assume such roles. Ultimately the socio-economic roles of gatherer and hunter are incorporated into the governance system that prevails in their society. As such, this primitive society becomes a "hunter-gatherer society" in which much higher gains from trade and economic wealth can be generated through the application of these roles. When socio-economic roles are no longer accidental and restricted to the extent of economic interactions themselves, we refer to these roles as "objective"; these socio-economic roles are now part of the fabric of this economy and have become elements of the institutional infrastructure or governance system that determines the socio-economic space.

The emergence of objective specialisations and socio-economic roles increases the ability of such a society to increase the generated economic wealth significantly. It is no longer necessary that individual economic agents interact only with a limited set of other agents; hunters can now interact with gatherers in an arbitrary fashion, thus extending the trade abilities significantly and, hence, forming a basis for the increase in economic wealth generated in this society. Therefore, there is a deepening of the socio-economic space in the sense that many productive economic relationships—between hunters and gatherers—emerge as a consequence of the social recognition of these roles. This allows the expansion of the productive community even further; thus, it allows the expansion of the socio-economic space itself, a process that can be denoted as "globalisation".

Therefore, an objective socio-economic role should be viewed as a well-accepted configuration of socio-economic institutions that determine the role that an individual economic agent can assume in the prevailing social division of labour. Usually this takes the form of "professions". Such an objective role is defined through appropriately given behavioural standards that are assumed by the economic agent through her role. This includes the use of a professional language; particular gestures and dress codes; a commonly expected workplace; and subject knowledge that accompanies the given role. For example, a *baker* uses chosen words—such as "wheat bread", "pretzel" and "scone"—to communicate with customers, wears a white overall and a hat, operates an oven and a shop, and, in principle, should communicate her knowledgeability about the subject of bread and cake baking.

Since the industrial revolution, the social division of labour has included vertical as well as horizontal chains of specialised labour. This implies that socio-economic roles now mainly refer to professional roles in hierarchical production organisations. Assuming such a socio-economic role requires the economic agent to collect certain credentials and training as a professional. In a purely horizontal social division of labour this was solely based on the fulfilment of an apprenticeship with a master artisan. However, the introduction of a vertical social division of labour introduced public education as the institutional setting in which training occurs.

Therefore, public education systems form a natural accompaniment to the emergence of objective socio-economic roles in the context of a vertical social division of labour. Here I not only refer to education provided by governments, but also open access private education as available in our contemporary global economy. Such open or public education differs considerably from the closed nature of education systems based on apprenticeships that were provided through the Roman collegia system and the medieval guild system. In those systems the apprentices were selected through social networks, their selection being based on subjective criteria.

The category of objective socio-economic roles as part of the governance system of a socio-economic space is subject to continuous evolution. A large part of the entrepreneurial force that induces change in the prevailing institutions focuses on the category of such objective roles. The innovation of socio-economic roles is contributed by economic agents assuming these roles, educators who train aspiring agents to assume such roles and entrepreneurial agents—in business as well as politics—who introduce new elements into such roles. Changes to these roles also occur through innovations in related elements, such as economic products, production processes and regulatory aspects.

### 3.2.2    An Illustration: Comparing Three Institutional Trade Infrastructures

To illustrate the significance of institutions in any socio-economic space, I consider a simple trade situation that can be resolved through different trade institutions. In particular, I consider three distinct trade institutions that have been studied extensively in the economics literature. The following analysis is based largely on the institutional comparison set out in Piccione and Rubinstein (2007) and the mechanisms discussed in Easley and Kleinberg (2010). For an elaboration I also refer to Rubinstein (2012).

I consider the assignment of indivisible economic goods to a given, fixed population of economic agents. In particular, consider a finite set of homesteads that have to be allocated to a finite population of citizens. We assume that there are exactly as many homesteads as there are citizens. In the economic and game theoretic literature this is known as an *assignment problem* or a *matching market*. An assignment problem is a useful setting to investigate the performance of different institutional arrangements.

As is common for an assignment problem, we represent each citizen as an economic agent, who has a certain purchasing power and a given preference over the available homesteads. I emphasise here that both elements are fundamentally social and dependent on the given socio-economic space. Hence, any purchasing power is a result of the implementation of certain socio-economic institutions, met importantly by the precise characteristics of the monetary system. Furthermore, preferences are social and reflect in a certain fashion a common underlying social preference ordering in which the citizens are embedded.[5]

I introduce eight homesteads to be assigned to eight citizens. The homesteads are represented by the set $\{H1, \ldots, H8\}$, where we assume that the numbering reflects the underlying social ranking of these homesteads. Thus, generally there is the perception in the represented society that $H1$ is the most preferred homestead, $H2$ is the second best homestead and so on, until $H8$ is the property commonly perceived as the worst homestead available.

This ranking therefore forms the foundation of the social preferences of the eight economic agents under consideration. Therefore, these eight citizens have individual preferences that adhere roughly to the social ordering on these eight

---

[5] The social or collective nature of preferences is an expression of the social embeddedness of individual citizens. Indeed, it is common for individuals to prefer one homestead over another based on social opinion rather than true individualistic reflection and investigation.

**Table 3.1**   Basic rankings of homesteads for different citizens

| Citizen | H1 | H2 | H3 | H4 | H5 | H6 | H7 | H8 |
|---------|----|----|----|----|----|----|----|----|
| A | 1 | 2 | 3 | 4 | 5 | 6 | 7 | 8 |
| B | 1 | 3 | 4 | 2 | 8 | 6 | 5 | 7 |
| C | 1 | 3 | 2 | 4 | 5 | 6 | 7 | 8 |
| D | 2 | 1 | 5 | 7 | 6 | 3 | 8 | 4 |
| E | 1 | 2 | 4 | 6 | 5 | 3 | 8 | 7 |
| F | 2 | 1 | 3 | 4 | 6 | 7 | 5 | 8 |
| G | 2 | 3 | 1 | 4 | 7 | 6 | 5 | 8 |
| H | 1 | 2 | 3 | 4 | 5 | 6 | 7 | 8 |

homesteads, but are not necessarily exactly the same. Citizens thus have individual deviations from this given social order on the set of homesteads. Some individual citizens might have more individualistically headstrong opinions than others.

**The Primitives of the Assignment Problem**   Table 3.1 gives a representation of the individual orderings on the eight homesteads of the eight citizens in the population. Both individuals $A$ and $H$ have individual preferences that exactly follow the common social preference order. Other individuals deviate from this ordering, some only in a minor fashion (Citizen $C$), while others deviate quite strongly (Citizen $D$). The latter can be identified as rather individualistic citizens, while others such as Citizens $A$, $C$ and $H$ act much more as social followers.

Second, I represent the social (purchasing) power of the given eight citizens exactly according to the given identifiers $A$–$H$, where Citizen $A$ is the most powerful, or wealthy, individual, while Citizen $H$ has the least power, wealth and standing. In different institutional settings this social power is represented and implemented in rather different ways.

Next I explore three very different institutional governance systems for the formulated assignment problem, including the provided preferences and the assumed social standing of the given citizens. First, I consider a "jungle economy" in which the strongest citizens take what they want at the expense of the weaker citizens. Second, I look at a pure barter system in which citizens are assigned ownership of the available homesteads prior to engaging in barter to achieve mutual gains from trade. Here, I apply the rule that the $n$-th ranked individual is assigned the $n$-th socially ranked homestead. Third, I consider a fully developed capitalist economy with a monetary system in which citizens are assigned wealth and homesteads are traded for market prices.

These three different trade environments result in unexpectedly varying equilibrium allocations for the same preferential data given in Table 3.1. The conclusion resulting from this analysis has to be that different institutional environments support very different outcomes. This confirms the fundamental idea that institutions matter and have an extraordinary influence on social conditions and fairness.

### 3.2.2.1    Case A: The "Jungle"—A Hierarchical Society

Piccione and Rubinstein (2007) introduced a formalisation of the Hobbesian idea of a primitive society based on the "law of the strongest". We can refer to this type of institutional framework as that of a hierarchical society or economy. There is a collectively accepted hierarchy of citizens and the hierarchical ranking is strictly adhered to in the allocation of goods and wealth.

The presence of a social hierarchy as a regulating institutional framework has been prevalent throughout economic history. Gilles et al. (2015) have shown in a mathematical model that the presence of a social hierarchy provides stability to the economy and a guarantee that an equilibrium can emerge in the complex networks of socio-economic interaction. The stabilising effects of a hierarchy are founded on the exclusion of interaction cycles, which can induce infinite regress and instability through retrading. This is a form of the problem that is also known as the *Condorcet paradox*.

Returning to our example, we have already introduced a social ranking of the eight individuals from Citizen $A$ to Citizen $H$. We have to assume that all individuals in this society adhere to this social hierarchy.

Trade is now conducted simply using this strict social hierarchy. The most powerful individual is allowed to select her most preferred homestead. In this case Citizen $A$ selects $H1$, which is now no longer available.

We then step down one ladder in the social hierarchy and let citizen $B$ select from the remaining set of homesteads $\{H2, \ldots, H8\}$. In this case, $B$ selects $H4$, since that is his second preferred homestead. As before, this homestead is removed from the set.

The next most powerful individual, Citizen $C$, now selects from the remaining, reduced choice set $\{H2, H3, H5, H6, H7, H8\}$. Her first-best selection is already allocated to $A$, but her second-best alternative $H3$ is still available and is now assigned to her.

We proceed in this fashion through all individuals in the social hierarchy, assigning their most preferred homestead from the set of remaining properties. Finally, the lowest ranked individual Citizen $H$ is assigned the only remaining property $H8$. I summarise the final allocation of homesteads to the hierarchically ranked individuals in Table 3.2.

The final assignment from the application of a social hierarchy as an allocation mechanism—or trade institution—results in a hierarchical allocation. The socially most preferred properties are indeed assigned to the socially most powerful individuals in this society. The only significant deviation from this regards the allocation made to Citizen $G$, although he only is assigned his 7-th most preferred homestead.

**Table 3.2**    A "jungle" equilibrium based on a discrete social hierarchy

| Individual | H1 | H2 | H3 | H4 | H5 | H6 | H7 | H8 |
|------------|----|----|----|----|----|----|----|----|
| A | 1 | 2 | 3 | 4 | 5 | 6 | 7 | 8 |
| B | 1 | 3 | 4 | 2 | 8 | 6 | 5 | 7 |
| C | 1 | 3 | 2 | 4 | 5 | 6 | 7 | 8 |
| D | 2 | 1 | 5 | 7 | 6 | 3 | 8 | 4 |
| E | 1 | 2 | 4 | 6 | 5 | 3 | 8 | 7 |
| F | 2 | 1 | 3 | 4 | 6 | 7 | 5 | 8 |
| G | 2 | 3 | 1 | 4 | 7 | 6 | 5 | 8 |
| H | 1 | 2 | 3 | 4 | 5 | 6 | 7 | 8 |

Piccione and Rubinstein (2007) showed some important properties with regard to the jungle equilibrium. They developed a model for a general class of socio-economic situations:

**Description 3.1**    *Let a hierarchical institution of a **discrete social hierarchy** in a socio-economic space be defined by a socially ranked set of individual economic agents and a set of indivisible goods of equal size. Every economic agent is assumed to have a strict preference over the set of indivisible goods.*
*An **allocation** is now a one-to-one mapping between the set of economic agents and the set of indivisible goods.*
*A **jungle equilibrium** is an allocation such that there is no economic agent who can improve her situation by taking an assigned property from an economic agent who is ranked lower than herself in the social hierarchy.*

The following properties hold for a jungle equilibrium:

**Proposition 3.2**

(a) *For every discrete social hierarchy there exists a unique jungle equilibrium.*
(b) First Welfare Theorem: *Every jungle equilibrium is Pareto optimal in the sense that no economic agent can be made better off without making at least one other economic agent worse off.*
(c) Second Welfare Theorem: *Every Pareto optimal allocation for a set of given strict preference rankings on a given discrete set of indivisible goods can be supported as a jungle equilibrium through an appropriately constructed social hierarchy.*

The stated properties in the formal description of a discrete social hierarchy and a jungle equilibrium are very powerful. First, the existence of a jungle equilibrium is guaranteed for any discrete social hierarchy. This is an important theoretical property, since it guarantees stability in the society and that there is no reason for social strife resulting from the allocation of goods in a social hierarchy under the given conditions. Stability guarantees that the economic processes could converge to a state in which there are no incentives to the economic agents to demand any major changes. Such stability is essential for the smooth functioning of the economy (Gilles et al. 2015).

Second, the two so-called "fundamental theorems of welfare economics" or "welfare theorems" hold:

- The **First Welfare Theorem** (FWT) states that a stable state in the institutional trade environment has to be *socially optimal*. The notion of social optimality in an economic allocation context was introduced by Pareto (1906).

  Pareto's optimality criterion requires that all available opportunities for further improvement are exhausted and that no gains can be generated without making additional social costs. Hence, we can only make certain individuals better off by taking resources and wealth away from certain other individuals. This formalisation is therefore also known as "Pareto efficiency".[6] Neo-classical economists have always viewed Pareto efficiency as a strongly desirable property.

  Indeed, the FWT can also be applied to the institution of a competitive market and is then recognised as the theoretical equivalent of Adam Smith's "invisible hand" mechanism: the competitive market economy—as if through an invisible hand—is guiding itself to a socially optimal state through the pursuit of self-interest.

- The **Second Welfare Theorem** (SWT) states that any Pareto optimal state can be supported through an appropriate modification of the initial distribution of wealth in that particular institutional setting of the economy. This refers to the possibility of affecting the state of the economy through appropriately chosen economic policy. Hence, a targeted (socially optimal) allocation of wealth is realised through appropriately selected redistribution of resources.

  We can illustrate this welfare analysis of the SWT in the hierarchical jungle economy further by looking at an alternative Pareto optimal allocation in this economy. This alternative Pareto optimal allocation is provided in Table 3.3, indicated by the bold numbers.[7]

  The corresponding social hierarchy for which the jungle equilibrium is exactly the chosen Pareto optimal allocation is given on the right-hand side of the table. In this example Citizens $F$, $G$ and $H$ are fully empowered, while $A$, $B$ and $C$ are ranked much lower than before. For this modified social hierarchy the resulting allocation transfers the most preferred properties to $F$, $G$ and $H$.

---

[6] I emphasise here that Pareto efficiency or optimality is a rather weak allocative property. Indeed, it does not impose any condition related to fairness or freedom. If all wealth is allocated to a single individual, say a dictator, then the situation is Pareto optimal: to make anybody else better off, one has to take wealth from the dictator.

[7] The interested reader is invited to check that the given allocation is indeed Pareto optimal.

**Table 3.3**  Illustration of the SWF for a discrete social hierarchy

| Individual | H1 | H2 | H3 | H4 | H5 | H6 | H7 | H8 | Social rank |
|---|---|---|---|---|---|---|---|---|---|
| A | 1 | 2 | 3 | 4 | 5 | 6 | 7 | 8 | 5 |
| B | 1 | 3 | 4 | 2 | 8 | 6 | 5 | 7 | 6 |
| C | 1 | 3 | 2 | 4 | 5 | 6 | 7 | 8 | 7 |
| D | 2 | 1 | 5 | 7 | 6 | 3 | 8 | 4 | 4 |
| E | 1 | 2 | 4 | 6 | 5 | 3 | 8 | 7 | 8 |
| F | 2 | 1 | 3 | 4 | 6 | 7 | 5 | 8 | 1 |
| G | 2 | 3 | 1 | 4 | 7 | 6 | 5 | 8 | 2 |
| H | 1 | 2 | 3 | 4 | 5 | 6 | 7 | 8 | 3 |

The SWT for an economy with a social hierarchy shows that we actually have a multitude of possible social equilibrium states in an institutional environment in which goods are allocated according to a social hierarchy. The fact that there are a (relatively) large number of equilibrium states shows that the economy organised around these principles of a social hierarchy has tremendous flexibility, like a market economy based on the perfectly competitive market mechanism (Mas-Colell et al. 1995, Part Four).

Finally, the FWT and the SWT for a discrete social hierarchy show that the welfare principles represented through them do not only hold for market economies, but also much more primitive economies. Indeed, efficiency and optimality are fully achievable and manageable in a system founded on the blunt application of a social hierarchy based on the exercise of authority rather than a bottom-up institutional design founded on the principles of individual liberty and self-interest.

**Relevance of Social Hierarchies in Our Contemporary Global Economy**
One would expect that the description of a jungle economy based on a discrete social hierarchy has no bearing on our contemporary global economy. However, I believe that to be far from the truth; the neo-liberal capitalist economy is actually rife with hierarchical structures and mechanisms that favour hierarchically positioned superiors over hierarchically positioned subordinates. The very fact that leadership is a major field in business studies illustrates that hierarchies still have a vital role in the contemporary economy.

The pretence is that social hierarchical positions have no influence on economic processes, since these processes are centred on and guided through so-called market forces. However, I view these forces to be rather limited in their effects. Instead, privilege is the rule and social mobility—the true effect of economic liberalism—is in decline in western capitalist societies, in particular in the USA and the UK.

### 3.2.2.2    Case B: A Barter Economy Based on Property Rights
The second trade institutional mechanism that I look at here to illustrate the importance of economic institutions is that of a pure barter mechanism based

on private property rights and ownership. I introduce the following hypotheses that define this institutional environment. This configuration is denoted as *barter system*.

- There are a finite number of economic agents and an equal number of indivisible goods ("properties") in the system;
- Each economic agent has a strict preference ordering over the set of available properties;
- There are private property rights that are enforced and commonly recognised;
- There is a public accounting system in which values of properties are registered and trades are recorded;
- Each economic agent is assigned exactly one property over which she exercises full ownership rights;
- Properties are traded one for one and these barters are registered in the public accounting system at agreed (accounting) prices, and;
- Trade continues until there is no incentives for any of the economic agents to barter their properties any further.

I emphasise that in a barter system there is no presence of or requirement for commodity or fiat money. Instead, a more primitive registration system of debts is implemented to register all executed barters and the debt balance of all economic agents. Ownership is thus translated into measured wealth levels in terms of a recognised value of the commodities available. This was the historical case in the ancient temple economies discussed in Chap. 1.

We can formalise a trade pattern or barter process in such a barter system through the introduction of some additional concepts, in particular that of an allocation and a price system:

**Description 3.3** *Let a barter system be given.*

- (i) *An **allocation** is a one-to-one mapping $h: N \to \mathcal{H}$ from the set of economic agents $N = \{1, \ldots, n\}$ to the set of properties $\mathcal{H} = \{H_1, \ldots, H_n\}$, assigning to each agent $i \in N$ exactly one property $h(i) \in \mathcal{H}$.*
- (ii) *A **price system** is a mapping that assigns a price or value to every property, $p: \mathcal{H} \to \mathbb{R}_+$.*
- (iii) *A **barter** between any set of agents $\{i_1, \ldots, i_k\} \subset N$ is a reallocation of the properties owned by these agents $\{h(i_1), \ldots, h(i_k)\} \subset \mathcal{H}$. A barter is **improving** if every agent in $\{i_1, \ldots, i_k\}$ prefers her after-barter property over her property at the outset of the barter.*
- (iv) *An allocation is **stable** if it does not admit any improving barter.*

In a barter system trade occurs using registered prices of the bartered properties. Hence, a group of economic agents report to the registration system and register trades that were agreed at given prices. This implies that in an agreed barter all properties should actually be exchanged exactly at the same price, preserving debt equalisation.

Trade is voluntary and only occurs under the condition of mutual gains from trade for the participants. Hence, a stable outcome is reached if all opportunities for mutual gains from trade are exhausted. This implies that there is no barter that results in a reallocation that strictly benefits all participating economic agents. This is the foundation of the definition of a stable allocation in the barter system given above.

Stability of allocations is insufficient to satisfactorily describe equilibria in a barter system. We require a higher form of stability. Indeed, the price or value of a property has to represent a wealth level. If one's property has a certain value it is normal to expect that one can afford any other property with a lower price.

We can now formulate a definition of an equilibrium concept using this more traditional economic concept of price equilibrium: there is no economic agent who is willing to barter her allocated property for an alternative property with a price that is equal or lower to the value of her property. This introduces the notion of a budget set of properties that have a value (price) less or equal to the property of that particular agent. Now, in equilibrium every economic agent is assigned the best property in her budget set under the prevailing equilibrium price system.

**Definition 3.4** Consider an allocation $h$ and a price system $p$ in a barter system outlined above. A property $H'$ is **affordable** under $(h, p)$ for economic agent $i \in N$ if $p(H') \leqslant p(h(i))$, where $h(i)$ is the property allocated to agent $i$.
An allocation-price pair $(h, p)$ is an **equilibrium** in the given barter system if for every economic agent $i \in N$, her allocated property $h(i)$ is exactly her best affordable property under the price system $p$.

Economic theory has provided us with a very extensive literature on the analysis of barter systems such as described here. We can summarise the main conclusions from this analysis in the following proposition:

**Proposition 3.5** *Consider an arbitrary barter system as introduced above. Then the following properties hold:*

(a) *There exists at least one equilibrium and at least one stable allocation in the barter system.*

(b) First Welfare Theorem: *Every equilibrium allocation is stable and every stable allocation is Pareto optimal.*

(c) Second Welfare Theorem: *Every Pareto efficient allocation can be supported as an equilibrium through an appropriate reallocation of the initial assignment of properties to agents in the system.*

Barter processes as introduced here are merely guaranteed to result in Pareto efficient allocations (Foley 2010). One needs stronger bargaining and bartering institutions to make sure that the resulting allocations have stronger properties. This is exactly guaranteed by the market-based processes introduced through the notion of an equilibrium. Indeed, by opening up demand to all properties that are affordable, one forces the number of resulting allocations to shrink considerably.

Usually the class of equilibrium allocations is strictly smaller than the class of stable allocations and the set of Pareto efficient allocations. The SWT again applies and makes sure that the barter system can be guided to any desirable Pareto efficient allocation.

**Computing Equilibria: The Top-Cycle Algorithm** One can compute the equilibrium allocations with appropriately chosen equilibrium price levels in a given barter system. This algorithm is based on a constructive proof of the existence of an equilibrium in a barter system devised by David Gale and restated in Shapley and Scarf (1974).

**Description 3.6 (Top-Cycle Algorithm)** *Let $N = \{1, \ldots, n\}$ be the set of economic agents in the barter system and let some initial endowment of properties be made, denoted by $H : N \rightarrow \mathcal{H}$, where $H(i) = H_i$ is $i$'s initially allocated property. We now construct a partitioning of the set of properties $\mathcal{H}$ denoted by $(L_1, \ldots, L_K)$ where $\cup_{k=1}^{K} L_k = \{H_1, \ldots, H_n\}$ and $L_k \cap L_m = \emptyset$ for all $k \neq m$. We follow the next procedure:*

   (i) *Start with agent $i_0 = 1$.*
   (ii) *At stage $k$, let $i_k$ be identified. Denote by $i_{k+1} \in N$ be the owner of $i_k$'s most preferred property. Continue through the stages until $i_{k+1} = i_m$ for some $m \leqslant k$. Now select $L_1 = \{H_{i_m}, \ldots, H_{i_k}\}$. (This group is known as a "top trading cycle".)*
   (iii) *Remove $L_1$ from the set of properties and the corresponding owners from the set of agents $N$. Next proceed to construct $L_2, \ldots, L_K$ as above until all properties are exhausted. This results in a well-defined partitioning $(L_1, \ldots, L_K)$ of the set of properties $\mathcal{H}$.*
   (iv) *Construct a price system $p$: select a sequence $p_1 > p_2 > \cdots > p_K > 0$ and for every $1 \leqslant k \leqslant K$ assign all properties $H \in L_k$ exactly the same price level $p(H) = p_k$.*

The resulting price vector and corresponding partitioning indeed define an equilibrium in the barter system. An agent with a property in $L_k$ buys a property from a fellow owner in $L_k$. If she prefers a property that is not in $L_k$, then it must be a property in $L_m$ with $m < k$, which is unaffordable for her given her wealth level $p_k$.

**Returning to the Example** Next I return to the example already explored in the discussion of discrete social hierarchies. Based on Table 3.1 we can now use the top-cycle algorithm to determine an equilibrium in the corresponding barter system in which every economic agent $i$ is initially assigned homestead $Hi$. Hence, we convert the social hierarchy into the corresponding ownership pattern in which higher ranked individuals are assigned socially preferred properties.

The application of the top-cycle trading algorithm results in a unique equilibrium, reported in Table 3.4. I point out that the starting point of the algorithm in every step can be selected arbitrarily, but the outcome is always the same. The price levels given in Table 3.4 are essentially set at an arbitrary level, even though the order is fixed by the partitioning made up of top-cycles identified in the algorithm.

Regardless of where one starts with the application of the algorithm, the first top cycle is $L_1 = \{H1\}$. Indeed, starting from 1 herself, her most preferred property is the one she is initially assigned, $H1$.

Starting next from agent $B$, her most preferred property among $\{H2, \ldots, H8\}$ is $H4$, which is owned by $D$. In turn, $D$ most prefers property $H2$, which is owned by $B$. Thus, this forms a top-cycle and, therefore, $L_2 = \{H2, H4\}$.

Starting from $C$, we note that $H3$ is her most preferred property in $\{H3, H5, H6, H7, H8\}$. Thus, $L_3 = \{H3\}$ is the resulting top-cycle.

This leaves the properties in $\{H5, H6, H7, H8\}$. Starting from agent $E$, we see that $H6$ is her most preferred property, owned by $F$. However, $F$ most prefers $H7$, which is owned by $G$. But $G$ herself most prefers $H7$ among the set of properties given. This implies that actually $L_4 = \{H7\}$ is the resulting top-cycle.

Repeating the procedure for the remaining properties $\{H5, H6, H8\}$ we finally get a trading cycle between agents $E$ and $F$, resulting in the top-cycle $L_5 = \{H5, H6\}$. This leaves $L_6 = \{H8\}$, completing the partitioning procedure.

Next, we assign appropriately selected price levels and we can check that the suggested prices in Table 3.4 instead support the allocation depicted as a barter equilibrium.

Table 3.4   Equilibrium in a barter system corresponding to Table 3.1

| Individual | H1 | H2 | H3 | H4 | H5 | H6 | H7 | H8 |
|---|---|---|---|---|---|---|---|---|
| A | 1 | 2 | 3 | 4 | 5 | 6 | 7 | 8 |
| B | 1 | 3 | 4 | 2 | 8 | 6 | 5 | 7 |
| C | 1 | 3 | 2 | 4 | 5 | 6 | 7 | 8 |
| D | 2 | 1 | 5 | 7 | 6 | 3 | 8 | 4 |
| E | 1 | 2 | 4 | 6 | 5 | 3 | 8 | 7 |
| F | 2 | 1 | 3 | 4 | 6 | 7 | 5 | 8 |
| G | 2 | 3 | 1 | 4 | 7 | 6 | 5 | 8 |
| H | 1 | 2 | 3 | 4 | 5 | 6 | 7 | 8 |
| Price | 80 | 70 | 60 | 70 | 40 | 40 | 50 | 30 |

Comparing this barter equilibrium with the jungle equilibrium in Table 3.2, we see that only agents $F$ and $G$ are allocated different properties. Indeed, $G$ seems to have improved herself, while agent $F$ now gets a lower ranked property. This is because of the different institutional environment that is imposed in the socio-economic space. I note that the difference is not significant, although agents are clearly treated differently in different institutional environments, as depicted here.

### 3.2.2.3   Case C: Trade Through a Competitive Price Mechanism

Easley and Kleinberg (2010, Chapter 10) discuss in detail a model of a matching market with a monetary competitive price mechanism. Instead of bartering properties for an accounting value, discussed above, all economic agents are endowed with purchasing power based on a certain monetary unit. Hence, we assume that there is money and that all values and prices are expressed in the corresponding monetary unit.

The Easley–Kleinberg model follows a rather standard neo-classical economic structure. All economic agents express their preferences in the monetary values that they are "willing to pay" for the various properties. These value levels are explicitly based on two sources: the preferences of the individual economic agent—informed by the social ordering of properties discussed before—and the wealth of that individual.

In this regard, these willingness-to-pay values are really social in nature. Indeed, individuals are only willing to pay higher monetary prices for a property if they have a higher preference as well as a higher budget or income to support these purchases. Hence, willingness-to-pay values reflect (social) preference as well as social hierarchy in monetary terms.[8]

Returning to the example of eight citizens and eight homesteads developed throughout our previous discussion, I now express their individual preferences through appropriately chosen willingness-to-pay values. The preferences in Table 3.1 are indeed represented in willingness-to-pay values in Table 3.5.

Again we see that the eight citizens are ranked in a similar social order as before and that this social hierarchy is now expressed in terms of individual purchasing power in monetary terms. Individual $A$ has the highest purchasing power and assigns a high willingness-to-pay for his most preferred property $H1$, namely a value of 100. This highest level of willingness-to-pay can be interpreted as an indicator of the purchasing power of that individual. We see a decreasing sequence of maximal willingness-to-pay values: 100 $(A)$, 90 $(B)$, 85 $(C)$, 80 $(D)$, 70 $(E)$, 65 $(F)$, 60 $(G)$ and 50 $(H)$. Each of these values acts as a proxy for the purchasing power of the corresponding individual economic agent.

---

[8] I emphasise here that the concept of willingness-to-pay has a purely individualistic meaning in neo-classical economics. There it is a purely individual expression of preference, and it is treated as such in the theory. There is a lack of reference to a strong relationship with purchasing power and social institutions such as societal hierarchy.

**Table 3.5**  Basic monetary willingness-to-pay values

| Individual | H1 | H2 | H3 | H4 | H5 | H6 | H7 | H8 |
|---|---|---|---|---|---|---|---|---|
| A | 100 | 80 | 70 | 65 | 60 | 50 | 30 | 20 |
| B | 90 | 80 | 50 | 85 | 10 | 40 | 45 | 30 |
| C | 85 | 70 | 80 | 60 | 55 | 45 | 40 | 30 |
| D | 70 | 80 | 45 | 30 | 40 | 60 | 20 | 50 |
| E | 70 | 65 | 50 | 40 | 45 | 60 | 20 | 30 |
| F | 60 | 65 | 55 | 50 | 35 | 30 | 45 | 10 |
| G | 50 | 45 | 60 | 40 | 20 | 30 | 35 | 10 |
| H | 50 | 45 | 40 | 30 | 25 | 20 | 15 | 10 |

We can now introduce a trade process that is based on the purchase of properties with monetary means. For this we introduce an objective of the economic agents in their purchasing behaviour. We assume that each economic agent tries to maximise the *gains from trade* expressed as the excess resulting from acquiring a property after paying a price for it.

Formally, let individual economic agent $i \in N$ consider a property $H$. Then her willingness-to-pay—representing the monetary value that this agent assigns to that property—can be denoted by $V_i(H) > 0$. If now a price $P_H > 0$ for property $H$ is charged, a *surplus* results that can be computed as

$$E_i(H, P_H) = V_i(H) - P_H. \qquad (3.1)$$

The imposed objective of individual $i$ is now to maximise $E_i(H, P_H)$ over all available properties $H$. A property $H^*$ is *maximal* if its acquisition generates a maximal, non-negative surplus in the sense that $E_i(H^*, P_{H^*}) \geqslant 0$ and

$$E_i(H^*, P_{H^*}) \geqslant E_i(H, P_H) \quad \text{for all } H \in \mathcal{H}. \qquad (3.2)$$

or, using set-theoretic notation,

$$H^* \in \arg\max\{E_i(H, P_H) \mid H \in \mathcal{H}\}.$$

If $E_i(H, P_H) < 0$ for all properties $H \in \mathcal{H}$, meaning that all properties are overpriced for $i$, then individual $i$ is assumed not to select any property and to abstain from trading. Hence, trade is voluntary and only engaged if there are gains from trade for all participating parties.

**Definition 3.7**  An allocation of properties to individuals—expressed as $H_i$ for all $i \in N$—is a **trade equilibrium allocation** if there exists a price system $P$ such that $H_i$ is maximal under that price system for every individual economic agent $i \in N$.

In a trade equilibrium all agents maximise the gains from trade and all agents are engaged in trade. Each economic agent is assigned a property that maximises the resulting trade surplus for that individual, which is the formulated objective of each trader.

This trade equilibrium concept is clearly based on a more advanced institutional framework than the barter equilibrium considered in the previous section. This equilibrium concept requires the implementation of a monetary system based on a common monetary unit rather than just an accounting or registration system. Moreover, properties are initially not assigned to individuals; rather individuals are endowed with purchasing power in monetary terms.

We can now state some properties of this equilibrium concept and the resulting equilibrium allocations.

**Proposition 3.8** *Let a monetary trade system be given.*

(i) *There exists at least one trade equilibrium.*
(ii) First Welfare Theorem: *A trade equilibrium allocation is Pareto optimal for the given preferences, expressed through the assigned willingness-to-pay values.*
(iii) *An trade equilibrium price system is efficient in the sense that the assigned prices express a social, competitive value of the properties.*
(iv) *A trade equilibrium allocation is stable in the sense that there are no improving barters as defined in Description 3.3.*

One cannot state the equivalent of a SWT in the context of a monetary trade system. Indeed, there is a fundamental problem with how we describe preferences and initial purchasing power: both are closely linked and represented through the same system of willingness-to-pay values. Therefore, it is unclear how a change in the initial conditions of the system can be described. In this regard, a monetary trade system as represented here is unambiguously *partial* rather than *general*. In this regard this approach falls under the remit of partial equilibrium analysis.

Nevertheless the stated properties regarding the existence of equilibria and the FWT make this a strong model, which results in a wide variety of applications. I will now return to the example introduced here and compute two equilibria for the system given in Table 3.5. For that purpose I introduce an algorithm described in depth in Easley and Kleinberg (2010).

**An Excess Demand Algorithm to Compute Trade Equilibria** Easley and Kleinberg devise a very simple algorithm that has applicability to a very wide range of pricing problems, not just in trade systems introduced here. I refer to Chapter 10 in their book for a full range of applications to network-structured pricing problems.

**Table 3.6**  Step 1—excess demands at zero prices

| Individual | H1 | H2 | H3 | H4 | H5 | H6 | H7 | H8 |
|---|---|---|---|---|---|---|---|---|
| A | **100** | 80 | 70 | 65 | 60 | 50 | 30 | 20 |
| B | **90** | 80 | 50 | 85 | 10 | 40 | 45 | 30 |
| C | **85** | 70 | 80 | 60 | 55 | 45 | 40 | 30 |
| D | 70 | **80** | 45 | 30 | 40 | 60 | 20 | 50 |
| E | 70 | 65 | 50 | 40 | 45 | 60 | 20 | 30 |
| F | 60 | **65** | 55 | 50 | 35 | 30 | 45 | 10 |
| G | 50 | 45 | **60** | 40 | 20 | 30 | 35 | 10 |
| H | **50** | 45 | 40 | 30 | 25 | 20 | 15 | 10 |
| Price | 0 | 0 | 0 | 0 | 0 | 0 | 0 | 0 |

**Description 3.9 (*Excess Demand Algorithm*)** *Let a monetary trade system be given for a set* $N = \{1, \ldots, n\}$ *of economic agents and a property set of similar size,* $\mathcal{H} = \{H_1, \ldots, H_n\}$. *Each individual economic agent* $i \in N$ *has a willingness-to-pay function* $V_i : \mathcal{H} \to \mathbb{R}_+$. *Now, follow the next steps to compute a trade equilibrium price system* $P : \mathcal{H} \to \mathbb{R}_+$ *and corresponding equilibrium allocation:*

(i) *Set* $P_H = 0$ *for every property* $H \in \mathcal{H}$.
(ii) *For the given price system* $P$, *identify for each property* $H \in \mathcal{H}$:

$$\mathcal{E}_H = \{i \in N \mid E_i(H, P_H) \text{ is maximal for } P\}.$$

*Now property* $H$ *is in excess demand if* $\#\mathcal{E}_H \geqslant 2$.
(iii) *Increase the prices* $P_H$ *of all properties in excess demand until the set of excess demand properties changes.*
(iv) *Return to step (ii) until an allocation can be made of exactly one maximal property under the resulting price system from (iii) to each individual economic agent.*

Easley and Kleinberg (2010) show that this excess demand algorithm always converges to an equilibrium in a finite number of steps.[9]

**Applying the Algorithm to the Example**  Let us return to the example posed in Table 3.5 and apply the excess demand algorithm to the willingness-to-pay values given there. Assigning zero prices to all properties leads to the conclusion that the willingness-to-pay values become pure gains from trade. In Table 3.6 all maximal properties are indicated in bold. Clearly properties $H1$ and $H2$ are in excess demand and identified in bold as well.

---

[9] In the analysis introduced by Easley and Kleinberg the set of excess demand properties is directly related to their notion of a *constricted set*. Their use of network analysis allows a much easier identification of equilibrium allocations in the absence of any constructed sets. This cannot be applied in the analysis with the representations through tables used here.

**Table 3.7**  Step 2—excess demand analysis

| Individual | H1 | H2 | H3 | H4 | H5 | H6 | H7 | H8 |
|---|---|---|---|---|---|---|---|---|
| A | 95 | 75 | 70 | 65 | 60 | 50 | 30 | 20 |
| B | 85 | 75 | 50 | 85 | 10 | 40 | 45 | 30 |
| C | 80 | 65 | 80 | 60 | 55 | 45 | 40 | 30 |
| D | 65 | 75 | 45 | 30 | 40 | 60 | 20 | 50 |
| E | 65 | 60 | 50 | 40 | 45 | 60 | 20 | 30 |
| F | 55 | 60 | 55 | 50 | 35 | 30 | 45 | 10 |
| G | 45 | 40 | 60 | 40 | 20 | 30 | 35 | 10 |
| H | 45 | 40 | 40 | 30 | 25 | 20 | 15 | 10 |
| Price | 5 | 5 | 0 | 0 | 0 | 0 | 0 | 0 |

**Table 3.8**  Step 3—excess demand analysis

| Individual | H1 | H2 | H3 | H4 | H5 | H6 | H7 | H8 |
|---|---|---|---|---|---|---|---|---|
| A | 85 | 65 | 60 | 65 | 60 | 50 | 30 | 20 |
| B | 75 | 65 | 40 | 85 | 10 | 40 | 45 | 30 |
| C | 70 | 55 | 70 | 60 | 55 | 45 | 40 | 30 |
| D | 55 | 65 | 35 | 30 | 40 | 60 | 20 | 50 |
| E | 55 | 50 | 40 | 40 | 45 | 60 | 20 | 30 |
| F | 45 | 50 | 45 | 50 | 35 | 30 | 45 | 10 |
| G | 35 | 30 | 50 | 40 | 20 | 30 | 35 | 10 |
| H | 35 | 30 | 30 | 30 | 25 | 20 | 15 | 10 |
| Price | 15 | 15 | 10 | 0 | 0 | 0 | 0 | 0 |

Increasing the prices of both excess demand properties to 5 already changes the gains from trade sufficiently to let $H3$ join as an excess demand property, as depicted in Table 3.7.

The next price increase amounts to 10 for all three properties that are in excess demand. This results in property $H4$ also becoming in excess demand. This is depicted in Table 3.8. Further price increases add property $H6$ to the set of excess demand properties (Table 3.9).

A further price increase enlarges the set of excess demand properties even further. Note that if there are more properties in excess demand it is easier to identify an equilibrium allocation. A property that is demanded by more than one individual can be assigned to one of them, as long as the other agents also get a property assigned that maximises their gains from trade.

Increasing the price of excess demand properties $H1$, $H2$, $H3$, $H4$ and $H6$ with 10 results in a fundamental shift of the set of excess demand properties. This is depicted in Table 3.10 after the fifth step in the algorithm.

Increasing the prices of the excess demand properties with a further 10 results in the gains from trade represented in Table 3.11. It is clear that many properties are in excess demand under the given price system. The only properties not in excess demand are actually $H6$ and $H8$.

**Table 3.9**  Step 4—excess demand analysis

| Individual | H1 | H2 | H3 | H4 | H5 | H6 | H7 | H8 |
|---|---|---|---|---|---|---|---|---|
| A | 80 | 60 | 55 | 60 | 60 | 50 | 30 | 20 |
| B | 70 | 60 | 35 | 80 | 10 | 40 | 45 | 30 |
| C | 65 | 50 | 65 | 55 | 55 | 45 | 40 | 30 |
| D | 50 | 60 | 30 | 25 | 40 | 60 | 20 | 50 |
| E | 50 | 45 | 35 | 35 | 45 | 60 | 20 | 30 |
| F | 40 | 45 | 40 | 45 | 35 | 30 | 45 | 10 |
| G | 30 | 25 | 45 | 35 | 20 | 30 | 35 | 10 |
| H | 30 | 25 | 25 | 25 | 25 | 20 | 15 | 10 |
| Price | 20 | 20 | 15 | 5 | 0 | 0 | 0 | 0 |

**Table 3.10**  Step 5—excess demand analysis

| Individual | H1 | H2 | H3 | H4 | H5 | H6 | H7 | H8 |
|---|---|---|---|---|---|---|---|---|
| A | 70 | 50 | 45 | 50 | 60 | 40 | 30 | 20 |
| B | 60 | 50 | 25 | 70 | 10 | 30 | 45 | 30 |
| C | 55 | 40 | 55 | 45 | 55 | 35 | 40 | 30 |
| D | 40 | 50 | 20 | 15 | 40 | 50 | 20 | 50 |
| E | 40 | 35 | 25 | 25 | 45 | 50 | 20 | 30 |
| F | 30 | 35 | 30 | 35 | 35 | 20 | 45 | 10 |
| G | 20 | 15 | 35 | 25 | 20 | 20 | 35 | 10 |
| H | 20 | 15 | 15 | 15 | 25 | 10 | 15 | 10 |
| Price | 30 | 30 | 25 | 15 | 0 | 10 | 0 | 0 |

**Table 3.11**  Step 6—excess demand analysis

| Individual | H1 | H2 | H3 | H4 | H5 | H6 | H7 | H8 |
|---|---|---|---|---|---|---|---|---|
| A | 60 | 50 | 35 | 50 | 50 | 30 | 20 | 20 |
| B | 50 | 50 | 15 | 70 | 0 | 20 | 35 | 30 |
| C | 45 | 40 | 45 | 45 | 45 | 25 | 30 | 30 |
| D | 30 | 50 | 10 | 15 | 30 | 40 | 10 | 50 |
| E | 30 | 35 | 15 | 25 | 35 | 40 | 10 | 30 |
| F | 20 | 35 | 20 | 35 | 25 | 10 | 35 | 10 |
| G | 10 | 15 | 25 | 25 | 10 | 10 | 25 | 10 |
| H | 10 | 15 | 5 | 15 | 15 | 0 | 5 | 10 |
| Price | 40 | 30 | 35 | 15 | 10 | 20 | 10 | 0 |

However, it is also clear from Table 3.11 that this configuration already allows an allocation under these given prices. Indeed, this allocation is given by $H1$ to $A$; $H2$ to $H$; $H3$ to $G$; $H4$ to $B$; $H5$ to $C$; $H6$ to $E$; $H7$ to $F$; and $H8$ to $D$. One can check that this allocation—denoted as allocation $\alpha$—indeed assigns maximal properties to all economic agents under the suggested price system.

However, we can further enhance the resulting equilibrium by a modification of the suggested prices. The large excess demand sets can be reduced by

**Table 3.12**  Allocation $\alpha$—an equilibrium allocation after price adjustment

| Individual | H1 | H2 | H3 | H4 | H5 | H6 | H7 | H8 |
|---|---|---|---|---|---|---|---|---|
| A | 55 | 45 | 30 | 35 | 45 | 30 | 15 | 20 |
| B | 45 | 45 | 10 | 55 | −5 | 20 | 30 | 30 |
| C | 40 | 35 | 40 | 30 | 40 | 25 | 25 | 30 |
| D | 25 | 45 | 5 | 0 | 25 | 40 | 5 | 50 |
| E | 25 | 30 | 10 | 10 | 30 | 40 | 5 | 30 |
| F | 15 | 30 | 15 | 20 | 20 | 10 | 30 | 10 |
| G | 5 | 10 | 20 | 10 | 5 | 10 | 20 | 10 |
| H | 5 | 10 | 0 | 0 | 10 | 0 | 0 | 10 |
| Price | 45 | 35 | 40 | 30 | 15 | 20 | 15 | 0 |

**Table 3.13**  Allocation $\beta$—an alternative equilibrium allocation

| Individual | H1 | H2 | H3 | H4 | H5 | H6 | H7 | H8 |
|---|---|---|---|---|---|---|---|---|
| A | 55 | 45 | 30 | 35 | 45 | 30 | 15 | 20 |
| B | 45 | 45 | 10 | 55 | −5 | 20 | 30 | 30 |
| C | 40 | 35 | 40 | 30 | 40 | 25 | 25 | 30 |
| D | 25 | 45 | 5 | 0 | 25 | 40 | 5 | 50 |
| E | 25 | 30 | 10 | 10 | 30 | 40 | 5 | 30 |
| F | 15 | 30 | 15 | 20 | 20 | 10 | 30 | 10 |
| G | 5 | 10 | 20 | 10 | 5 | 10 | 20 | 10 |
| H | 5 | 10 | 0 | 0 | 10 | 0 | 0 | 10 |
| Price | 45 | 35 | 40 | 30 | 15 | 20 | 15 | 0 |

increasing all prices of excess demand properties with 5 and to levy an additional price increase of 10 for $H4$ as the property with the largest excess demand. This clarifies the equilibrium much as depicted in Table 3.12. Here the identified equilibrium allocation is given in bold italics, while all other maximal properties are given in plain bold.

There is a second equilibrium allocation under the price system given in Table 3.11, which remains valid after the price adjustment depicted in Table 3.12. This alternative equilibrium allocation assigns $H1$ to $A$; $H2$ to $F$; $H3$ to $C$; $H4$ to $B$; $H5$ to $H$; $H6$ to $E$; $H7$ to $G$; and $H8$ to $D$. This equilibrium allocation $\beta$ is depicted in Table 3.13 under the adjusted price system as given in Table 3.12.

From the analysis in this example we come to some interesting conclusions about the monetary trade system and the resulting equilibrium allocations. Foremost, we note immediately that in both identified equilibrium allocations socially lower ranked individuals with low purchasing power are assigned highly socially ranked properties: $H$ is assigned the second highest ranked property in equilibrium allocation $\alpha$ and is assigned the fifth highest ranked property $H5$ in equilibrium allocation $\beta$. Similarly, the second lowest ranked individual $G$ is assigned the third-best property $H3$ in allocation $\alpha$.

This stands in marked contrast with the allocations considered under the jungle equilibrium concept in an institutional economy that is founded on a social hierarchy and the equilibria emerging in a barter economy. Those cases resulted in similar allocations that followed pretty much the social order of both individuals and properties: higher ranked individuals are assigned socially more preferred properties. This principle seems to be missing in this most market-like of environments considered here.

As in the cases of the jungle and barter economies, an institutional system of trade based on a competitive price mechanism does not affect the inequalities that are built into the representative values. Indeed, individuals with a higher purchasing power—based on higher willingness-to-pay values for the properties on offer—generally obtain the socially higher ranked properties. The trade mechanism itself does not affect these inequalities; the market cannot be recognised as being particularly "fair". In particular, I emphasise that the competitive price mechanism does not perform better in this regard than a social hierarchy, although the latter might be perceived as "obviously" more unequal and unfair.

It is even stronger than that. Looking at the individual willingness-to-pay evaluations, there does not seem to be a competitive price system that would assign agent $H$ property $H8$. This is because of the high value that agent $D$ assigns to $H8$, even though it is a lower ranked property in her individual preference order. This was the case neither for the jungle nor for the barter system.

The conclusion is that the introduction of a monetary system also includes the consideration of *cardinal* preference rankings in the procedure that determines the equilibria in the system. Here, this is signified mainly by the high value that $D$ assigns to property $H8$. This cardinal feature draws the equilibrium allocation process away from the diagonal and to a completely different allocation, even assigning the second highest socially preferred property to the lowest ranked individual in the social hierarchy. In contrast, jungle equilibria and barter systems are firmly founded on ordinal considerations only, without computing how more valuable one property is from another for some individual economic agent.

Thus, the introduction of a system in which money is a social medium of account to express individual purchasing power—rather than just a unit of account as in the barter system—alters the performance of the economy in unexpected ways. Allocations are not just based on ordinal considerations, but also on the cardinal levels of value.

A second feature of the resulting equilibria is that the equilibrium price system indeed assigns generally higher values or "prices" to socially higher ranked properties. This seems sensible in this context: higher ranked properties are likely to be "scarcer" than lower ranked objects and therefore more frequently subject to excess demand as a consequence. This justifies a higher price. In this regard, the equilibrium price system in a monetary trade system truly reflects social scarcity of the commodity under consideration.

## 3.3    INTERACTION INFRASTRUCTURES

The second element of a socio-economic space is the interaction infrastructural sphere. This describes and represents the embodiment of the social division of labour itself, founded on the application of the socio-economic roles that individual economic agents can assume in the social division of labour. The social division of labour results in horizontal production networks of specialised economic agents and/or hierarchically structured social production organisations, the latter being founded on the exercise of authority in relationships between superiors and subordinates. Since the infrastructure embodies the prevailing social division of labour, a significant element of the interaction infrastructure is related to the trade, exchange and barter of economic commodities. Trade is not only conducted through lateral interactions, but also through hierarchical interactions in the infrastructures. This is discussed below.

One can discern three subspheres in the interaction infrastructural sphere of a socio-economic space: the *subjective subsphere* consisting of weak socio-economic interactions and basic socio-economic institutions guiding behaviour of the constituting economic agents, mainly representing networking activities; the *objective subsphere*, guided by the advanced socio-economic institutions imposed through the governance system—mainly through objective socio-economic roles and trade institutions; and the *superstructure*, consisting of advanced organisations such as social production organisations and markets. I elaborate on these fundamentally different sub-spheres in the trade infrastructure in a socio-economic space.

**Subjective subsphere:**    The weakest relationships in the trade infrastructure are based on the individual attributes and skills of the economic agents that conduct these interactions. This refers to *networking* between economic agents in its purest form. These relationships are fluid or "subjective" in the sense that the roles of the economic agents in such a relationship are not completely fixed and can be adjusted according to the perceived needs. This describes relationships and interactions by acquaintances and occasional trade relationships. In principle, these relationships have no regularity to them and no true expectations are attached to the interactions that these relationships represent.

An example of a multilateral relationship in the subjective subsphere of a socio-economic space is that between university students spending time in class, in which they interact in their capacity as participants in a collaborative learning process, and on Thursday or Friday night in the pub, where they are acquaintances entertaining one another with banter and casual discourse. These relationships are fluid and roles are not necessarily fixed. There are not necessarily fixed expectations of the different socio-economic roles that these students assume in the various contexts in which they interact.

The fluid relationships and the temporal nature of the interactions in this subjective subsphere act as a conduit to build more permanent relational infrastructures in the socio-economic space. These interactions clearly have a critical role in making the social division of labour flexible and responsive to outside influences and inside disruptions.

**Objective subsphere:**    Subjective relationships can become more objectified if there is a regularity to that relationship or if the relationship is underwritten by a formalisation. This formalisation can take the form of a legal contract, but also of a pattern of fixed expectations in the parties that interact in that relationship.

The formal interactions in the objective subsphere embody the most productive features of the social division of labour. These interactions are supported by objective socio-economic institutions that guide the interactions in the socio-economic space. In particular, such objective relationships are conducted by economic agents in fixed, objectively accepted socio-economic roles. For example, a trade relationship between a shop owner and a client is an objective relationship that is founded on objective expectations of that shop owner as a supplier of certain economic commodities and the client as a demander of those same commodities. These objectively defined and commonly accepted interactions form the main source of economic wealth generation through a social division of labour.

**Superstructure:**    Advanced forms of multilateral and hierarchical socio-economic interactions make up the superstructure. These structures include social production organisations—also referred to as firms or corporations—that are founded on hierarchical authority relationships between superiors and subordinates. These also include the formal authority relationships between citizens and social organisations and the nation-state. The latter refers to the exercise of governmental oversight and the enforcement of systems of laws. Finally, the superstructure includes the contracted relationships between large corporations and their clients as well as their providers. The superstructure also includes the so-called "gig economy" in which relatively powerless individual providers of services subject themselves to the contracts imposed by these corporations.

The common feature of the interaction structures that make up the superstructure is the *exercise of authority* in the relationships that constitute these structures. This authority can be formal, as is the case in an employment relationship, or informal, as is the case of employment in the gig economy.

The complex of production networks and hierarchical structures that make up the collective of interaction infrastructures in a socio-economic space result in a complex of network structures. Thus, the interaction infrastructures generated in a socio-economic space can also be viewed as networks of interacting economic agents. This viewpoint provides us with the necessary perspective to develop a mathematical representation of the interaction infrastructures that are generated in a socio-economic space. We pursue that here in some detail, but for a full development I refer to Gilles (2018).

Before that, however, I turn to an alternative interpretation of these interaction infrastructures founded on the social division of labour itself. Instead of considering these infrastructures as networks in the subjective and objective sphere as well as organisations in the superstructure, we can view them as representing two distinct incarnations of the social division of labour.

### 3.3.1    Forms of the Social Division of Labour

The socio-economic space incorporates the social division of labour into its constituting interaction infrastructural sphere. This social division of labour transects the three subspheres in the infrastructure of a socio-economic space, as discussed above. Indeed, in the functioning of a social division of labour these three subspheres are present quite prominently. Networking as part of the subjective subsphere is critical in the functioning of the social division of labour; formal trade relationships between specialised individuals are captured by the objective subsphere, while the superstructure captures the hierarchical structures that make up the social production organisations in the social division of labour.

From a relational point of view, the social division of labour mainly takes two fundamentally different forms, which are founded on two of the three identified subspheres in the interaction infrastructure of a socio-economic space: a horizontal social division of labour and an incorporated division of labour.[10] These two forms enhance our insights into the functioning of the objective sphere in the socio-economic space as well as the organisational activities in the superstructure. The horizontal social division of labour is firmly placed in the objective subsphere, while the incorporated division of labour has to be considered as a foundation of the superstructure in the socio-economic space.

I consider the subjective subsphere to be made up of fluid, flexible relationships and networking efforts that let the social division of labour function effectively. Indeed, without informal contacts and networking activities, the social division of labour cannot be sustained or enhanced.

**The Horizontal Social Division of Labour** A horizontal social division of labour refers to the assumption of well-defined socio-economic roles of independent economic agents, which result in generated economic values to every economic agent in the resulting networks. Hence, individual economic agents assume a certain socio-economic role in a position in the resulting supply chain networks; values can therefore be attributed directly to their activities.

**The Platonian division of labour:**    The Platonian division of labour refers therefore to two main implementations, namely the product provision chains structured around the role of artisans. Here, individuals assume an objective role in the supply chain for a certain class of goods, usually supported only

---

[10] The incorporated division of labour has been referred to as the manufacturing division of labour by Babbage (1835) and Marx (1867).

by a few apprentices or employees. This was the main form that the social division of labour took prior to the industrial revolution. These supply chains and artisan production networks form the core of the social division of labour in the ancient polis economy—discussed in detail by Plato (380 BCE) and Aristotle (340 BCE, 350 BCE)—as well as in the premodern economy in the era before the industrial revolution.

The supply chains in the Platonian division of labour structured around artisans are supported through socio-economic institutions and organisations from a relatively small economy, such as a town or a city. The main organisations were the city markets for various categories of goods, the guilds organising succession and training in their supply chains, and a law system imposed by authorities, much influenced by the guilds.

**Capitalist production networks:** The second form of a horizontal social division of labour refers to the one that emerges among social production organisations, possibly mixed with traditional artisan production units or so-called "self-employed" individual entrepreneurs. Here, positions in a product provision chain are occupied by firms or corporations that interact with each other, customers and individual suppliers in their supply chains. These complex, mixed product provision chains form the core of the social division of labour in a capitalist economy.

This second form of the horizontal social division of labour is fundamentally different from the first form in that the interacting parts are much larger and much more diversified. As a consequence the product diversity is much larger than through a traditional, artisan-based, horizontal product provision chain in a Platonian economy. Therefore, it is preferable to refer to this form of a social division of labour as a *production network*, a term accepted in recent contributions to the literature (Acemoglu et al. 2012; Carvalho 2014; Huremovic and Vega-Redondo 2016).

Contrary to a traditional horizontal supply chain, the constituting parts are no longer necessarily approximately equal in size as well as control. In our contemporary global economy size and control power are essential elements in the functioning of a supply chain. Large corporations aim to fully control the supply chain from its roots through its logistics to the final consumers. Corporate strategies are devised to enhance the control of the supply chain, and corporations such as Wal-Mart, Tesco, Google and Apple are successful in achieving near complete control over operations extending beyond their direct remit.

**The Incorporated Social Division of Labour** The second main form of the social division of labour occurs within a social production organisation and refers to the assignment of objective productive roles in a hierarchical production organisation that is guided through the exercise of authority. These roles are not directly value-generating, but indirectly through partial and compartmented contributions to the production process, which lead to final products that are traded onward in a (horizontal) supply chain to other corporate entities.

Hierarchies are usually understood as authority-driven structures. Hence, hierarchical relationships are between superiors and subordinates only. Such relationships mainly represent employment situations: an employer has the authority to assign tasks to the subordinate as her employee. This constitutes a hierarchical relationship between the employer as a superior and the employee as a subordinate. This allows for the interpretation of social production organisations and firms as hierarchical organisation forms.

In economic theory, the employment relationship has gone through several interpretations. The most simple interpretation is that of a command relationship, in which the superior instructs the subordinate in detail about the tasks to be executed (Coase 1937). The Coasian conception of the employment relationship conforms with the Marxian viewpoint of the role of labour in the incorporated division of labour. Indeed, Marx (1867) postulates that workers as the providers of labour force in the social division of labour have no direct access to the means of production themselves. Their access depends on the owners of these means of production, the "capitalists".

The previous discussion of the employment relationship neglects the main *agency problem* in such a relationship: the superior does not necessarily have the complete knowledge to instruct the subordinate in sufficient detail. Usually the agency problem is formulated as a *principal–agent* construct in which the superior is a principal pursuing a certain goal. The subordinate acts as her agent and pursues the task on the principal's behalf. Failure to attain the desired objectives can be caused by environmental factors, but also by a lack of effort on the part of the agent. The principal cannot distinguish between these two fundamentally different causes. A full theoretical approach is based on applications of advanced game theory (Grossman and Hart 1983). The conclusion from this theory is that a combination of an outcome-based bonus and monitoring will guarantee that the agent will exercise sufficient exertion to fulfil the assigned task.[11]

Hart and Moore (1990, 1999) point out that the agency problem is insufficient to understand hierarchical production organisations. Indeed, the problem is worse; the principal cannot actually identify anything and monitoring is not effective. Ultimately the principal can only deny the subordinate access to the proactive assets by firing him.

More recent developments in the economic theory of the hierarchical production organisation point to more advanced understandings of authority relationships, distinguishing formal authority from real, effective control (Aghion and Tirole 1997). For a discussion of the most recent developments I refer to Dessein (2013).

---

[11] This theory clearly can be used as a theoretical justification for the bonus culture in our contemporary global economy. In particular, the prevailing remuneration culture in transnational corporations is affected by this. The theory is, however, more subtle than the bonus culture lets us believe: the balance between bonus and monitoring is very precise, requiring advanced structures for proper implementation. For a full and enlightening treatment of this subject, using elementary mathematical techniques, I refer to Ricketts (2003).

A very general framework for the study of hierarchical social production organisations has been developed in Brink and Gilles (2016). In that study we consider a general framework based on arbitrarily complex hierarchical networks in which superiors decide to exercise authority. We show that if subordinates are rational, they would actually anticipate the exercise of authority without it being exercised explicitly. These insights conform with the standard binary principal–agent framework discussed above.

Although the source for hierarchical inequality in an interaction is usually to be understood as the presence of authority, it is not the only form by which the incorporated divisions of labour can be interpreted. In our contemporary global economy we distinguish two other fundamental sources of hierarchy.

In many economic situations, we can distinguish the presence of a *first-mover advantage*. This refers to competitive situations in which one party has a distinct advantage over another owing to inside knowledge or simply the adherence to some precedence order. A well-established corporation in a certain trade network can be contested by an entrant, but it will be very difficult. The incumbent has a substantial advantage for knowing the market and having established long-running trade relationships with suppliers and customers. The entrant has to recreate these networks usually from scratch, at a high cost of networking.

A similar first-mover advantage is obtained from inside information. If one of the parties in a market or trade network has information that is relevant to all trading parties, it can base its strategy on this additional information. This advantage might result in a leadership position by the informed trader, where its competitors would adjust their strategies in response to the informed market leader.

A second fundamental source of hierarchy is socio-economic *power*. Such power can be based on size—(being the largest trader in the network results naturally in a leadership position)—or on advantages from strategic networking—(as exemplified by leadership positions in global supply chains that allow corporations to dictate terms to the other parties in the network). The most prevalent contemporary example is that of the gig economy, in which corporations dictate terms to their self-employed providers.

For example, the relative size of corporations such as Uber and Deliveroo—in comparison with their individual self-employed service providers—allows them to obtain a natural leadership role in the provision relationship and dictate unfavourable terms to their providers in the contract for those services. On the other hand, leadership in supply chains by logistics TNCs such as ADM and by retailers such as Tesco and Wal-Mart is a result of highly strategic networking and the development of new forms of contracting. In either case, leadership is founded on power in those relationships and results in excess rents.

**Mixed Forms of the Social Division of Labour** It should be clear that in our contemporary global economy we observe a mixture of all forms of the social division of labour that we have discussed here. Indeed, there are clearly horizontal supply chains, in particular capitalist production networks. Furthermore, the hierarchical, incorporated social division of labour remains the main organisational form within corporations and firms in those capitalist production networks. Both descriptors of the social division of labour remain crucial in understanding our contemporary global economy.

### 3.3.2    A Primer on Network Analysis

The previous discussion makes clear that a proper development of models of the interaction infrastructure in a socio-economic space has to be founded on the descriptive notion of a *social network*. In the past two decades a significant literature on the study of social networks has emerged (Jackson 2008; Newman 2010; Barabási 2016). Using these tools, we are able to describe the various organisational forms that emerge in the interaction infrastructure of a socio-economic space. In this subsection I explore the main descriptive concepts from this literature.

As discussed in the previous section, the social division of labour results in two types of network structure: horizontal division of labour, based on *lateral* interactions, and the incorporated division of labour, founded on hierarchical relationships. Both forms will be formalised using different constructs from network science, namely regular (undirected) networks and directed networks.

**Networks** Lateral interactions between two or more economic agents in a horizontal division of labour are founded on equality or parity of the interacting parties. Here I introduce a formal description of these lateral relationships and the resulting networks from these interactions. These mathematical definitions and the resulting analysis of these networks and related concepts form a basis for developing a theory of the analysis and building of infrastructures within a socio-economic space. The comprehensive definition that follows captures a network's formal mathematical definition as well as related concepts.

**Definition 3.10 (Networks)**  Let $N = \{1, \ldots, n\}$ be some set of (individual) economic agents, network, technically denoted as **nodes**. We now introduce the following concepts:

(a) A (lateral) **link** between two nodes $i \in N$ and $j \in N$ with $i \neq j$ is formally defined as the binary set $ij = \{i, j\}$.[12]

(b) A **network** on population $N$ is any set of links,

$$G \subset \{ij \mid i, j \in N \text{ with } i \neq j\} \tag{3.3}$$

---

[12] I emphasise here that this implies that a link $ij$ is exactly the same as a link $ji$. This reflects that both parties that constitute this link are equal and that the link represents an interaction that is founded on parity between the two parties involved.

such that every $i \in N$ is connected to at least one other agent; that is, for every $i \in N: N_i(G) = \{j \in N \mid ij \in G\} \neq \emptyset$, where $N_i(G)$ is the set of **neighbours** of node $i$ in the network $G$.

The definition above introduces a variety of formal concepts representing socio-economic notions introduced previously. A *link ij* represents an equal bilateral relationship or binary socio-economic activity in which $i$ and $j$ participate. Links are formal representations of interactions between two equal parties. They can be used to describe contracting relationships in a horizontal social division of labour on the population of economic agents $N$.

The notion of an undirected *network* introduced above is simply a collection of links in which all nodes are connected to at least one other node. So, autarkic or unattached nodes are excluded from a network in this formal representation. This is illustrated in Fig. 3.2, which depicts a network consisting of nine nodes and a set of links—describing binary relationships between these nodes.

Recent contributions to network science have focused on certain properties of nodes and links in networks. In particular the *centrality* of a node in a network is considered to be important. A variety of centrality measures aim to attach numerical values that express the importance of a node's position in the network.

The most straightforward centrality measure is the *degree* of a node in the network—being the number of links to other nodes it has in the network under consideration. Formally, the degree of a node $i \in N$ in a network $G \subset \{ij \mid i \neq j \text{ and } i, j \in N\}$ is defined by

$$d_i(G) = \#N_i(G) \quad \text{where } N_i(G) = \{j \in N \mid ij \in G\}. \tag{3.4}$$

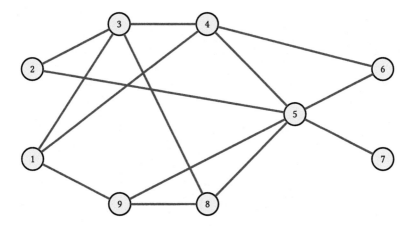

**Fig. 3.2**  An example of a lateral network

In this definition $N_i(G)$ again refers to the set of neighbours of node $i$ in the network $G$. Node $i$'s connectivity in the network is described by its neighbourhood $N_i(G)$ and the degree of that connectivity is captured by the magnitude of that neighbourhood, being the number of direct neighbours of node $i$ in the network $G$. The degree $d_i(G)$ exactly quantifies this.

Nodes can be ranked by their degree, describing how well these nodes are connected. "Hubs" are nodes with a relatively high degree, being connected to a large number of other nodes. On the other hand, "leaves" are minimally connected, with $d_i(G) = 1$, being connected to a single other node. An interesting finding of empirically observed large-scale social networks is that the *degree distribution* in such networks satisfies a power law or a Pareto distribution. This means that there are a few, extremely well-connected hubs, while there are a lot of leaves in these networks. Another expression of this finding is to paraphrase Pareto's Law and to say that 20% of the nodes have 80% of the connections, while 80% of the nodes have only 20% of the connections in these networks.

There is a wide variety of centrality measures that are fundamentally based on the degree of a node. For example, the *β-measure* is defined by

$$\beta_i(G) = \sum_{j \in N_i(G)} \frac{1}{d_j(G)} \tag{3.5}$$

and reflects a much more sophisticated approach to identifying more connected nodes from less connected nodes in a network (Brink and Gilles 1994, 2000). The $\beta$-measure can be interpreted as a version of the PageRank centrality measure that is at the foundation of the Google internet search engine (Brin and Page 1998).

**Application to Platonian Divisions of Labour**  I introduced the notion of the Platonian division of labour as a social division of labour made up of individual economic agents that are specialised in one of the traditional artisan professions. A Platonian division of labour can be fully represented by a network model. It generates commodities through a chain of intermediate products produced by a variety of specialised artisans.

This is illustrated in Fig. 3.3, which depicts a production network for bread. There are five distinct roles in this simple Platonian production network, namely that of a farmer producing wheat as an intermediary product; a dairy producer, usually a dairy farmer, who produces butter and milk as intermediary products; a miller who converts wheat into flour at his mill; a baker who combines flour and butter to bake bread; and finally a consumer, who purchases the bread from the baker as a consumption good. Note that each artisan profession is attached to the production of at least one economic commodity, most of these being intermediary products necessary in the production processes of other commodities.

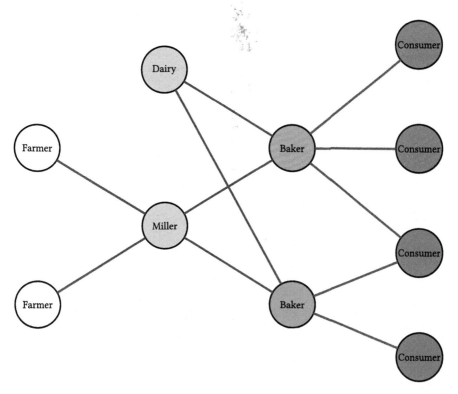

**Fig. 3.3**  A Platonian production network for bread

I emphasise that a Platonian production network reflects the nature of the social division that underlies the production of economic commodities. Indeed, there is a natural order in which the social division of labour conducted through specialised artisans takes the production of a good through its various stages of development. Wheat is a necessary product for the milling of flour, which in turn is used in the production of the final consumption good, bread. This natural order is fully reflected in the production network depicted in Fig. 3.3. The links in the production network connect the producers of the various intermediary goods that are connected through the natural production order. In that regard the production network is fully characterised by the underlying technical production processes.

This implies that links only occur between the subsequently sequenced intermediary production stages in the underlying technical production processes. Farmers deliver their output (wheat) to the miller for the production of flour. There is no natural reason why farmers should directly trade with the bakers in the production network.

This gives rise to the ability of producers of intermediary product to take control of a certain stage in the production process underlying the production network. Historically this explains the success of (trade) guilds of artisan professions (Ogilvie 2014). Indeed, the guild of millers controls fully the production stage between wheat and flour, while the guild of bakers exercises control over the production of bread itself. Under certain conditions, the power of a professional guild might extend to the whole production network.

Historically, the power of these guilds was expressed in the elaborate guildhalls that they were able to erect, based on the excess rents from the control they exerted over the production networks in their jurisdiction. These excess rents resulted in significant riches for some of the most influential guilds. Testament to these riches is still on display in cities such as Bruges, Antwerp and Brussels, where there are elaborate guildhalls in the market squares.

I emphasise that technically the relationships in a Platonian production network are principally bilateral. Indeed, some artisan professions organised themselves more successfully in guilds than others, but from a technical point of view the artisans involved in the different stages of production in a Platonian division of labour are on parity: all artisans are equally powerful in these production networks. This justifies the use of undirected links as the mathematical tool of choice to represent the underlying trade relationships. If one party is principally more powerful than the other, a directed link or "arc" has to be used to express the power relationship.

**Directed Networks** Hierarchical relationships are at the foundation of the social production organisations that form the backbone of the incorporated division of labour. In network science, such hierarchical relationships can be represented by directed links or arcs. Networks made up of such arcs only are denoted as *directed*. The next definition captures the formal concepts of this notion.

**Definition 3.11 (Directed Networks)** Let $N = \{1, \ldots, n\}$ be some set of nodes, representing some economic agents. We now introduce the following concepts:

(a) An **arc** from node $i$ to node $j$ is formally defined as a coordinated pair $(i, j) \in N \times N$ and represents a directed relationship from node $i$ to node $j$, where node $i$ has the predecessor position and node $j$ has the successor position in the directed relationship represented by this arc.

(b) A **directed network** on population $N$ is any set of arcs

$$D \subset \{ (i, j) \mid i, j \in N \text{ with } i \neq j \} \tag{3.6}$$

such that the structure $G(D) = \{ij \mid (i, j) \in D\}$ is a network on $N$.[13]

---

[13] This implies that each node in $D$ is connected to at least one other node, either as a predecessor or as a successor or both. It excludes the existence of unattached nodes in the directed network as is the case for (undirected) networks.

*(c)* A **chain** on population $N$ is a directed network

$$D \subset \{ (i, j) \mid i, j \in N \text{ with } i \neq j \}$$

such that $D$ does not contain any cycles, where a **cycle** in $D$ is a subset of arcs in $D$ given by $C = \{ (i_1, i_2), (i_2, i_3), \ldots, (i_{K-1}, i_K) \} \subset D$ such that $i_1 = i_K$.

An *arc* can be used to represent a relationship between two economic agents that has a directed nature in some sense. An arc can, therefore, be used to formally describe a hierarchical authority relationship between a superior and a subordinate, in which the superior is in the predecessor position and the subordinate in the successor position. Arcs can also be used to represent weaker forms of directness such as a formal representation of a relationship between a sender and a receiver in a communication situation or the direction of an information flow in a social production organisation. Furthermore, the concept of an arc can describe a supply relationship, where a supplier, represented as a predecessor, delivers goods to a customer, represented as a successor. These type of arcs are important in the analysis of (Platonian and capitalist ) production networks.

A network is *directed* if it is composed of arcs rather than links. In that case there is a direction to the network represented by the flow of each arc. This diffraction can represent rather benign properties such as the direction of the flow of products or money, but it can also represent coercion or authority. I next discuss an example that represents a common economic process that can be represented as a network as well as a directed network.

**Chains** Chains, as a specific class of directed networks, can be used to describe certain properties of flow systems. For example, the chain depicted in Fig. 3.4

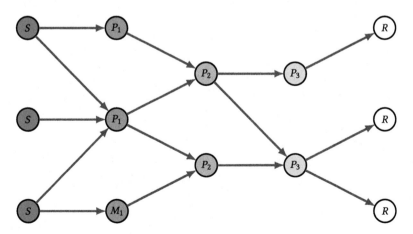

**Fig. 3.4**  A neural network for information processing

models the flow of information from a number of sources (the $S$ nodes), from which raw information originates, through a number of intermediary processors (the $P$ nodes) to an number of reporters (the $R$ nodes). Such an information processing network is also denoted as a *neural network*.

The neural network depicted in Fig. 3.4 is a typical example and application of a chain. A chain has a general direction or flow from one side, described by the source nodes, to the other side, represented by sink nodes, in this case the reporter nodes. Between the sources and the sinks in a chain, there are usually a number of intermediary nodes through which the information flows and is transformed. In Fig. 3.4 these intermediary nodes are denoted as "processors" of the information that flows through them.

Chains can also be used to represent production networks from a certain perspective, even though these production networks are in principle undirected. The most simple application is to use the direction of the arcs to describe the general direction of the production process, namely how one form of intermediate product is converted into another. The direction of the arcs provides additional information about the production process represented by a production network, such as depicted in Fig. 3.3.

The corresponding undirected network $G(D)$ provides us with a representation of the *architecture* or *topology* of the directed network $D$. It depicts the basic relationships as links that make up the arcs in the directed network. Clearly, the topology $G(D)$ contains less information that the original directed network $D$.

It should be clear from this discussion that *chains* are useful tools to describe and analyse product provision chains and structures emerging from the social division of labour in a socio-economic space. This is supported by a general property of chains:

**Proposition 3.12** *Let $G$ be a chain on the population $N$. Then $N$ can be partitioned into three distinct classes of nodes:* **Sources** *being nodes that only have outgoing arcs in $G$;* **Intermediaries** *being nodes that have incoming as well as outgoing arcs in $G$; and* **Sinks** *being nodes that only have incoming arcs in $G$.*

**Power Relations in a Production Network**  Directed networks made up of arcs can also be used to depict the power relationships in a production network. We return to the Platonian production network for bread, depicted in Fig. 3.3, to discuss this. In that production network, we debated the possibility for guilds for each of the professions to arise. For example, a baker guild can emerge to regulate and control the production of bread. Under certain circumstances, such a guild can extend its power to the control of the Platonian production network as a whole. This is the case in the directed network depicted in Fig. 3.5.

In the directed network depicted in Fig. 3.5, the arcs represent the relationships of control between the various parties in this production network. So, an arc $(i, j) \in D$ represents that $i$ sets the terms of trade for $j$. Here, $i$ is in the predecessor position and $j$ in the successor position, reflecting that

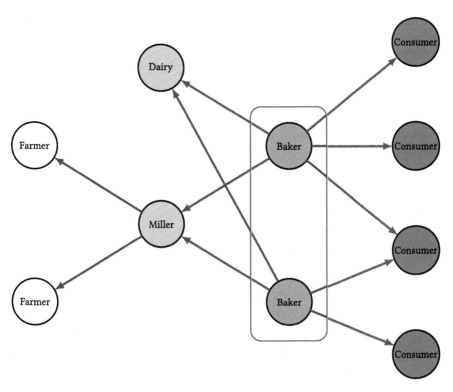

**Fig. 3.5**   A production network for bread with power relationships

the control is with $i$. In the directed network depicted in Fig. 3.5, the guild of bakers has supremacy and is assumed to control the production network. Thus, both bakers set the terms of trade with their customers (the buyers of bread) as well as their suppliers, the dairy producer and the miller. The terms of trade are also imposed further through the network by imposing that the miller has control over the trade relationships with the farmers.

The power of the baker guild in this example is emphasised by the red box around the two baker nodes in the network depicted in Fig. 3.5. It signifies that these two bakers form a *block* in this production network and exert control throughout the network. I refer to Chapter 5 in Gilles (2018) for further discussion and a formal analysis of the consequences of this control.

I also point out that the directed network depicted in Fig. 3.5 is in fact a chain. The two source nodes are the two bakers, while the sink nodes are made up of the dairy producer, the two farmers and the four consumers. The sole intermediary node is the miller. Since the arcs represent power relationships, the interpretation imposed by the chain structure is interpretatively correct. Indeed, the two bakers are the source of the power exerted in this production network. The sinks are clearly the least powerful participants in this network.

**Hierarchies**  A special class of chain networks represents the common features of authority structures that provide the framing of the social production organisations in the contemporary global economy. In a hierarchy, we impose that the arcs represent the exercise of authority between a superior and a subordinate and that this hierarchical network emanates from a single "source", called the *root* of that hierarchy. The root position in a hierarchy is assigned to the highest authority in the production organisation. Furthermore, a hierarchy imposes a tier-like structure: the organisation encompasses multiple *tiers* such that relationships only occur between positions in two subsequent tiers of the organisation.

We can formalise this concept in two fundamentally different mathematical notions. In a regular hierarchy, we impose the two properties introduced above. In a strict hierarchy we impose further that every position in the organisation— except the root position—has a unique superior. In a strict hierarchy, therefore, the exercise of authority is unambiguous.

**Definition 3.13 (Hierarchies)** Let $N = \{1, \ldots, n\}$ be some set of (individual) economic agents, network-technically denoted as **nodes**. We now introduce the following concepts:

> (*a*) A **hierarchy** on node set $N$ is a directed chain network $H \subset \{(i, j) \mid i, j \in N \text{ with } i \neq j\}$ such that there are classes of economic agents $N_1, N_2, \ldots, N_m \subset N$ with $\#N_1 = 1$, $N_p \cap N_q = \varnothing$ for all $p \neq q$, and $(i, j) \in H$ if and only if there is some $p \in \{1, \ldots, m-1\}$ with $i \in N_p$ and $j \in N_{p+1}$.
> The unique node $r \in N_1$ is denoted as the **root** of the hierarchy $H$.
>
> (*b*) A **strict hierarchy** is a hierarchy $H \subset \{(i, j) \mid i, j \in N \text{ with } i \neq j\}$ on node set $N$ such that for every non-root node $i \in N \setminus N_1 = N \setminus \{r\}$ it holds that
>
> $$\#\{(j, i) \mid j \in N\} = 1. \tag{3.7}$$

A hierarchy is a concept that represents social organisations in which authority is exercised between superiors and subordinates. These positions can be ranked using a tier system. Positions in a lower numbered tier are ranked higher than positions in higher ranked tiers. Direct authority is only exercised between positions in subsequent tiers; relationships do not cross tiers. Brink and Gilles (1994) introduce a more general class of directed networks and derive the properties under which these networks are hierarchical. This allows for the endogenous determination of the different tiers in the organisation.

The chain representing the power relations in the bread production network depicted in Fig. 3.5 is *not* a hierarchy, since there is more than one source. This does not accommodate the identification of a unique root. As stated, a hierarchy is a chain with exactly one source. On the other hand, the chain depicted in Fig. 3.5 has a clear tier structure in which all arcs occur between two subsequent tiers in the hierarchy. The top tier is made up of the two bakers. The second

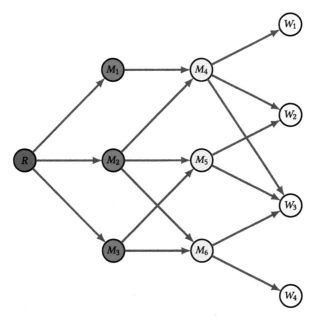

**Fig. 3.6**  A hierarchical network

tier consists of the four consumers, the dairy producer and the miller. The third tier consists of the two farmers.

A proper hierarchical network is depicted in Fig. 3.6. This could depict a hierarchical manufacturing organisation. In this structure the top tier consists of a single root; the second tier consists of three managers $M_1$, $M_2$ and $M_3$; the third tier consists of a second group of three lower ranked managers $M_4$, $M_5$ and $M_6$; and, finally, the fourth tier consists of four workers $W_1$, $W_2$, $W_3$ and $W_4$ that provide the labour on the work floor of the factory.

Note that the hierarchy depicted in Fig. 3.6 is not strict. Indeed, all lower ranked managers in the third tier have multiple superiors, as do two of the four workers on the work floor. This might create ambiguity in the organisation, since conflicting instructions from superiors could lead to confusion among the various subordinates. This can only be remedied properly by excluding the possibility of a subordinate to have multiple superiors. This is guaranteed in the notion of a *strict* hierarchy.

Figure 3.7 depicts a strict hierarchy that is derived from the hierarchy in Fig. 3.6. The multiplicity of superiors has been corrected by removing some authority relationships in the organisation represented in Fig. 3.6. Note that a strict hierarchy has a much sparser structure than a regular hierarchy, but it can also be expected to be much less ambiguous in its operations.

**Networking**  The building of networks is usually known as "networking". Indeed, networking is at the foundation of the formation of infrastructures

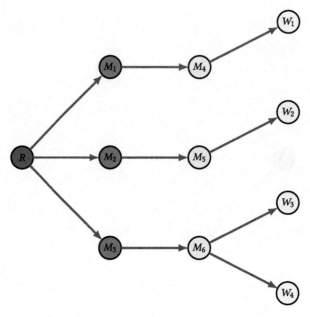

**Fig. 3.7**   A strict hierarchy

in the socio-economic space and is subject to as well as supported by the prevailing socio-economic institutions that make up its governance system. The networking process is subject to rituals prescribed through these institutions. In our contemporary capitalist society this is supported by organised events and parties at which business and society's leaders gather to create new and strengthen existing relationships.

Furthermore, networking also refers to other, much more organised, collective efforts to build and enhance an organisation. This takes the form of building personal relationships between industrial leaders, but it also refers to other more mundane processes. In particular, any hiring process is a networking activity. Hiring enhances a production organisation and thereby changes the existing infrastructures in the prevailing socio-economic space. As such, hiring should be categorised as a network building process.

It is clear that networking refers to the conduct of most aspects of "doing business". This also includes activities generated by government agencies and non-governmental organisations. It summarises most human economic conduct.

I emphasise as well that networking is intimately linked to entrepreneurship as the feedback process in the socio-economic space. Indeed, entrepreneurial activity enhances the infrastructural capacity of that socio-economic space. Networking is therefore part of that entrepreneurial feedback function in the socio-economic space. It is clear that our common understanding is that entrepreneurship includes networking as a major component. This fits clearly with the perception of the socio-economic space defined here.

As such, networking activities are clearly part of the *subjective subsphere* of the interaction infrastructure in a socio-economic space. Networking is explicitly fluid and entrepreneurial. This implies that the relationships that are forged need to settle and objectify before they become effective in the regular process of economic wealth creation.

### 3.3.3   Commodity Markets as Trade Networks

In the context of a socio-economic space, markets are explicitly represented as specific trade networks. As discussed earlier, there is ample empirical evidence that markets can best be understood as networks of trade relationships. Here I simply construct the definition of a market as a network of potential trade relations or simply as a *trade network*.

**Description 3.14** *Consider a socio-economic space.*

(a) *A **trade relationship** is a bilateral relationship in the given socio-economic space in which economic values are generated through the exchange of at least two economic commodities, where an economic commodity is a physical or non-physical bearer of consumption properties in the sense of Lancaster (1966), which is scarce in the sense that it cannot be provided without cost or productive effort.*

(b) *A **commodity market** is a network of trade relationships such that the trade represented through these relationships concerns mainly a single economic commodity or, alternatively, a set of multiple closely related commodities.*

This definition explicitly limits the notion of a commodity market to the trade of economic commodities; other economic interaction is not subject to the market and is explicitly excluded from consideration.[14] A market facilitates the trade of one specific commodity. An example is the (global) oil market. A market facilitating the trade of multiple, closely related commodities is, for example, the car market. In this market, an extensive set of differentiated commodities is traded. In particular, these commodities are differentiated through pricing and branding. This is contrary to the oil market where there is a single product traded at one price, "the" oil price.

Networks consisting of trade relationships usually represent trade systems that are different from commodity markets. First, a commodity market concerns usually a single commodity, or at most a set of closely related commodities; a

---

[14] Note that I avoid the many philosophical complications that the proper definition of a market has to incorporate such as the voluntary nature of economic trade. Here I base the given definition on a practical consideration only. For an account of the complexities of the concept of a market and its proper definition I refer to Rosenbaum (2000).

trade network usually refers to the handling of multiple, possibly very diverse, commodities. Second, a trade network is founded on physical infrastructures such as shops, road systems and cities; markets, instead, refers to certain places where all trade in a certain commodity is concentrated. In short, a trade network clearly refers to a provision chain approach to economic exchange, while a commodity market points to a single, possibly abstract or virtual gathering point at which all trade takes place. Obviously, supply chains are at least as common as marketplaces in our globalised economy and certainly more prevalent in our daily economic trade activities.

**Organised Markets** I debate the modelling of commodity markets within a relational framework. There are three possibilities for describing a commodity market in our contemporary capitalist economy as a network of trade relations. An *organised market* is a star-shaped network of potential trade relations. At the centre of this star is the *market master* or *market convener* and the other participants are potential suppliers and demanders in the market. Each potential supplier and demander only has a trade relation with the market auctioneer. This market convener in the guise of the auctioneer gathers all market price information, and thus "market clearance" happens at a relatively low cost.

In practical implementations of organised markets, the position of the market convener is usually occupied by a market owner or an organisation that controls the market. In medieval times this used to be the local lord or town council, who protected the market and provided market rights to his cities.[15] In modern times, a convener could refer to the auction house of Christie's, the New York Stock Exchange (NYSE) corporation, the NASDAQ company or eBay; in all cases all realised trades are controlled and guided through the approved processes and systems of that market convener, either through the information board at the NYSE or NASDAQ or through the online auction system at eBay. Usually the market auctioneer will charge a brokerage fee on every realised trade as well as an admission fee for participation in the market. As such, "running a market" is just a business in our capitalist society.

I refer to Fig. 3.8 for a graphical representation of an organised market. Here the $M$-node depicts the market auctioneer or market convener and the five $T$-nodes refer to the various traders in this market. These traders are usually the suppliers and demanders of the commodity or commodities traded in this market.

An organised market can also be interpreted as a *club* that is structured around a single "convener". This was the model pursued in Gilles et al. (2015) to describe collaborative or cooperative platforms for economic wealth generation. This approach implies that membership of the market is regulated and that it is certainly not an open arrangement. This provides the market

---

[15] In actuality, the lord was represented by a professional market master, who levied fees on the market participants on behalf of the lord. In many European cities, public markets are still run in this way, the market master nowadays usually being a municipal employee.

**Fig. 3.8**  An organised market

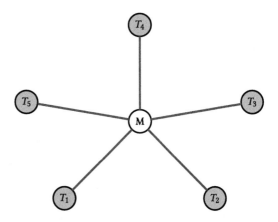

convener or maker with significant control of the trade that takes place and has the power to levy charges on other market participants. It is clear that a market is explicitly organised by the market maker in these cases and functions as an enterprise that is controlled by that market maker or convener.

Gilles et al. (2015) also discuss the implications of an open market structure. In that case the convener cannot reject the participation of a potential market participant. Examples of such open markets are much more difficult to identify, since a proper implementation of a centralised trade mechanism requires regulation by a convener. Therefore, open market structures usually attain the features of an unregulated, decentralised matching market, which is discussed next.

**Matching Markets**  A second form of commodity market is the *matching* or *two-sided market*, which essentially refers to a group of potential traders that gather to make trades. A matching market has an *open* architecture and any trading party can in principle gain access. There is no or very little regulation of such markets and trades are conducted according to general rules and regulations—usually imposed by general contract law. Therefore, matching markets are not organised and omit a convener or regulator.

Examples of such matching markets are medieval markets and fairs, flea markets and farmers' markets. There are relatively low barriers to participation in these markets and there are sufficiently low trading fees levied by a market master or organiser. In such markets, price information has to be gathered by the market participants without the aid of a central market auctioneer as a gatherer of such information. Other contemporary matching markets are the housing market and the schooling of children. In most contemporary matching markets, the traded commodities are indivisible and there is a limited supply of these commodities.

A matching market can be represented by a "bipartite" network of potential trade relations between all market participants on the demand and supply side in the market. Formally, a network is *bipartite* if there are two groups of economic

**Fig. 3.9** A network representation of a matching market

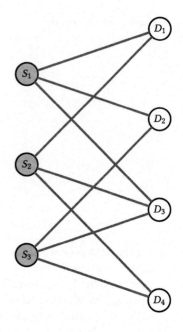

agents—say $A$ and $B$—and every economic relationship in the network is a bilateral economic interaction of one agent from group $A$ and one agent from group $B$. A bipartite network is *complete* if all agents in $A$ have a bilateral economic relationship with all agents in $B$. An example of such a network representation is depicted in Fig. 3.9.

In Fig. 3.9 a matching market is depicted as a bipartite network between a set of three suppliers (the $S$-nodes) and a set of three demanders (the $D$-nodes). The depicted network is "nearly complete" in the sense that only a few potential links between suppliers and demanders are not present in this network.

Organised and matching markets are prime examples of market*places*. Indeed, both markets forms refer to physical or virtual spaces in which people meet and trade. These two forms also represent the traditional markets that are studied in neo-classical economics. In fact, neo-classical market theories refer mostly to the organised market form and explicitly assume complete information exchange at a central level through some auctioneer.

**Provision Chain Markets** A rather different market design is the third organisational form in our relational approach, the *provision chain market*. This is a very common organisation type in our contemporary global economy and refers to the chains of trade relations between middlemen, one acting as a supplier and one acting as a demander in these relationships. The chain is terminated in a set of final consumers and originates in a set of basic input suppliers. I refer to the discussion of the production network for bread depicted in Fig. 3.3.

As discussed before, in Fig. 3.3, the basic input suppliers—or "sources"—are represented by the nodes representing the two farmers and the dairy producer. These raw inputs are processed by the intermediary producers, being the miller and the two bakers. The bakers produce the final consumption good, bread, which is sold to the consumers, who are the "sink" nodes in this representation.

There are four intermediary commodity markets in this product provision chain: (1) a wheat market between the two farmers and the miller; (2) a flour market between the miller and the two bakers; (3) a butter market between the dairy producer and the two bakers; and, finally, (4) a bread market between the two bakers and the four final consumers. In these intermediary commodity markets, the trading parties are in parity with each other. More complex supply chain networks are possible as well, in which suppliers of more basic inputs enter at a later stage in the supply chain.

It should be clear that the intermediary markets in this product provision network have the form of matching markets. Hence, the provision chain market is actually a chain of intermediate product markets that have the form of matching markets. I emphasise that these markets are linked and that the prices at which the intermediary products are traded in these matching markets are affected by prices emerging in the other markets in the chain. The product provision chain has to be viewed as a general framework that is composed of matching markets.

For a more elaborate and mathematical analysis of such chain markets I refer to the discussion and analysis of network economies in Chapters 5 and 6 in Gilles (2018).

### 3.3.4    A Network Perspective on the Laws of Demand and Supply

Mainstream, neo-classical economics is essentially founded on the introspection of two "forces" to explain the emergence and change of a market equilibrium price. The *Law of Demand* hypothesises that there is an inverse relationship between market demand and market price: the quantity demanded in the market decreases if and only if the market price increases. Thus, the Law of Demand refers to a fundamental market force that guides the demand decisions in relation to the market price. The Law of Demand has been used to explain phenomena in our economies innumerable times by economists and non-economists alike. For example, statements are made such as "the oil price goes up since worldwide demand for oil products increases owing to the growth of the Asian economies, in particular India and China".

The *Law of Supply* is the hypothesis that states there is a positive relationship between market supply and market price: the quantity supplied in the market decreases if and only if the market price decreases as well. Again the Law of

Supply refers to a fundamental force in the economy and is used in numerous ways to explain observed economic phenomena. For example, the oil price is increasing because market supply is sluggish in adapting to the higher levels of world demand for oil products.

Both the Laws of Demand and Supply play a central role in economic analysis and cannot be omitted. In this regard it is imperative to be able to formulate these laws in our relational framework as put forward here. I limit my discussion of these laws to the context of network models of markets only. Thus far, we have discussed three types of market forms in our relational framework of a socio-economic space. Besides the organised and matching market forms, I have also introduced the provision chain market form. In my subsequent discussion I limit myself to the Law of Demand rather than both the Laws of Demand and Supply. Indeed, the discussion of the Law of Demand transfers rather straightforwardly to the development of a Law of Supply based on dual principles.

**The Law of Demand in Organised Markets** First, I consider the Law of Demand primarily within the context of an organised market. This model of a star network centred around a market auctioneer or convener is the most fundamental network representation of the standard theoretical model of a competitive market. The Law of Demand here refers to the ability to either activate new trade relationships between demanders and the auctioneer or enlarge the traded quantities on existing trade relationships. These modifications occur in the context of a certain division of the gains from trade that are generated in those trade relationships, determined by the prevailing market price.

An increase of demand for the traded commodity is expressed here by the desire of more potential demanders to activate new trade relationships with the auctioneer and/or that existing demanders increase their requests for quantities of the commodity. The auctioneer cannot meet these demands and, thus, will undertake two actions. First, the auctioneer can discourage the demanders in their desire to activate new trade relationships with her or increase the quantities requested from her. This is done by increasing the share of the gains from trade that the demander has to relinquish in this trade relationship. Second, the auctioneer can attempt to attract more supply by encouraging potential suppliers to engage in trade relationships with her or to request existing suppliers to increase their supplied quantities. This in turn is done by increasing the share of the gains from trade that are transferred to these (potential) suppliers. Both of these actions from the auctioneer result in a market price increase that has to be paid by the demanders in this market.

From this discussion, it is clear that the Law of Demand is a dynamic aspect of the structural development and adjustments in a trade network. Here, it is particularly related to the use of prices by the market auctioneer to guide the extent of her demand and supply network. As such, the Law of Demand is a hypothesis concerning the dynamic development of the extent of the trade network of the auctioneer. Thus, the adjustment of the market price of a commodity is very much the outcome of a *visible hand* in that market, namely that of the market auctioneer.

In many organised markets the role of the market auctioneer is devolved to institutions that regulate the trade in that market. These could be rules on how to publicise the prices at which trades are contracted (stock exchanges) or algorithms to determine trade prices (eBay). In most cases, these institutional implementations of the auctioneering function lead to similar adjustments to those discussed above.

**The Law of Demand in Matching Markets**  On the other hand, if we turn to the second network market form, the matching market, the Law of Demand has a rather different formulation, since the trade relations are independent and direct between demanders and suppliers. The principle, however, remains the same: the mechanism that determines the division of the gains from trade in a relationship between a supplier and a demander is guided by the extent of the trade network as a whole. If demand increases, this is reflected in the attempts to form trade relationships by demanders for the commodity in question. This in turn triggers that suppliers have the opportunity to demand higher shares of the gains from trade that are generated. Thus, in general the prices charged for the commodity traded will increase over all trade relationships in the matching market network.

It should be emphasised here that the Law of Demand is and remains a *hypothesis* of how the gains from trade are distributed among trade partners in these networks. As such, the Law of Demand has the form of a behavioural assumption for the various traders in the network that has to be formulated mathematically in a certain way.

**The Law of Demand in Production Networks**  Finally, I consider the third network model of a market, the provision chain network. This is the most complex representation of a market, but also the most realistic. Here the Law of Demand has to be considered on the activated chains between the source supplier of a basic input and a final consumer. I emphasise that the Law of Demand concerns the activated trade chains and that as such the desires of the final consumers drive the activation of these supply chains.[16] In this regard the Law of Demand can be considered to be a hypothesis of how supply chains are activated in response to desires of demanders to obtain more units of the commodity under consideration.

So, if more consumers at the local Starbucks ask for café mochas, more cups of this brown beverage will be produced and the higher demand for ground coffee will be translated into higher demand for raw coffee beans. Ideally this would result in the activation of more supply chains or otherwise an increase in

---

[16] This activation could happen with a certain delay. Indeed, if there are fewer final consumers interested in obtaining units of a certain commodity provided through a supply chain there is naturally a lag before these supply chains are de-activated.

trade streams on the existing supply chains. The incentive mechanisms would normally require that higher rents are attributed to the various suppliers of basic inputs (the coffee bean farmers) and the middlemen (ADM, Starbucks and the like) that form these supply chains. This means that the price paid by the final consumers for their cup of café mocha will necessarily increase.

**Toward a Theory of Network-Based Markets** The details of the incentive mechanisms that embody the apparent "Law of Demand" in these three different market forms refer to the institutional framing of these markets. In the economics literature, there has been little attention given to the study of these complex processes.

I limit my discussion to that of the most realistic and complex market form, the provision chain network or the production network. The provision chain network allows for the application of multiple mathematical theories about how such incentive mechanisms can be implemented. This is at the moment a relatively unexplored part of economic theory, in particular owing to the complexity of such chained market networks. I refer to Spanjers (1997) for a pioneering theory of trade chains and auctioneering in such chained trade environments. The mathematical complexities of these structured markets are very significant, and at this moment there is no satisfactory solution to the mathematical modelling of such chained market networks.

This brings up an interesting question about how such production networks are regulated in the daily economic practice of trade and exchange. It is clear that these trade processes rely heavily on the dimension of time and the availability of monetary instruments of credit to bridge gaps in their resolution. Indeed, the distance between coffee bean farmer and the final consumer of café mochas is substantial, even in our highly networked global economy. Only the availability of debt can bridge this otherwise insurmountable divide.

**Globalisation** In the context of the notions of the Laws of Demand and Supply, it is useful to mention the issue of globalisation. This refers to the currently popular account that the application of markets as well as the opening of many developing economies to multinational corporations has generated opportunities for increased growth and the generation of economic wealth throughout the developing world.

Within our relational setting, the notion of globalisation can be understood from two different perspectives. First, globalisation could refer to the extension of the trade network to include more traders within the *same* socio-economic space. This implies that it is assumed that all participating economic agents have adopted and use the same governance system of media and institutions to establish communication and trade. As such, this could be understood as a form of *local* extension of trade networks. Examples are the development of new markets for existing products and/or firms, such as the building of more Wal-Mart supercenters in communities throughout certain regions of the USA or the construction of new outlet centres in the EU.

A second interpretation of globalisation seems to be more appropriate. This interpretation refers to the extension of the socio-economic space itself in which trade networks are formed. This is based on the addition of new economic agents to the original set $N$. This reflects the idea that more economic agents adopt the governance system of media and institutions that govern a specific socio-economic space. This seems to capture the idea of globalisation better, since it refers to developing Asian countries in particular adopting western economic standards and the opening of these economies to western business practices and corporations (Zakaria 2008).

## 3.4    THE ENTREPRENEURIAL FUNCTION

The schematic representation of a socio-economic space depicted in Fig. 3.1 includes the feedback process of economic agents on the prevailing institutions through entrepreneurship. As stated there, it is more precise to denote this feedback process as the *entrepreneurial function* in the socio-economic space. This entrepreneurial function can be executed in various forms, but the two main ones are individualistic and collective. In the first case we refer to individual "entrepreneurs", while the second form is rather neglected in the economics literature and should be denoted as "collective entrepreneurship".[17]

The entrepreneurial function primarily focuses on the activities developed within the infrastructural networks in the socio-economic space and/or the process of networking and the resulting network architecture itself. We can denote these two primary forms of entrepreneurship as Schumpeterian and Burtian. Schumpeterian entrepreneurship is activity-based and refers to developing innovative products or services, production processes and designs (Schumpeter 1934). Burtian entrepreneurship refers to the idea that smart networking can result in significant increases of social capital and successful exploitation of new markets and supply chains. These opportunities are also known as *structural holes*, which are a central concept in network analysis (Burt 1992). I refer to Chap. 5 for an elaborate discussion of entrepreneurship from Schumpeterian and Burtian perspectives.

Regardless whether the entrepreneurial function is initially Schumpeterian or Burtian in nature, *entrepreneurship can only be deemed successful if it actually affects the institutional governance system of the prevailing socio-economic space.* Indeed, any change in a product or service is only truly successful and deemed entrepreneurial if it results in a significant profit. This informs potential competitors of the innovative activity in question, which is copied, accepted and responded to. This, in effect, institutionalises the innovative activity, thereby changing the institutional fabric of the socio-economic space.

---

[17] These historical episodes of collective entrepreneurship are usually just viewed as part of a process of economic development. In our managerial economy, they can also be referred to as research and development processes.

Some of the most important historical examples of individual entrepreneurship are inventors such as James Watt (steam engine), Thomas Edison (electric appliances), Alexander Graham Bell (telephony) and Tim Berners-Lee (the World Wide Web). These entrepreneurs can all be categorised as "Schumpeterian". Through their innovations in products and production processes, each had a huge influence on how the economy itself functions. James Watt's improvements to the steam engine in the eighteenth century were at the foundation of the Victorian British economic rise and affected production processes throughout the economy; after the introduction of mechanisation of production and the building of a railway network there was no return to premodern labour intensive production technologies. Thomas Edison and Alexander Graham Bell are exponents of the rise of the consumer capitalist economy after the 1870s; their products fundamentally changed how we live. Finally, Tim Berners-Lee is an exponent of the recent computing revolution who made personal computing an integrated part of the global virtual network that we know now as the World Wide Web. For many this final advance in technology is the harbinger of the "Fourth Industrial Revolution".

A similar argument holds for Burtian entrepreneurship: successful networking and innovative supply chain design affects the institutional landscape as well. Indeed, these innovative networking practices and designs will be copied, assimilated and countered through competing networking activities. The effect is again that these innovations will be institutionalised and will be subsumed in the prevailing system of governance institutions.

A historical example of a Burtian entrepreneur is Steve Jobs, who introduced innovative ways to distribute and consume music through iTunes. He created cloud computing as a viable system and anchored consumers in closed computing delivery systems such as the iPad and the iPhone. This changed the institutional fabric of our contemporary global economy immeasurably, integrating it more fully with the emerging World Wide Web.

**Institutional Entrepreneurship** From the discussion above, our conclusion has to be that any successful entrepreneurial process is effectively institutional in nature. There are an extraordinarily large number of would-be entrepreneurs who can be deemed unsuccessful owing to their lack of impact on the institutions that govern our global economy. The entrepreneurial function is first and foremost institutional in nature and, as such, is a fundamental force in the evolution of a socio-economic space. Entrepreneurship should be judged at a higher standard than that of merely (successfully) managing some corporation.

Institutional entrepreneurship also acts as its own separate form of the entrepreneurial function in the global economy. In fact, it is quite common, since every aspiring politician is essentially an aspiring institutional entrepreneur. Again, many of them are not successful and have minimal impact; others have a tremendous influence on the functioning of the economy. Obvious examples of political institutional entrepreneurs are Napoleon Bonaparte and Margaret Thatcher, two controversial figures who influenced the economy in surprising and fundamental ways: Napoleon through the export of French enlightenment principles and regulatory law codes; Thatcher through the promotion of her neo-liberal ideology and policies.

Institutional entrepreneurship as an independent category is strangely neglected in economics and the social sciences. This is mainly because many political institutional entrepreneurs introduce changes to the governance system through non-economic channels; they do not head some corporation, but affect the institutions directly through political decision making. Non-political institutional entrepreneurs are more scarce, although the examples noted above had an immediate impact on the prevailing economic practices and institutions of their time.

**The Entrepreneurial Spirit: Risk, Uncertainty and Luck**  The entrepreneurial function is characterised by two important properties. First, entrepreneurship is subject to dealing with highly risky and uncertain processes. Knight (1921) already recognises that entrepreneurs have an extraordinary ability to deal with risk and uncertainty.[18] He even goes on to characterise an entrepreneur as an individual who can process and tolerate uncertainty beyond what "normal" individuals can cope with.

Modifying activities, network structures and institutions is subject to very high levels of uncertainty owing to the prevalence of unintended consequences to these modifications. Therefore, entrepreneurship has a significant failure rate. Only a very few lucky individuals have a straightforward ascent in the business rankings. Steve Jobs is well known for his multiple failures, including that of Apple Corp and his NeXT Corporation in the early 1990s (Isaacson 2011).

Closely related to the aspect of uncertainty is that entrepreneurial success is mainly based on *luck* (Alchian 1950). One has to be at the right place in the right time under the appropriate conditions to be successful and mitigate the related risks and uncertainties. Chance and luck therefore form an extraordinarily important factor in establishing successful entrepreneurship. One significant aspect in this context is the environment that results from the socio-economic space itself—in particular the prevailing socio-economic institutions in the governance system. This explains how individuals in different societies are more successful at innovation than others under objectively similar conditions. So, in the eighteenth century Britain was known for its extreme industrial innovation, while in the twentieth century the USA had taken over as the most entrepreneurial nation in the world. Both phenomena can be attributed to the prevailing institutions and cultural aspects in these nation-states in those two different historical eras.

---

[18] The fundamental difference between risk and uncertainty is that risk can be assessed through statistical methods (in particular it is subject to a probability distribution), while uncertainty is also known as unmeasurable risk and cannot be assessed through these methodologies. Uncertainty is usually assessed purely subjectively. Knight argues that entrepreneurship required the ability to handle uncertainty quite well, while risk could be assessed through designing and implementing appropriate managerial contingencies.

Although I refer above to individual entrepreneurs only, Alchian (1950) points out that in general collective entrepreneurship is also subject to the same aspects of risk, uncertainty and luck. Indeed, "Silicon Valley" as a collective entrepreneurial hub evolved in California owing to its prevailing institutional setting and the collective spirit of entrepreneurship in the information technology industry at the end of the twentieth century. This collectively brought about a "can-do" attitude that countered the inherent uncertainty of the rapidly evolving industry.

**Is Entrepreneurship Always a Force for "Good"?**   It is natural to assume that entrepreneurship refers to positive socio-economic innovation, which increases wealth creation and enhances people's lives. However, that is not necessarily the case. Entrepreneurship also refers to innovation that decreases the functionality of the socio-economic space. In these cases it refers to institutional changes that might even be detrimental to wealth creation or undermine the cohesion of socio-economic space.

Furthermore, it should be pointed out that every entrepreneurial innovation in itself is actually good as well as bad. Indeed, change itself causes certain parties in the socio-economic space to suffer losses. For example, the collapse of the guilds at the conclusion of the premodern era introduced "free" labour markets into the economies of that time (Epstein 1991). This was one of the most important factors for the emergence of the capitalist economy during the industrial revolution. The collapse of professional guilds resulted in the vanishing of many artisan professions and their replacement by industrial production methods. This resulted in a very significant growth of economic wealth, but it had a direct impact on these artisans themselves. They lost control of the production networks in the premodern economies, resulting in financial losses and bankruptcies. A formal analysis of this point was developed in Gilles and Diamantaras (2003).

Recent examples illustrate exactly the opposite. The introduction of financial derivatives in the decade prior to 2007 enhanced the portfolio of tradable goods, which in itself is a good thing. However, it allowed the rise of the ability to exploit owing to the complexity of these innovative products, ultimately even resulting in a rise in financial corruption that undermined the overall functionality of the global economy.

### 3.4.1    Individual Entrepreneurship

Individual entrepreneurs have been explored in the economics literature quite exhaustively. Many theories of entrepreneurship that centre on individualistic industrial leadership have been developed. I have already touched upon the most important ones. I will also mention the theory put forward by Shackle (1979), who assesses entrepreneurs as individuals with extraordinary abilities to imagine possible futures resulting from their choices, thus being able to overcome inherent uncertainty. In some sense these imaginative individuals make their own luck.

I argue here that these theories neglect the institutional environment—the socio-economic space itself—as a determining factor of how we deal with uncertainty and how we imagine possible futures. The institutional perspective is that the entrepreneurial function is central to economic development and the evolution of the institutions themselves.

Individual decision-makers have a central position in this process, but always in the context of a cooperative setting. There are always collaborators, customers and suppliers. That is also clear from the descriptions of successful individual entrepreneurs such as James Watt, Bill Gates and Steve Jobs. An exceptional case of institutional entrepreneurship is that of Gaius Octavius, also known as Augustus, who initiated extraordinary institutional entrepreneurial innovation in government organisations and Roman cultural practices to create one of the most successful economies of all time, the *Roman Empire*.

### Case: Augustus, the First Emperor of Rome

Gaius Octavius (63 BCE–14 CE) can be categorised as one of the most extraordinary institutional entrepreneurs in human history. He took the Roman Republic, which was in a state of complete collapse and bankruptcy, and transformed it through revolutionary innovation into an extremely economically successful state, known as the *Pax Augusta*, and provided the foundation for the emergence of the Roman Empire, which lasted half a millennium.[19]

Gaius Octavius also combined the standard traits of an individual entrepreneur, namely combining particular skills to deal with highly risky situations, to be tremendously lucky, to be extremely ruthless, and—despite this ruthlessness—to have the right temperament to build deep trust relationships with a large number of people. At multiple times in his career, his existence was under direct threat and illness may have shortened his life. However, his luck was that he survived these episodes and continued to build his career and empire. In the end he was able to forge an extremely stable organisation of the empire that secured economic prosperity for several centuries after his death, even though his successors ranged from lazy and incompetent to cruel. He laid the foundation for the apogee of the Roman Empire and economy during the second century CE.

Everitt (2006) and Goldsworthy (2014) provide a detailed account of the exploits of the young Gaius Octavius. He was born into the decaying world of the Roman Republic, which was constituted on the precarious balance of two classes in society: the ruling aristocracy and the underclass of the working poor, the plebeians—or "plebs". The republican society and economy was ripped apart by a nearly permanent state of civil war in the first century BCE. The war raged between opposing factions—the "optimates" and the "populares"—in the ruling aristocratic elite of Rome. The populares built their political power on their appeal to the plebs directly, while the optimates tried to continue the elitist

---

[19] The Roman Empire actually continued in the east as the Byzantine Empire for another millennium after that.

rule of the aristocracy. Actually, these factions were quite fluid, with shifting alliances and ever-continuing strife. Julius Caesar tried to settle the disputes, but was unsuccessful and was assassinated in 44 BCE by a coalition of foes and allies, having lost the trust of many in the ruling elite.

As his nephew, Gaius Octavius inherited the wealth as well as Caesar's obligations, as Caesar adopted him posthumously as his son. This adoption allowed him to change his name to Gaius Julius Caesar Octavianus—or Octavian as modern historians refer to him. This formed the foundation for a political career at the top of the Roman world. After a further decade of constant civil war, Octavian was able to settle the disputes by defeating his foes in 30 BCE and being "the last man standing".

Octavian built a new governmental institutional system through two *constitutional settlements*, in 27 and 23 BCE. The resulting settlement was renewed several times after 18 BCE and has been known as the *Principate*.[20] Before 27 BCE, Octavian combined a variety of republican institutional positions, most importantly those of consul and tribune. In the constitutional settlement a new position of *Princeps* was created, which combined traditional republican powers corresponding to these positions in a single person. Hence, the republican traditions were not abolished, but amended; the Princeps was not a king, but rather a republican constitutional role. Octavian received the honorary name *Augustus* ("the venerable one") in 27 BCE.

Augustus enhanced institutional trust by avoiding the formal abolishment of the republican institutions, since these were viewed to be at the core of Roman culture and tradition; these institutions represented "being Roman". Instead, he created new institutions that de facto ended the Roman Republican constitution, but retained its spirit and traditions. This system of the Principate embodied a major institutional innovation in the Roman society and economy. It resulted in a very stable and economically wealthy period in the history of the Roman Empire, culminating in the second century CE under the Antonines.

Augustus founded his Principate on an extensive set of institutional innovations, described by Everitt (2006), Eck (2007) and Levick (2010). I look only at differences between the rule of Caesar and Augustus to see how the latter modified institutions concerning the use of finance, the elections of the Senate, the structure of the judiciary and social legislation:

**Public finance:**    Although Caesar feigned that the Senate had autonomy over control of the Roman finances, he was able to render the Senate powerless in 49 BCE. During this time, Caesar broke into the *Aerarium*—the State

---

[20] The period of the Principate ended with the assumption of the title "Dominus" by the emperor Diocletian in 284 CE, introducing the *Dominate* era of the Roman Empire. During the Principate the Roman Republican constitution was formally upheld, but with Diocletian this was formally abolished, together with republican institutions such as the Consulate and the Senate. The Dominate was a system that focused on the supremacy of the Dominus as the sole ruler of the Empire, making it a purely autocratic system of government.

Treasury—and commandeered it for his own financial needs to conduct and perpetuate a civil war. For the first time, "a Caesar" was richer than Rome itself. He also put his own slaves in charge of the mint and the tax system as opposed to members of the Senate, as tradition prescribed.

On the contrary, Augustus publicised widely that he had four times replenished the *Aerarium* with his own personal wealth. Under the reforms of 27 BCE, Augustus not only handed back provinces and armies, but also sources of revenue to the control of the Senate. Shortages of funds weakened the *Aerarium*, affecting the Senate's ability to act and empower its agents. Augustus felt that an economy's finance should always come first. Decentralised control of state funds and the vast private wealth of Augustus which was used for the state's benefit won the confidence and trust of the troops and the plebs of Rome.

**The Senate:**    Caesar not only controlled the *Aerarium*, distributing funds as he chose, but he also promoted men at will, helping them to lucrative and prestigious positions, or alternatively blocked their way or even exiled them from the Republic altogether when they seemed minded to potentially oppose him.

Caesar's "prefecture of morals" enabled him to determine whether men should take part in the Senate and as provincial governors or not. The Senate was purged of uncooperative aristocrats, but Caesar was accused of unjustly bringing in new citizens—even Gauls—to replace known provincial senators. The system became so corrupt owing to Caesar's actions that there was no rationale for any serious participants in politics to join the system and the Senate.

Augustus was more subtle in maintaining his power, doing so in a more trustworthy fashion. He coped with the Senate's membership by implementing the *Lex Saenia* in 30 BCE. This regulated the *adlection* of plebeians to the patriciate and the Senate.[21] Specifically, it also gave Augustus a way to create new patricians and appoint them to priesthoods, which was required at the time by the republican tradition of the *Lex Saenia*.

Augustus refused the "curatorship of morals" that would have given him the same powers as Caesar's prefecture, that is, the ability to add and remove members of the Senate at will in a tyrannical fashion. Augustus also renounced the direct methods that Julius Caesar had used to ensure that his favoured candidates reached the highest office, instead bringing back the republican free-for-all elections. There was, however, an inconvenience that came with free-for-all elections when they did not specifically favour Augustus's interests. He circumvented this by canvassing and promoting

---

[21] Definition: those chosen to fill a vacancy in any office or collegium.

his favoured candidates.[22] Indeed, he did not directly give these candidates membership to the Senate, but would indirectly do so by promoting them, indicating to voters and other members that the candidates were supported by him. The personal weight and prestige of Augustus therefore naturally gave him control of large parts of Rome's government. Subsequently, one routinely talks about Augustus "giving" the consulship to a certain candidate. By 14 CE it became expected to thank the Princeps for the post. Bribery was a perpetual fact in Roman politics. The plebs were bribed not only to demonstrate, but also to vote for specific candidates. Augustus attempted to reduce this by introducing a law against bribery, which he passed in 18–17 BCE. Although this attempted to build foundations of trust among candidates and members of the Senate, it was not necessarily followed by Augustus himself. Indeed, in 8 BCE Augustus bribed members of two voting tribes so that they themselves would not be influenced by any other bribes from other members of the Senate. It is not known how long this went on for, although it is assumed that it was continuous.

**Judiciary:**    The last century of the Republic saw the establishment of jury courts, presided over by a *praetor*, for the trial of defined offences such as misconduct and the extortion of senatorial officials in the provinces. At the time the law determined the penalties and the jury was only allowed to decide whether the defendant was guilty or innocent. The make-up of the juries were always a source of controversy and changed with every swing of power. Augustus was given special power of appeal in 30 BCE in order to judge all legal disputes in the Empire, as well as a deciding vote in the case of a tie. Moreover, Augustus continued to exercise his *imperium* in deciding the fates of dependent monarchs and tribal leaders. Therefore, he was as tyrannical in the judiciary as his predecessors in the Roman Republic had been. However, in the settlement of 28–27 BCE the rights of magistrates and judges were restored and Augustus began to take less of a role.

**Civil society:**    Augustus issued a raft of legal reforms regarding how plebs could act. Specifically, he imposed laws that would exile people for adultery by men with married woman, he penalised celibacy, regulated marriage between the two orders, and forbade the intermarriage of those of senatorial rank with persons of servile origin or ill repute. The legislation regarding marriage and inheritance helped to keep wealth within families by encouraging the propertied classes to raise true heirs and put off legacy hunters.

Under Roman law, the more heirs a man had the less could be passed down to each individual heir. This led to a decline in birth rates in the aristocratic senatorial class. This was in Augustus's favour, since fewer potential rivals would be born. On the other hand, the rule on inheritance and his promotion of in-

---

[22] There was no evidence that Augustus would have the right to deny any man's candidature for office. Nor did he take over any running of elections from the magistrate whose function it was at any time.

class marriages meant that a well-structured social and economic hierarchy was formed within the Roman Empire. This strengthened his position. These changes were also part of spreading a sense of well-being throughout society. Although this legislation regulated the conduct of Roman citizens concerning their sexual affairs, both the legislation and the assumption of patronage were part of a tightening of control after the political crisis of 19 BCE. Indeed, it is unlikely that Augustus was obsessed with sexual reform but more with class stability and decorum.

Augustus promoted orderliness; this was seen in the form of new ranks, new posts, new voting centuries[23] and new privileges. People were physically segregated by class in public spaces such as the baths and the theatres to stop mingling between the classes. These purity laws gave the upper classes reassurance regarding the stability of their position in civil society.[24]

**The "Cult of Augustus":**    The first Princeps introduced an ideology based on paternalistic and conservative values. In this ideology the Princeps was presented as the very incarnation of all virtues attributed to an ideal ruler, in particular the virtues of clemency and justice. This required the Princeps to play this designated role within Roman society, as his political insurance as well as a moral duty. The Princeps had to find a balance between the demands of the people and the requirements of these imposed conservative values: distribution of subsidised grain for Romans on the dole and the organisation of lavish games was offset by displays of frugality and the fulfilment of religious duties.

This was reinforced with building a cult around the personality of the Princeps. His statues and public works were everywhere and the Roman citizens were always in his "presence". Furthermore, Augustus was always depicted as a vibrant, young man rather than the aged ruler he became after assuming sole leadership in the empire; Augustus was eternally youthful.

I consider Augustus to be the most convincing historical example of an institutional entrepreneur, who affected the functioning of the global Roman economy in a profound way. He fully embodied the abilities of a Schumpeterian as well as a Burtian entrepreneur. His Principate settled the Roman Empire in the *Pax Augusta* for several centuries and allowed the Roman economy to develop successfully and fruitfully (Temin 2012).

---

[23] A voting century refers to a class of eligible Roman citizens that are allowed to participate in the republican voting system. A century was based on ancient tribal heritage, but was expanded over time to include more and more new classes of (new) citizens.

[24] Surprisingly, not much upheaval has been recorded. These laws were intrusive and restricted freedom. It is not clear why there was no more resistance. It could be that the large emphasis on sport and games in the circus and amphitheatres was leveraged in order to show Augustus to be a benevolent ruler of the Roman population.

### 3.4.2    *Collective Entrepreneurship*

My interpretation of the entrepreneurial function in the context of a socio-economic space as set out here brings together many of the elements discussed above in a comprehensive vision. Individual entrepreneurship is only one possible state of this process of socio-economic institutional renewal and development. Collective entrepreneurship is at least as important, even though much more persistent, continuous and resilient a force for change.

Collective entrepreneurship shares many characteristics with individual entrepreneurship. First, it only emerges strongly in an environment that is conducive to an innovative spirit. Thus, the institutions that make up the governance system in a socio-economic space support a spirit of free-thinking, innovation, risk-taking and taking opportunities that are presented.

Second, collective entrepreneurship builds upon diversity in a community of sufficient critical mass and size. The diversity refers to the make-up of the population represented in the community, in particular the variety of experiences and the ability to draw upon a variety of ideas. The experience of highly functioning entrepreneurial communities such as Silicon Valley is that these are drawing heavily on a wide range of sources and experiences. These feed into a communal spirit of empowered and self-guided individuals who recognise the value of these experiences.

Third, collective entrepreneurship is subject to high risk, uncertainty and luck—as is the case in similar measure for individual entrepreneurship. People in a community have to take on the high risk and uncertainty as well as take advantage of any opportunity that presents itself. Luck therefore plays an important role in the innovation process that is triggered by collective entrepreneurial activities.

Fourth, collective entrepreneurship has to have a lasting institutional impact to be fully effective and to lead to increased economic wealth. This is similar to individual entrepreneurship. However, collective entrepreneurial activities focus more directly on institutional innovation, since they usually combine many facets of economic life and the social division of labour; innovation of commodities and products as well as networking have a larger and more immediate impact on the institutional fabric of the society in which these changes take place.

Collective entrepreneurship is more permanent and important a force of institutional innovation in a socio-economic space than individual entrepreneurship. Individual entrepreneurs need to develop a very comprehensive and deep impact to trigger permanent changes to the institutional structure underlying the socio-economic space. This is illustrated by the case of Augustus, who would have failed without his extraordinary luck of survival. However, collective entrepreneurship is usually more gradual and longer lasting.

Fifth, collective entrepreneurship is a permanent force that is a normal part of any socio-economic space as its *entrepreneurial function*. Clearly, the entrepreneurial function is subject to waves of innovation and change: longer periods of relatively minor and steady development are interrupted by bursts of extreme innovation. These bursts are accompanied by financial and economic crises or trigger shortly after a financial and economic crisis, as was the case in 1873, 1929, 2000 and 2008. In this regard the entrepreneurial function exhibits the features of an evolutionary process with *punctuated equilibria*.

These aspects of collective entrepreneurship are illustrated by the historical case of the economic rise of Amsterdam as a trading hub in the fifteenth and sixteenth centuries. During this period the economy of Amsterdam went through multiple transformations, from a small fishing village to a religious centre and, ultimately, to a global trade hub. This case has been exhaustively described and analysed in Mak (1994) and Shorto (2013).

*Case: The Rise of Amsterdam as a Global Trade Hub*
Amsterdam emerged as a village that was gathered around a dam on the river Amstel in the marshlands of Holland in about 1200. From the onset, this village emerged in an institutional environment that was conducive to entrepreneurship and self-determination. The farmers that made up the population were engaged upon a constant struggle to make a living in the surrounding marshlands. In particular, they attempted to manage these marshlands through the building of water-regulating infrastructure such as canals and dams. The struggle developed a spirit of self-determination in the population as they addressed these essential problems. This is exemplified by the fact that Amsterdam emerged at a human-made dam in the Amstel river that was part of the water management of the marshlands.

Second, the prevalence of the marshlands prevented the authorities from exercising strict control, as was normal in other parts of western Europe at that time. The lack of direct oversight and strict suppression enhanced a spirit of self-control and communal reliability.

A religious miracle in Amsterdam in 1345 made the town a place of pilgrimage. This, in turn, brought about an enormous influx of visitors and immigrants, thus increasing the population to a critical and diverse mass.[25] The town experienced a second surge in its population after Emperor Maximilian of Austria experienced a miracle cure there in 1489. The street names in the city centre still remind visitors of the religious origins of this initial stage of economic development.

The growing city expanded into the marshland surrounding it through a system of canals that dealt with the ever-present water and dried the marsh. The city also became much more wealthy through the influx of wealthy religious patrons and the building of convents and parish churches to accommodate them. Thus, a sufficiently large and diverse foundation was created for the next step of economic development through collective entrepreneurial innovation.

---

[25] The miracle itself was rather trivial from a modern perspective. The host given to a dying man in the sacrament of Holy Communion remained unburnt after it was thrown in a hearth fire. For a full account I refer to Shorto (2013, pp. 30–31).

**First Stage of Economic Development**  The main collective entrepreneurial activity concerned a major development in the fishing industry that was based there. Herring fishing has been part of the food supply chain in Holland, and northern Europe in general, since ancient times. The herring were caught, hauled ashore, gutted and preserved in barrels with brine. The results were acceptable, but the preserved fish was no delicacy and could only be kept for a limited period.

In the fourteenth century, however, anonymous Dutch fishermen introduced a major innovation in the treatment of herring, which transformed the industry and indirectly Europe as a whole. This innovation was a minute change in how to gut the fish: instead of cleaning the herring completely, one preserves little pouches in the stomach of the fish that contain certain enzymes. This modified cleaning process is known as *gibbing*. Putting the fish—including these enzymes—in brine improves the flavour of the fish and extends its preservation time.

The Dutch fishing industry gained an advantage over its competitors, and demand for Dutch herring increased owing to these improved properties. This required the Dutch fishermen to go further out on the North Sea to the so-called Dogger Bank to increase their haul. The introduction of innovative means of production was required for this to take place, and in 1416 the Dutch introduced long boats with bulging sides and a large hold. The gibbing could now take place during the fishing trip itself, increasing even further the efficiency of these production processes. Dutch fishing vessels could now stay out for weeks at a time, preserving the gibbed herring in brine during the trip. The barrels of herring were ready for consumption when they were hauled ashore.

**The Second Phase of Economic Development**  The transformation of the fishing industry had major consequences for Amsterdam. First, it required very significant cooperative support from the community and resulted in a very advanced social division of labour based on a variety of socio-economic roles. Amsterdam thus became the centre of an industrial complex that included ship-building, saw-milling, netting, processing and sale of the herring. These industries were each subject to entrepreneurial innovation owing to the prevailing spirit in Dutch society. For example, Dutch saw-milling became a world leader in high quality processed wood for ship-building for centuries.

Two further developments followed quickly. Based on the wealth generated—thanks to 200 million herring being caught each year—Amsterdam became a financial centre to support these industrial activities and expansions into other industries. The ability to build financial asset portfolios and to spread risk resulted in the ability for the Dutch East Indian Company (VOC) to support very risky ventures in the seventeenth century.[26] By that time the very first stock exchange had been established in Amsterdam.

Second, the Dutch were able to diversify into different trade streams. Herring runs initially often resulted in the return of empty vessels, but return trips were used to trade rye and wheat from the northern European ports to the southern European ports and vice versa, with products such as wine. Consequently, the Dutch merchants monopolised the Baltic trade and discovered the high quality of the available rapeseed, hempseed and potash for soap production. This introduced yet another industry, one based on "green soap", which became famous throughout Renaissance Europe.

By about 1500 Amsterdam was a powerhouse shipping centre as well as a religious pilgrim destination. This lay the foundation for the Dutch *Golden Age* in the seventeenth century, when Holland became a global trade nation and the first economic superpower or "hegemon" (Wallerstein 2011a,b).

The collective entrepreneurial force for economic development illustrated by the case of Amsterdam was successful mainly thanks to its impact on the way that business was conducted and how opportunities were exploited. These point to major institutional innovations that changed the face of Dutch society and of Europe in general.

## REFERENCES

Acemoglu, D., V. M. Carvalho, A. Ozdaglar, and A. Tahbaz-Salehi. 2012. The Network Origins of Aggregate Fluctuations. *Econometrica* 80: 1977–2016.

Aghion, P., and J. Tirole. 1997. Formal and Real Authority in Organizations. *Journal of Political Economy* 105: 1–29.

Albanese, J. 2011. Neanderthal Speech. *Totem: The University of Western Ontario Journal of Anthropology Totem: The University of Western Ontario Journal of Anthropology Totem: The University of Western Ontario Journal of Anthropology Totem: The University of Western Ontario Journal of Anthropology* 1(1): 99–105.

Alchian, A.A. 1950. Uncertainty, evolution, and economic theory. *Journal of Political Economy* 58: 211–221.

Aristotle (340 BCE). *Ethica Nicomachea*. 2009 ed. Oxford: Oxford University Press.

Aristotle (350 BCE). *The Politics: A Treatise on Government*. 1995 ed. Oxford: Oxford University Press.

Babbage, C. 1835. *On the Economy of Machinery and Manufacturers*. 4th enlarged ed. London: Augustus M. Kelley Publishers.

Barabási, A.-L. 2016. *Network Science*. Cambridge: Cambridge University Press.

Bowles, S., and J.-K. Choi. 2013. Coevolution of Farming and Private Property During the Early Holocene. *Proceedings of the National Academy of Sciences* 110: 8830–8835.

---

[26] The Vereenigde Oost-Indische Companie was established as a joint venture of merchants in Amsterdam to finance expeditions to the East Indies. They were able to establish profitable trade routes to these regions for the trade of spices and other goods. The success of the VOC resulted in the creation of a global trade network that was governed from Amsterdam.

Bowles, S., and J.-K. Choi. 2016. The Neolithic Agricultural Revolution. SFI Working Paper 2016-09-016, Santa Fe Institute.

Brin, S., and L. Page. 1998. The Anatomy of a Large-Scale Hypertext Web Search Engine. *Computer Networks* 30: 107–117.

Burt, R.S. 1992. *Structural Holes: The Social Structure of Competition.* Cambridge, MA: Harvard University Press.

Campbell, B.M.S. 2016. *The Great Transition: Climate, Disease and Society in the Late-Medieval World.* Cambridge: Cambridge University Press.

Carvalho, V.M. 2014. From Micro to Macro via Production Networks. *Journal of Economic Perspectives* 28: 23–48.

Coase, R.H. 1937. The Nature of the Firm. *Economica* 4: 386–405.

Dediu, D., and S.C. Levinson. 2013. On the Antiquity of Language: The Reinterpretation of Neandertal Linguistic Capacities and Its Consequences. *Frontiers in Psychology* 4(397). https://doi.org/10.3389/fpsyg.2013.00397.

Dessein, W. 2013. Incomplete contracts and firm boundaries: New directions. *The Journal of Law, Economics, & Organization,* 30 (suppl 1): i13–i36.

Easley, D., and J. Kleinberg. 2010. *Networks, Crowds and Markets: Reasoning about a Highly Connected World.* Cambridge: Cambridge University Press.

Eck, W. 2007. *The Age of Augustus.* Oxford: Blackwell Publishing.

Epstein, S.A. 1991. *Wage Labor and Guilds in Medieval Europe.* 2006 reissue ed. Raleigh, NC: University of North Carolina Press.

Evans, D.S. 2003. Some Empirical Aspects of Multi-sided Platform Industries. *Review of Network Economics* 2(3): 191–209.

Evans, D.S., and R. Schmalensee. 2013. The Antitrust Analysis of Multi-Sided Platform Businesses. NBER Working Paper 18783.

Everitt, A. 2006. *Augustus: The Life of Rome's First Emperor.* London: Random House.

Foley, D.K. 2010. What's Wrong with the Fundamental Existence and Welfare Theorems? *Journal of Economic Behavior & Organization,* 75: 115–131.

Gilles, R.P. 2018. *Economic Wealth Creation and the Social Division of Labour Volume II: Network Economies.* London: Palgrave Macmillan.

Gilles, R.P., and D. Diamantaras. 2003. To Trade or Not to Trade: Economies With a Variable Number of Tradeables. *International Economic Review* 44: 1173–1204.

Gilles, R.P., E.A. Lazarova, and P.H.M. Ruys. 2015. Stability in a Network Economy: The Role of Institutions. *Journal of Economic Behavior and Organization* 119: 375–399.

Goldsworthy, A. 2014. *Augustus: From Revolutionary to Emperor.* London: Weidenfeld & Nicolson.

Graeber, D. 2011. *Debt: The First 5,000 Years.* Brooklyn, NY: Melville House Publishing.

Grossman, H., and O.D. Hart. 1983. An Analysis of the Principal-Agent Problem. *Econometrica* 51: 7–45.

Hagiu, A., and J. Wright. 2011. Multi-Sided Platforms. Harvard Business School Working Paper 12–024.

Hart, O.D., and J. Moore. 1990. Property Rights and the Nature of the Firm. *Journal of Political Economy* 98: 1119–1158.

Hart, O.D., and J. Moore. 1999. Foundations of Incomplete Contracts. *Review of Economic Studies,* 66: 115–138.

Hudson, M. 1994. Land Monopolization, Fiscal Crises and Clean Slate 'Jubilee' Proclamations in Antiquity. In *A Philosophy for a Fair Society*, ed. M. Hudson, G.J. Miller, and C. Feder, 33–79. London: Shepheard-Walwyn.

Hudson, M. 2002. Reconstructing the Origins of Interest-Bearing Debt and the Logic of Clean Slates. In *Debt and Economic Renewal in the Ancient Near East*, ed. M. Hudson, and M. van de Mieroop. Bethesda: CDL Press.

Huremovic, K., and F. Vega-Redondo. 2016. Production Networks. HAL Working Paper 01370725.

Isaacson, W. 2011. *Steve Jobs: The Exclusive Biography*. London: Little, Brown Publishers.

Jackson, M.O. 2008. *Social and Economic Networks*. Princeton, NJ: Princeton University Press.

Johnson, N., G. Zhao, E. Hunsader, H. Qi, N. Johnson, J. Meng, and B. Tivnan. 2013. Abrupt Rise of New Machine Ecology Beyond Human Response Time. *Scientific Reports* 3: 2627.

Knight, F.H. 1921. *Risk, Uncertainty and Profit*. Boston, MA: Houghton Mifflin.

Lancaster, K.J. 1966. A New Approach to Consumer Theory. *Journal of Political Economy* 74: 132–157.

Levick, B. 2010. *Augustus: Image and Substance*. London: Pearson Education Ltd.

Mak, G. 1994. *Amsterdam: A Brief Life of the City*. Amsterdam: Olympus.

Marx, K. 1867. *Capital: A Critique of Political Economy — Volume I: The Process of Production of Capital*. 1967 ed. New York, NY: International Publishers.

Mas-Colell, A., M. Whinston, and J. Green. 1995. *Microeconomic Theory*. Oxford: Oxford University Press.

Mazzucato, M. 2014. *The Entrepreneurial State: Debunking Public vs. Private Sector Myths*. London: Anthem Press.

Newman, M.E.J. 2010. *Networks: An Introduction*. Oxford: Oxford University Press.

Ogilvie, S. 2014. The Economics of Guilds. *Journal of Economic Perspectives* 28: 169–192.

Pareto, V. 1906. *Manual of Political Economy*. 1972 Reprint ed. London: Macmillan Press.

Piccione, M., and A. Rubinstein. 2007. Equilibrium in the Jungle. *Economic Journal* 117: 883–896.

Piketty, T. 2014. *Capital in the Twenty-First Century*. Boston, MA: Harvard University Press.

Plato (380 BCE). *Republic*. 2007 ed. London: Penguin Classics.

Ricketts, M. 2003. *The Economics of Business Enterprise: An Introduction to Economic Organisation and the Theory of the Firm*. 3rd ed. London: Edward Elgar Publishing Ltd.

Rochet, J.-C., and J. Tirole. 2003. Platform Competition in Two-Sided Markets. *Journal of European Economic Association* 1(4): 990–1029.

Rosenbaum, E.F. 2000. What Is a Market? On the Methodology of a Contested Concept. *Review of Social Economy* 58(4): 455–482.

Rubinstein, A. 2012. *Economic Fables*. New York, NY: Open Book Publishers.

Sargent, T.J., and F.R. Velde. 2002. *The Big Problem of Small Change*. Princeton, NJ: Princeton University Press.

Schumpeter, J. 1934. *The Theory of Economic Development: An Inquiry into Profits, Capital, Credit, Interest and the Business Cycle*. Cambridge, MA: Harvard University Press.

Shackle, G.L.S. 1979. *Imagination and the Nature of Choice*. Edinburgh: University of Edinburgh Press.

Shapley, L.S., and H. Scarf. 1974. On Cores and Indivisibility. *Journal of Mathematical Economics* 1: 23–37.

Shorto, R. 2013. *Amsterdam: A History of the World's Most Liberal City*. New York, NY: Doubleday.

Spanjers, W. 1997. *Hierarchically Structured Exchange Economies: Models with Bilateral Exchange Institutions*. Boston, MA: Kluwer Academic Publishers.

Stiglitz, J.E. 2011. Of the 1%, by the 1%, for the 1%. *Vanity Fair*.

Stiglitz, J.E. 2013. *The Price of Inequality*. London: Penguin.

Temin, P. 2006. The Economy of the Early Roman Empire. *Journal of Economic Perspectives* 20(1): 133–151.

Temin, P. 2012. *The Roman Market Economy*. Princeton, NJ: Princeton University Press.

van den Brink, R., and R.P. Gilles. 1994. A Social Power Index for Hierarchically Structured Populations of Economic Agents. In *Imperfections and Behavior in Economic Organizations*, ed. R.P. Gilles and P.H.M. Ruys. Theory and Decision Library, chap. 12, 279–318. Boston, MA: Kluwer Academic Publishers.

van den Brink, R., and R.P. Gilles. 2000. Measuring Domination in Directed Networks. *Social Networks* 22: 141–157.

van den Brink, R., and R.P. Gilles. 2016. Explicit and Latent Authority in Hierarchical Organizations. Working Paper, Queen's Management School, Queen's University Belfast.

Vignes, A. 1993. Dispersion de prix et marchés décentralisés: le cas du marché au poisson de Marseille. Ph.D. thesis, European University Institute, Florence.

Vignes, A., and J.-M. Etienne. 2011. Price Formation on the Marseille Fish Market: Evidence from a Network Analysis. *Journal of Economic Behavior and Organization* 80: 50–67.

Wallerstein, I. 2011a. *The Modern World-System I: Capitalist Agriculture and the Origins of the European World-Economy in the Sixteenth Century*, vol. 1, Reprint edn. Berkeley, CA: University of California Press.

Wallerstein, I. 2011b. *The Modern World-System II: Capitalism and the Consolidation of the European World-Economy, 1600–1750*, vol. 2, Reprint edn. Berkeley, CA: University of California Press.

Zakaria, F. 2008. *The Post-American World*. New York, NY: W.W. Norton & Co.

# CHAPTER 4

# Economic Relationships and Trust

Since the Great Panic of 2008 descended upon the global economy, trust—mainly the lack thereof—has been on the mind of many people. Many economists now recognise that the nature of socio-economic trust is a neglected part of economic theory. There is an urgent need to clarify this crucial aspect of our global economy and to understand it better. However, thus far little has been gained in our understanding of this complex issue.

Economists have mainly focused on the study of trust at the level of individual decision-making and behaviour. As such, the study of trust is firmly founded in the setting of non-cooperative game theory and behavioural economics. The latter aims to explain the observed behaviour in economic and game theoretic experiments. There are numerous "trust games" investigated in this literature (Berg et al. 1995; Glaeser et al. 2000; James 2002). The perspective that is promoted in this literature is firmly founded on the hypothesis of methodological individualism: trust is a trait of individual, rational decision-making in a social environment. This limits the scope of this theory significantly, making it less significant for the study of the role of trust in wealth creation processes in a social division of labour.

There are only relatively few economists who have attempted to understand the role of trust and trustworthiness in the context of the social division of labour. Seabright (2010) studies the general principles of economic wealth creation and dedicates his complete monograph to understanding trust, since he realises that it is indeed central to understanding the nature of human interaction in general and of capitalist economic development in particular—as he states in his introduction. Seabright's central theme is that *Homo sapiens* somehow learned to trust strangers and was able to develop a very complex, structured economy that is able to achieve very high levels of wealth by accessing increasing returns to specialisation. Thus, only by trusting strangers outside one's kin group is one able to build and maintain a complex society that achieves high levels of economic wealth.

© The Author(s) 2018
R. P. Gilles, *Economic Wealth Creation and the Social Division of Labour*,
https://doi.org/10.1007/978-3-319-76397-2_4

Similarly, Beaudreau (2004) dedicates most of his analysis and discussion to trusting behaviour in trade situations. He contends that trust emerged through human evolution. In his view, trust evolved with the human species and is embedded into the design of our brains. Without trust there is no cooperation; without cooperation there is no exchange and trade; without trade there cannot be a social division of labour; and without such a division of labour there is no wealth and we are doomed to go extinct, exactly as was the case with the Neanderthals (Horan et al. 2005).

Unfortunately, neither Seabright nor Beaudreau is able to successfully define trust at a social or societal level. Instead, they mainly refer to the concept of *reciprocity* in economic behaviour. This refers to the observation that repeated interaction among individuals sustains trusting behaviour, in particular if the repeated behaviour indicates that one's trusting behaviour is reciprocated. So, by repeatedly making economic transactions, one learns the rules that support such transactions; the repeated interactions also instil expectations of how people interact with each other. Thus, if a miller and a baker interact frequently and repeatedly with each other, both individuals will learn to trust each other until one of the individuals does not reciprocate the expectations of the other. Therefore, repeated trade between that miller and baker will support the expectation that each of them will honour the implicit trade contract made. This expectation in turn supports the development of trust of one trader in the other and vice versa.

Reciprocity not only applies to interpersonal economic interaction, but very much also for institutional elements in our economy. For example, by buying lots of cups of mocha at the local Starbucks over time, one builds a certain expectation of how business is conducted at that shop and the expected quality of the coffee that is produced. If the coffee again and again meets the expected quality standard, one's beliefs are confirmed and this strengthens one's expectations about the quality offered. This process of reciprocal behaviour supports the trust in the Starbucks brand and, therefore, in the accepted trade standards in the prevailing governance system of our globalised economy.

Therefore, any accepted notion of trust has to fit the fundamental property that repeated interaction and reciprocal behaviour sustain and enhance it. It also needs to take account of the fact that trust extends not just to other persons, but also to the rules, customs and media that are part of our economic governance system.

**Toward a Social Theory of Trust**  My objective in this chapter is to go beyond the limited individualistic perspective considered in the economic literature. Instead I aim to develop a comprehensive model of trust and trustworthiness that incorporates the various accepted aspects of trusting behaviour. This model is set firmly within the context of the model of a socio-economic space that I constructed in the previous chapter.

I propose a particular perspective on economic trust that is founded on the institutional–relational approach to economic activity discussed in the previous chapters. Central to this approach is that all economic interaction is embedded into a governance system, the so-called *embeddedness hypothesis* (Lemma 1.4). In this chapter I will interpret trust to be an accompaniment to any economic interaction and, as such, intimately connected with the embeddedness hypothesis.

The proposed model transcends the specific aspects of the socio-economic space and therefore does not refer explicitly to the different elements in the interaction infrastructure. Instead, the proposed perspective is founded on the overall functionality of human socio-economic interaction, namely its embeddedness in a system of governing socio-economic institutions and the accompanying entrepreneurial function. In particular, my theory proposes that trust stands actually in a *dual relationship* to the socio-economic interactions captured in a socio-economic space. Thus, trust is the dual of embeddedness.

Trust and trustworthiness manifest themselves in the different spheres of the interaction infrastructure of the socio-economic space. Reciprocity and reputation are far more important in the subjective sphere than in the objective sphere or the superstructure. Indeed, networking is firmly founded on the reputation of the networkers and is rooted in repeated interaction. In fact, networking is far more based on *trustworthiness* than blind trust. The appropriate perspective, therefore, fits much better with the behavioural model of a calculating decision-maker (networker) than the social actor who relies blindly on the goodness of the other persons she interacts with, as promoted in social theory (Hardin 2006).

For example, if a miller and a baker interact and configure a trade relationship in the subjective sphere of a socio-economic space, it is the outward signals and the professional attitude of these individuals that sustains their mutual trusting behaviour. The baker will look at the outward signs that are exhibited by the miller to deduce something about the quality of the flour that he tries to sell to the baker. Similarly, the miller will look at the outward signs exhibited by the hunter—such as the different aspects of the bakery—to determine the trustworthiness of the baker as a trading partner. Furthermore, hand gestures, facial expressions and the use of language affect how we perceive the other person. It is our trust in assessing these signals that makes us trust the other person, not the actual nature of that person. The nature of another person is fundamentally unknowable and, therefore, interpersonal trust can only exist as an ideal category in our daily life.

Reciprocity is here simply the mechanism that sustains the functioning of that socio-economic embeddedness and thereby supports and enhances the required trust. It also implies that trust is primarily placed in elements in the governance system in the economy rather than in other individuals. Hence, even in the context of networking, the trust between interacting partners is really founded on the trust that one has in the governance instruments and tools.

In the objective sphere and the superstructure of a socio-economic space, trust is much more blind and far less calculating. Buying a mocha at Starbucks is not a networking activity, and we do not calculate the trustworthiness of

Starbucks, its store and its employees. Instead, we blindly rely on the various signals and institutional features of the other trading party. Thus, we have blind faith in the socio-economic institutions that guide our behaviour and use these institutions to engage with our trading partners in the social division of labour. If these potential trading partners exhibit and use the socio-economic institutions as I expect them to be used, then I will trust these trading partners blindly. So, even in situations where I cannot directly assess the trustworthiness of a coffee shop, since it has no socially recognised and reputable brand name, I will enter that shop to buy a beverage if it emits the proper institutional signals.

Therefore, trust emerges in most interactions in the objective sphere based on the institutional embeddedness of our potential trading partners. We mostly calculate the trustworthiness of potential trading partners if there is uncertainty about their institutional embeddedness or if the interaction takes place in the subjective sphere. I argue, however, that the calculation of trustworthiness is founded on the same principles as the designation of blind trust. It is based on the institutional nature of the networking relationship, in particular the use of behavioural conventions. This will be captured in a categorical theory, founded on the theory of a socio-economic space developed in Chap. 3.

From the perspective that trust accompanies the embeddedness of all our economic interaction, I subsequently develop a complete framework. This is founded on a reconstruction of economic interaction using a tripolar matroid structure, the so-called *Fano plane*. This approach is founded on the theory set out in Ruys (1974, 2008) and further developed in Gilles (1990, Chapter 2). Here, I develop a complete description of the interaction and the dual structure that describes different categories of socio-economic trust.

Before embarking on the development of this theoretical framework, I first provide a short overview of accepted notions of trusting behaviour or confidence. This makes clear that our understanding is rather limited.

## 4.1   THE BEHAVIOURAL ECONOMIC PERSPECTIVE OF TRUST

In the social sciences and economics there has emerged a substantial literature on trust and trustworthy behaviour, beginning with the seminal contribution of Coleman (1990). However, this literature mainly addresses the issue of trust from a purely individualistic perspective—adhering to the methodological individualistic foundations of neo-classical economics. Hence, it mainly focuses on trust as *interpersonal* trust only.

In this methodological individualistic view, trust is subject to *choice* and as such trust is *rationalisable*. Thus, Person A makes a rational decision to trust Person B, prior to engaging in an interpersonal interaction. In this view, trust is construed as part of the interaction decision itself and fully individualistic. Hardin (2006) provides an in-depth discussion of this literature. Hardin (2006, p. 16) reports that "In the current literature there are essentially three distinct conceptions of trust. All three are in fact conceptions of trustworthiness or, one could say, conceptions of how someone's trustworthiness of a particular kind leads us to trust that someone with respect to some matter or range of matters." The behavioural perspective therefore conceptualises trust as trustworthiness only. It is the act of calculation that defines this form of trusting behaviour.

For trustworthy behaviour to emerge and to be successful, there has to be a purpose to that behaviour. This implies that there are common or shared objectives over which parties have to coordinate their (individual) actions.[1] Hence, these parties have coincidental interests: "our" interests. This refers to trust as an set of encapsulated interests in the sense that one's interests are encapsulated in the interests of the other trusted party. It should be clear that this is different from applying a behavioural norm. Indeed, following a behavioural norm is actually based on one's self-interest rather than a shared interest.[2] On the other hand, the existence of the behavioural norm implies that we have a common or shared understanding of that norm.

**Behaviour in Trust Games** Furthermore, trust between individuals can also be viewed as being founded on reputation and repeated interaction. This is a distinctly game-theoretic approach, in particular the theory of repeated non-cooperative games. This theory predicts that players settle on a certain equilibrium in which players coordinate their actions to achieve shared interests. This equilibrium state can be understood as a "convention". Within this convention, individual players' choices can either support it or undermine it. Supporting actions build reputations of these individual players, and as a consequence their behaviour becomes fully predictable (Berg et al. 1995; Mailath and Samuelson 2006).

A game-theoretic approach to trustworthy behaviour also fits with the idea that individual players make sacrifices to maintain and strengthen an emerging convention. Indeed, from a perspective of pure self-interest, a player might invest in a strategy to strengthen the state of the economy. We do this daily; we incur transaction costs to make sure that these transactions are secure and thereby strengthen the prevailing transaction system or infrastructure.[3] This is

---

[1] The most common framework in which trustworthiness has been investigated is the Prisoners' Dilemma (PD) game. In the social sciences this is used as a benchmark to discuss cooperative behaviour among decision-makers. In the repeated PD the issue of cooperation versus non-cooperation comes most forcefully to view. For a review of trust issues in this context I refer to James (2002).

[2] This in turn implies that there is a perfectly methodological individualistic foundation to the emergence of a governance system. Namely, the various elements captured in the governance system simplify decision-making for the members of the prevailing socio-economic space. It allows these members to fully individualise their social interaction system through the adherence to certain behavioural norms and media, in particular. However, this brings up the issue of the trust we put in these institutional elements in the governance system. This is what I address in the next section.

[3] An example is paying by credit card, even though paying with cash is an option. The credit card incurs fees to the user, the consumer, as well as the recipient, the merchant. These costs are accepted by these parties to solidify their transaction through protections offered by the credit

closely related to the idea that as economic agents we build reputations through reciprocal behaviour and that the person who has a "good" reputation is willing to incur sacrifices to maintain that good reputation. This is in light of the purely selfish motive that a good reputation has large benefits in the future for the person who has it.

The ultimate conclusion of this literature is put forward in Fehr (2009): trust is simply a purely individual trait that is literally etched in our brains. Neuroeconomic experimentation has shown that when people make social decisions certain areas of the brain are used.[4] These areas are related to prosocial behaviour and decision-making. Through experiments, this has resulted in the conclusion that the chemical oxytocin is directly involved with trustworthy behaviour of individuals; higher levels of this chemical in the brain cause people to act more trustworthy. Fehr concludes that institutions and institutional design can guide decision-makers to behave in a more trustworthy fashion.[5]

**Some Problems with the Behavioural Approach to Trust**  The main problem with the behavioural approach founded on the conceptualisation of trust as a form of social behaviour is that it leads to something that cannot fully explain the fundamental questions about human cooperation in an economy with a social division of labour. Namely, these methodological individualistic foundations do not allow for a proper understanding of individual economic agents and the social institutions that they create collectively. In other words, this approach to trusting behaviour and cooperation does not explain how institutions emerge and are adhered to; in particular it neglects to account for human sociality.

Indeed, Fehr (2009) points to a chemical explanation of trusting behaviour and that this behaviour is guided by institutional designs, but he does not explain how these institutions emerge and are adapted through individual behaviour. It shows that trusting behaviour is literally in our genes, but it does not explain what we do with it. We need a workable approach to trusting behaviour and how we interact in an institutionally structured society.

A parable was put forward in Leijonhufvud (1995) that offers an illuminating perspective on human economic life in different historical periods.[6] He considers the life of Bodo, a tenth-century serf attached to the abbey of St-Germain-des-Prés, about whose life and economic circumstances the British historian Eileen Power (1924), unearthed an amazing amount of concrete information in the archives. Leijonhufvud invented a fictional character, "M. Baudot",

---

card system—Visa or MasterCard. Note that this refers to a rather institutional feature of the economy; trustworthiness emanates from a financial institution rather than from the reputation of the individual involved.

[4] Neuroeconomic experimentation consists of measuring brain activity while the human subjects are involved with economic interactions such as certain non-cooperative games.

[5] See also Onyeiwu and Jones (2003) for an earlier discussion of the same perspective.

[6] An updated version of this paper is available as Leijonhufvud (2007).

who lives in twentieth-century St-Germain. I would like to add the character "M. Baudot Jr", being the son of M. Baudot, who lives in our contemporary twenty-first-century global platform economy.

As Leijonhufvud (2007) (and I) describe, Bodo, M. Baudot and M. Baudot Jr live in a social environment that is made up of socio-economic networks of cooperation. All three are involved with productive and consumptive activities. But we also see that M. Baudot and M. Baudot Jr operate in networks that are several magnitudes more complex than the simple network in which Bodo operated.

> Relatively few people cooperated, directly or indirectly, with Bodo in producing his output and, similarly, few people cooperated in producing his real income, that is, for his consumption. Moreover, Bodo's network was relatively permanent. It tied him to the same people from day to day, year to year. This contrasts with the flexibility of the network sustaining M. Baudot. The people who have contributed to the production of what he consumes today are likely to be a rather different set from those who happened to supply him yesterday—even taking the regularity of the Frenchman's daily routine into account.
>
> (Leijonhufvud 2007, p. 1)

This contrasts with the virtual networks in which M. Baudot Jr operates. His Facebook account gives him access to people across the globe, no longer confining his social contacts to people in his physical location in Paris. His Amazon.com purchases let him access commodities from other parts of the world through direct sales. It should be clear that M. Baudot Jr's economic interactions have a far larger scope in his economic activity than they did for his father, M. Baudot, let alone Bodo.

Bodo could count on his hands the people who provided for his existence: his direct family members, his neighbours and the other inhabitants of his village. This would make up close to 100% of his social environment and the value added to his economic interactions. Bodo's networks would be very strong. The constituting relationships are based on strong personal bonds. Therefore, Bodo's networks are limited in scope but very strong, giving him an excellent support network throughout his life.

In comparison, M. Baudot operates in a socio-economic environment that stretches much further. Particularly, he interacts with a vast international network of providers through the global social division of labour. Nevertheless, his local network, the shops he frequents, the local markets he visits and the people he interacts with through his job as a factory worker would probably account for 50% of the value added to his economic interactions. M. Baudot's network is much weaker, but more extended than Bodo's. Throughout his life, M. Baudot will be supported through anonymous government-provided facilities and networks of acquaintances, rather than strong familial and friendship networks, as was the case with Bodo.

If we consider the life of M. Baudot Jr, this assessment changes even further. His local networks are far less important and his local shops are primarily used to access the global supply chains, rather than locally produced commodities. Possibly only 25% of the value added to his economic interactions comes from his local network. His job as a real estate agent requires him to interact with Russian and Chinese clients, who are investing vast sums in the purchase of Parisian apartments. M. Baudot Jr casts a much wider and weaker network. He is supported by fully anonymous global networks. He is financially secured through global banking and financial networks and support from government-provided facilities is much reduced when compared with his father's situation.

It is clear that these three different stories describe vastly different economies. In each of these three economies, trust and trustworthiness take on fundamentally different forms. I again quote Leijonhufvud:

> Every society must of necessity have some social mechanism that controls the amount of resources that individual members can appropriate and ties this amount to the respective members' contribution to that society, according to whatever framework of rights and obligations is in force. In Bodo's case, this control is enforced on a bilateral basis. The bailiff or steward of the abbey will hold him accountable for the obligations on which his rights in the community depend. For it to be feasible to change over from this redistributive economy to an entirely voluntary one—wherein the typical agent chooses what to do and for whom and, quite independently, what to acquire and from whom—requires an accounting system encompassing the entire society.
>
> (Leijonhufvud 2007, pp. 4–5)

Leijonhufvud goes on to argue that *money* plays the role of the primary enforcing institution in our contemporary, capitalist societies. This is related to individual or private property rights and the role of the individual in these contemporary societies. This points to the institutional nature of trust. Indeed, human sociality is fundamentally expressed through the human ability to believe collective narratives. These take the form of behavioural rules and other socio-economic institutions in the contemporary capitalist economy. Thus, trust has to be viewed as fundamentally institutional in nature.

Linking back to the human evolutionary and anthropological perspective developed in Chap. 1 of this book, it should be clear that trust emanates from the human ability to fully buy into and accept as belief our collective narratives. The stories that we tell each other form the basis of the human ability to cooperate flexibly and to build a society around a functioning social division of labour. In essence, trust refers to the human ability to blindly accept such collective narratives and, therefore, the socio-economic institutions at the foundation of our human economy.

From the fundamental insight that trust refers mainly to the blind belief and acceptance of our collective socio-economic institutions, we can now build a more comprehensive theory of trust and trustworthiness. Such a theory also conforms with Hardin (2006)'s perspective that trust *cannot* be understood as behaviour, but rather has been assessed as fully cognitive; trust is not subject to choice, but is inalienably embedded within us. Here I amend Hardin's perspective by adding that human trust extends to our collective socio-economic institutions and that other forms of trusting behaviour can be derived from this fundamental form of trust. This also seems to be supported by the insights from neuro-economic experimentation that are reported above (Fehr 2009).

In particular, this implies that there are institutional arrangements that enforce and strengthen trustworthy behaviour.[7] This implies that we are acting in a trusting and trustworthy manner in nearly all economic circumstances.

In the following discussion I consider the consequences of the lemma that trust is inalienably embedded within every economic activity we undertake. As such, trust should be recognised as the "dual" of that economic activity: it is simply the other side of any economic activity or interaction.

**A Critique of the Behavioural Perspective on Trust** From the previous discussion it might be clear that in the behavioural conceptualisation of trust and trustworthiness there is an emphasis on trust as an interpersonal cohesive force. Thus, trust is actually fully personalised as a behaviour trait and implemented through the standard of methodological individualism. This implies that individuals are endowed with trust in other individuals.

As pointed out above, there some serious problems with this conceptualisation. Besides Hardin's critique that trust is cognitive and not subject to choice, I introduce three additional reasons to contend that interpersonal trust only exists as an idealised state, at an aspirational level, in our behaviour.

- First, individuals can never develop the required senses about each other that allow them to know each other fully or totally; individuals are restricted in their perceptions of exterior signals, in particular the observed actions of those other individuals. Thus, trust can only be informed and built upon through the external signals of the other person and the observation of the actions that the other person undertakes. This reduces the actual trust of one person to trusting the exterior signals and observed actions of the other person rather than his innermost motivations.
  I support this with the observation that in our contemporary neo-liberal global society, we put a lot of effort into our personal appearance and our signals of belonging to certain groups and professions in that society. The way we dress, the expressions that we use, the activities we pursue and the social recognitions we collect determine fully who we are or

---

[7] In Bodo's case these institutions refer to the whole make-up of the community in which Bodo lived; that is, the whole community enforces reciprocal behaviour and contributions to collective actions. In our contemporary global economy these institutions are the monetary system and the implementation of property rights in an individualistic philosophy of life—as described in the fictional cases of M. Baudot and M. Baudot Jr.

pretend to be. In this respect our "personality" is fully socialised rather than individualised.[8] I have already referred to this as an individual's *socio-economic role* that is resulting from his or her embeddedness in the governance system. This implies that we put trust in another individual's socio-economic role rather than her hidden, inner personality, which is fundamentally unknowable.

- Second, as economic agents and members of our societies and communities, we rely heavily on the social institutions and organisations that support our very survival and existence.[9] This includes foremost the media and socio-economic institutions that make up the governance system in the socio-economic space that we participate in. We fully submit and abide by these institutional rules and symbols to communicate with other members of that socio-economic space. In this regard, we fully trust the governance structure. This was denoted as *institutional trust* in the previous discussion. It might be clear that this is rather different from interpersonal trust, since the trust afforded to media and socio-economic institutions cannot be derived from the trust of other individuals.

  Furthermore, we trust elements from the superstructure in the socio-economic space. For example, we put faith in shops to deliver goods to us at the right moment, in the ability of the financial system to deliver the necessary capital to provide for our existence and in government agencies to regulate the undesirable behaviour of other individuals. Thus, trusting behaviour is somehow extended to the networks in the objective sphere and to the many organisational structures in the superstructure of the socio-economic space, including the networks that we form through interpersonal interaction.

  The trust put in organisations and other elements in the superstructure goes well beyond interpersonal trust or even institutional trust. This type of trusting behaviour is founded on institutional trust, but has a more practical tone to it. I therefore refer to this type of trusting behaviour as *operational confidence*; it refers to a daily usage of elements in our society that alleviate our problems to accomplish things and establish relationships with other individuals and organisations.

- Third, for the fulfilment of our socio-economic objectives, interpersonal trust is actually irrelevant. When considering economic interaction in our

---

[8] We love to pretend that we are fully individualised persons in our contemporary neo-liberal society. We usually play up our so-called individuality, since in our neo-liberal economy that is fully expected; we are, of course, "free" individuals and allowed to fully individualise our personality. However, this is not really true, since true individualism would undermine the fundamental ability of others to trust us and, thus, the functioning of the very society we rely on.

[9] I refer here to this discussion of the Social Organisation of Production principle (Hypothesis 5) and the role of the *Res Publica* as the ancient source of our well-developed relationship with the governance structure in the economy. This includes the emergence of such institutional trust among the citizens of a society.

institutionally well-developed global economy, we are struck by the fact that individuals do not actually interact personally with each other, but mostly in more anonymous fashions as representatives of larger groupings, networks and/or organisations. In other words, we always play socio-economic roles; we are rarely completely individually personalised in our interactions. Even as consumers we execute expected actions and contemplate social categories; we do not purchase an item because it fits with our inner, highly personal desires, but rather because it fits with the exhibited characteristics of the community that we belong to.

For example, if you purchase a cup of mocha at Starbucks, this is mostly an expression of a learned behaviour. As a young person one first has to be trained to like coffee; next, we purchase a mocha because that fits our station in life and the community we operate in; finally, we are expected to purchase the café mocha at Starbucks because the chosen provider contributes to our social image as well. The latter is at the core of what is known as branding: brand names and their advertisements play into the cognitive features of our socialised personality.

The conclusion is that our preferences are not individual, but largely institutional or social. The myriad of socio-economic institutions and organisations that influence us determine what we pretend to like and affect our choices in unexpected ways. I refer to the ability of social. networks such as Facebook and Twitter to influence our choices and behaviour in profound ways. This even extends to the deliberate influencing of national elections in Europe as well as the USA.

In this critical discussion of the behavioural approach to socio-economic trust, I argue that the embeddedness of human decision-makers in the governing socio-economic institutions fully socialises our behaviour as well. Trust and trustworthiness are expressions of this. Individualism is a non sequitur in a social, institutional perspective on wealth creation in a human economy. I next turn to the full development of an institutional perspective to replace the behavioural approach to socio-economic trust and trustworthiness.

## 4.2   TRUST AS A DUALITY

The discussion above refers to several categories of trusting behaviour that can apparently be distinguished. I will carefully consider these identified forms of socio-economic trust.

First, I identified interpersonal trust as an aspiration in our interactions only. We cannot know another person fully and have to rely on our assessment of that other person just in her socio-economic role. Thus, we trust the signals and observable actions that the other person emits through her socio-economic role. I argued above that this refers to our blind faith and trust in the socio-economic institutions in which we are embedded.

Second, our trust of the governing socio-economic institutions extends beyond the objectively construed socio-economic roles. Even in less well-defined circumstances, we rely on these institutions to determine the trustworthiness of an individual. Indeed, when we operate in the subjective sphere of the interaction infrastructure, our networking activities are guided by these institutions. We read the signals emitted by other individuals to identify whether they are trustworthy or not.

I argue that, apart from the aspirational form of interpersonal trust, we can essentially identify two principal types of trusting behaviour here. I distinguish institutional trust—our trust in the governing socio-economic institutions—from our trust of other individuals in their socio-economic roles—our "operational confidence". Moreover, I argue that institutional trust is the more fundamental form of trusting behaviour and that operational confidence is a derived trust category.

### 4.2.1    Institutional Trust as the Dual of Embeddedness

Let me again stress that institutional trust refers to the confidence that an individual economic agent exhibits in the elements of the governance system in the prevailing socio-economic space. It is her usage of these elements that is supported by this form of trust. Hence, this trusting behaviour is directly related to the embeddedness of that individual in the governance system. So, to further understand this idea of institutional trust, I discuss the embeddedness hypothesis in detail.

Embeddedness of an individual in a system of governing socio-economic institutions is closely related to the act of role-building in an institutional economy. An individual economic agent devises herself a socio-economic role in the prevailing social division of labour. These roles can be understood as configurations of expressions of certain socio-economic institutions. The role usually is associated to a dress code, a set of practices and behaviours, and a membership of certain networks in the prevailing interaction infrastructure of the socio-economic space in which this individual operates.

More formally, consider a socio-economic space $S$ with a population of economic agents $P$ and a governance system $G$ of prevailing socio-economic institutions. We assume that this socio-economic space is sufficiently developed and that there exist a subjective sphere, an objective sphere and a superstructure within its context.[10] As discussed in Chap. 3, the elements that make up this governance system $G$ can be categorised as follows:

**Media:** This category refers to all elements that are used to establish and maintain communicative abilities between the economic agents in $P$. This

---

[10] This implies that I assume the socio-economic space to be rather advanced. If I assume a more primitive socio-economic space, say without a superstructure, the levels of extended trust are much lower. The sustained society is much less developed and the generated wealth is lower; we would probably then consider a Malthusian economy such as prevailing in preindustrial times.

includes natural language, technical terminology related to economic activity, cultural norms and accepted symbols and expressions. Here, natural language is the language that is common to all economic agents in $P$. The technical terminology mainly refers to collection of names of commodities, services and socio-economic roles that are accepted within $S$. Finally, the cultural elements are the accepted gestures and symbols that we use and carry with us. This includes, for example, our dress, hand gestures while talking and facial expressions. Of course, this category overlaps with the category of behavioural rules in $G$, since some of these rules are closely founded on the media that are accepted within the context of $S$.

The trust extended to these media is a natural and fundamental form of institutional trust. Economic agents cannot operate in the socio-economic space and build networks without common media such as those listed here. It should be clear that the institutional trust of media is deep, strong and fundamental.

**Behavioural rules:** The second category of institutions refers mainly to the social conventions that we have collectively adopted in the socio-economic space $S$. This includes greeting rituals, the rituals that accompany agreements to economic contracts and the acceptance of certain (pricing) systems from the superstructure to support meaningful economic interaction. Contracts can be written or agreed upon verbally, usually accompanied by certain rituals to seal the contract such as the slapping or shaking of hands, the rubbing of noses or drinking an alcoholic beverage. These contracts are usually supported by a system of recognised property rights and a legal system that enforces these property rights. Contracts are usually guided through a pricing system in our capitalist economies, the so-called price mechanism. Pricing rules structure how prices are "posted" and/or negotiated. This category of behavioural rules also includes non-economic rules that affect our economic interaction in a meaningful way.

Behavioural rules surprisingly might also include cultural requirements and directives that guide choice. This refers mainly to production and consumption habits that are anchored in the prevailing culture. For example, the Japanese do not put sugar in their green tea and the French do not condone putting ice cubes in their red wine. It might be the case that these cultural norms are enforced through habits and service standards in the retail industry.

The trust extended to this category of behavioural rules is fundamental to any meaningful socio-economic interaction. Nevertheless, it is less deep than the trust in media. Rules can occasionally be questioned and discussed. Property rights and contracting law can be adjusted to accommodate certain solutions to problems that arise. This has to be imposed hierarchically by an authority rather than the natural adjustments that adapt the media in the governance system—as discussed above.

**Socio-economic roles:** The third main category in the governance system $G$ consists of the set of socially recognised and accepted socio-economic roles in $S$. Individual agents in $P$ are understood to be able to assume these roles with the required training and specialisation. Each of these roles refers to an economic profession that involves the specialisation of an economic agent that assumes the role and is accompanied by activities with certain economic commodities and services. As such, a role is closely related to certain media and behavioural rules that are attached to that role. This refers to dress, language usage and rituals. For example, a banker is expected to wear a suit, to talk about financial instruments and to fill out long forms if financial contracts are written—such as opening a checking account.

Socio-economic roles are highly trusted, but are more adaptable than the behavioural rules and the media discussed above. These roles are the fundamental building blocks of the social division of labour and can be adapted rather easily by the agents that assume these roles. Clearly, these roles also can be viewed as trust builders in the sense that agents assuming these roles can enhance and deepen the social division of labour, resulting in enhanced economic wealth.

**Monetary system:** The monetary system—which encompasses the implemented notion of money, the related banking system and the larger financial sector, as well as the governmental financial regulatory system—is an integral part of the governance system $G$ in the socio-economic space $S$. It essentially combines elements from the three other defining components in relation to the implemented concept of money. Indeed, strictly speaking, money is a medium of exchange and as such belongs to the media. However, it is accompanied by strict (behavioural) rules of how this medium of exchange is used. Furthermore, money generates a complicated set of derived institutions that guide the saving of money, the issuing of credit and the storage of money in banks; money has a socio-economic role in the functioning of the social division of labour and the wider socio-economic space $S$. All this is supported through an elaborate set of laws enforced by specialised governing agencies, private as well as public.

From this description it is clear that the monetary system is present throughout the various spheres of the prevailing interaction infrastructure in the socio-economic space $S$. The medium of exchange is crucial for the development of the subjective and objective spheres. For the growth of the objective sphere and the superstructure in particular, a fully developed financial system is required. Enhancing these spheres is closely related to the emergence and enrichment of the monetary system and the financial sector.

The institutional trust afforded to the monetary and financial system in a socio-economic space is, therefore, rather fundamental. Without such trust, the functionality of the social division of labour would be compromised severely.

Now the embeddedness hypothesis (Lemma 1.4) essentially asserts that all individual economic agents in a socio-economic space use the institutions in the prevailing governance system in all economic activities that they participate in and undertake. Hence, an individual has a reciprocal relationship with the governance system that is founded on several aspects of her embeddedness. This relationship will be explored further.

**The Embeddedness Relationship**  First and foremost, embeddedness is fully relational in a bidirectional sense—comprising the embeddedness hypothesis itself and the entrepreneurial function.

On the one hand, through the embeddedness hypothesis the governance system fully subsumes the individual. Individuals completely adapt their behaviour by becoming a member of the community, in particular through assimilating themselves into the socio-economic space centred around the given governance system. In this sense, the governance system is *internalised* in an individual member of the socio-economic space; the governance system thus fully assimilates these individuals.

On the other hand, through the entrepreneurial function an individual can affect and modify the socio-economic institutions that make up the governance structure through her behaviour and actions. Thus, by using certain media, behavioural rules or other institutions from the governance system, an individual might affect how others perceive these elements. Moreover, an individual—possibly in interaction with other individuals—might actually innovate and modify the socio-economic institutions in the governance system directly. This refers to the entrepreneurship initiated by the members of the socio-economic space.

I emphasise that membership of a socio-economic space and using the prevailing governance system is not truly a choice. Indeed, at most instances all individuals just use governance elements without explicit contemplation of their use or their nature. We just use our natural language and our money, and adhere to the posted price mechanism in our economic interaction without questioning these elements. In this regard embeddedness is fully cognitive (Hardin 2006).

The bidirectional embeddedness relationship of individual and the governance structure is stylised in Fig. 4.1. Here $i$ refers to an individual and $G$ to the governance system. The embeddedness relationship between $i$ and $G$ is now depicted as a line between the two nodes.

The intermediary node $R$ in Fig. 4.1 refers to the embodiment of the embeddedness of individual $i$ in to the governance system $G$; $R$ represents the socio-economic role that individual $i$ assumes. The embodiment $R$ essentially refers to how $i$ uses the elements in the governance structure and what third parties observe of individual $i$ in interactions with her. So, $R$ is a *reflection* of $i$ in $G$ and, vice versa, an expression of $G$ in $i$. The configuration $R$ therefore consists of the media and behavioural rules that $i$ uses—such as the language she speaks, the gestures she makes, the money she uses and the shops she frequents—and

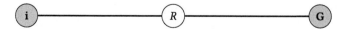

**Fig. 4.1**  Graphical representation of an embedded relationship

the socio-economic role that she builds and assumes. The latter is as well based on the media and behavioural rules that accompany that role, but also on the abilities that she has to show to others to make that role plausible.

In this regard embeddedness itself refers to the construction of such a reflection $R$ of an agent $i$ in the governance system $G$. This aspect of embeddedness can be referred to as *role-building*. A socio-economic role is constructed through the assumption of certain elements of the governance system that are available to the economic agent $i$. This assumption can be conscious or subconscious. The first also might refer to the rational act of constructing a socio-economic role of oneself.

One of the remarkable conclusions from the contemplation of the embeddedness of an individual $i$ in a governance system $G$ is that actually $i$ and $G$ are unobservable; only the reflection $R$ of this embeddedness relationship is actually observable. Indeed, we exercise our language by speaking and writing it; language itself remains elusive unless it is actually used. Similarly, for all other elements in $G$, only the actual usage of these elements by individuals gives them meaning. On the other hand, I have already pointed out that an individual $i$ is fundamentally unknowable; it is the usage of governance elements of that individual that informs us of her individual person. In other words, we have to glean an individual's personality through observation of $R$.

Furthermore, as mentioned above, I point out that embeddedness is founded on the same principle as trust. As Hardin (2006, pp. 18–20) points out, trust can be viewed as encapsulated interests. When two individuals have common or coincidental interests, this is a foundation for trust among those individuals. I disagree with Hardin that interpersonal trust is relevant for economic activity; rather *an individual identifies coincidental interests with other individuals in the setting of a socio-economic space through the adherence to the elements in the governance system in that socio-economic space*. Thus, within a socio-economic space, the constituting members in the population identify common interests, "our interests", that are embedded within the governance system and certain organisational structures in the superstructure of the socio-economic space.[11]

Taking the properties of embeddedness into consideration leads us to the conclusion that it is relational and reflects a set of common interests. This coincides exactly with the constituting properties of trust according to Hardin (2006). In this regard, embeddedness fully reflects an understanding of trust. I refer to this as *institutional trust*.

I would like to strengthen this conclusion by adding that institutional trust stands in an ontological relationship to embeddedness. Indeed, this form of trust is not the same as embeddedness, but accompanies and supports it. On the other hand, embeddedness cannot function properly without the existence

---

[11] This also refers to the relationship between citizens and the *res publica* in ancient societies, where the *res publica* clearly extended the citizens' brains to allow wealth creation.

of trust. The proper terminology for this relationship between embeddedness and institutional trust is that it is a *duality*. Both embeddedness and institutional trust are two constituting aspects of the same thing. This was formulated as the trust hypothesis, stated as Lemma 1.6 in Chap. 1.

Trust centres on the reflection $R$, including the socio-economic role assumed by an individual, rather than on the individual $i$ herself or on the governance system $G$ itself. It is through her constructed reflection $R$ that an individual $i$ interacts with others in a socio-economic space. Trust only pertains to that reflection $R$, not the individual herself.

Furthermore, the trust hypothesis (Lemma 1.6) refers to a primary and general form of trusting behaviour. It does not distinguish between different forms of trust, trusting behaviour and trustworthiness that emerge from closer inspection, such as interpersonal trust, institutional trust and operational confidence. In that sense, this approach considers trust to be a generalised category: being a member of the same socio-economic space and being subject to the same governance system implies the presence of a fundamental form of trust and trusting behaviour.

Next, through an extended model of embeddedness and trust, I will explore a more complete analysis of the duality between embeddedness and institutional trust. From this analysis we can develop a mathematical meaning of this duality.[12]

### 4.2.2   Daily Life: Operational Confidence

From our discussion it is clear that institutional trust refers to our usage of the governance system in our economic interaction with others. It describes a deep, cognitive form of trust that is not really subject to choice. It refers to how an individual uses the governance system to build herself a reflection or embodiment, in particular a socio-economic role. Thus, institutional trust is limited to the relationship of an individual with the elements in the governance system that she uses to build her position and role in the community. It does not refer to how third parties perceive this individual and attempt to interact with her.

In our daily life we continuously observe others and interact with them. How we perceive these others is crucial in our assessment of our own position in this community or society. This refers to the operational form of trusting behaviour and it is founded on how one individual perceives and responds to another individual's reflection in the governance structure.[13] So, if I purchase

---

[12] Duality theory is a fully developed part of algebra and can be represented formally through isomorphisms. This is explored more fully in the next sections of this chapter.

[13] In this regard, how we use elements from the governance system in our daily life is very Shackleian (Shackle 1972, 1979). Shackle builds a philosophical approach to economic behaviour around the fundamental idea that economic subjects construct mental images of future events to make decisions. Thus, I imagine that a green apple tastes in a certain way and subsequently

bread from a baker, I build an expectation or mental image of how a baker behaves and uses elements from the governance structure. This might refer to how a baker is expected to dress (e.g. in white), the terminology he uses (e.g. words such as "whole wheat bread", "croissants") and the shop he has constructed (e.g. displaying the bread in rows). If the actual baker fulfils my mental image of a "baker", this provides a foundation for me trusting him and an actual economic transaction.

I refer to this operational form of trusting behaviour as *operational confidence*. It is a secondary or derived form of trust, which is firmly founded on the embeddedness of individuals in the governance system of the socio-economic space under consideration. In this regard, operational confidence is much more subject to choice. Indeed, even though both the baker and I are fully embedded in the governance system, I make a conscientious and even rational decision to interact with the baker or not. That decision is informed by my perception of the baker's reflection or socio-economic role.

Operational confidence as the form of trust that informs our daily economic interactions is closely related to *trustworthiness*. Indeed, our socio-economic interactions and trades are informed by the role assumed by the other party. If this role is "proper", we have a high level of confidence that the interaction will be fruitful and properly conducted; however, if the other party has assumed a less proper implementation of that role, it would affect our confidence. This in turn would affect how we interact, and we would take a more calculating approach to such socio-economic interaction. We would assess the other party more carefully, determining the other party's trustworthiness.

Furthermore, socio-economic roles simplify the decision-making process that is informed by our operational confidence and trustworthiness. Indeed, a baker is expected to have expert knowledge of producing bread and pies; moreover, he is expected to exhibit certain behaviour, such as wearing a white outfit. A police officer should satisfy a very different set of expectations and behavioural standards. Both of these socio-economic roles have been created to standardise economic interaction and to allow for deeper specialisation, leading to higher returns for the community as a whole.

If an individual assuming the role of a baker or a police officer answers consistently to the social expectations regarding her assumed socio-economic role, she supports the socialisation of such roles and enhances the trusting behaviour or trustworthiness received by individuals in the same socio-economic role in other interactive situations. Thus, operational confidence relates to the social category induced by a particular socio-economic role. Clearly, socio-economic roles such as a baker and a police officer induce high operational confidence,

---

decide to purchase a pound of green apples or not. This mental image is based on past experiences and transferred knowledge through education. This is closely related to the theory of case-based decision-making (Gilboa and Schmeidler 2001; Gilboa et al. 2002).

while socio-economic roles such as a thief and a terrorist induce no trust in any interaction.[14]

**Trustworthiness: Expectations and Reputations**  From the discussion above it should be clear that operational confidence refers to the expectations with regard to the socio-economic roles assumed by agents in economic interactions. It has no personal nature or foundation, but as such is purely based on the social category induced by the socio-economic role. This can be extended to production teams in the superstructure as well. A production team as a whole can assume a certain socio-economic role by associating itself with certain social categories of productive activities. For example, a hospital can be perceived as a coalition of physicians, nurses and administrative staff that provides certain health care services to patients. Here, the terms "physician", "nurse" and "patient" refer to socio-economic roles, while the term "hospital" refers to a non-personal, collective entity that has also assumed a certain socio-economic role. A hospital is usually a hierarchy and as such an economic organisation that has assumed this role, which comes with certain expectations and behavioural rules; if fulfilled, it results in institutional trust. This in turn facilitates the building of mutually beneficial relationships with the various patients.

Furthermore, I refer here to the trustworthiness instilled by a brand name as operational confidence.[15] We might even view a brand name essentially as a particular incarnation of a socio-economic role at the level of the super-structure. Indeed, the brand names Ford or Coca-Cola promote very different expectations, but also correspond to clear (institutional) expectations. Again, these expectations facilitate the building of mutually beneficial relationships and interactions. In this regard, brand names promote a similar purpose to the assumption of any other socio-economic role.

A similar social convention is that of the shop sign. Such signs have been used since antiquity, as shown in the many Greek and Roman ruins around the Mediterranean. Signs are used to indicate the socio-economic role of the shop in question. In Pompeii, a fishmonger was indicated by a fishing boat with nets to communicate the shop's nature, while a poultryman would be advertised with a mosaic of chicken legs in a pan. Our contemporary signs have exactly the same function, namely to communicate the socio-economic role of the shop and its proprietor. Again this refers to elements that support the development of operational confidence with regard to organisations in the superstructure

---

[14] This is the reason why thieves and terrorists usually obscure their socio-economic role in the economic interactions they pursue; a thief opening a checking account at a bank will certainly not list his job as such on the application form.

[15] As such, a brand name is a very recent invention, part of the rise of the consumption economy in the first half of the twentieth century. Brands and branding have completely subsumed personal or even professional categories of behaviour. In this regard, they supersede socio-economic roles to the level of the superstructure of the socio-economic space.

rather than at the individual level, in particular the objective sphere related to the socio-economic space.

This discussion shows that operational confidence is a flexible notion and is fundamentally different from interpersonal and institutional trust. Indeed, interpersonal trust refers to an aspiration level or ideal form of interaction, while institutional trust embodies the embeddedness of individuals in the governance system of media, behavioural rules and socio-economic roles. Operational confidence, however, is subject to actual decision-making and refers to how we put our trust in other individuals as well as socio-economic organisations in the superstructure to support our interactions with them. It should be clear that operational confidence is a secondary or derived notion of trusting behaviour, which is firmly founded in our institutional trust and aspires to emulate interpersonal trust.[16]

Operational confidence is not the only category of trusting behaviour that can be derived within this approach. The functioning of the socio-economic space is also much influenced by the application of "notional trust", which refers to how the community as a whole considers the quality of the governance system to be. To properly explore this latter category of trusting behaviour, I develop a complete analysis of the interaction of individuals in the setting of a socio-economic space. Only by modelling the specific details of such an interaction in an appropriate model can we flesh out the details to show the trusting behavioural categories that affect this interaction. This is pursued in the next section.

## 4.3   A Reconstruction of Embeddedness and Trust

In this section I extend the discussion of embeddedness in the previous section to an analysis of the nature of an economic relationship between two economic agents. The embeddedness hypothesis recognises that such economic interactions or activities are formed within a socio-economic space that is founded on the prevailing governance system—being a collection of media and economic institutions that are collectively recognised. Next I address how this embeddedness hypothesis can be used to develop a workable theoretical framework in which we can analyse economic activities from a relational perspective. This results in the next stage in the development of a relational approach to economic interaction.

The first consequence of the embeddedness hypothesis is that economic interaction has to be understood as evolving completely within the context of a matrix founded on these media and economic behavioural rules and

---

[16] The latter point also makes it clear why there might be confusion about interpersonal trust as a viable, functional form of trust. Many authors assume that interpersonal trust is the only true or viable form of trust, while in my approach this place is occupied by institutional trust; that is, the trust we put in the elements that make up our governance system.

institutions. This governance system of media and economic institutions can therefore also be denoted as an *institutional matrix*. It is only within the context of such an institutional matrix that economic interaction can emerge and evolve. Moreover, the media and institutions that make up the institutional infrastructure actually shape and largely determine the form of these economic interactions; in many regards these media and institutions fully determine the costs and benefits of these interactions or activities as well as their form.

The matrix of socio-economic institutions in which the economic agents are embedded largely determines and shapes the interaction infrastructure in the socio-economic space. The networks of these interactions are guided by these institutions and through their embeddedness, economic agents shape their interactions in accordance with the institutional matrix. Thus, it is not only the individual economic agents that are embedded within the governance system, but also the economic activities that they engage in. This implies that if we contemplate an economic relationship between two individual economic agents, we have to take account that both individuals are embedded and that their interaction is embedded as well.

**A Reconstructionist Perspective** For the formal development of a proper description founded on this embeddedness hypothesis, I employ a reconstruction theory that decomposes economic interaction into multiple relationships. First, we recognise the fundamental mutually beneficial relationship between the two economic agents. This relationship describes the potential value that can be generated between the two economic agents if they interact, and as such this relationship functions as an ideal or aspiration level. Subsequently, we connect this ideal relationship with the embeddedness of both economic agents in the prevailing governance system. This reconstruction theory is an implementation of the reconstructive approach to general representation seminally introduced in Ruys (1974, 1999) and further developed in Ruys (2008). One can denote this approach as *reconstructionism*.

Reconstructionism allows us to understand binary, mutually beneficial economic interaction from a comprehensive perspective founded on a force field. One considers interaction to be shaped by certain socio-economic forces that are embedded in the different elements in that interaction and its environment. In particular, I use this methodology to decompose a socio-economic interaction between two agents in the context of a socio-economic space using *three* fundamental socio-economic "forces". These form the three "polar positions" on which this binary interaction is founded; this allows us to denote this representation theory as *tripolar*. In a tripolar representation the three forces span a force field in which the interaction takes shape and is conducted. More precisely, this force field represents the embeddedness of the interaction in the prevailing system of socio-economic institutions.

The three fundamental socio-economic forces on which this reconstruction is founded, are categorised as centrifugal (repelling) or centripetal (binding). In particular, I consider two centrifugal forces and one centripetal force.

The two centrifugal forces are the individual desires and abilities that are embodied within the two individual economic agents who form the mutually beneficial relationships. The centripetal force is the embeddedness of these individuals in the institutional matrix on which the prevailing socio-economic space is founded. To illustrate this reconstructionist approach intuitively, I use two simple examples of economic interaction: the simple exchange of two commodities and the delivery of a simple service, namely the execution of a haircut.

Furthermore, as a consequence, this reconstruction of a socio-economic economic interaction can explain trust as related to that interaction. In fact, reconstructionism allows us to analyse the dual of the decomposition of economic interaction into these three fundamental forces. This dual exactly fleshes out the various forms of trust and their relationships that emanate from such economic interaction. Thus, we arrive at a comprehensive model that places institutional trust and operational confidence—identified earlier—in a proper context as related to socio-economic interaction. This results in a much richer theory of trusting behaviour than until now has been pursued in the literature (James 2002; Buskens 2002; Nooteboom 2002; Hardin 2006). In particular, there emerges a third fundamental form of trust that can be denoted as *notional trust*. This describes the relationship that economic agents have as a collective with the prevailing institutional matrix in the socio-economic space. It describes how such a community of agents steers the various media and institutions to support the pursuit of its economic objectives more efficiently. Notional trust points to the collective nature of the institutional governance in the socio-economic space. This refers to the political debate among these agents that shapes the socio-economic space and that forms the foundation of the entrepreneurial function in that space.

Finally, I point out that reconstructionism allows us to delineate economic interaction from non-economic activities and to identify the basic processes that sustain value-generating activities in the prevailing socio-economic space. Indeed, is a conversation between two persons an economic activity? It is actually value generating for both participants and as such it is mutually beneficial. However, it would be going too far to denote such activity as "economic". Reconstructionism allows us to formulate what separates non-economic activities from economic interaction.

The remainder of this discussion consists of three parts. First, I develop a complete representation of a mutually beneficial economic relationship using the methodology of scientific reconstructionism. Next, I use this representation to develop a complete theory of trust emanating from economic interaction, including institutional trust, as one of the fundamental constituting elements and operational confidence as a derived concept. Finally, I delineate economic activity from non-economic activity using the constructed theories.

### 4.3.1    Reconstructing Embedded Economic Interactions

It is universally recognised in economics that socio-economic interaction only emerges in the context of the fundamental tension between a certain desire on the one hand and the ability to relieve this desire on the other.[17] For example, if we consider the exchange of an apple for an orange, this interaction is founded on the presence of a desire for consumption properties generated by an apple in one economic agent and for the consumption properties of an orange in the other economic agent. These consumption properties may refer to the calorific nutritional value of these fruits as well as their smell, colour, texture and/or shape. The desires of these two economic agents constitute the centrifugal forces in this interaction, while the institutions on which these two agents can interact with each other form a centripetal force that binds these two agents in a relationship. The relief of these desires is accomplished through the exchange of the apple for the orange in that binding relationship.

Now consider a more general setting of an arbitrary socio-economic interaction. We postulate that there are two individual economic agents $i$ and $j$ that intend to engage in a mutually beneficial economic interaction or relationship. What is exactly required for such an interaction to come to fruition and actually generate mutual benefits?

First, we recognise that $i$ and $j$ indeed perceive the potential benefits from such an interaction. Thus, both individuals are aware that the potential interaction would result in benefits for themselves as well as the other agent. We should also recognise that this awareness only has a potential nature; it is not yet realised. In this regard, the relationship between $i$ and $j$ has principally a potential nature and other elements have to be brought into it to actually realise this recognised potential. These other elements are the building blocks offered through the institutional matrix or governance system of the socio-economic space in which these two economic agents are embedded and operate.

I will discuss two examples, one interaction within the subjective sphere and one interaction in the objective sphere in the prevailing socio-economic space between two individual economic agents, to illustrate this.

- First, suppose that agents $i$ and $j$ are aware that exchanging apples for oranges would result in mutual benefits, satisfying their desires for consumption properties emanating from these two commodities. Note that I interpret this as an interaction in the *subjective* sphere of the socio-economic space, since in the context of a fully developed (objective) social division of labour the facilitation of this exchange is embodied in a different fashion. (I refer to the next example to make this clear.)

---

[17] This refers to the fundamental, neo-classical definition of economics that emerged from a thorough debate in the first half of the twentieth century among neo-classical economists. The most pointed formulation of this economic principle was presented by Robbins (1932).

In the context of a subjective interaction, being part of these agents' networking activities, these two individuals would rely on relatively simple tools from the institutional matrix to accomplish such a subjective exchange relationship. Indeed, for a successful exchange, both agents have to employ certain tools from the institutional matrix to establish and realise such an economic relationship.

- Certainly, the traders have to meet physically. This might imply that both use a common marketplace that is offered in the market town.
- Moreover, the traders are expected to communicate their wares to each other through the use of a common natural language.
- Finally, both traders have to use common bargaining rules and a monetary system to accomplish the actual trade. This is further supported through the use of mutually understood hand gestures, clothing options and physical facilities such as a stand or basket to present the offered wares.[18]

  The postulated subjective interaction is founded on the relative *social scarcity* of the commodities considered for exchange. Thus, the availability of apples and oranges is not plentiful enough to costlessly satisfy all desires within the community of economic agents that are embedded in the prevailing socio-economic space.

- A second example would be that of the delivery of a haircut service by a trained provider, a hair stylist, to a customer or client. This example has to be placed in the context of a more advanced economy with a completely developed social division of labour, and as such the delivery of a haircut is an interaction that takes place within the *objective* sphere of the prevailing socio-economic space. Indeed, the realisation of this interaction requires more advanced institutional instruments that govern the actions of these economic agents.

  Both agents in this case would rely on distinct sets of commonly accepted socio-economic institutions.

  - The provider of the service relies heavily on rather advanced commonly accepted instruments to position herself before any trade can take place. Foremost, she has to be trained as a hair stylist; she has to procure a reasonable outfit, including tools of the trade; she has to prepare bank accounts to collect revenues from services provided; she has to establish a well-advertised place of provision or shop in a mall or on the high street in the city centre; she has to advertise the provided services using well-

---

[18] It should be clear that the usage of elements from the governance system is costly and that, consequently, the mutual benefits from the relationship are lower than potentially available or realisable. Thus, the realised gains from an economic interaction are always lower than the potential benefits owing to the costly nature of the interaction. This mainly refers to *social* costs of the common trade infrastructure.

recognised and -established channels, such as a sign outside the shop, a web site on the internet, a Facebook circle of friends and regular clients, as well as an entry in the yellow pages.

– The procurer of the service also prepares himself before the trade itself takes place. He identifies a potential service provider and tries to identify the expected quality of the service provided. This amounts to using word-of-mouth information and searching the internet or yellow pages for potential providers. Usually a successful interaction results in a long-term relationship that does not require continued investment in these information tools.

Finally, the interaction itself is established and executed. This requires the usage of the same tools as already pointed out in the discussion of the subjective relationship between two agents trading apples for oranges: natural language, commonly understood pricing rules (i.e. the price mechanism) and a common monetary system based on fiat money and an advanced financial system. As a consequence, the objective relationship between the hair stylist and the client is embedded in the prevailing institutional matrix or governance system as well.

These examples illustrate the embeddedness of the relationship or interaction itself in the prevailing governance system. From this discussion it should be clear that both economic agents assume certain elements from the governance system to establish the mutually beneficial interaction. Therefore, these socio-economic interactions are founded on role-building by the two engaging parties in the institutional matrix of the socio-economic space.

Next I develop the reconstruction of a socio-economic interaction between two economic agents $i$ and $j$ into a tripolar force field through several steps,

**Postulating the Tripolar Force Field** We consider the potential socio-economic interaction between two agents $i$ and $j$ in the context of a socio-economic space that is founded on a system of governing institutions that we denote by $G$, as before. The two economic agents $i$ and $j$ themselves embody the two centrifugal forces in the force field, while the governance system $G$ embodies the centripetal force of the prevailing institutions in the socio-economic space.

Schematically we now arrive at a triangular construct. First, we postulate that the relationship between the two agents $i$ and $j$ potentially provides mutual benefits to these economic agents. Second, we postulate that both agents $i$ and $j$ are embedded within the prevailing governance system and build a socio-economic role through the adoption of instruments from the system of governing institutions $G$. These socio-economic roles are mutually communicated to the other agent. We have to recognise that the potential value that the relationship might generate can only be realised if both agents use tools from the governance system in which they are embedded.

I now introduce a formal representation of the described structure as the foundation for a tripolar reconstruction of economic interaction between $i$ and $j$. The ideal or potential, mutually beneficial relationship between $i$ and $j$ is denoted by $I$. The symbol $I$ stands for the *aspirational ideal or potential* of the relationship, not just the potential values it can generate, but also the effects it has on other aspects related to this interaction. Therefore, $I$ has a *potential nature* and cannot be assumed to be fully realisable. This potential remains an "ideal".

In the case of the exchange of apples for oranges, the potential values refer to the utilitarian benefits from the acquired consumption properties this exchange will bring to both traders, while the two agents can additionally get mutual benefits from the interaction itself—such as the conversation that ensues between the two traders. Thus, $I$ embodies the utilitarian values from the commodities as well as the external benefits from the interaction itself. In the more advanced example of the delivery of a haircut, $I$ stands for the financial revenues for the provider, the utilitarian benefits for the procurer and also the reputational effects of a successful delivery for both parties involved. The latter refers again to external effects related to the interaction itself.

Subsequently we recognise that both $i$ and $j$ are embedded in the governance system $G$. Thus, both $i$ and $j$ represent themselves in $G$ through socio-economic roles that they adopt. As before in Fig. 4.1, I denote the reflection or socio-economic role that $i$ creates for herself by $R_i$. Similarly, the reflection or socio-economic role of $j$ is denoted by $R_j$. This is analogous to and an extension of the representation of the embeddedness hypothesis given in Fig. 4.1.

These three elements are now brought together in the triangular representation depicted in Fig. 4.2. At the top is depicted the aspirational relationship

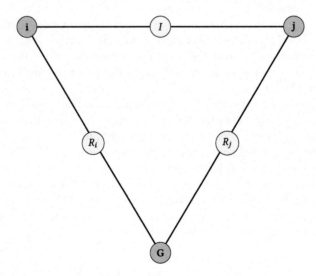

**Fig. 4.2**   Basic tripolar representation of an economic interaction

between $i$ and $j$, which potential is given by $I$. Both individual agents $i$ and $j$ are embedded in $G$, resulting in the socio-economic roles $R_i$ and $R_j$.

**Centrifugal and Centripetal Forces** Note that the tripolar representation in Fig. 4.2 brings together the desires and abilities of two economic agents $i$ and $j$ in the two red upper corner points. Therefore, these corner points refer to the fundamental *centrifugal* forces that are founded on the individualised abilities of the two economic agents. These agents might have opposite desires and abilities, but can still engage in mutually beneficial interaction. In fact, it is the desires of both economic agents and their diverse abilities that bring these agents together in the first place.[19] The centrifugal nature of these individualised forces creates the space between them that is also indicated with the symbol $I$, being the potential wealth that can potentially be generated through the interaction between these two agents.

There is a second fundamental tripolar force represented in Fig. 4.2, namely the binding force of the common governance system in which both agents are embedded. This force can therefore be categorised as *centripetal*. In Fig. 4.2 the centripetal force is represented as a blue node that binds or embeds the two centrifugal forces. The interaction between the centripetal force $G$ with the two centrifugal forces $i$ and $j$ generates the two socio-economic roles $R_i$ and $R_j$ in which the two agents represent themselves. It should be emphasised that the centripetal force $G$ not just binds, but mainly facilitates in the sense that it offers opportunities to the two agents to realise the potential gains represented by $I$, which would remain unattainable without such a facilitating system.

To summarise, Fig. 4.2 brings together the fundamental building elements of the interaction: the two centrifugal forces based on the desires and abilities of the two individual agents (red nodes) and the centripetal force of the governance system (blue node) that binds the centrifugal forces into a productive construct. There result three derived concepts from the confrontation of these three forces represented in the yellow nodes: the ideal potential of the interaction between the two individual agents and the representations of the two agents in the governance system.

**Socio-Economic Roles as Reflections** I emphasise here that Fig. 4.2 only represents the preamble to the imperfect realisation of the potential interaction $I$, not this realisation itself. The tripolar framework of Fig. 4.2 sets the boundaries and fundamental forces of the interaction between $i$ and $j$; it describes the *span* of the tripolar reconstruction of the interaction of $i$ and $j$.

Here, the two reflections $R_i$ and $R_j$ represent the tools that the two agents use to realise as best as possible the potential $I$ in their interaction. Indeed, $I$

---

[19] It should be recognised that the differences between $i$ and $j$ might be fully a result of endogenous differentiation through the adoption of different socio-economic roles $R_i$ and $R_j$ by these two agents. This is the fundamental hypothesis of economic wealth creation through a social division of labour: the embeddedness itself generates the social wealth around which societies are built.

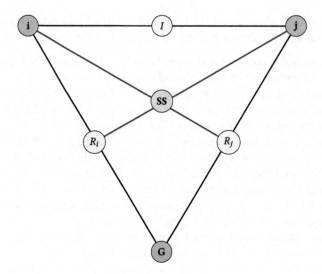

**Fig. 4.3** Reconstruction of the actualisation of an economic interaction

represents the unrealised potential of the interaction between $i$ and $j$, while $R_i$ and $R_j$ refer to the governance tools employed by the two economic agents $i$ and $j$ to communicate a willingness to interact with other economic agents. In the example of the delivery of the haircut, the stylist $i$ assumes a socio-economic role $R_i$ based on her training, her shop and facilities, and her advertising. This is directly based on her institutional trust in the tools that the prevailing governance system offers her to prepare for the delivery of her services. These elements are supposed to be represented fully in the symbol $R_i$.

Therefore, the socio-economic role $R_i$ truly *reflects* the economic agent $i$ in the system of governing institutions $G$. As such, $R_i$ is the role that $i$ assumes to prepare for the realisation of the potential interaction $I$. It does not yet represent the actual realisation of the interaction between $i$ and $j$; this requires a missing element that points to the interactive nature of $i$ and $j$ through $G$.

In Fig. 4.3 I extend the tripolar structure with two additional elements that actually describe the realisation of the mutually beneficial interaction represented by $I$.

The interaction between the two economic agents does not occur directly at the personal level, but travels through the governance tools that are available in the socio-economic space in which these agents operate. In terms of the language introduced in Fig. 4.2, agent $i$ really interacts with the image of agent $j$, being $R_j$. Vice versa, agent $j$ actually deals with the image $R_i$ of agent $i$. The two additional relationships depicted in Fig. 4.3 represent these interactions. Where they "meet", a resolution of the forces results and a stable state emerges, indicated by the node $SS$ in Fig. 4.3. In this regard the node $SS$ represents the imperfect realisation of the potential $I$ of the interaction between $i$ and $j$.

To be more concrete, I again return to the two examples discussed earlier. I discuss the resulting relationships and the resolution point $SS$ in some detail for both cases:

- In case of a subjective exchange of apples for oranges, the adopted roles by the two traders are rather primitive and coarse, as indicated before. The apple seller observes the orange seller through the chosen representation $R_o$ and vice versa, the orange seller contemplates the offering made by the apple seller $R_a$. Both react to the generated roles or reflections comprising of the chosen trade location, the baskets used and the chosen clothing options of both sellers. This affects how they decide to react and ultimately interact. The point $SS$ represents the ultimate trade that is agreed upon.

  It should be emphasised that the chosen tools are primitive and the interaction is very limited in nature. Thus, the realised trade represented in $SS$ is simple as well and not burdened by advanced expectations. Furthermore, the realised trade $SS$ only captures partially and imperfectly the potential $I$ that could be accomplished in the relationship between $i$ and $j$. For example, the exchange rate between apples and oranges in this trade relationship might deviate from the theoretical perfectly competitive price based on the demand and supply in this relationship. As a consequence, the realised division of the potential surplus from this trade (represented by $SS$) can be substantially different from the potential ideal based on the perfectly competitive exchange rate (represented by $I$).

- The case of the delivery of the haircut is rather different. Advanced instruments are used to construct the objective socio-economic roles that are required to build a proper social division of labour. In particular, as described above, the hair stylist has constructed a very advance and complex configuration $R_s$ to represent herself. As discussed, this comprises a shop, branding and alliances with other brands.

  The client has a much simpler role $R_c$ consisting mainly of dress (clothing options) and demeanour. The client is also expected to inform himself about the hair styles on offer and which hair style to request from the hair stylist.

  For the establishment of the delivery and execution of the haircut, represented by $SS$, the client is significantly affected by the exact role $R_s$ as built by the hair stylist, while the hair stylist is affected by the client in his role $R_c$. The client selects the store and informs himself about the price of the haircut based on $R_s$ completely; the hair stylist allows the client to enter the premises based on her observation of $R_c$. The trade is executed if both agree, which is simplified as the fact that the client enters the store and allows the hair stylist to engage in the delivery of the haircut.

The distances and distinctions in the schematic representation in Fig. 4.3 indicate an abstraction of the various types of costs. Thus, the distinction between $i$ and $R_i$ reflects the cost that are incurred to create the socio-economic role $R_i$ for agent $i$. Similarly, the distinction between the realised interaction $SS$ and the ideal interaction $I$ reflects an efficiency loss owing to the imperfections of the interactions that are possible within the socio-economic space based on the governance tools that are part of $G$.

With regard to the two additional relationships between $i$ and $R_j$ and between $j$ and $R_i$ in Fig. 4.3, I note that these relationships are the prime interactive elements in this reconstruction. These relationships are actually *operational*. As such these operational relationships are informed by the level of operational confidence that is present in the relationship between $i$ and $j$. Indeed, the operational confidence of $i$ reflects how much trust or confidence she puts into the role $R_j$ built by agent $j$. This holds in the reverse for agent $j$ in his relationship to the role $R_i$ assumed by $i$. I will return to the discussion of operational confidence in relation to these operational relationships in the next section of this chapter.

**Introducing the Notional Relationship** Two more relationships can be added to the construct depicted in Fig. 4.3. First, I consider the fundamental relationship between $I$ and $G$, which also links both these elements to the realised interaction represented by $SS$. This is depicted in Fig. 4.4, which enhances the construct in Fig. 4.3 with the additional relationship $I - SS - G$.

The relationship $I - SS - G$ between the idealisation $I$, the outcome $SS$ and the governance system $G$ can be denoted as the *notional relationship*. It reflects the collective perception of the functionality of the media, behavioural rules and other socio-economic institutions in the governance system $G$, in relation to the ideal values that we perceive to get from our potential economic activities—represented by $I$. Thus, the resulting stable state $SS$ can be viewed

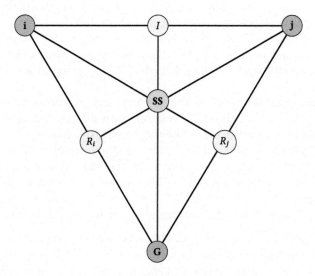

**Fig. 4.4** Introducing the notional relationship in the tripolar reconstruction

as the expression of the realisation of $I$ in the socio-economic space carried by the governance system $G$.

The notional relationship should be understood more as a dynamic relationship than a static one. Indeed, it refers to an aspirational relationship that points to the functionality of the governance system in relation to the realised values from the interaction between $i$ and $j$. Therefore, the collective of all economic agents that populate the socio-economic space under $G$ aims at improving the functionality of $G$ in the sense that they aspire to higher realised values $SS$ from their economic activities, which potential is given by $I$.

Improving the functionality of $G$ is an important dynamic force in the socio-economic space that it supports. This refers to the entrepreneurial function in the socio-economic space. In principle, this is a continuous process that is informed and guided by all members of the socio-economic space.[20] Only if the functionality of $G$ in relation to $SS$ and $I$ fails does the entrepreneurial function transform itself into a more revolutionary and disrupting force, which can be denoted as a revolution.[21]

I emphasise that the entrepreneurial function relates directly to the notional relationship $I - SS - G$. Only through collective action or collectively accepted actions by individual entrepreneurs will $G$ change and accommodate an improved performance in the socio-economic space. Thus, the entrepreneurial function is enacted and effectuated through the discourse that is represented in the notional relation $I - SS - G$.

**Role-Building as a Balancing Act**    The second relationship to be added to the construct depicted in Figs. 4.2, 4.3 and 4.4 is that between the two assumed socio-economic roles $R_i$ and $R_j$ and the ideal interaction $I$, which is actually the last remaining relational triple in this tripolar representation. This last circular relationship can be denoted as the *balancing* relationship. This final component

---

[20] However, in the capitalist economy that arose after the industrial revolution there emerged an *entrepreneurial elite*. This elite consists of a minority of population members, who have disproportional influence on the goings-on in the socio-economic space and have the qualities associated with entrepreneurship. These entrepreneurs have significant influence on the direction of the development of elements in the governance system $G$. In our contemporary global economy, there are three obvious entrepreneurial elites: the leaders in the financial sector of the global economy, in particular large, institutionalised bankers and institutional investors; the leading managers of the global energy industry; and the entrepreneurs in the information technology sector of the global economy, particularly the business leaders of Apple, Google, Facebook and Amazon.

[21] The most obvious and famous examples of such revolutions are the French and Russian revolutions of 1789 and 1917 (Schama 2004; Acton 1990). The collapse of the socialist states in 1989–1991 belongs to this class of revolutions, although many old elites transformed themselves during the latter period. But also less obvious examples such as the collapse of the Roman Republic in the period of 100–28 BCE (Schotter 2005) and the American revolution of 1776 can be explained as such (Bailyn 1992).

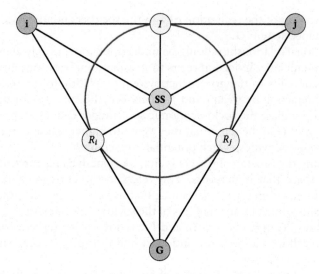

**Fig. 4.5**    A fully developed tripolar reconstruction of economic interaction

is introduced in Fig. 4.5 to arrive at the completely developed reconstruction of the economic interaction between $i$ and $j$.[22]

The balancing relationship introduced in Fig. 4.5 is that of the relationship between the two socio-economic roles or reflections $R_i$ and $R_j$ of the two economic agents $i$ and $j$ with the idealisation $I$ of the interaction between these two agents. Again, this balancing relationship should be considered as primarily a dynamic relationship. It refers to the two agents reflecting on the performance of the assumed socio-economic roles in relation to the potential value that the interaction between these two agents could generate. Thus, it refers to the evaluation and assessment of the assumed roles and whether these roles indeed achieve the stated goal of attaining sufficient wealth from the interaction between the two agents.

In this regard the circular relationship between $R_i$, $R_j$ and $I$ refers to the balancing of the assumed roles in light of their objective, being the realisation of $I$. Here, we essentially assume that the two economic agents assess and fine tune the assumed roles; it refers to role-building as an essential part of the activities of economic agents in our global economy. This role-building has to be tuned with the objectives of the economic interaction one pursues and engages in. Thus, an apple seller constructs the role he assumes in the market

---

[22] The construction depicted in Fig. 4.5 represents the *Fano plane.* This is a well-known matroid as well as a symmetric graph from discrete mathematics. It is the unique minimal fully symmetric and non-trivial matroid, generated by three poles and their derived interactions. If the three poles are represented binary by {100, 010, 001}, then the four derived elements can be given by {101, 011, 110, 111}. These seven elements exactly form the Fano plane depicted in Fig. 4.5. I refer to Ruys (1974) for an elaborate discussion.

square with the objective of meeting other sellers and buyers. The apple seller will seek to distinguish himself as a trustworthy and reputed seller, who delivers high-quality fruit.

Similarly, the hair stylist constructs her role in light of the profitable business she engages in with clients who want to be styled. Again, it is the objective of the role-building that guides decisions of the hair stylist: she will design a salon that promotes her ability to deliver high-quality hair styles and that exudes confidence in the pursuit of the highest possible realisation of the potential wealth captured in $I$.

*Summary*

Starting from three fundamental "forces"—being the abilities and desires of the two individual economic agents and the centrifugal force of the institutions in the governance system—we have arrived at a complete reconstruction of the potential interaction between the two agents. We have derived a set of four positions, being the socio-economic roles of the two economic agents, the idealised potential of the relationship and the resulting stable state in which the interaction is resolved.

I can now bring these elements together in a summary, which presents the various elements of the tripolar reconstruction of an economic interaction in a comprehensive fashion. The elements brought together in Fig. 4.5 have the following aspects:

1. The two centrifugal forces are made up of the capabilities embodied in the two economic agents $i$ and $j$, mainly referring to their individual productive abilities and consumptive desires;

2. The unique centripetal force consists of the media, tools, socio-economic roles and behavioural rules collected in the governance system $G$;

3. The interpersonal relationship between $i$ and $j$ is viewed as purely aspirational and results in its idealisation $I$. This idealisation also represents the potential value or wealth that can be generated in this interpersonal relationship;

4. Each agent constructs or builds a socio-economic role reflecting herself in the system $G$ of governing socio-economic institutions. This results in the reflections $R_i$ and $R_j$. This construction is based on the institutional trust that these individual agents have with regard to the governance instruments in $G$. This construction is costly, represented by role-building costs for each agent;

5. The operational relationships of each agent with the socio-economic role assumed by their counterpart result in a realisation of the pursued interaction, represented in $SS$. This realisation $SS$ represents an outcome in which all forces are balanced. Therefore, $SS$ can be interpreted as the embedding of the ideal $I$ in the governance system $G$;

6. The two socio-economic roles $R_i$ and $R_j$ and the realised interaction $SS$ are the only elements in the reconstruction that are observable

and measurable. All other elements remain hidden and are principally unobservable;

7. The relationship between the idealisation $I$ and $G$ reflects on the functionality of the socio-economic space to generate benefits from the interactions it supports. This is known as the notional relationship. The distinction between the idealisation $I$ and the realisation $SS$ represents the interaction inefficiency that is present in this particular interaction. Therefore, the notional relationship $I - SS - G$ represents the entrepreneurial function and the collective discourse about the effectiveness of $G$ in relation to the social goal $I$;

8. Finally, the balancing relationship of the idealisation $I$ with the generated socio-economic roles $R_i$ and $R_j$ describes the dynamic functionality of the constructed and assumed roles within this potential interaction. If the agents assume well-functioning roles, it is reflected in the value of these roles in the context of the idealisation: the socio-economic roles have to reflect the idealisation and make it possible to achieve higher returns on their activation.

**Representing Efficiency Losses in the Tripolar Reconstruction**  One could consider the complete tripolar representation in Fig. 4.5 to be flexible, in the sense that the node $G$ is placed at various distances from $I$. The closer $G$ is placed to $I$, the more efficient the socio-economic institutional matrix represented by $G$ will be in achieving the potential gains from the interaction between $i$ and $j$, represented by $I$. Now, the actual distance between $SS$ and $I$ could signify the actual efficiency loss owing to institutional imperfections in this representation.

In such a flexible representation, the farther the distance between $i$ and $R_i$ the higher the role-building costs are and the further the distance between $I$ and $SS$, the higher the overall inefficiency of the governance structure is in relation to its intended purpose of achieving and emulating interpersonal trust. Formally, $\delta_i = i - R_i$ can be called the *role-building costs* of agent $i$ in context of $G$. Analogously, $\Delta = I - SS$ can be called the *trust inefficiency* within the context of $G$, also denoted as the "trust inefficiency of governance system $G$".

This implies that the overall functionality of the socio-economic space is actually measured through $\Delta$ for all interactions that members of the socio-economic space engage in.[23] If the distance $\Delta$ is significantly large, we may conclude that there is room for improvement of the functionality of the governance system; relatively low levels of wealth from interaction are realised in comparison with the potentially available wealth levels represented in $I$.

---

[23] This reasoning can be extended to the distance of $I$ and $G$, which represents a similar measure of overall functionality of the socio-economic space, and its governance system $G$ in particular. I refer to the discussion of Fig. 4.5 for an elaboration of this point.

### 4.3.2    The Tripolar Reconstruction of Trust as a Duality

In the previous section I developed a reconstructive theory of simple economic interaction between two economic agents. This theory introduced three fundamental forces that span this interaction and four derived positions that explain the resolution of that interaction. This tripolar reconstruction was fully developed as depicted in Fig. 4.5. Based on this we can now interpret trust and trusting behaviour as the dual of that reconstruction.

Indeed, the tripolar reconstructionist perspective allows us to consider the underlying impulses that support the various relationships in Fig. 4.5. We distinguished seven different relationships in the tripolar reconstruction of simple binary socio-economic interaction. Each of these relationships corresponds to a different *impulse*. The construct of impulses corresponds again to a tripolar model that combines the resulting seven impulses into a relational structure similar to the one depicted in Fig. 4.5.

The main argument here is that the underlying support of the primary economic interaction between $i$ and $j$ in the context of the institutional matrix $G$ is a form of trust. This implies that trust is a supporting impulse to a certain relationship in the reconstruction of that economic interaction. Moreover, this trusting impulse is dualistic in nature; that is, it is the other or opposite side of the relationship under consideration.

To illustrate this fundamental principle, consider the simple case that two persons have a (social) relationship. The impulse that actually sustains the relationship is the trust between these two persons. Without such trust there is simply no relationship possible. This indeed refers to the idea that trust is the *dual* of that relationship: the trust is in that regard a supporting impulse for that relationship, while the relationship itself is actually an embodiment of the trust between those two individuals.

I can state this principle in the form of a derivative of the trust hypothesis, Lemma 1.6. This form of the trust hypothesis is more pragmatic in nature and allows the modelling of trust.

**Trust Hypothesis**  *Trust has a dualistic nature with regard to a relationship between reconstructive categories describing the nature of a socio-economic, value-generating interaction.*

**The Tripolar Dual**  The formal dual of the tripolar reconstruction of binary interaction represented in Fig. 4.5 is depicted in Fig. 4.6. As indicated, it has the same architectural structure as the original tripolar reconstruction given in Fig. 4.5, since it is self-dualistic.[24] However, the interpretation of the seven nodes and the relationships in Fig. 4.6 are dualistic in nature. Next, I discuss the seven trust concepts and their relationships in detail.

---

[24] I refer to Ruys (1974) and Evers and Maaren (1985) for further elaboration.

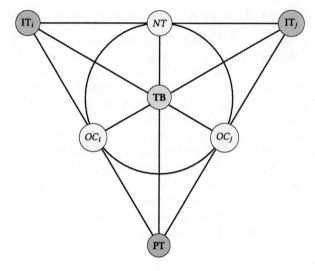

**Fig. 4.6**  Trust as the dual of reconstructed interaction

As argued, socio-economic interaction as reconstructed in Fig. 4.5 is founded on three fundamental forces, being the individual abilities and desires of the two economic agents under consideration and the binding force of the institutions and media provided through the governance system. These three forces result in three fundamental relationships in the context of the interaction between the two individual economic agents. The first one is the direct interactive relationship between $i$ and $j$, which is purely idealistic in nature. The other two are the relationships between each of the two individuals and the governance system itself.

Each of these three fundamental, spanning relationships con be interpreted as a form of socio-economic trust. I discuss these first:

**Interpersonal Trust (PT).** As discussed before in this chapter, in neo-classical economics, behavioural economics and game theory trust is generally considered to be interpersonal and based on individual characteristics of the persons involved. Trust is afforded by choice and supported through a computational comparison. In other words, trust in general is simply equated to interpersonal trust. In this regard trusting behaviour only applies to other persons, not to socio-economic institutions and media.[25]

In our comprehensive approach represented in Fig. 4.5, interpersonal trust is still recognised, but no longer as an attainable form of trust. Here,

---

[25] In the reconstructive approach promoted here, this limited perspective on trusting behaviour is replaced by a more comprehensive view founded on the embeddedness of socio-economic interaction in a system of media, behavioural rules and socio-economic institutions. This includes these other forms of trusting behaviour as a natural consequence.

interpersonal trust is considered as the supporting impulse of the idealistic interaction—represented by the relationship $i - I - j$ between the two economic agents $i$ and $j$. As such, this interaction is considered to be aspirational in nature and, therefore, interpersonal trust is non-realisable and purely aspirational as well. As stated before, interpersonal trust is an ideal form of trusting behaviour and as such fundamentally non-realisable.

Interpersonal trust has to be realised through the building of relational elements through the governance system of the prevailing socio-economic space. It is only through the use of media such as a common language and cultural elements that interaction can be established, but the interpersonal relationship—expressed in its idealisation $I$—remains an aspirational guide in the use of the institutions called upon by the prevailing governance system. And in this regard, interpersonal trust forms an ideal form of trusting behaviour; as such, it also acts as a guide in the interaction between $i$ and $j$. From the above, it should be clear that interpersonal trust is a guiding impulse and an *aspirational* form of trusting behaviour. Therefore, as such it can be recognised as a *centripetal force* itself. That is why interpersonal trust is placed at the anchor position in the tripolar diagram depicted in Fig. 4.6: interpersonal trust is depicted as the node **PT**, acting as the unique centripetal force in the trust force field. It binds the other trust forms through its aspirational guidance. In this regard, its dual nature is made clear, since interpersonal trust **PT** is the dual of the relationship $i - I - j$ between the two centrifugal forces embodied by the individual agents $i$ and $j$ in Fig. 4.5.

**Institutional Trust (IT).** The relationship of an individual economic agent and the governance system of media, behavioural norms and socio-economic institutions is supported by the trust that each individual has in those elements. This form of trust does not extend to other people, but rather relates an individual to institutional settings that she observes in her socio-economic environment, represented by the prevailing socio-economic space. This type of trust I denoted before as "institutional" trust.

Institutional trust refers to the ability of an individual to use the governance elements to her advantage in her socio-economic interactions with other individuals. The hair stylist relies on the reputation of her place of business, usually a street or district in her city of residence,[26] and the pricing rules of various elements of the services provided in order to be able to properly attract clients in the competitive industry.

---

[26] Cities emerged in economic history as major governance structures that guide business to appropriate locations and at appropriate facilities. Thus, in a medieval European city retail business was placed in the city centre, close to the market square, while bulk trade was located at the harbour area where large merchants interacted to write large-scale trade contracts concerning bulk goods that were imported into the city. These locations were appropriately indicated with street names to guide potential customers (Pirenne 1952; Gies and Gies 1969).

In this capacity, institutional trust can be assessed as the dual of role-building. This form of trust informs and supports the construction of the appropriate socio-economic role of an individual in the prevailing governance system. On the other hand, the resulting expertise of role-building results in an enhancement of the institutional trust that is present in the socio-economic space in which these agents operate. Hence, institutional trust begets role-building and role-building enhances such trust.

In Fig. 4.5, role-building by agent $i$ has been represented as the embeddedness relationship $i - R_i - G$ itself. Its dual—institutional trust—is now denoted by $\mathbf{IT}_i$ in Fig. 4.6. Similarly, we can consider $j - R_j - G$ as the role building relationship, supported by $j$'s institutional trust $\mathbf{IT}_j$. Now, $\mathbf{IT}_i$ and $\mathbf{IT}_j$ represent the two centrifugal forces in the tripolar force field representing trusting behaviour underlying economic interaction. In this regard, institutional trust gives expression to the desires and abilities of an individual. Institutional trust relates to the ability of an agent to express herself in the tools and instruments that the prevailing governance system provides. The better an individual is at building an appropriate and effective socio-economic role, the higher the institutional trust is of that particular individual. Well-functioning individuals indeed rarely make good rebels and revolutionaries. This refers to the centrifugal nature of institutional trust in comparison to interpersonal trust that actually acts as a binding force in this tripolar force field.

I emphasise here that institutional trust is limited to the relationship of an individual with the institutional environment created by the elements in the governance system $G$. In this regard, it has no bearing on the interaction between the two individuals directly. The underlying impulse of that relationship is represented by interpersonal trust and the other derived forms of trusting behaviour that I will address below. It should be clear that institutional trust in this respect acts as a fundamental force as well, independently from the other forms of trust in Fig. 4.6.

The three fundamental forms of trusting behaviour now correspond to the three corner points in Fig. 4.6, $\mathbf{IT}_i$, $\mathbf{IT}_j$ and $\mathbf{PT}$, being the two main manifestations of centrifugal trusting force and a single manifestation of centripetal trusting force.

**Derived Forms of Trust**  As we pursued in the reconstruction of economic interaction, we now may derive four further forms of trusting behaviour from these three fundamental trust forms. These result from the relationships between these three fundamental forms. The derived forms are two forms of operational confidence, denoted by $\mathbf{OC}_i$ and $\mathbf{OC}_j$, one form of notional trust NT and finally a form of trust balance **TB**. I discuss these derived forms of trust in detail below.

**Operational Confidence (OC).**  The first derived form in the trust force field is that of operational confidence, which refers to the impulse that supports the usage of derived forms of governance instruments in our daily economic interactions. Thus, it refers to the trust of clients in the persona created by the hair stylist to run her business: the layout of the store; the production technologies used by the hair stylist; her outfit or uniform; and the marketing tools employed by her. As argued before, it refers to the trust we have in the usage of other of the elements (media, behavioural rules and socio-economic institutions) in the prevailing governance structure.

In Fig. 4.5 this refers to the relationship between an individual and socio-economic role representing the other individual. In terms of the symbolic language used here, operational confidence supports the relationships $i - SS - R_j$ and $j - SS - R_i$. Hence, we introduce the two nodes $OC_i$ and $OC_j$ in Fig. 4.6 as the duals of these two operational relationships.

From Fig. 4.6 it is also clear that operational confidence embodies the relationship between institutional trust and interpersonal trust. In other words, operational confidence is the meeting point of our trust in the governance system (institutional trust) and the support of the idealised form of the binary interaction (interpersonal trust). As stated, interpersonal trust guides the usage of the governance system by individuals and interacts with the institutional trust these individuals have concerning the elements in the prevailing governance system $G$. This finds its expression in our operational confidence.

More practically, operational confidence reflects our institutional trust and our belief that the idealised interaction that we all pursue can be realised. It brings together our aspirations and our trust in the governance system. If our aspirations are lofty, our operational confidence will be enhanced as a consequence. On the other hand, if we believe more in the institutional environment we operate in, implying higher institutional confidence, the more we aim at in our interactions and the more we expect from these interactions. This is reflected in our operational confidence as well.

This refers to a much deeper, underlying principle of the connections between these various forms of trusting behaviour. Operational confidence in this regard combines the aspirational ideal of interpersonal trust and the trust in the prevailing governance system that should make it possible to realise some of these ideals.

Finally, I point out a secondary dualistic relationship. Namely, the relationship $IT_i - OC_i - PT$ is fully captured by the individual economic agent $i$ herself. Indeed, within our individual being, we bring together our trust in the prevailing institutional setting in which we operate, the aspirations we have to interact with others and the operational confidence that we exhibit in the actions of others. In other words, our individual nature is determined through these three forms of individualistic trust. If any of these three types of trust is weak, it is questionable whether an individual can successfully construct an effective socio-economic role for herself and operate successfully within the socio-economic space supported through $G$.

In this respect, an individual essentially forms an incarnation of the delicate balance between these three forms of trusting behaviour.

Technically, this refers to the fact that the relationship $IT_i - OC_i - PT$ in Fig. 4.6 is the actual dual of $i$ in Fig. 4.5.[27]

**Notional Trust (NT).** The trust impulse that supports the notional relationship $I - SS - G$ in Fig. 4.5 has been rather neglected in the trust literature. This type of trust is of a different category. Namely, individual human beings also base their behaviour on trust in the community or society as a whole. This form of trust, therefore, refers to one's trust in the totality of the socio-economic space.

This form of trust is denoted as *notional trust* and refers to our collective trust in the very media and socio-economic institutions on which a community or society is founded. In some sense this type of trust is the belief that one's institutional trust acts as a good proxy for the ideal of true interpersonal trust. Hence, one trusts that a baker will do a good job of baking bread *as if* he were one's close personal friend (Seabright 2010).

Therefore, notional trust refers to the acceptance of and full compliance with the media and institutions at the foundation of the socio-economic space under consideration. Using game-theoretic terminology, notional trust refers to the hypothesis that all economic agents within a given socio-economic space have *common knowledge* of all socio-economic institutions that form the foundation of that space.

Obviously, the prevailing media have to be trusted completely to be useful among individuals. Indeed, one has to rely fully on the language one speaks, whether verbal or in gestures and signs. For example, consider the use of *posted prices* in economic interaction and trade. Using such prices to more quickly reach a trade deal among trading parties is something that these parties have to be familiar with. Only if they know and are fully confident that the other party has knowledge of the usage of posted prices and accepts them, can one easily establish these standardised trade contracts. I argue that the usage of posted prices has to be common knowledge among the trading parties: each party knows that the other party knows that they have knowledge of the usage of posted prices; each party knows that the other party knows that they know that the other party has knowledge of the usage of posted prices; and so on. Only common knowledge of these media and institutions makes such institutions actually useful and have value.

I view notional trust as a fundamental form of social cohesion that is present in any human society, which facilitates socio-economic interactions. This form of notional trust goes beyond the individual level and refers to the

[27] I emphasise here that the reconstructionist approach applied here opens up numerous interesting avenues and insights. First, we identify multiple forms of trusting behaviour as relevant for the understanding of economic interaction. Second, these innovative forms of trust exhibit surprising interpretations through their relationships with other trust categories and elements in the reconstruction of the economic interaction itself.

very social fabric of the community itself: notional trust refers to acting in accordance with the social contract at the foundation of human society. It refers to the fact that human interaction is impossible without those media and other institutions. In our lives these social media and skills are hard wired as much as our desires and abilities are. We grow up in a social environment and the rules of social interaction including language and social habits become part of our innermost being. As such, notional trust refers to a belief in the social governance system that is part of ourselves.

In this regard notional trust refers to a political factor in human socio-economic interaction. It refers to the collective discourse that a society has about the functionality of its governing institutions. This indeed refers to a political discussion rather than purely individualistic considerations such as represented by each individual's institutional trust.

In Fig. 4.5 notional trust supports the dynamic notional relationship $I - SS - G$, which was discussed extensively in the previous section. In Fig. 4.6 the dual of this notional relationship is represented as the node NT, which is spanned between the two incarnations of the two centrifugal trust forces, $IT_i$ and $IT_j$. Indeed, this refers back to the common knowledge aspect of the interaction between the two individuals $i$ and $j$. Where the two individuals' institutional trusts meet is in the common knowledge to fully trust that the other economic agent adheres to the prevailing social contract, in this case the prevailing governing institutions.

Again I point out that the trust relationship $IT_i - NT - IT_j$ has a dual as well, which corresponds to the governance system $G$ itself. Alternatively, we can interpret this as meaning that the governance system is the incarnation of our collective notional and institutional trusts. It gives a full expression to these forms of trusting behaviour and responds to these trust forms. Indeed, the governance system actually responds and changes to our usage of its prevailing elements. It also responds to our collective satisfaction dissatisfaction with the governance system or its specific elements.

This also refers to the many evolutionary and revolutionary changes that have taken place throughout history. In a primitive market, prices are mainly established through direct bargaining. This is still the case in many markets in our global economy, such as the Moroccan suq and the Egyptian bazaar in Istanbul. However, in our supermarkets we only use and adhere to posted prices; bargaining is not accepted at the cash register. These posted prices reduce transaction costs significantly by eliminating bargaining costs, mainly in the form of time preference and labour costs. This evolution has now further progressed in the internet economy, in which online shopping is based on completely individualised posted prices.[28]

---

[28] This refers to the ability of online traders to individualise prices fully based on collected information about shopping behaviour. In advanced assessment methods a customer's credit score, Facebook friendships and past shopping behaviour could inform Amazon to set a completely individualised posted price for the commodities considered by that customer.

The evolutionary change of pricing rules in trade is informed by our use of the price mechanism and the aspirations we have regarding its usage. Increased transaction efficiency is critical in this respect and guides the change from bargaining to posted prices. It requires in some sense a higher level of institutional trust, since it eliminates a check on the fair pricing of the traded commodities, which is certainly protected by direct bargaining. Furthermore, it requires a sophisticated form of notional trust that opens the way for society to accept this pricing tool. Indeed, posted pricing relies highly on the perceived fairness of the suppliers that price these commodities. To summarise, the trust relationship $IT_i - NT - IT_j$ is the dual of the governance system $G$ itself. The governance system thus *incarnates* these forms of trusting behaviour and is fully formed through the forces that are represented in these types of trusting behaviour. In this regard, the governance system is viewed as a social contract that is accepted and trusted by all members of the socio-economic space.

**Trust Balance (TB).** Finally, the balancing relationship $I - R_i - R_j$ in Fig. 4.5 has a dual in the form of the underlying impulse denoted as the trust balance. As the balancing relationship itself, the underlying trust has in principle a dynamic character. It is reflecting the confidence of the two interacting parties $i$ and $j$ in their constructed socio-economic roles to generate sufficient value in their relationship.

To return to the example of our hair stylist, she constructs a socio-economic role for herself in response to the socio-economic roles assumed by her clients. Clients will enter her shop seeking a new hairdo while observing her outfit and shop. This informs them about the potential value that they can expect from the service provided by this particular hair stylist. Vice versa, the hair stylist through interaction with a potential client will identify the potential profitability of delivering a service to this client. In this regard, the two parties interact with the objective of achieving a realisation of the potential ideal value of their relationship. This is exactly captured by the balancing relationship, which describes the metaphorical dance of the interacting parties $i$ and $j$ through the assumed socio-economic roles $R_i$ and $R_j$, with the objective to realise a substantial portion of the ideal value $I$.

The underlying impulse for this dynamic interaction is now denoted as the trust balance between $i$ and $j$. In turn, the trust balance describes a rest point—or "dynamic equilibrium"—of the various forms of trust that emerge in the interaction between $i$ and $j$. Thus, the trust balance is also a steady state of the forces generated between the institutional trusts of the two parties as well as the aspirational interpersonal trust between these agents. This steady state is in principle dynamic in the sense that the interaction is in flux and socio-economic roles are adapted in response to the needs of the agents, as well as the availability of instruments in the prevailing governance system.

The trust balance has a central position in the trusting force field depicted in Fig. 4.6. In this regard, it plays a central role in explaining a variety of concepts in the reconstruction of the interaction between $i$ and $j$ as depicted in Fig. 4.5.

First, the relationship $IT_i - TB - OC_j$ can be understood as a description of the socio-economic role $R_i$ assumed by agent $i$. Indeed, through that role, agent $i$ seeks to engage with $j$, and so the role that she assumes is founded on her own institutional trust in the instruments provided through the governance system $G$ and the operational confidence of the other agent $j$ in his response to the role $R_i$ assumed by $i$. Central in this interpretation is the trust balance that brings together these various elements; it is the binding underlying force that holds the assumed socio-economic role $R_i$ together.

Second, the relationship $NT - TB - PT$ actually represents the idealisation $I$ of the interaction between $i$ and $j$. Indeed, notional trust and interpersonal trust are aspirational in nature and, as such, also collective with regard to the two interacting parties $i$ and $j$. From this perspective, the trust balance binds notional trust and interpersonal trust together in the idealisation $I$.

Finally, I mention that the circular relationship $OC_i - NT - OC_j$ actually reflects the realisation $SS$ itself. In the equilibrium state, the operational forms of trust are brought together with notional trust. Operational confidence reflects how both agents use their own socio-economic role and interact with the other's socio-economic role to generate value from their interaction. On the other hand, notional trust describes how the governance instruments on which these socio-economic roles are based are modified and enhanced in light of the idealisation $I$ of the relationship between $i$ and $j$. The relationship between these forms of trust now are brought together in the actual realisation $SS$ of that interaction.

This final piece of the puzzle completes the reconstruction of the interaction between two agents within a socio-economic space founded on a set of governance instruments $G$. It should be emphasised again that this reconstruction of the interaction of two economic agents is purely conceptual in nature.

## 4.4   WHAT CONSTITUTES ECONOMIC ACTIVITY?

To conclude this chapter, I discuss the delineation of economic activity in contrast to non-economic, social activity. The first is the prerogative of economics, while the second is in principle covered by social science, social psychology and/or sociology. Therefore, we ask the question what exactly the boundaries of economics are and where activities become the subject of other subjects.

I have already mentioned the case of a conversation between different people. Although a conversation generates consumption values for all conversationalists, it can be argued that such an activity is actually *not* an economic interaction. Next, I will introduce some rules that make it possible to make such a delineation.

I promote the rule that an economic interaction should be representable using the tripolar reconstruction developed here. The categorisation of interaction as being "economic" is therefore based on the embeddedness of this interaction in the prevailing system of governing socio-economic institutions and our agreement to categorise it as such.

The main feature of economic activities is therefore that these activities are founded on the assumption of participants in these interactions of appropriate socio-economic roles. These roles should be firmly within the economic realm of human experience. In other words, the "economicness" of interaction is founded on the same foundations that we consider throughout our approach: activities are principally economic if they are recognised as such by the constituents of these activities.

For practical purposes it is preferable to define an interaction as economic if it can pass a test. I refer to this test as the *replacement principle*:

**The Replacement Principle** *A social interaction is **economic** if it is value generating and it is* either *embedded in the prevailing social division of labour,* or *it can be replaced by an appropriate extension of that social division of labour.*

If interactions take place within the social division of labour, they can easily be recognised as being economic in nature. Obviously, these interactions are embedded in the prevailing system of governing socio-economic institutions. Indeed, any trade relationship is founded on an underlying economic interaction and it can be analysed using the tripolar reconstruction.

On the other hand, activities that occur outside the setting of the social division of labour are much harder to assess as being economic in nature. The Replacement Principle introduces the test that an interaction is categorised as economic if it can be conducted through an appropriately constructed extension of the social division of labour. So, if one can reconstruct the interaction using appropriately chosen new economic commodities, new socio-economic roles and institutional rules, it should be able to categorise it as economic. Namely, such an extension of the social division of labour is founded on embedding the interaction properly in the prevailing system of socio-economic institutions.

Below I will argue that a conversation between friends is not economic in nature. It cannot be reconstructed through an appropriately configured social division of labour, since the values it generates are not economic in nature. On the other hand, the preparation of a family meal is economic in nature. This activity can be conducted through a social division of labour using a cook, a server and appropriate sums of monetary compensation for these professionals.

**Reconstruction of a Conversation** Returning to the example of a conversation, we distinguish no clear economic roles assumed by the participating conversationalists. No physical economic output is generated in a conversation; just consumption values from the pleasant spending of time in company. Mainly this conclusion is based on the social conventions that surround an activity such as a conversation among friends. Even if other economic goods are consumed during the conversation, such as some pints of Guinness, we collectively do not recognise this activity as being economic. Thus, the social conventions surrounding the activity of a "conversation among friends" only allow its classification as a purely social activity rather than an economic or socio-economic activity.

However, if we consider a debate by candidates for the American presidency or the position of UK prime minister, the economic consequences are very clear. Such a debate therefore fits in with the definition of an economic interaction. It is in fact a (public) performance by individuals who assume clear socio-economic roles, in particular the roles of the Democratic and the Republican candidate for the presidency of the USA. The debate takes place in public, possibly in front of a television and internet audience, is moderated by a professional political journalist and generates commercial values: corporations will generate revenues from activities surrounding the debate. This includes the sale of television time and space on web pages carrying the debate for commercial use.

A conversation in a pub is much less clear. Indeed, the conversation itself can be understood as a pure consumption activity, but it takes place within the context of a clear corporate setting. A pub is a commercial enterprise and in principle sells products that are socially consumed to generate revenues for the pub. In this regard the conversation between consuming clients of the pub is part of the productive activity or production process of the pub itself. The conversationalists in the pub all assume the same socio-economic role, namely as clients of the pub. Therefore, it is clear that a conversation in a pub is part of a larger economic activity, namely between the pub and its clients, which is essentially a simple economic trade activity embedded in the prevailing social division of labour.

**Reconstructing the Cooking of a Family Meal**   Another category of activities that is of interest to consider here is related to home-keeping tasks. If one cooks a meal at home and consumes it with one's family, is it an economic activity? In nature, it seems very similar to having a conversation while consuming some pints of Guinness, as mentioned above. Indeed, purchased commodities are converted into a meal at the family table, similar to drinking a few pints of purchased beer at one's home with visitors. In that regard, why should it be considered to be a purely social activity rather than a socio-economic one?

The main difference between cooking a meal and consuming it with one's family and having beers with visitors is the act of producing the meal. Cooking is clearly a considerable productive task, requiring certain skills that point to some degree of specialisation. In this regard, it is much more than opening a few cans of beer, and as such it indicates the possibility that cooking a meal and its consumption is a socio-economic activity than can actually be *outsourced*. This implies that we could visit a restaurant and purchase a prepared meal to replace the described home activity. Thus, the Replacement Principle is directly applicable, and this in turn indicates that the home cooking of a meal has true, measurable economic value.

We can therefore conclude that cooking a meal is actually a *household production* task. Household production is defined as the class of productive activities that result in the creation of non-tradable goods. Household production usually involves the members of a household and is limited to the production or creation of goods that are consumed directly in the home.[29]

The Replacement Principle makes clear that the outsourcing of household production tasks is a central feature of the deepening of the social division of labour. The history of the consumer capitalist economy can also be interpreted as an embodiment of the steady deepening of the capitalist social division of labour through the outsourcing of household production activities. The development of a hospitality industry to replace the production and consumption of home-prepared meals has resulted in significant increases in the economic wealth generated, defining the very nature of the consumer capitalist economy.

**Reconstructing Social Production** Household production contrasts with *social production* in which one creates tradable goods or "commodities". Social production activities are firmly part of the socio-economic networks in our global economy; these activities are clearly part of the social division of labour.[30] Household production can only be the endpoint of such a chain of specialised productive activities; it signifies a final consumption task, even though certain inputs are still converted into consumables in the household as part of that final "consumption".

Social production activities are usually conducted within the setting of a *firm*, which can be defined roughly as a production organisation and as such is part of the superstructure in a relational economy. Firms are crucial elements in the socio-economic infrastructure of our contemporary global economy. As such they clearly form elements in the supply chains in the economy. In that regard, this again emphasises that social production is very much a socio-economic activity that is a fundamental part of the fabric of the relational economy.

The distinction between household and social production is simply that of placement. Household production can easily be replaced with or converted into social production and, therefore, as a consequence of the Replacement Principle should very much be denoted as a socio-economic activity. Converting

---

[29] In a primitive economy, nearly all productive activities are conducted in the home and should be categorised as household production activities. Only after there emerges a primitive social division of labour within such an autarkic economy can the economic agents start to build trade networks, and consequently move away from household production as the main productive organisation mode.

[30] With reference to the previous footnote, it is clear that moving away from an autarkic economy is founded on the introduction of social production organisations. This implies that social production is a crucial element of the development of the subjective and objective spheres in the relational economy represented by a socio-economic space.

household production into social production is essentially an entrepreneurial activity.

**A Concluding Remark** Now we can compare the discussed activities with our conventions about what we denote as "economic" versus "non-economic". As indicated, having a beer with friends in one's home is not an economic activity, but on the other hand cooking a meal and consuming it is recognised as such. This is firmly founded on the stated Replacement Principle. This is further supported by the historical fact that over time economic activities are more and more subsumed into the social division of labour.

The discussion about what delineates household production from social production activities indicates that the social recognition of certain activities as economic is based on the defining elements of these activities. It is in fact the social recognition of these underlying properties of these activities that determines what we denote as economic versus non-economic. These defining properties are clearly stated in the Replacement Principle: these activities and interactions can be subsumed in a social division of labour and as such can be reconstructed using the tripolar methodology developed in this chapter.

## REFERENCES

Acton, E. 1990. *Rethinking the Russian Revolution.* London: Hodder Education.

Bailyn, B. 1992. *Ideological Origins of the American Revolution.* 2nd revised ed. Cambridge, MA: Harvard University Press.

Beaudreau, B.C. 2004. *World Trade: A Network Approach.* New York, NY: iUniverse.

Berg, J., J. Berghaut, and K. McCabe. 1995. Trust, Reciprocity, and Social History. *Games and Economic Behavior* 10:122–142.

Buskens, V. 2002. *Social Networks and Trust.* Boston, MA: Kluwer Academic Publishers.

Coleman, J.S. 1990. *Foundations of Social Theory.* Cambridge, MA: Belknap Press.

Evers, J.J.M., and H.v. Maaren. 1985. Duality Principles in Mathematics and their Relations to Conjugate Functions. *Nieuw Archief voor de Wiskunde* 3: 23–68.

Fehr, E. 2009. On the Economics and Biology of Trust. *Journal of the European Economic Association* 7: 235–266.

Gies, J., and F. Gies. 1969. *Life in a Medieval City.* New York, NY: HarperPerennial.

Gilboa, I., and D. Schmeidler. 2001. *A Theory of Case-Based Decisions.* Cambridge: Cambridge University Press.

Gilboa, I., D. Schmeidler, and P.P. Wakker. 2002. Utility in Case-Based Decision Theory. *Journal of Economic Theory* 105: 483–502.

Gilles, R.P. 1990. Core and Equilibria of Socially Structured Economies: The Modelling of Social Constraints in Economic Behaviour. Ph.D. thesis. Tilburg: Tilburg University.

Glaeser, E., D. Laibson, J. Scheinkman, and C. Soutter. 2000. Measuring Trust. *Quarterly Journal of Economics* 115(3): 811–846.

Hardin, R. 2006. *Trust.* Cambridge: Polity Press.

Horan, R., E. Bulte, and J. Shogren. 2005. How Trade Saved Humanity from Biological Exclusion: An Economic Theory of Neanderthal Extinction. *Journal of Economic Behavior and Organization* 58(1): 1–29.

James, H.S. Jr. 2002. The Trust Paradox: A Survey of Economic Inquiries into the Nature of Trust and Trustworthiness. *Journal of Economic Behavior & Organization* 47: 291–307.

Leijonhufvud, A. 1995. The Individual, the Market and the Industrial Division of Labor. In *L'individuo e il mercato*, ed. C. Mongardini, 61–78. Rome: Bulzoni.

Leijonhufvud, A. 2007. The Individual, the Market and the Division of Labor in Society. *Capitalism and Society* 2(2), Article 3.

Mailath, G.J., and L. Samuelson. 2006. *Repeated Games and Reputations: Long-Run Relationships*. Oxford: Oxford University Press.

Nooteboom, B. 2002. *Trust: Forms, Foundations, Functions, Failures and Figures*. Cheltenham: Edward Elgar Publishing.

Onyeiwu, S., and R. Jones. 2003. An institutionalist perception of cooperative behavior. *Journal of Socio-Economics* 32(3): 233–248.

Pirenne, H. 1952. *Medieval Cities: Their Origins and the Revival of Trade*. Princeton, NJ: Princeton University Press.

Power, E. 1924. *Medieval People*. London: Methuen.

Robbins, L. 1932. *An Essay on the Nature and Significance of Economic Science*. London: Self published.

Ruys, P.H.M. 1974. *Public Goods and Decentralization: The Duality Approach in the Theory of Value*. Dordrecht: Kluwer Academic Publishers.

Ruys, P.H.M. 1999. The Role of the Medium in an Interaction Structure. In *Logic, Game Theory and Social Choice: Proceedings of LGS 1, May 13-16, 1999*, ed. H. de Swart, 314–329.

Ruys, P.H.M. 2008. A Constructive Theory of Representation. In *CentER Dicussion Paper Series*. Tilburg: Tilburg University.

Schama, S. 2004. *Citizens: A Chronicle of The French Revolution*. New ed. London: Penguin.

Schotter, D. 2005. *Fall of Roman Republic. Lancaster Pamphlets in Ancient History*. 2nd ed. London: Routledge.

Seabright, P. 2010. *The Company of Strangers: A Natural History of Economic Life*. Revised and enlarged ed. Princeton, NJ: Princeton University Press.

Shackle, G.L.S. 1972. *Epistemics and Economics: A Critique of Economic Doctrines*. Cambridge: Cambridge University Press.

Shackle, G.L.S. 1979. *Imagination and the Nature of Choice*. Edinburgh: University of Edinburgh Press.

# CHAPTER 5

# The Entrepreneurial Function

## Coauthored with Owen Sims

As the social division of labour is at the centre of our perspective on wealth creation, its evolution and institutional development is of major significance to our discussion. In Chap. 3 we have already discussed that the development of a socio-economic space and the structure of the social division of labour depend on two major factors: *institutional embeddedness* and the *entrepreneurial function*.

We elaborated on the embeddedness of economic agents in Chap. 4 and developed a duality approach to socio-economic trust, trustworthiness and other forms of trusting behaviour. In particular, we argued that trust is founded in our fundamental trust of the socio-economic institutions that govern our collective wealth creation.

Embeddedness shapes the division of labour, in particular its architecture, in the context of a given governance system—which consists of all socio-economic institutions in which interactions are embedded. Embeddedness informs the context of all economic interactions and relationships within the space. This takes the form of the emerging socio-economic roles and the associated productive possibilities for agents. Thus, all interaction in a socio-economic space is ultimately formed through the institutions that govern and guide these interactions.

In this chapter we turn to the further development and discussion of the entrepreneurial function that drives innovation in the socio-economic space. As argued in Chap. 3, in a socio-economic space innovation is lasting and effective if it is institutional in nature and if it affects the fundamental functioning of the wealth creation processes in the prevailing social division of labour. The entrepreneurial function represents the innovative processes that shape and change the prevailing governing institutions in the socio-economic space.

---

This chapter was developed in close cooperation with Owen Sims. A previous draft of this chapter was part of Owen's PhD dissertation, where it is presented as Sims (2017, Chapter 4).

© The Author(s) 2018
R. P. Gilles, *Economic Wealth Creation and the Social Division of Labour*,
https://doi.org/10.1007/978-3-319-76397-2_5

In particular, entrepreneurial actions drive the deepening of the social division of labour extended; an initial insight made by Smith (1776). Outlining a theory of the entrepreneur, and with it an elaboration of the theory of the entrepreneurial function within our relational perspective, is the main focus of this chapter.

We develop a holistic perspective on the entrepreneurial function within a socio-economic space built on a basis that is founded on the well-known contributions of Schumpeter (1926, 1929, 1934), Baumol (1968, 1983, 1990, 2002), Burt (1976) and Henrekson and Sanandaji (2011). Subsequently, we develop our own institutional perspective from the foundations of the socio-economic space as a model of economic wealth creation through a social division of labour. We apply our framework to the case offered by the rise of the House of Medici in the Florentine economy in the fourteenth and fifteenth centuries. By doing this we add a theoretical perspective to the business history contributions by de Roover (1946) and others regarding the rise of the Medici Bank, the change in both the informal and formal perception of usury and the partnership system architecture of banking at this time.

**Progressive Institutional Innovation** In Chap. 3, we argued that the entrepreneurial function refers to the force of institutional innovation that propels the development of the socio-economic space. This form of innovation can be *progressive*—meaning that the innovation improves the functionality of the social division of labour, generally improving the lives of the participating economic agents—or it can be *regressive*—meaning that the innovation worsens economic performance and productivity in the social division of labour.

Our discussion in Chap. 2 shows that periods of progressive institutional innovation are interspersed with periods of regressive innovation. In this regard, progression and regression are natural parts of the institutional waves in economic history. Overall, however, the past three centuries constitute a period of significant progressive institutional development and change. During this period the institutional foundations of the industrial incorporated (capitalist) economy were laid out through several stages. The emerging capitalist institutional matrix was adopted throughout the global economy. During this historical period, economic wealth creation was significantly amplified and the lives of individuals throughout the world were enriched significantly.

On the other hand, the decline and collapse of the Roman Empire in the fourth and fifth centuries CE is usually considered to be a period of institutional regression. The economy restructured itself as a feudal hierarchy in which subsistence and serfdom of the peasantry were the norm. Economic performance and productivity declined significantly through the shrinking of the scope and depth of the social division of labour during this historical period.

More recently, the rise of the neo-liberal institutional framework in our contemporary global economy since the 1980s has resulted in socio-economic developments that many would consider to be regressive. Increased inequality and discontent have emerged from these institutional modifications—founded on the favouring of transnational corporations (TNCs) over democratically structured nation-states. This wave of institutional change is still playing out, and it is too early to state with certainty where this process will lead the global division of labour.

**Entrepreneurs and the Entrepreneurial Function**  In Chap. 3 we elaborated on the distinction between "entrepreneurs" and the "entrepreneurial function". We introduced entrepreneurs as individual economic agents that play a critical role in the process of institutional innovation within a socio-economic space.[1]

It has to be emphasised that in the context of the entrepreneurial function, entrepreneurs have to be assessed only from the aspect of institutional innovators. We refer to the discussion in Chap. 3 of the first Roman emperor Octavian Augustus as an institutional, political entrepreneur to illustrate that entrepreneurship is not restricted to the strict confines of business only. Indeed, institutional developments are mostly political through our public discourse of socio-economic performance and functionality. This implies that the adoption of institutional innovations and even the instigation of such innovations are well within the political realm of public discourse. As such, true institutional innovation is very much political and its success also depends on the political abilities of such entrepreneurs to network and build coalitions to support its adoption.[2]

This institutional perspective on entrepreneurship aligns rather well with the perspectives put forward in the economics literature. We discuss these established theories in the first part of this chapter, before turning to the case of the Medicis.

**Motivating Case: The Rise of the House of Medici**  One of the most influential and acclaimed pieces of business history is Raymond de Roover (1946)'s investigation into the rise and fall of the Medici Bank. His analysis chronicles the evolution of the House of Medici from its establishment by Giovanni di' Bicci de' Medici, and later growth by his son and heir Cosimo di' Giovanni de' Medici. This study, although deficient in overarching theory, provides an impressively intricate analysis of the financial accounts and business practices of the Medici Bank at the centre of the entrepreneurial activities of the Medicis. This chapter therefore contributes to the work on the House of Medici by developing a theoretical analysis of the entrepreneurial function in

---

[1] This is rather different from the practice in our neo-liberal economy to denote any so-called "self-employed" individual and every senior manager of a large corporation as an entrepreneur. These individuals do not contribute significantly enough to the process of institutional innovation in the global division of labour to be denoted entrepreneurial from the perspective of the entrepreneurial function discussed here.

[2] This is shown very clearly in the rise of the House of Medici as our main case in this chapter; the Medici very effectively combined socio-economic institutional innovation with political networking and the building of social networks to further their causes.

a socio-economic space and applying it to the actions of the entrepreneurial agents that drove the rise of the Medici Bank. Our specific application assesses the actions of Giovanni and Cosimo de' Medici.

De Jong et al. (2012) identify a need for the creation of a "new business history". The focus of new business history, according to these authors, is to complement case study research with a firm theoretical foundation. The continued focus on single firms within business history, as noted by De Jong et al. (2012), is not the source of the methodological problems faced by business historians. Studying single firms may highlight the need for more general models.[3] This use of analytic narrative to illustrate the application of the theory on entrepreneurship is an important methodology, and one that we use here in the case of the rise of the House of Medici.

Analytic narratives are a subset of a more inclusive approach to business and economic history—one that is arguably more general and thus compatible with business history than standard cliometrics—itself a branch of empirical economics. The standard approach of economists in motivating an in-depth investigation is to formulate a set of puzzles. A number of interlinked elements can be identified when considering the establishment and rise of the Medici Bank and the change in institutional governance structure of the Florentine economy during this time.

The first element regards the institutional change in moneylending and the provision of financial credit that allowed it to move out of the ghettos of Florence—and away from the faith-based assessment as the work of the devil—to become the legitimate preserve of banks. This transition was symbolised by the rise of international moneylending practices and the rise of the Medici Bank in this international financial network.

The second element concerns the phenomenal economic prosperity of the Medici Bank and the political dominance of the Medici family in Florence within the first two generations of the family. The Medici family rose from obscurity to become one of the most powerful families in Europe. Prior to the establishment of the Medici Bank, the Medici family were renowned criminals in Florence. Indeed, within a seventeen-year period five members of the Medici clan were sentenced to death by the criminal courts for capital crimes. The causes of the rise of the Medicean hegemony are addressed with respect to an analysis of institutional entrepreneurship. In relation to this we also look at the interrelationship between the political and economic spheres of the society, and how the Medici rose to dominate both spheres.

---

[3] In a recent paper, Brownlow (2015) acknowledges the call of De Jong et al. (2012) for a new business history. In doing so, Brownlow provides an analytic narrative regarding the establishment of the *DeLorean Motor Company* in Northern Ireland during the "Troubles". He provides a convincing depiction of DeLorean as a rent-seeking entrepreneur who exploited governmental policies and institutional responses to the deficient Northern Irish economy relative to the rest of Britain.

Beyond these two elements of this case, the motivation for analysing the Medici is related to the fact that there exist few other entrepreneurial families that have had such an impact on the cultural and economic composition of a historical period. Indeed, one can ask oneself whether the world we see today would have been the same if the Medici had not come to power in Florence during the late Middle Ages. It is of interest to see how a family gained so much economic and political control; how the actions and innovations of a small group punctuated the direction of a civilisation. More specifically, it is important to see how a theory of entrepreneurship can explain how individuals attain power within an economy. The Medicis were able to amass so much power and success because of their entrepreneurial ability, in particular their potential to innovate, network and build their own socio-economic role within the late medieval Florentine socio-economic space.

## 5.1    Established Perspectives on the Entrepreneurial Function

Jean-Baptiste Say initially coined the term of *entrepreneur* around the beginning of the nineteenth century, proclaiming that the entrepreneur was an economic agent who owned a large quantity of resources and transferred them out of an area of lower productivity into an area of higher productivity and greater yield (Hindle 2008).[4] To a large extent, this perspective has been embraced by neo-classical theories of entrepreneurship. Indeed, the Sayian concept is firmly founded on methodological individualistic principles, and the neo-classical models of static market equilibrium provide mechanisms in which to integrate the individual's decision to be an entrepreneur as an "occupational choice", meaning that individuals allocate their talents to either becoming an entrepreneur and setting up their own enterprise or becoming an employee for an existing firm, depending on the prevailing market wage level to the corresponding actions.[5]

**The Knightian Perspective**   Frank Knight (1921) enhanced the Sayian view and defined an entrepreneur and entrepreneurship as the profitable bearing of non-measurable economic uncertainty. For Knight all forms of entrepreneurship must have "uncertainty" and "profit" involved. His central thesis suggests in particular that entrepreneurs profit from the bearing of uncertainty.

Indeed, Knight's notion of uncertainty relates it to unique events in which probability and outcome can only be subjectively assessed. Unlike risk,

---

[4] This is not dissimilar to the perspective developed in Kirzner (1979), who perceives such entrepreneurial agents to bring the market to an improved equilibrium.

[5] Note that the Sayian concept fits very well with the neo-liberal perspective of an entrepreneur as any person who is not employed through a traditional employment relationship with a firm. In the neo-liberal perspective, these individuals are elevated to be the bearers of economic growth and development in the global economy.

uncertainty cannot be estimated and insured against. Profit is the reward for those willing to bear such non-measurable, inestimable and uninsurable uncertainty.[6] Entrepreneurs are thus those who are willing to incur the uncertainty of a potentially profitable course of action. This distinction between risk and uncertainty typically does not, however, filter into conventional economics. As a consequence, Knight (1935, p. 282) notes that "in the idealised society of equilibrium theory, there would be no occasion for assigning the distinctive name of profit to any type of return".

Next we explore three established theoretical perspectives of the entrepreneurial function and entrepreneurship that go beyond the narrow interpretations proposed by Say and Knight. The first is the neo-classical market theory that entrepreneurship is a result of occupational choice, linked to models of endogenous growth developed within the neo-classical framework. The second is the Schumpeterian perspective on capitalist economic development through the waves of creative destruction spurred by the entrepreneur. The third perspective is the Burtian perspective on the entrepreneur, developed on the basis that all economic activity is embedded in a social network.

### 5.1.1   The Deficiency of the Neo-Classical Perspective

Traditionally, neo-classical economic theory of a market economy has suffered from a failure to state clearly the role and actions of the entrepreneur—and, consequently, the entrepreneurial function in the economy. William Baumol (1968, p. 66) summarises how neo-classical economics has investigated this elusive economic entity since the Marginalist Revolution: "The theoretical firm is entrepreneurless—the Prince of Denmark has been expunged from the discussion of Hamlet." This discrepancy should be emphasised with the consideration that many economists believe the entrepreneur to be the driving force of the prevailing capitalist ideology and economic prosperity (Schmitz 1989; Wennekers and Thurik 1999; Baumol et al. 2007). As Lazear (2002, p. 1) suggests, "the entrepreneur is the single most important player in the modern economy". This omission within mainstream economics is certainly perplexing given its recognised importance.

Ultimately, Baumol (1968)'s argument is that the traditional theory of the firm does not allow for the full integration of the entrepreneur into a comprehensive theory of the economy. The production function suggests that the firm considers the costs and benefits attached to the employment of certain, well-defined factors of production, including capital and labour. All firms within the economy optimise and operate at maximal profit in equilibrium and, consequently, the induced market structure is inert.

---

[6] This is the opposite of the reward for supporting risky ventures. Indeed, returns to the bearing of measurable, estimable and insurable risk can be denoted as "interest" or "usury" rather than profit.

In the extreme case of perfect competition, one additionally assumes certainty, homogeneity, absence of barriers to entry and pursuit of self-interest only. A paradox follows whereby at the equilibrium of perfect competition there is actually no competition: all firms operate independently earning normal returns to business without being given the opportunity to innovate. Innovation, reorganisation of trade networks, the leveraging of unique social networks and product or process diversification are removed from these static models. The eventual failure of marginal firms only derives from an exogenous change in the market as opposed to endogenous factors such as uncertainty, bad networking or poor managerial decision-making due to bounded rationality.

This discrepancy extends to the adopted perspectives on the firm as an entity in the market economy that goes beyond the narrow black box model of production. Coase (1937) seminally introduced the thesis that the firm exists owing to its role as a shelter against market transaction costs for capital providers as well as workers as labour providers. This has been extended to a more comprehensive perspective through the seminal contributions of Grossman and Hart (1983) and Hart and Moore (1990), but was never abandoned as a main *raison d'être* of the firm. For neo-classical economics, entrepreneurship is closely linked to the notion of a firm as a social production organisation from this Coaseian perspective. Entrepreneurship is never really extended to the Platonian artisan who functions as a singular producer in a horizontal division of labour; in this regard the neo-classical perspective offers no affinity with the notion that economic production occurs through a social division of labour.

**Occupational Choice Models** To suggest that neo-classical economics has continued to disregard the entrepreneur since Baumol (1968) would be incorrect. The models of Lucas (1978) and Kihlstrom and Laffont (1979) form the foundations of an approach to entrepreneurship as an *occupational choice* for economic agents. Entrepreneurship is considered to be a chosen role in the market and, as such, subject to rational reasoning based on the optimisation of stated objectives. Being an "entrepreneur" is a rational choice, and entrepreneurship in this regard is an occupation.

Some deficiencies of occupational choice models are due to their market-centric perspective. Specifically, market equilibrium theories of entrepreneurship make three assumptions. First, every economic agent can recognise all entrepreneurial opportunities, which derives from their *ex ante* homogeneity.

Second, individual attributes—rather than information about opportunities or the encompassing structure of the socio-economic environment—determine who becomes an entrepreneur. Although human action is the result of individual ability there is no doubt that external and social factors also play a role in determining entrepreneurial action (Shane et al. 2003; Aldrich and Martinez 2007).

Third, being an entrepreneur is a rational choice. We remark that, in contrast, our institutional-relational perspective of the socio-economic space developed in Chap. 3 postulates that most individuals cannot just "choose" to specialise in some role of an "entrepreneur". Rather, it will be seen that individuals create or build their own role to their socio-economic environment; they specialise subjectively. Indeed, they do not adopt a preexisting occupation, but rather create their own role and, thus, spur the deepening of the division of labour.

Endogenous neo-classical growth models have been created to incorporate the notion of the entrepreneur (Peretto 1998; Sanders 2007). The most influential of these are the Aghion and Howitt (1992) model and its later adaptations (Aghion and Howitt 1998; Howitt and Aghion 1998), which facilitate the integration of entrepreneurial innovation as a driver of economic growth. Indeed, they do this by having firms invest resources in research to achieve new products that render the existing products obsolete. Capital is excluded from the basic model while economic growth results from technological progress, being a result of competition among firms that generate these innovations. Firms are motivated by the prospect of temporary monopoly rents after a successful innovation is patented. In the Aghion-Howitt framework, further innovations will subsequently destroy these rents as other entrepreneurial agents make existing goods obsolete.

Although Aghion-Howitt developed highly influential models attempting to capture the Schumpeterian notion of creative destruction, these models fail to capture the characteristics of the agent that leads to the destabilisation of the economy through the process of creative destruction—the very essence of entrepreneurship. Indeed, although Aghion and Howitt (1992), for example, regards creative destruction as a driver of growth, the paper does not mention the word "entrepreneur". Instead it is simply suggested that it is the firm, investing in research and development, which drives technological advancement and therefore economic prosperity. This is undeniably true; firms that invest in research and development can create innovative products—but innovation is still assumed to emerge from sources outside the firm. Thus, these neo-classical attempts to capture the entrepreneurial function are fundamentally flawed.

The development of entrepreneurial models to encompass institutional and social aspects are of paramount importance. From our discussion above, neo-classical theory has difficulty in modelling economic evolution through the entrepreneurial function. We suggest that the problems of neo-classical theory derive from the very fundamental axioms that underpin it: methodological individualism, methodological instrumentalism and methodological equilibration.

### 5.1.2    The Schumpeterian Theory of Entrepreneurship

Although progressively sidelined over the past decades (Aldrich 2005), one of the most prominent perspectives of entrepreneurship was developed by Joseph Schumpeter, who discusses entrepreneurship and the entrepreneurial function in two contributions: in Chapter 2 of Schumpeter (1926, 1934) and in a contribution prepared in 1928 (Schumpeter 1928).

Schumpeter provides a novel perspective on entrepreneurship that is fundamentally differentiated from the neo-classical rational choice perspective.

Realising the limitations of general equilibrium analysis in explaining economic evolution and development, Schumpeter rejects any notion of equilibrium, instead emphasising that the economy needs to be analysed in a purely dynamic manner propelled by the waves of *creative destruction* (Schumpeter 1942). From this dynamic viewpoint he builds a relatively loose conceptual narrative on the premise that, even if markets were to approach equilibrium, they would disequilibriate over time owing to the advancement of product and process innovation. Through the entrepreneurial function new products and markets would be created, thus provoking a deviation from equilibrium in the economy.

The process of Schumpeterian creative destruction assumes that all entrepreneurial activity is progressive, and that the entrepreneurial agent is a heroic entity productively influencing production and process techniques and introducing new technologies and specialisations to the socio-economic space. We argue that this perspective is rather limiting, since history has shown that many entrepreneurial innovations have resulted in regressive institutional developments.

***Entwicklung* and Entrepreneurship** Schumpeter's overall perspective on entrepreneurship fundamentally deviates from neo-classical economics and, thus, the Sayian outlook of a process of economic development that ultimately allocates resources in a more efficient manner. Instead, he initially took a more literal definition of the term "entrepreneur" as an agent who stimulated economic progress by finding new and better ways of doing things. In doing so Schumpeter emphasises the importance of innovation as a dynamic process that emerges from a stagnated state of affairs so that a new state of affairs can emerge. Innovation is a concept notably absent from the neo-classical models of comparative statics, where the types of goods and services are given. These models describe market economies in which the goods and services in the future are fully specified as well, which allows for intertemporal trade.[7]

However, in emphasising innovation, Schumpeter takes a relatively social perspective on the entrepreneur's socio-economic environment. Moreover, he fully accepted that not every agent could be an entrepreneur. Each entrepreneurial agent specifically required two attributes. The first is the existence of technical knowledge or "know-how" in order to produce new, innovative outputs. Second, entrepreneurial agents are required to have the power of disposal over the factors of production in the form of access to capital markets. In effect an entrepreneur requires access to the financial capital to fund the innovation's development and its diffusion through the relevant commodity markets. We note here that in Schumpeter's perspective such an innovation is essentially technical in nature, referring to an innovative production technology or a new product.

---

[7] This is formally modelled through Debreu's concept of a contingent commodity, which forms the cornerstone of neo-classical general equilibrium theory (Debreu 1959).

Considering his theory of economic innovation, Schumpeter's acceptance of evolution—or *entwicklung* (Schumpeter 2005)—is particularly notable. However, despite flirting with the Darwinian concept of evolutionary selection, Schumpeter did not follow up his insights with any major evolutionary discussion (Smelser and Swedberg 2005). Despite his efforts, he failed to provide any formal model in which to specifically link entrepreneurship, the entrepreneurial function, creative destruction and economic development (Witt 2002). He did attempt, however, to conceptually couple his discussion of entrepreneurship with one on internal economic development.

Schumpeter specifically saw that development was a process that emerged from actions endogenously occurring within the economy itself and not necessarily from the impact of some form of exogenous shock. He perceived an economy that is simply adapting to exogenous shocks as being dragged along by the changes in the surrounding world. According to him, this adaptation to an exogenous factor cannot be considered as proper development; economic development comes from innovative entrepreneurial action within the economy itself:

> By "development" we shall understand only such changes in economic life as are not forced upon it from without, but arise by its own initiative from within. [···]
> By this we should mean that economic development is not a phenomenon to be explained economically, but that the economy, in itself without development, is dragged along by the changes in the surrounding world, that the causes and hence the explanation of development must be sought outside the group of facts which are described by economic theory.

> Joseph Schumpeter (1934, p. 63)

Despite his efforts to integrate entrepreneurship into endogenous economic development, Schumpeter largely fails to accomplish this successfully. As Becker et al. (2006) already note and as pointed out in the introduction to Schumpeter (2005, p. 111): "Development's dismissal of entrepreneurship as the explanation of discontinuities is the rare instance where Schumpeter himself indicates that he is still searching for an entirely adequate explanation of the novel social phenomena he had characterised as discontinuities."

In discussing economic development, Schumpeter is adamant that development was not a self-organising process. Specifically he suggests that "[t]he economy does not grow into higher forms by itself" (Schumpeter 2003, p. 75). When considering situations of increased complexity, the difficulty of self-organisation becomes notable. Subsequently it becomes apparent that the entrepreneur does not just act as a diffuser of an innovation, but acts as an organising force that drives development of an economy from inside (März 1991). Entrepreneurs actively organise society and the divisions of labour in the production of innovative outputs. With this, Schumpeter makes an interesting argument: that homogeneous and fully autonomous agents may not necessarily produce systems that organise successful development when considering complex economies. Forces in terms of entrepreneurship and governance must actively organise society in effective production. Even if this organisation is imperfect or lacking, such fruitful economic development can still emerge.

**Personalisation and Depersonalisation of the Entrepreneur**  There remains controversy over whether Schumpeter's perspective on the entrepreneur changed during his lifetime. There does seem to be an implicit distinction between what he considered to be an entrepreneur and entrepreneurship, and what he considered to be the function of entrepreneurship. However, his views on these are not mutually exclusive; he simply views the same innovative process from two different perspectives. In his later work, Schumpeter's analysis becomes more depersonalised, focusing on the process and outcome of the entrepreneurial function within the economy. In doing so, he places more of an emphasis on the entrepreneurial activities and actions as opposed to the entrepreneurs' personal attributes. Becker and Knudsen (2003) imply that this made entrepreneurship seem to be a much more contingent activity; that the entrepreneurial function did not have to specifically emerge from a single individual, but may emerge from a group activity or a collective process.

With respect to a depersonalised entrepreneurial function, Schumpeter stresses that the function of the entrepreneur is to reform or revolutionise the pattern of production. They can do this in many ways: by exploiting an invention; or, more generally, by exploiting an untried technological possibility for producing a new commodity; by producing an existing product in a new way; by opening up a new source of supply of materials or a new outlet for products; by reorganising an industry; and so on. From this definition, the Schumpeterian entrepreneur is focused on production technology as well as firmcentric; specifically providing the link between the innovative function and firm organisation and productive output.

Despite the difference in approaches, Schumpeter—alike the neo-classical perspective—stresses a direct link between the development of technology and resulting economic prosperity. However, he suggests that technological advancement comes from the fruition of an entrepreneur's innovative idea embodied within the economy and the production of heterogeneous output as opposed to a mere exogenous shock. This provides a general consensus that the entrepreneur has to be considered as an entity which blurred the distinction between the micro- and macro-spheres of the economy: the entrepreneurial function is a microeconomic action with potential macroeconomic implications.

Thus, Schumpeter contends that the entrepreneurial function, and therefore the acts required to become an entrepreneur, is *not* the same as choosing an occupation or a profession; one cannot learn to become an entrepreneur as if it were any other profession. To be an entrepreneurial agent, one must specifically carry out an innovative process, which is outside the predefined actions of a socially accepted socio-economic role. Being an entrepreneur is specifically the converse of simply following the established procedures and institutions to conform to an established and socially accepted specific socio-economic role. Moreover, Schumpeter argues that one should not be considered to be an entrepreneur forever; an agent should only be considered to be entrepreneurial during the period in which the agent is carrying out any entrepreneurial innovation.

**Entrepreneurial Disequilibriation** Schumpeter's earlier work looks more at the characteristics of the entrepreneurial agent—or a 'man of action'—as an entity. Schumpeter (1934) considers the entrepreneur to be an exceptional, disruptive individual who actively *disequilibriates* the economy with the introduction of new products or processes, thus carrying out the aforementioned entrepreneurial function.

Schumpeter emphasises that entrepreneurial success is derived from the utilisation of an exogenous skillset. In his first rendition of the entrepreneur, Schumpeter attributes almost superhuman powers of leadership to the entrepreneur. Much like Lucas (1978), he perceives the entrepreneur as an agent with an innate leadership talent; indeed, what differentiates a successful entrepreneur from other agents within the economy is his ability to lead a firm or act on an innovation. Schumpeterian entrepreneurs exhibit such qualities as the ability to take the initiative, being authoritative, having imaginative foresight. This is best personified by the figure of a "captain of industry"—as long as he or she is innovative—as opposed to the "plain businessman" or manager who only executes and manages business as usual.

**Invention and Innovation** Within his perception of an entrepreneur, Schumpeter proposes a distinct dichotomy between inventor and entrepreneurial innovator:

> Economic leadership in particular must hence be distinguished from "invention". As long as they are not carried into practice, inventions are economically irrelevant. And to carry any improvement into effect is a task entirely different from the inventing of it, and a task, moreover, requiring entirely different kinds of aptitudes. Although entrepreneurs of course may be inventors just as they may be capitalists, they are inventors not by nature of their function but by coincidence and vice versa…It is, therefore, not advisable, and it may be downright misleading, to stress the element of inventions as many writers do.
>
> Joseph Schumpeter (1934, pp. 88–89)

Given this, an *inventor* is considered a person who creates a new product or process, but does not necessarily distribute it throughout the economy. On the other hand, an entrepreneurial *innovator* is a leader who economically commercialises, puts into practice and distributes an invention through his own efforts. Therefore, it is the innovator, as opposed to the inventor, who provides the shock to the economy and thus initiates the process of creative destruction through the entrepreneurial function.[8]

So, importantly, Schumpeter's analysis highlights that the innovating entrepreneur does not necessarily have to be the one that creates the novel product or process, but rather uses his superior networking abilities to distribute the innovation throughout the relevant economic network. Most notably, although attempting to depersonalise the entrepreneurial process in his later work, Schumpeter still suggests that the successful entrepreneur is endowed with some form of exogenous leadership talent, which leads to the diffusion of the innovation and the resulting disequilibriation of the economy.

**Assessing Schumpeter's Perspective**  Within his analysis of entrepreneurship Schumpeter provides a number of insightful notions. Not only does he put forward the concept of creative destruction, which is propelled by innovation through the entrepreneurial function, but he also provides an insight as to where this innovation is likely to emerge: in innovative production processes and the distribution of new products. The fact that he has to provide an exogenous leadership characteristic to explain successful entrepreneurial action, much as in the occupational choice models, is one of the major deficiencies of Schumpeter's theory of the entrepreneur, and one that was noted by other economists of his time.

For our purposes we claim that the Schumpeterian perspective on entrepreneurship is deficient in two main ways. First, we note the lack of a socio-economic institutional framework of reference in Schumpeter's theory. As he emphasises, entrepreneurship is endogenous, but he does not recognise that it occurs in an institutional environment. This has been identified and partially remedied by Baumol (1990). We discuss Baumol's approach in detail below with reference to the socio-economic space.

A second deficiency is that Schumpeter does not take into consideration the foundational networks of entrepreneurial activity. His ideas are still embedded firmly within the theory of markets as the interaction of household preferences and firm production functions. Indeed, it is suggested that an entrepreneur needs to be well placed in order to collect and disseminate ideas and resources. This relational element is integrated prominently in Burt's sociological perspective on entrepreneurship. This is the subject of the next discussion.

### 5.1.3   The Burtian Theory of Entrepreneurship

Whereas the Schumpeterian perspective explains economic development through product and process innovation, the theory of Ronald Burt (1992, 2005, 2010) discusses the act of entrepreneurship on the basis of the

---

[8] At the time, Schumpeter suggested that the inventor and the innovator would be two distinct entrepreneurs; however, he still noted possible situations when the inventor's role may coincide with that of the innovator. Although these situations were not considered to be typical, instead they were seen as mere exceptions to the rule.

socio-economic infrastructure that underpins economic interaction. This perspective is based on the premise that economic processes operate within social networks, and are as such socially embedded. As a consequence, and keeping in line with other economic sociologists, development occurs not just through the process of Schumpeterian innovation, but it also occurs from the reorganisation and exploitation of positions within social networks.

Specifically, Burtian entrepreneurs are individual agents who benefit from exploiting bridge relations that span structural holes of a social network or architecture of an economic organisation. The notion of the Burtian entrepreneur builds on the inherent infrastructural topology that naturally emerges within a networked economy. Burt's line of discussion follows that of the theory of weak and strong ties developed by Mark Granovetter (1973, 1983). We provide a short introduction to the notion of weak and strong ties in a social network before discussing Burt's theory of entrepreneurship.

**Strong and Weak Ties**  With reference to Definition 3.10, a *network* has been introduced formally as a set of nodes $N$ endowed with a set of links $G \subset \{ij \mid i, j \in N\}$. A node $i$ represents an economic agent, while a link $ij$ represents a socio-economic relationship or interaction between two agents represented as nodes $i$ and $j$.

A link $ij \in G$ is referred to as a *strong tie* if the two parties invest significant resources into its establishment and maintenance. A strong tie is a close relationship on which multiple processes and aspects interact and develop. This implies that a strong tie is deeply "socially embedded". On the other hand, a link $ij \in G$ is referred to as a *weak tie* if it is structurally weak in the sense that it is not socially embedded and that relatively few resources are invested in its maintenance. This implies that far fewer processes and aspects are conducted through these weak ties.

Strong ties are typically between close friends and family members. These include relationships that cover multiple aspects, ranging from familial relationships to mentoring relationships. On the other hand, weak ties are prominent in singular processes such as trade, casual social interaction and political discourse.

Mark Granovetter (1973, 1983) introduced the hypothesis that weak and strong ties can be distinguished and identified by their network topological properties. In particular, strong ties are relationally embedded in the sense that they are part of relational *triads* in the social network, while weak ties are not part of such triads.[9] This theory, therefore, directly links a strong tie to a subnetwork of high clustering, while a weak tie is part of no clusters. This implies in turn that strong and weak ties can be identified by the value of their *clustering coefficient*.[10]

---

[9] A triad is a completed triangle of links in a network. Formally, a triple $i, j, h \in N$ form a triad in network $G$ if $ij, ih, jh \in G$.

[10] We refer to a standard textbook sources on network theory such as Newman (2010) and Barabási (2016) for a formal treatment of these concepts.

**Fig. 5.1** A network with strong and weak ties

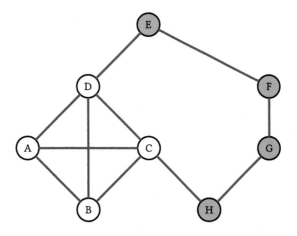

To illustrate these notions, we refer to Fig. 5.1. This figure depicts a network with a highly clustered subnetwork consisting of nodes $A$, $B$, $C$ and $D$, while the other nodes are more dispersed. All links between the nodes in the highly clustered subnetwork are strong ties, signified by their high clustering. The blue links involving the blue coloured nodes $E$, $F$, $G$ and $H$ depict weak ties, having a much lower clustering coefficient. These weak ties typically refer to relationships that concern a certain activity, or simple one-dimensional relationships. The black ties in Fig. 5.1, on the other hand, refer to multidimensional relationships.

Granovetter (1973) seminally points out that weak ties are remarkably strong in a completely different and unexpected way. Indeed, a weak tie can act as a conduit to link different parts of a larger network. So, even though these weak ties refer to certain dimensions or aspects only, they are valuable in connecting separated parts of the network. The control of these weak ties is very valuable as a consequence; in particular, this control can be a source of positional rents in the prevailing network. This is expressed by the notion of the "strength of a weak tie", as coined by Granovetter.

The strength of a weak tie is also expressed by the property that its removal can separate two or more clusters of nodes by a substantial distance; the removal of strong ties does not suffer from this problem. Indeed, the removal of a strong tie between a pair of nodes still means that the nodes can connect to each other through a path length of 2. Although ties can be weak in the structural sense, they are strong with regard to the quantity and quality of information that they are able to transmit from one agent to the other. Strong ties, on the other hand, are weak with regard to the diversity of information that can flow along them. Weak ties have a lack of redundant information that comes with the connection of cohesive and structurally equivalent contacts when strong ties are formed.

**Structural Holes and Bridges** We note that in the network depicted in Fig. 5.1 the group of nodes $C$, $D$, $E$, $F$, $G$, $H$ forms a circular structure that has no links between nodes on opposite sides of that circular structure. This is a typical example of what Burt (1992) calls a *structural hole*: a part of the network that lacks sufficient links to be a well-functioning social infrastructure. It is rather costly to establish communication between the nodes that are part of such a structural hole and information travels only with great difficulty in such a part of the network. A structural hole is signified by very low clustering and the abundant presence of weak ties.

The functionality of a structural hole is significantly improved by the addition of a single weak tie to bridge the different sides of the hole. Indeed, a link between nodes *C* and *F* in the network of Fig. 5.1 would significantly increase its infrastructural performance. A link such as *CF* is usually referred to as a *bridge*. A bridge is more valuable if the distance that it bridges is higher. The highest value is attained through the bridging of two completely separated parts of the network. This is referred to as a *network bridge*. The network bridge concept is defined as a link which, if removed, would cause two groups or cliques of nodes to become fully disconnected. The two nodes that make up a network bridge are also denoted as *middlemen*.

This is illustrated in Fig. 5.2 below. The black links represent strong ties that are part of one or multiple triads and have a high clustering coefficient. The red link between the two white nodes depicts a network bridge linking the left and right side of the depicted network, represented by a minimal clustering coefficient. Furthermore, the blue links represent regular bridges, while the grey links represent other weak ties.

At the basis of the Burtian theory of entrepreneurship is the utilisation of bridges and the building of such bridges in a network. Building a bridge across a structural hole creates a competitive advantage for the parties involved with this bridge; these individuals connect multiple hitherto distant components in the network and facilitate potential transactions between the different clusters in the network. It is clear that such "bridging" refers to a common part of any entrepreneurial networking activity. The introduction of a bridge means that

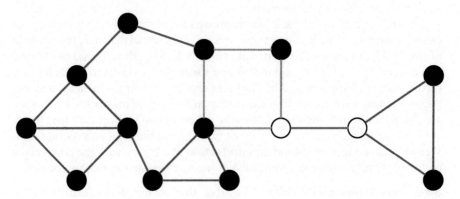

**Fig. 5.2**   The role of bridges in a network

the entrepreneur acts as a *gatekeeper*. Her reward is the extraction of rents from the exceptional middleman position in the network. Because of the structural position of a Burtian entrepreneur as a middleman, she could also be seen as a *market-maker*.

Although Burt's theory focuses on an individual as opposed to a firm or other non-personal entity, there are clear examples of institutions and other non-personal entities which act as bridge builders or middlemen. These include financial brokers and platform providers such as Google, Uber and eBay. Indeed, eBay acts as a middleman to facilitate interaction between groups of buyers and sellers. In doing so, eBay reduces search costs—or more generally transaction costs—between the two otherwise disconnected groups of traders. It receives revenue from providing this networking service, representing a typical example of a platform provider.

**Extending the Burtian Perspective** The network bridge theory of entrepreneurship does not explicitly express the creation of new products, processes or professions in society, which are emphasised in the Schumpeterian perspective. It is rather a representation of arbitrage and resource allocation through the entrepreneurial function. However, the dissemination of information and the exchange of ideas are typically required for the development of new technologies which can be easily integrated into this perspective. Indeed, Burt's theory goes beyond the positional theory of the entrepreneur. He subsequently extended the structural hole theory in a more philosophical and less formal network theoretical framework. This extension primarily focuses on how new, innovative ideas are generated and disseminated in a social network (Burt 2004).

The core of his argument is that agents with bridge relations are critical to learning, creativity and dissemination. Agents whose set of links span structural holes have unique access to diverse and even contradictory information and interpretations, giving them an advantageous opportunity in forming and exploiting innovative and productive ideas. Undoubtedly, ideas come from a variety of sources, divisions of labour and over a variety of paths; but the generation of ideas involves at some point transferring specific knowledge and information from one group to another, bringing agents together or combining knowledge across clusters.

This role of the entrepreneur alludes not just to the brokerage of information, but rather to the arbitrage, recombination and practical application of specific knowledge and information; the result of which may lead to the formation of a new firm. Burt (2005) furthers his proposition by suggesting that agents who create and control network bridges across multiple structural holes and multiple divisions of labour are more likely to have their ideas evaluated. Indeed, social networks are amazing tools for filtering and criticising good ideas: with more people evaluating an idea there is an increasing probability that a productive idea will emerge.

Moreover, value accumulates as ideas disseminate. Indeed, dissemination of ideas across clusters and diverse groups of agents allows for the creation of a tight feedback loop, which is needed for successful innovation. Therefore, people whose links span multiple network groups have a competitive advantage in the creation of such productive ideas. An idea of low impact in one group may be extremely valuable in another. An idea is only really valuable to agents and entities when these agents recognise it as such. This is more likely when ideas are diffused, discussed and evaluated throughout society.

Although Burt does not discuss this, these processes of the generation of ideas by spanning multiple networks could be linked to the processes underlying Schumpeterian creative destructionism. In this regard these seemingly disparate perspectives on entrepreneurship and the entrepreneurial function in an economy have more in common than one would expect at first glance.

## 5.2   INSTITUTIONS AND THE ENTREPRENEURIAL FUNCTION

Next we consider the role of entrepreneurship and, more generally, the entrepreneurial function in the context of the social division of labour. We argued before that entrepreneurship is driving institutional change in a socio-economic space: "Institutional change in the human economy is driven by the entrepreneurial function that represents how economic agents change the prevailing socio-economic institutions through their actions and behaviours." (Lemma 1.5) Thus, we argue that entrepreneurship is closely related to institutional innovation and widely impacts on the functioning of the social division of labour.

Entrepreneurship, therefore, impacts mainly on the institutions that govern the wealth creation processes in a social division of labour. The institutional governance system contains all of society's socio-economic roles and therefore determines the depth of the social division of labour. Moreover, these governing institutions guide and coordinate all socio-economic interactions and, thus, determine the relative payoffs of such economic interaction to the economic agents.

In this section we develop the theory of the entrepreneurial function and entrepreneurship in the context of a socio-economic space in much more detail. We first summarise some perspectives on institutional entrepreneurship in the existing literature. Subsequently we carefully construct a comprehensive perspective of institutional change in a socio-economic space. In doing so, we distinguish between entrepreneurship and the entrepreneurial function as two incarnations of the same socio-economic phenomenon.

### 5.2.1   *Institutional Entrepreneurship: A Literature Survey*

The idea that entrepreneurship is institutional in nature has already been put forward in the literature by multiple authors. Moreover, recent historical research has put the spotlight on the role of political and constitutional institutions on economic development (Acemoglu and Robinson 2012). Naturally this can be extended to entrepreneurship and its role in the institutional causes of economic development.

Baumol (1990) seminally introduces an institutional perspective on entrepreneurship. Baumol contests Schumpeter's perspective on the entrepreneur as a driver of economic development through generating waves of creative destruction. Baumol instead observes that the distinct form of entrepreneurship within a society is determined by the institutional structures of that society, and thus integrates institutional structures into the analysis of entrepreneurial action.

Baumol suggests that some institutional environments and arrangements have historically been more compatible with productivity-increasing technological innovations than others. Thus, institutional arrangements allow a Schumpeterian entrepreneur to be more or less successful. However, Baumol also notes that entrepreneurship has historically not always been of the Schumpeterian variety. Hence, institutions tend to determine both the level and type of entrepreneurship.

Baumol identifies three types of institutions in relation to entrepreneurial support: productive, unproductive and destructive. Institutions ensure that generated wealth is allocated in certain ways to promote or discourage entrepreneurial innovation: allocated payoffs could be skewed towards rewarding redistribution favouring sectional interests rather than in return for productive entrepreneurship. This distinguishes productive from unproductive institutional arrangements.

Dysfunctional institutions—those that are ill-defined or provide poor incentives—may provide a basis for entrepreneurs to exploit weaknesses in the infrastructural fabric of the socio-economic space. These institutional arrangements may provide incentives for entrepreneurs to rent seek—lobbying for barriers to entry or exploiting employment loopholes—as opposed to expending resources on more productive and socially beneficial endeavours. Institutions may be operating with such malfunction that they are created only to be exploited by entrepreneurs, who will ultimately damage the wider economic performance of the economy. These institutional arrangements can be deemed to be destructive.

**Extending Baumol's Perspective**  Murphy et al. (1991) discuss the distribution of entrepreneurial effort within an economy and the impact that this has on economic growth. The authors are interested in how the most entrepreneurial choose to seek returns and how incentives in a society promote rent seeking or profit seeking. As such, they identify factors that encourage rent-seeking and productive entrepreneurship. These factors are mainly institutional in nature, extending Baumol's thought framework.

For Murphy et al. (1991), productive entrepreneurship is founded on sufficiently large commodity markets; effective communication and transportation infrastructures that facilitate efficient trade flows; low barriers to market entry and business expansion; accessible capital markets and an effective banking sector; clear property rights; patent protection; and an ability to start firms that can make rents on talent. Owing to their socio-economic embeddedness in the prevailing institutional governance system, talented individuals are assumed to abide by the institutional framework and respond appropriately to them.

Acemoglu (1995) extends the thesis posed by Baumol (1990) and Murphy et al. (1991) by identifying reward structures as the main determinant of the distribution of entrepreneurial effort. Thus, the distribution of entrepreneurial effort and the ensuing entrepreneurship are endogenously determined in the institutional matrix in the economy. The endogeneity of the distribution of entrepreneurial effort allows for the existence of path dependency such that initial differences in rewards will have long-run effects, as these distributions in one generation shape the rewards for the next. Acemoglu argues that there might be situations in which there exist two-way causality between the rewards structures of society and the distribution of entrepreneurial effort.

**A Fundamental Critique of Baumol's Perspective**  Baumol (1990)'s perspective on entrepreneurship, which was enhanced through subsequent contributions discussed above, is that institutions provide a constrained framework in which entrepreneurship occurs. Too little attention is given to the fact that this institutional framework itself is a canvas on which an entrepreneur can actually develop innovative structures. In the setting of a socio-economic space, entrepreneurship is indeed concerned with institutional renewal and innovation, thereby affecting economic wealth generation at its core.

Our argument is that the institutional matrix in a socio-economic space creates itself the potential for entrepreneurship and institutional change through the entrepreneurial function in general. Certain institutional arrangements are more open and conducive to institutional innovation than others. This is illustrated by the differentiated forms of economic development and entrepreneurial successes in the US economy versus the EU economy: Silicon Valley emerged in California, not in northern Italy or in the Scottish lowlands. As such, the entrepreneurial function reflects the overall functioning and performance of the socio-economic space as a whole and its institutional matrix in particular.

More precisely, the schematic of the socio-economic space provided in Fig. 3.1 represents the principle that the entrepreneurial function works to affect the institutional environment of the economy; it embodies a force that is opposite to the direction of socio-economic embeddedness. The institutional framework determines the attainable payoff configurations for individual economic agents. In this regard, socio-economic embeddedness is unidirectional, abiding to pressures and payoffs from an existing institutional matrix. To assume, like Baumol (1990), that entrepreneurship is subject to socio-economic embeddedness is far too restrictive. The entrepreneurial function instead embodies the socio-economic force of institutional innovation and, as such, is not subject to embeddedness, but rather its counterforce.

Baumol perceives entrepreneurship as responsive to the payoff structure defined by institutional pressures without actively altering the environment in which entrepreneurial agents operate. As such, his analysis indicates that institutions can determine the balance between productive, unproductive and destructive actions undertaken by entrepreneurial agents. However, as put forward by public choice theory (Buchanan and Tullock 1965) and as indicated in Acemoglu's work, feedback loops can emerge whereby opportunistic individuals can actively alter the institutional environment they operate in to improve their own payoffs. This is indeed the essence of the entrepreneurial function depicted in Fig. 3.1: entrepreneurship acts in the opposite direction of embeddedness. Entrepreneurial agents modify the institutional environment that they operate in, the outcome of which can lead to positive outcomes for themselves and potentially for society as a whole. But it could also result in unproductive institutional change. Whether the entrepreneurial agent alters the governance system in a progressive or regressive fashion will largely depend on the institutions already in place within the economy.

**Institutional Entrepreneurship** This interaction between socio-economic institutions and entrepreneurial agents is partially captured in the work of Henrekson and Sanandaji (2011), which integrates James Buchanan's insights into Baumol's model of the entrepreneur. Buchanan (1980) notes that entrepreneurial effort can affect institutions in multiple ways, by market innovations that alter institutions or the effect of institutions, evasion of institutions and direct political entrepreneurship. Just as Baumol notes that the supply and allocation of entrepreneurial effort depends on the institutional framework of society and, therefore, on the relative payoffs to profit seeking and rent-seeking activities, Henrekson and Sanandaji note that the allocation of entrepreneurial effort depends on the ability for agents to abide, evade or alter institutional frameworks. Moreover, they acknowledge that the same individual can switch between different forms of behaviour.

This bidirectional relationship extends Baumol's perspective and leads to the notion of *institutional and political entrepreneurship* (Boettke and Coyne 2009). Already Dahl (1961) had discussed individuals who recombine resources in an effort to bring about change in policies that effect the wider economy, thereby introducing a restricted notion of institutional entrepreneurship. Within Dahl's framework, political entrepreneurs are effectively Schumpeterian entrepreneurs acting within the political space.

A distinction can be made between so-called political entrepreneurs and market entrepreneurs, who "refer to traditional Schumpeterian entrepreneurs, distinct from political entrepreneurs" (Henrekson and Sanandaji 2011, p. 50). The authors claim that not only is there a distinction between these types of entrepreneur, but that they are interdependent: political entrepreneurs must create the environment for market entrepreneurs. The economic system can thrive or collapse as an outcome of the actions provided by political entrepreneurship.

Eisenstadt (1980) and Hwang and Powell (2005) discuss a form of institutional entrepreneurship which involves entrepreneurship over the structure of government—that is, decisions regarding the general institutions within which ordinary political discourse and decision-making take place. Institutional entrepreneurship specifically involves changes to the fundamental constitution of the formal and informal rules of the game. DiMaggio (1988) used the term institutional entrepreneurship in reference to those individuals who have the resources and ability to generate changes in institutions. Institutional entrepreneurs can be driven by a variety of factors including monetary gain, prestige or power. This discussion of the entrepreneur extends beyond the political sphere of the economy and focuses on more ingrained institutional features, such as informal rules of the game, including beliefs, behavioural rules, religion and scientific knowledge. Such institutional entrepreneurship may have a less obvious but more distinct and longstanding impact on society (Abrutyn 2013).

Overall there emerges some consensus regarding how entrepreneurial efforts can impact the institutional architecture of an economy, whether in the political or the market domain. The impact of an entrepreneurial agent's actions on the institutional architecture can be either productive or unproductive. A productive entrepreneurial impact provides an environment with greater market opportunities and subsequently enhanced wealth generation within society, but requires an incentive structure for entrepreneurs to provide it. An unproductive or destructive entrepreneurial impact, conversely, provides an environment with more restricted economic activities and opportunities, resulting in rent-seeking as opposed to enhanced productivity.

### 5.2.2   Entrepreneurship in the Socio-Economic Space

The established theories on institutional entrepreneurship described above constitute two strands of thought. The first strand describes entrepreneurial actions as subordinated to the institutional matrix. These theories emphasise that innovation and development is subject to the institutional matrix that is present in the socio-economic space. Thus, economic development through the social division of labour is embedded in the governing institutions and, as such, is subject to socio-economic embeddedness.

The second strand focuses on a bidirectional interaction between institutions and entrepreneurship. As such, governing institutions are seen to provide the relative payoff structure that guide entrepreneurial actions and therefore affect the allocation of entrepreneurial effort. Further, entrepreneurial activities can impact the institutional matrix itself and the incentives that they in turn provide for further subsequent entrepreneurial effort. Such theories can easily be integrated into the relational perspective represented by our notion of the socio-economic space.

A missing element is the acceptance that effective entrepreneurship stimulates a deepening of the social division of labour and facilitates increased specialisation, as initially discussed by Smith (1776). Indeed, successful entrepreneurship affects economic wealth creation directly and translates into significant changes in the social division of labour itself. This takes the form of new socio-economic roles, innovative exchange mechanisms and novel forms of socio-economic interaction. This reengineering of the socio-economic space thus provides the basis for greater interactions and the development of innovations. A feedback loop between the extension of the division of labour and entrepreneurial activity is implied.

In this regard, our understanding of entrepreneurship is very similar to the Schumpeterian perspective. Indeed, by using the established theories of the entrepreneur we provide an integration of the notion of entrepreneurship to the relational perspective discussed.

**Definition of Entrepreneurship** Within a socio-economic space, *entrepreneurship* refers to an advanced form of *adaptive specialisation*: the agent builds a role that lies outside the existing matrix of governing institutions in the socio-economic space.

Entrepreneurship is therefore a form of behaviour by individual economic actors that goes beyond the choice space that is defined and imposed through the prevailing governance system or institutional matrix. These efforts affect two categories of institutional structures—the institutions making up the governance system itself as well as the networks making up the interaction infrastructure of the socio-economic space. All actions that result in new developments in the governance structure or in the trade infrastructure underlying the economy can be regarded as "subjective innovation", since they usually derive from the actions already exhibited by individuals within a given socio-economic space.[11]

**Description 5.1** *Consider a socio-economic space made up of a set of economic agents, an institutional governance system and an interaction infrastructure.*

  (a) **Entrepreneurship** *refers to actions that significantly modify elements of the institutional governance system and the resulting interaction infrastructure in the socio-economic space, thus directly or indirectly impacting the wealth creation processes in the socio-economic space.*
  (b) *An* **entrepreneurial agent**—*or entrepreneur—is an economic agent who engages in actions that constitute entrepreneurship.*

Entrepreneurship refers to major or significant changes in the institutional matrix on which a socio-economic space is founded. It has the effect of a major

---

[11] The entrepreneurial function is a weaker form of entrepreneurship and will be considered separately.

institutional shock to the processes that occur in that socio-economic space. In this regard, entrepreneurship refers to "revolutionary" changes or processes of change. This categorises the actions of Augustus as the first emperor of the Roman Empire—discussed in Sect. 3.4.1. Similarly, the processes executed in medieval Amsterdam discussed in Sect. 3.4.2 are a case of collective entrepreneurship; these changes were major and revolutionary, although spread out over a longer period of time.

**Reconsidering the Entrepreneurial Function** Entrepreneurship is a certain incarnation of the entrepreneurial function in a socio-economic space. As pointed out, it constitutes a process of major change and is revolutionary in that regard. On the other hand, the entrepreneurial function itself is simply the underlying process of institutional adaptation and innovation that propels change in the socio-economic space. The entrepreneurial function is normally incarnated as an evolutionary process of change rather than a revolutionary process instigated by acts of entrepreneurship. We refer to the regular, evolutionary process of institutional innovation, renewal and change as a *weak* form of the entrepreneurial function.

Both entrepreneurship and the weak entrepreneurial function impact the socio-economic space in some way, but the most notable difference between entrepreneurship and the weak entrepreneurial function is that the latter is not necessarily carried out by entrepreneurial agents and as such affects the structure of the socio-economic space in a more minor way. Indeed, the weak entrepreneurial function, as distinct from entrepreneurship, is the process of modifying a given socio-economic role for operation in a given context or the formation of new economic interactions and relationships with a given socio-economic role and some recognisable output.

Therefore, as such the weak entrepreneurial function can, and is, conducted by all economic agents in a given socio-economic space. It does not directly lead to the deepening of the division of labour, the formation of new socio-economic roles, new outputs and technologies, a reformation of the socio-economic space or new influential positions in the network, and thus does not spur radical development of the socio-economic space. However, any economic agent can spur growth through the process of the weak entrepreneurial function.

**Description 5.2** *The **weak entrepreneurial function** refers to actions that modify in a minor way institutional elements of the socio-economic space, thus directly impacting the individual economic agent and her social neighbourhood.*

For clarity we note two main differences between entrepreneurship and the weak entrepreneurial function from the definitions above. These two differences can be distinguished as "scope" and "depth". With regard to *scope* we note that entrepreneurship is conducted at a larger scope than the weak entrepreneurial function. Indeed, the impact of entrepreneurship leads to a change in the institutional matrix represented by the governance system that is used by all agents within the socio-economic space; therefore the process of entrepreneurship directly impacts all agents of the socio-economic space.

This is not the case with regard to the weak entrepreneurial function: the entrepreneurial activities subject to this only directly impact the economic agents conducting it and their social neighbourhoods. It may impact others in the population indirectly, but the effects of the weak entrepreneurial activities are directed and do not necessarily lead to changes in the institutions of the governance system.

With regard to *depth*, we note that entrepreneurship is inherently innovative and, as such, all subsequent changes to the governance system are new. The depth of impact of these changes is considerable, as a consequence. Therefore, the depth of the actions conducted by entrepreneurial agents is reflected in the formation of new socio-economic roles, novel products, innovative mechanisms of exchange and modifications of the interaction architectures, which are subsequently widely embedded in the socio-economic space.

On the other hand, the depth of the weak entrepreneurial function is limited, and by itself does not necessarily generate anything inherently new in the economy. This distinction with regard to the innovativeness of the entrepreneurial agent is important when making a general distinction between these two forms of the entrepreneurial function.

**Freedom and Entrepreneurship**  There is a close relationship between the freedom to pursue economic objectives and entrepreneurship. This has been recognised since the foundations for the industrial revolution were laid in the historical period of Enlightenment. In many regards, one can read Smith (1759, 1776) as a promotion of economic liberty in an institutional matrix that suffocated most economic endeavours. From this viewpoint, political economy was concerned with convincing nineteenth-century politicians to implement policies of laissez-faire and to promote the free spirit of classical capitalism.

Within the context of a socio-economic space, freedom becomes closely linked to the pursuit of entrepreneurship and the entrepreneurial function in general. In our network-institutional approach, individual freedom—so much promoted by economists from Smith to Buchanan—is essentially impossible. As social beings, individuals only have freedom in relationship to others. The "freedom to choose" is a misnomer, since any chosen action impacts others in their ability to choose and pursue their interests.

Therefore, freedom is fundamentally *social* and has to be assessed from that perspective. We can distinguish two forms of freedom that are closely related to entrepreneurship and the entrepreneurial function. First, there is the *freedom to network*—or social freedom in the sense as discussed in Chap. 1—which refers to the unhampered possibility to network and to build one's social capital. This refers strongly to the Burtian conception of entrepreneurship. Networking might have an impact on the institutional matrix, but not necessarily. Therefore, the freedom to network affects the functionality of the interaction infrastructure, but as such might not be related to the entrepreneurial function.

There is a higher form of freedom: *entrepreneurial freedom*. This form of freedom refers to the ability to alter one's institutional environment and, thereby, the institutional governance that guides one's and others' actions. This is directly related to the entrepreneurial function, making it possible to pursue entrepreneurial activities. In the context of a socio-economic space, entrepreneurial freedom or the liberty to design institutions is actually the highest form of freedom.

From the previous discussion, it should be clear that entrepreneurial freedom is determined by the prevailing institutional matrix in the socio-economic space. If the established institutions facilitate the emerge of new institutions or the alteration of these institutions, then it refers to a state of effective entrepreneurship and institutional change. Clearly, the promotion of entrepreneurial freedom requires the promotion of the two weaker forms of freedom, namely individual and social freedom. It also implies that individual or even social freedom is not sufficient for effective entrepreneurship to develop in a given socio-economic space. This could explain why Silicon Valley emerged in California rather than in Northern Italy; the openness to institutional change is different in the USA—and California particularly—than in the EU.

**The Impact on Wealth Creation** Whereas entrepreneurship is the main workhorse for the development of the socio-economic space, the weak entrepreneurial function along with external parameters such as population growth and technological progress are the main forces of the growth of economic wealth creation in the socio-economic space. The evolutionary nature of economic development through the weak entrepreneurial function is punctuated by changes due to radical entrepreneurship in the socio-economic space. Thus, the social division of labour expands through the weak entrepreneurial function and population growth, while it deepens owing to entrepreneurship.[12]

Our approach to entrepreneurship is restricted relative to the existing literature. Within the relational perspective represented through the socio-economic space, entrepreneurship refers to more than simply self-employment—as is the typical indicator for many analyses of the topic (Evans and Jovanovic 1989; Lazear 2004; Cagetti and De Nardi 2009; Sanandaji and Leeson 2013)—but must include actions that alter the governance system of the economy in a substantial way. As a consequence, the notion of entrepreneurship coincides with Schumpeter's perception of the entrepreneur as representing a disequilibriating force in the economy.

---

[12] We refer to Gilles and Diamantaras (2003) for a mathematical formulation of the selection of market institutions, allowing the deepening of the social division of labour and the significant increase of the generated economic wealth. Moreover, Gilles et al. (2015) propose the formation of a stable socio-economic space based on a social division of labour of objective socio-economic roles as initially emerging from a state of chaos. Here, we extend the notion to include the actions of the entrepreneurial agent and the weak entrepreneurial function.

Our point of departure is to claim that the entrepreneur should not be perceived as simply an agent that interacts within a market context, but can actively disequilibriate a socio-economic space through influencing a radical change to its institutional governance system. Further still, and perhaps most importantly, we argue that entrepreneurship leads to the deepening of the social division of labour through the development and introduction of new socio-economic roles and novel commodities. As a consequence, new positions emerge in the social division of labour, so entrepreneurial individuals can build on those positions and potentially earn rents and profits from this. These entrepreneurial earnings last until these positions are contested in a structural sense by entrepreneurial actions of other individuals.

### 5.2.3    Institutions and the Unique Network Positions of Entrepreneurs

In properly integrating entrepreneurship into the socio-economic space through its entrepreneurial function, we provide a discussion about the interaction between entrepreneurship, institutions and the unique positional attributes that economic agents attain from the development of new socio-economic roles within the social division of labour.

Below we provide a deeper insight into how the entrepreneurial function performs by exploring the interdependencies between the advancement of socio-economic roles and the development of positional attributes within the context of the institutional matrix. Given the definition of entrepreneurship above we discuss the relationship of the interaction between institutions, entrepreneurship and the unique positional attributes that entrepreneurial agents attain from the development of a new socio-economic role within the social division of labour.

**Entrepreneurship and Entrepreneurial Positions** In Chap. 1 of this book we already made the argument that the implementation of a social division of labour leads to the formation of social and economic positions. This is because of the social and economic networks that form as a consequence of the employed specialisations, socio-economic roles and enacted trade relationships. As such, individual economic agents have a tendency to form similar socio-economic relationships if they have similar socio-economic roles: there is positive *assortativity* in social and economic networks in the interaction infrastructure based on a social division of labour.

We can therefore postulate that, owing to the positional attributes of socio-economic roles in a social division of labour, the assumption of a particular socio-economic role leads to the formation of a unique set of socio-economic relationships and therefore a unique position within the interaction infrastructures represented in a socio-economic space. Thus, a socio-economic role is characterised by its uniquely associated *social capital*—the relationships it attains in the networks making up the interaction infrastructure generated by that social division of labour. We conclude that a role's characteristics define a *unique* relational position with that role in the interaction infrastructure.

Therefore, if an entrepreneurial agent creates a new socio-economic role, she also creates a unique position for that role in the modified interaction infrastructure. We can refer to this as that agent's (unique) *entrepreneurial position* in the interaction infrastructure. The uniqueness of this entrepreneurial position fits well within the relational perspective and integrates some aforementioned theories of the entrepreneur, such as those from Smith, Schumpeter and Burt.

**Lemma 5.3 (Entrepreneurial Positions)** *If through a process of entrepreneurship an entrepreneurial agent creates a new socio-economic role in the prevailing social division of labour, then this role embodies unique positional attributes and social capital within the generated interaction infrastructure.*

As a consequence of the creation of an entrepreneurial position in the prevailing interaction infrastructure, an entrepreneurial agent has access to higher levels of social capital, in particular through the formation of unique global and local bridges. This aspect of entrepreneurship builds on Burt's insight: an entrepreneur adds value to this unique set of relations through entrepreneurial actions. Specifically, an entrepreneur creates value through the creation of a novel product or an innovative production process that requires a hitherto unrelated set of specialisations and socio-economic roles; or through the potential rent-seeking and increased bargaining power that comes with brokering information and outputs.

In some cases, the implementation of a new socio-economic role necessitates the flow of information from the entrepreneurial position to other positions, particularly with the formation of a novel output and the generation of ideas. In other cases, the introduction of a new socio-economic role provides incentives to block the flow of information from one position to another; this may be the case where the exchange of knowledge does not directly benefit the entrepreneurial agent, or where that agent wishes to exploit some bargaining power to influence the institutions of society. The prevailing institutional matrix also affects the strategies of entrepreneurial agents; the governance system determines the actions associated with the new socio-economic role.

**The Interaction of Institutions and Network Positions**  We have discussed two aspects of entrepreneurship thus far. First, the process of entrepreneurship can lead to the development of new socio-economic roles. As the division of labour deepens, new specialisations are introduced and new (entrepreneurial) positions are formed within the interaction infrastructure in the socio-economic space.

Second, entrepreneurial agents create and occupy unique positions within the connected fabric of the socio-economic space. Owing to their positional attributes they can either be rent-seeking or wealth-generating with their actions. For example, a middleman can exploit their position at a network bridge within a network through the process of rent-seeking or can facilitate exchange between individuals and markets that were previously unconnected by providing a platform for interaction.

Consequently, entrepreneurial agents can act in a positive-sum, zero-sum or negative-sum way (Krakovsky 2015). Much depends on the context of the prevailing institutional matrix and, thus, the relative payoffs to rent-seeking or profit-seeking actions. If institutions are ill defined or if the rules of the game regarding the expropriation of rents from intermediating interaction are poorly enforced, then the entrepreneurial agent has an incentive to act opportunistically. On the other hand, if institutions are imposed to effectively mitigate opportunistic behaviour, it incentivises these agents to be more productive with their positions and as a consequence add wealth to the network as a whole by facilitating exchange.

*Example 5.4 (Financial Brokers During the Great Panic of 2008)* The exploitative potential of entrepreneurial positions are particularly sensitive to the prevailing institutions in the governance structure of a socio-economic space. As a simple illustrative example, Crotty (2009) discusses the architecture of the financial system that evolved during the run-up to the Great Panic of 2008. Whilst noting a number of theoretical problems that underpinned the financial crisis, Crotty also notes the perverse incentives and exploitative power given to mortgage and financial brokers.[13]

Without correct and well-defined institutional regulation of their actions, bankers granted mortgages without mortgagers being correctly scrutinised. Moreover, owing to the commission basis by which mortgage brokers are remunerated, they have incentives to exploit their unique position based on asymmetric information that accompanies their gate-keeper role in the mortgage provision network. The rules of the game informed by the institutions of the prevailing socio-economic space provide incentives for the brokering middlemen to be opportunistic and, therefore, exploit their unique position. Thus, mortgage brokers pursued destructive actions; they effectively were rent-seeking at the expense of society at large.                                                ◆

The example of the mortgage brokers during the Great Panic of 2008 shows that the institutional matrix in a socio-economic space needs to be sufficiently developed in order to reduce the unproductive and destructive acts of the entrepreneurial agents; particularly the creation of middleman positions in the interaction infrastructure. However, the relationship between entrepreneurship and institutions is bilateral; we specifically contend that agents with high levels of social capital and unique positional attributes can influence a change to the

---

[13] We emphasise that these bankers and brokers acted as entrepreneurial agents in the run-up to the Great Panic of 2008. They innovated the financial sector of the global economy significantly during the 1990s and 2000s by introducing new socio-economic roles and innovative financial products that resulted into their occupation of middleman positions in the global financial networks. We refer to Chap. 2 for a detailed discussion.

institutional governance system owing to their increased bargaining power from their entrepreneurial position.

As pointed out, entrepreneurial agents can modify the institutional matrix through the creation and assumption of unique entrepreneurial positions in the interaction infrastructure. Productive entrepreneurship and profit-seeking can naturally lead to unproductive or destructive entrepreneurship through rent-seeking and the unproductive modification of institutions. Owing to their unique positional attributes, entrepreneurs also have the opportunity to accumulate excessive wealth and rent, potentially gaining economic prominence within the socio-economic space, and using this prominence to impact other elements of the governance system.

Indeed, the creation of social and economic capital through entrepreneurial acts, the deepening of the division of labour and the attainment of unique entrepreneurial positions in a socio-economic space increase the bargaining power for individuals who occupy these positions. By monopolising the flow of information and/or outputs throughout a networked space, one can gain economic prominence and affect the rules governing the economic wealth creation processes.

**The Fused Nature of Entrepreneurship**  Infrastructural positions, entrepreneurship and institutions are fundamental in the analysis of economic development through the deepening of the social division of labour. The notion of the entrepreneurial function in a socio-economic space indicates that it is often difficult to separate these components: entrepreneurs create new socio-economic roles which provide them with new positional attributes and potentially high economic and social capital that can be leveraged to actively alter institutional elements of the governance system.

Furthermore, disequilibriation through innovation of products and production processes has a fundamental impact on the institutional matrix of the socio-economic space. On the other hand, it also benefits these entrepreneurial agents with increased levels of social capital through bridge formation, specifically through the acquisition of ideas and dissemination of innovations. This fuses our perspective with the Burtian and Schumpeterian perspectives on entrepreneurship.

Our conclusion here is that these concepts—infrastructural positions, entrepreneurship and institutions—are intertwined or *fused*. Their fused nature is captured by the historical case describing the rise of the House of Medici. We turn to this next.

## 5.3    CASE: THE ENTREPRENEURSHIP OF THE HOUSE OF MEDICI

The proposed institutional perspective of entrepreneurship and the entrepreneurial function can be assessed using the historical case of the rise of the House of Medici. The Medicis played an extremely important and illustrative part in the transformation of the medieval, feudal economy into the premodern economy.

A notable achievement from this historical period was the conception of modern banking as a pillar of financial capitalism. We provide a brief analysis of the roots of capitalist banking and the fruition of the incorporated economy and relate this analysis to the theories of entrepreneurship as discussed in this chapter. Of specific interest are the entrepreneurial efforts of the Medici family, particularly Giovanni di' Bicci de' Medici and his son Cosimo di' Giovanni de' Medici, both of whom can be considered to be the grandfathers of modern banking because of their innovations in financial accounting and the organisation of banking. Cosimo furthered the cause of the House of Medici by building a dominant position in the political networks of Renaissance Florence. The entrepreneurial actions of Giovanni and Cosimo laid the foundation to the positions of power—economic as well as political—that the Medici heirs were able to attain.

This case clearly describes a historical period of entrepreneurial activity that resulted in significant socio-economic change. In this regard, the rise of the House of Medici refers to progressive institutional change that was instigated by the Medicis' entrepreneurial actions. These actions were clearly *multidimensional*. Indeed, institutional innovations occurred in the economic as well as the political sphere and interacted to create a major change in the economy at that time.

**The Consequences of the Black Death**  To make possible an analytic narrative and to trace the roots of modern capitalism and European banking, we first provide a brief account of the institutional framework in which the Medicis were able to emerge and establish themselves. These institutional settings are rooted in the *Black Death* in Italy—with a particular focus on Florence. This shock to the Italian city-states and economy set the scene for a period of fruitful, progressive entrepreneurial activity that resulted in the Italian Renaissance.

The Black Death had a major, devastating impact on the Italian economy in the fourteenth century. The consequences included the institutional restructuring of the economy. It was through this that the Medicis were able to flourish and to establish themselves as leading bankers in the European economy and, subsequently, as political leaders in Florentine society and Europe as a whole.

The Black Death was relatively egalitarian in its impact. As such, it affected the ruling classes of medieval Italian society, including members of both the government and Church who were instrumental in the enforcement of formal societal rules. Moreover, cities such as Florence became inhabited and ruled by a relatively consolidated oligarchy of elitist families whose power became unconstrained by artisan guilds, some of which had dissolved completely in the wake of the Black Death.[14]

---

[14] Indeed, despite its egalitarian impact, some of the best off in society were able to shelter themselves from the exogenous shock of the Black Death and therefore strengthen their power at the detriment of the rest of society.

The population of Florence grew quite quickly as the devastating effects of the Black Death subsided. This led to a divergence of both social class and political power of various groups in Florentine society. A large and evident wealth gap emerged, which was exacerbated by a lack of institutions to facilitate wealth redistribution and stop the exploitation of the poor by the elite. Over time the ruling oligarchy physically separated themselves from the rest of society in their bombastic city palaces.

### 5.3.1    Restructuring the Institutional Matrix: The Ciompi Revolt

This striking segregation of Florentine society between the elites and the lower classes and the resulting opportunity inequality were fuelled by inherited networks and class homophily that emerged after the Black Death. This segregation could not be addressed through the local government system, since any government policy would inevitably be favourable to the oligarchic elites rather than emancipating the lower classes.[15] This quickly led to a societal tipping-point, which became known as the *Ciompi Revolt*.

The Ciompi Revolt hit Florence in 1378.[16] The revolt was a revolution in which groups of wool carders,[17] vegetable sellers and crockery vendors lobbied to demand a voice in Florentine society. These disadvantaged social groups—collectively known as the *popolo minuto*—had no representation through the Florentine guild system of governance in the wake of the Black Death.

The Ciompi Revolt had a lasting effect on the social, political and economic networks in Florence. It induced a gradual and lasting deterioration of the social stratification through a restructuring of marriage and economic networks, a partial liberation of the lower classes and a favourable lean towards a more democratic political system. Importantly, the revolt split the incumbent oligarchic elite into two factions: those who sympathised with and fought alongside the Ciompi, and those who did not and resisted the induced changes.

**The Roots of the House of Medici**  The Ciompi Revolt in Florence is a pivotal historical moment that allowed the emergence of the Medici family, and the roots of the Medici Bank stretch back further. The Medici family participated in the moneylending business that supported much of the rebuilding of the Italian

---

[15] The government system in medieval and Renaissance Florence can characterised by both "oligarchy" and "plutocracy" (Chaplin 2016). The city-state was essentially controlled completely by a few major families or houses through the most powerful guilds in the main city-state governing bodies.

[16] There is a striking parallel with the Peasants' Revolt of 1381 in England. This is also attributed to the emancipation of the lower classes as a result of the effects of the Black Death on the economy (Barker 2014).

[17] This class of workers in the cloth workshops of Florence were also known as the *Ciompi*, from the sound that their wooden clogs made on the work floor. This nickname gave the revolt its historical indicator.

economy after the Black Death. Vieri di' Cambio de' Medici (1323–1396) was conducting moneylending operations immediately following the Black Death.

Salvestro de' Medici (1331–1388), a first cousin of Vieri, initially paved the way for Medici influence and economic significance. During the critical period of the Ciompi Revolt in July 1378, Salvestro was selected as the *Gonfaloniere of Justice*, the de facto presiding public representative of the ruling elites. This meant he was given a notable degree of power and access to the social networks of the ruling elite.

During Salvestro's rule, Vieri's Bank was in its maturation stage of growth and was accepted into the well-established *Arte del Cambio* guild in Florence, specifically because of the influence of Salvestro. Owing to the increased reputation of the Medici name, Vieri was approached to provide financial services to the municipal government of Florence and the Curia of the Catholic Church, located in what is now Vatican City. Owing to the trusting functional relationship that was established, the financial trade continued even after Salvestro ceased to serve as the Gonfaloniere of Justice.

Giovanni di' Bicci de' Medici (1360–1429) came from a separate family line from Salvestro and Vieri. Although once influential in Florence, Giovanni's side of the family experienced a fall from grace, after which they became associated with low-level criminal activity. Giovanni, however, reaped fortune from misfortune: the death of his father during the Black Death and his subsequent orphaned state led to a de facto adoption by Vieri, who provided Giovanni with a position at his bank and an introduction to financial and banking management.

**The Oligarchic Counter-Revolution** In 1382, a few years after the revolt and the establishment of the Ciompi government, the Ciompi alliance was successfully overthrown by the partisan elite of previously ruling oligarchs. This counter-revolution led to a further split between those elites who sympathised with the Ciompi and those who did not. Those who strictly opposed the Ciompi eventually controlled Florence for the remainder of the fourteenth century despite further intra-elite conflicts between families, through the rise of the House of Albizzi (Chaplin 2016, Chapter 1). During these conflicts, the ruling oligarchs fractured the faction of Ciompi-sympathising patrician families. These Ciompi sympathisers subsequently fragmented into detached houses with only a few social and economic connections between them. The elitist solidarity thus dissolved in the decades following the Ciompi Revolt.

When considering the social structure of the oligarchic houses after the counter-revolution, it can be seen that the elite marriage networks shifted permanently during the period from 1385 to about 1420; from a quasi-feudal pattern of parallel marriage hierarchies, which had incorporated most patrician families, toward a city-wide elitist pattern of marriage cycles, which coopted "politically correct" patrician families while structurally isolating patrician "class-traitors" who had collaborated with the Ciompi and the less powerful artisan guilds, representing the minor professions.

This marriage network transformation prevented Ciompi-type challenges from ever arising again and safeguarded the now successful oligarchic elite from another uprising. No longer were there fluid elite factions to play off one another. The progressive fracturing of all facets of society led to the creation of structural holes in the social network and the opportunity to span them in a Burtian entrepreneurial manner. The Medicis played a pivotal role in the restructuring of the marriage and economic networks that followed the counter-revolution of 1382.

Giovanni's intelligence and prudence allowed him to excel at Vieri's bank. His natural ability, desire and dedication to reestablish the legitimacy of the Medici name meant he was promoted to become the manager of the bank's Rome branch. In this position he became one of the most trusted papal moneylenders. However, the Medici Bank remained second to the Alberti Bank—the largest bank in Italy and the main recipient of the Catholic Church's fortune. In this regard, the Albertis were the Medicis' main competitors at the time.

Vieri stepped down from his bank in 1392 and died a few years later. On his death the bank was immediately liquidated and his fortune was divided into three separate inheritances. All three inheritors were direct family members and they went on to establish their own banks. Although Giovanni did not inherit from Vieri, he was able to continue his Roman banking operations independently. He built his banking empire on a foundation of significant entrepreneurial innovations in both the financial and political spheres.

### 5.3.2   Giovanni de'Medici as an Institutional Entrepreneur

The success of the Medici Bank has been largely attributed to the entrepreneurial actions and organisational architecture established by Giovanni di' Bicci de' Medici. Specifically, two prominent factors are considered to be at the foundation of the rise of the bank. One factor concerns its accounting practices; particularly in the area of double-entry bookkeeping, in combination with the commission—the *discrezione*—placed on foreign exchange trades, which made financial services more profitable and set the stage for interest payments to become acceptable for Christian lenders.

The second factor is the innovative partnership system introduced by the Medici Bank, which provided the basis for a decentralised banking system that was subsequently adopted throughout Europe. This structure allowed for a vas relational network of credit ties under the Medici name. The decentralised nature of the Medici Bank's organisational architecture was particularly novel when compared with traditional banking across Europe during the Middle Ages. In Florence, many of the dominant banks that collapsed during the Black Death were unitary organisations that operated solely in the city.

Interestingly, the Medici banking network under Giovanni expanded where the needs of his social ties were greatest as opposed to his needs for economic value generation. He therefore took advantage of the information and opportunities that arose within his social and economic network. In other words, Giovanni's social capital was clearly directed towards his entrepreneurial activities.

**Entrepreneurial Innovations**   Giovanni's first innovation concerns the bank's accounting practices, which ultimately evaded the *usury doctrine* imposed as an embedded rule of finance by the Catholic Church. The imposition of this forbade interest-based moneylending throughout Europe and ultimately meant that the constitution of modern banking systems was largely impossible.

**The *discrezione*:**   The Medici Bank did not strictly perform moneylending services; rather they acted as foreign exchange brokers who relied on bills of exchange in order to trade in multiple currencies. Their accounts highlight their reliance on these bills of exchange specifically because of their ability to impose implicit usury. The Church strictly prohibited charging interest on loans; the formal and informal rules of credit influenced the nature of banking and the architecture of banking organisations.

On the other hand, brokers could make money from transactions that included the exchange of multiple currencies. Therefore, instead of charging interest, the Medici Bank imposed a commission for transferring one currency into another. If the money was in the hands of the broker for any substantial period of time, then the charged commission would be larger. Subsequently, if depositors put their money into the bank they were given a *discrezione*—which referred to the return paid by the banker for this privilege and the risk that the depositor accepted. This was considered to be credit, again concealing any interest charged. This was one of the first times that bank deposits were created.

To earn *discrezione*, the bank would claim the transfer of currencies without a trade actually being realised. This act of creative accounting was used as a mechanism to bypass the laws of usury. It was a progressive act, particularly favouring the oligarchic elite and the Catholic Church who used the Medici Bank to transfer money initially across Italy and then to the rest of Western Europe as Giovanni's banking network expanded. With the application and social acceptance of this entrepreneurial innovation, Giovanni de' Medici evolved the institution of moneylending into what would now be considered to be the foundations of modern banking.

Henrekson and Sanandaji (2011) suggest that entrepreneurs can evade and potentially alter society's institutions through their acts. Instead, we claim that the Medici Bank, particularly under Giovanni, altered the institutional configuration of the economy; in particular, concerning the accepted beliefs regarding the usury doctrine. The *discrezione* substantially increased the payoffs of holding deposits and exchanging currency for bankers, allowing the Medicis to amass significant levels of wealth. From our perspective, we assess the evasion and ultimate alteration of the usury doctrine as a productive form of entrepreneurship. Moreover, *discrezione* became a widely accepted practice in Florence and was later adopted by other banking houses throughout Italy and Europe.

Only through the Medicis' social network did Giovanni's invention become socially recognised and embedded into Florentine banking practices, therefore being accepted and imitated by the rest of society.[18]

**Organisation of the Medici banking networks:**   The second entrepreneurial innovation focuses on the organisational architecture of the Medici Bank. It used a different organisational structure than the typical one of the time. Traditionally banking was centralised and strictly hierarchical—like the Alberti Bank. Owing to the bank's initial roots in Rome it quickly established a branch-based organisational structure in both Rome and Florence.

Subsequently, the bank retained an organisational structure that was more decentralised and governed by a set of harmonised lending rules within all of its branches. This decentralised network allowed for the diversification of loans and ultimately the reduction of risk, lowering the cost of banking. This architecture reflected that of a joint stock company whereby the parent company, located in Rome, controlled the subsidiary partnerships by owning more than 50% of the capital of its branches. Other partners also owned substantial amounts of stock within the subsidiary banks, meaning that their compensation was tied in closely with the bank's performance.

Instead of salaried employees, branch managers were junior partners who received a share in the profits plus an allowance for living expenses. The system provided incentives for increasing effort levels and lowering risk. Moreover, a hierarchical promotion system incentivised high-performing managers, giving them the possibility of becoming a full partner, and thereby greatly increasing their earnings.

The Medici Bank retained the power to condemn partners at any time. In effect, it created an organisational architecture similar to that of a limited liability holding company. Under this structure decision-making was decentralised and the risk for the Medicis was diluted by being split across the activities of other branches. Moreover, the structure gave them easy oversight, a clear locus of control and therefore the ability to create rules and bylaws that was imposed on the bank's branches.

The Medici Bank's organisational structure evolved to respond to the high transaction costs of international banking at that time. Decision rights were decentralised throughout the organisation to make use of local information. As a consequence, partners could be opportunistic with their resources and abilities.

---

[18] We can observe the acceptance of the Medici family into patriarchal Florence and the profession of moneylending through the Renaissance paintings commissioned by banking houses, including the Medici Bank. Indeed, Botticelli's *Adoration of the Magi* and *Portrait of a Man with a Medal of Cosimo the Elder* show the Medici family in a well-regarded and powerful manner. With Giovanni's innovations and the Medici Bank's successes, banking went from being stigmatised to next to divine.

On the other hand, partners could potentially damage the Medici Bank's reputation and profitability through risk-shifting or through privately capturing the gains from lending activities. Partners within the organisation require monitoring and evaluation from central authorities; however, monitoring and the transfer of information between Florence and these branches was costly. The costs of monitoring partners were reduced significantly through aligning the partners' incentives, as discussed above: these partners de facto became the residual claimants of the firm, preventing excess rent-seeking and corruption in the bank's branches.

There are some reasons why Giovanni's entrepreneurial effort was so successful. The first is that his main competitor, the Alberti Bank, collapsed and the Alberti family was expelled from Rome in 1393. This mainly derived from its strongly hierarchical organisational structure, which did not allow for flexibility and correct oversight of its moneylending practices. Specifically, the bank's dealings in civil wars in Italy, prior to the wars in Lombardy during the fifteenth century, cemented its political disrepute and eventual collapse. Moreover, the Alberti family was considered Ciompi sympathising during the Revolt, and was thus punished after the counter-revolution.

Furthermore, Giovanni essentially took over Vieri's Rome branch under a different name, giving him immediate access to a source of funds from the Church's Curia. Finally, Giovanni could use his social connections and the extended knowledge he had amassed when working in Vieri's bank to successfully secure banking services across Italy.

### 5.3.3   The Political Entrepreneurship of Cosimo de'Medici

Our theory of entrepreneurship developed above highlights the importance of the positional attributes of economic agents for the exploitation of power and influencing change. Although the *discrezione* and the bank's organisational innovations were pioneered by Giovanni, the positional power of the Medicis within the Florentine elite can be attributed mainly to Giovanni's son, Cosimo, as a political networker. After laying the foundations, Giovanni stepped down from the bank and ownership transferred to Cosimo, who subsequently led the Medici family to political dominance.

Cosimo consolidated political and economic power in an entrepreneurial manner by leveraging a central middleman position in the networks of elite inter-family marriages, economic relationships—centred on the Medici Bank—and political patronage. Cosimo's success was down to his superior networking ability and patronage of the arts, which became of increasing importance as the Renaissance began to flourish. He was therefore multiply embedded in various aspects of the socio-economic space, playing a role in complex and overlapping Florentine marriage, economic and elite political patronage networks. He took advantage of the vast macro-political and macro-economic forces far beyond his control.

Thus, he founded a political dynasty that dominated Florence and Europe at large for over three centuries. He consolidated a Europe-wide banking network that helped induce both international trade and state-making elsewhere. He also oversaw and sponsored the Florentine intellectual and artistic effervescence that we now call the Italian Renaissance. Such sprawling success of a single individual is largely due to two factors: the economic success of the Medici Bank and Cosimo's positional power within the socio-economic networks in Florence at the time.

We can apply the notion of multivocality to explain the prominence of Cosimo's position in Florentine society.[19] To do this we must first note that the Medici benefited from the restructuring of the marriage networks which occurred over the decades following the Ciompi Revolt and the subsequent counter-revolution.

**Social Structure of the Florentine Political and Economic Elite** Elite marriage networks were strategically restructured in order to segregate those who sympathised with the Ciompi and those who did not.[20] Intra-elite marriages were conceived partially in political alliance terms and were used to strengthen the elite's position, such that further revolutions by coalitions of workers could not emerge again. The elite families that did not sympathise with the Ciompi tended to marry with other non-sympathisers. This resulted in a tight-knit marriage network of socio-economic equals within their oligarchic neighbourhoods. Conversely, Ciompi sympathisers, also called "New Men", did not tend to marry into other sympathising families—each elite family remaining relatively isolated.

Giovanni had already crafted very carefully a neutral position in the volatile political period following the Ciompi Revolt and the counter-revolution of 1382. The Medicis' stance during this period—as well as their aforementioned economic successes owing to Giovanni's entrepreneurial innovations—made them attractive to both sides of the oligarchic elite. Over time, the House of Medici both strategically and fortuitously married into both sides of the Florentine elite. This resulted in a unique middleman position in the social network, which allowed the Medici family to build and control an early forerunner to a political party, while the other elite families of the time suffered from internal strife. This allowed Cosimo to engage in a process of Burtian political entrepreneurship.

**Mapping the Florentine Elite Network** Our claim is made evident with the aid of the set of graphs in Fig. 5.3. These figures provide five networks on the same set of Florentine elite houses. Each network focuses on a certain type

---

[19] *Multivocality* refers to an agent who specialises in a number of different roles and thereby directly operates in a number of different dimensions of a socio-economic space.

[20] We should point out that all elite marriages were strategically arranged by patriarchs or their equivalents in the two participating families. As Padgett and Ansell (1993, p. 1259) describe it, "[the] Medician political control was produced by network disjunctures within the elite, which the Medici alone spanned".

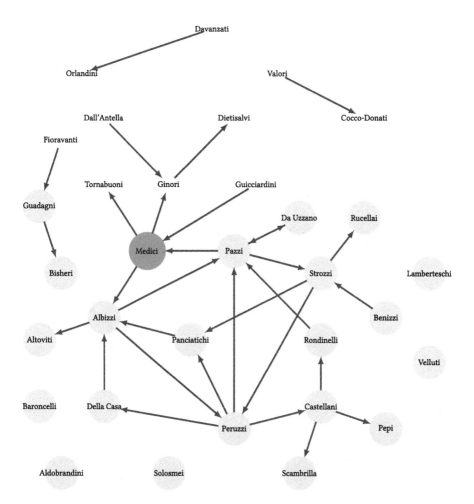

**Fig. 5.3** Marriage network of Florentine houses, c. 1429

of relationship. In each depiction, the "new men" houses or former Ciompi sympathising houses are indicated without a circular structure. The established oligarchic houses, which took control in the counter-revolution of 1382, are depicted as grey nodes.

Specifically, the network in Fig. 5.3 shows marriage relationships that were strategically formed between the various families in the Florentine elite. The red links in Fig. 5.4 map the lending relationships between the different houses at Cosimo's time. The direction of the link shows which house lent to which.

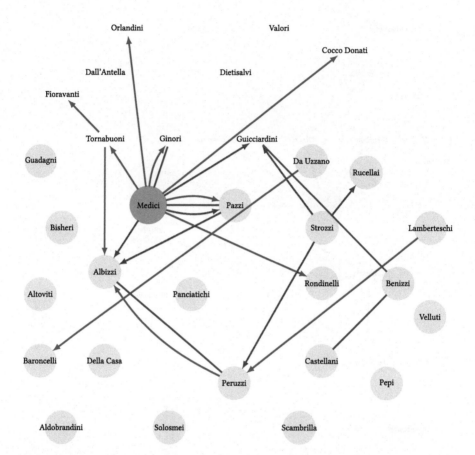

**Fig. 5.4** Lending (red), partnership (blue) and patronage (black) relationships between Florentine houses

Similarly, blue links in Fig. 5.4 map partnership relationships and the black links show patronage relationships.[21]

The marriage network, the loan network and the patronage network all indicate that the Medici occupied a central, bridging position in the structural hole between the two opposing sides in both a social and an economic sense. Cosimo created a new and unique socio-economic role through his network position, based on a combination of marriage, lending and patronage. Although

[21] The data that has been used for the construction of the networks depicted in Figs. 5.3 and 5.4 was based on the reported sources in Padgett and Ansell (1993).

he never occupied any formal governmental position, through this unique entrepreneurial network building he took control of the political governance and therefore the institutional and economic environment of Florence, Tuscany and even Northern Italy.

There are some interesting points to note with regard to the depicted networks. The first point concerns the importance of the composition of both marriage and economic linkages within the houses in Florence. Each family's respective actions depended not only on independent rationalised decision-making, but also on how they were interlinked. Power and influence were enhanced through the marriage relationships, meaning that the very composition of the marriage network mattered.

**The Consolidation of Cosimo's Political Position**  During the second half of the 1420s, the Lombardi war with Milan and Lucca increased tensions within the oligarchic networks of Florentine society. The economic costs of the war were significant and the manipulations of the oligarchic leader Rinaldo degli Albizzi resulted in the banishment of the most influential "new men", including Cosimo in 1433. In 1434 Cosimo used his unique middleman position in the Florentine oligarchy and his considerable social capita to take control of the Florentine city-state. This was mainly accomplished through the entrepreneurial manipulation of Florence's political institutions.

In particular, the lack of proper coordination through a functional network architecture undermined the actions of the "new men" faction before 1433. This structural problem transformed into a leadership crisis in 1433. Instead, a focal point in the form of a leader could have properly strategised and initiated action. Similar coordination issues undermined the response of the established oligarchic houses under the leadership of Rinaldo in 1434. Both sides suffered from coordination and leadership problems.[22] This case shows that social ties can provide constraints as well as opportunities in the pursuit of self-interest without any clear governing rule-sets or leaders.

While the oligarchs under Rinaldo hesitated, Cosimo was able to solve the collective action problem through the utilisation of the Medicis' unique middleman position between the various factions and houses to effectively mobilise a faction as a political party in 1434.[23] Again, this was largely because of the architecture of the social network underlying the party which formed around the House of Medici. Indeed, the Medicis were married directly into three other families: the Tornabuoni, the Ginori and the Guicciardini. The Medicis combined this middleman position in the marriage network with the fact that the other member families were not heavily interlinked through

---

[22] The composition of the social network clearly affected the cohesiveness in these times of crisis. Opposing stratagems arose between the different interlinked houses, ultimately generating tensions within the ruling elites, irrespective of their affiliation. In effect, they became bound by their own network neighbourhood.

[23] This became known as the *Medicean faction* over time.

marriage, as was pointed out for the oligarchic partisans. This provided a focal point which allowed for collective action, coordinated by Cosimo.[24]

This discussion highlights the entrepreneurial characteristic which brought the House of Medici and Cosimo to a position of political prominence. The main characteristic refers to the Medicis' unique middleman position within the social network of the ruling elite, mentioned above. As depicted in Fig. 5.3, Cosimo developed a star network which spanned both the oligarchic partisans and the former Ciompi sympathisers in various aspects. Such a position meant that Medici followers could only interact with the rest of the followers through mediation of the Medici family. Moreover, if they wished to discuss issues with the oligarchic rulers, all information had to pass through the Medicis and vice versa. From their strategic position in the social network they were able to remain in power as the main brokers of critical information.[25]

## 5.4    The Interaction of Networks, Institutions and Entrepreneurs

Our theory of institutional entrepreneurship and the entrepreneurial function in the context of a socio-economic space has some commonalities with the perspective of Henrekson and Sanandaji (2011). These authors highlight the interaction between political and market entrepreneurship. In doing so they explain how the economic and political spheres of the socio-economic space can interact with each other and facilitate development. Particular attention is paid to how entrepreneurial agents can affect the institutional rules governing the economy.[26]

Similarly, the interaction between the infrastructural and political spheres of the socio-economic space is also notable with respect to the successes of the Medicis. We suggest that the positional attributes of individual agents in the networks that make up the interaction infrastructure impact their influence on the institutional governance system of the socio-economic space. This is

---

[24] It is easy to appreciate how the dependence on a powerful and respectable family would provide the necessary leadership for collective action. For a seminal discussion of this phenomenon we refer to Emerson (1962).

[25] To illustrate the powerful role of the House of Medici and of Cosimo himself, Pope Pius II proclaimed: "Political questions are settled in his [Cosimo's] house. The man he chooses holds office. [· · · ] He it is who decides peace and war and controls the laws. [· · · ] He is King in everything but name" (Hibbert 1980, p. 87).

[26] In particular, entrepreneurship affects the relative payoffs to entrepreneurial activity as well as the allocation of entrepreneurial effort within the social division of labour. Henrekson and Sanandaji (2011) illustrate this interdependency with the example of Silvio Berlusconi, who used his economic power from market activities to fuel his political dominance in contemporary Italy. His media empire provided him with a platform to promote himself and to influence the beliefs of the voters. Berlusconi's entrepreneurial efforts can be labelled as unproductive and potentially destructive to society's welfare. Indeed, there is evidence that throughout his career he used his political ties to seek and capture rents.

particularly apparent with the aforementioned network of the Florentine elite and our theory of entrepreneurship: in the socio-economic space capturing the Florentine economy at that time, Cosimo and the House of Medici instigated institutional change and the actions of elite Florentine factions primarily owing to their positional attributes, which in turn were formed as a consequence of their entrepreneurial strategy.

Our perspective on entrepreneurship, therefore, extends the insights of Henrekson and Sanandaji (2011), noting that the position of an individual agent within the interaction infrastructure in a socio-economic space can inform her ability to broker information and trade, and thus potentially gain a powerful position within a network. Therefore, entrepreneurial agents can form and exploit unique network positions, which can subsequently result in institutional impact.

The unique position attained by entrepreneurial agents can emerge as a consequence of the development of new socio-economic roles. As such, the relational perspective provides a way to investigate the interaction between these three important elements: institutions, socio-economic networks and entrepreneurship. The interacting elements of institutions, socio-economic networks and entrepreneurship can be easily applied to the case of the rise of the House of Medici.

## References

Abrutyn, S. 2013. *Revisiting Institutionalism in Sociology: Putting the "Institution" Back in Institutional Analysis.* New York: Routledge.

Acemoglu, D. 1995. Reward Structures and the Allocation of Talent. *European Economic Review* 39: 17–33.

Acemoglu, D., and J.A. Robinson. 2012. *Why Nations Fail: The Origins of Power, Prosperity and Poverty.* London: Profile Books.

Aghion, P., and P. Howitt. 1992. A Model of Growth Through Creative Destruction. *Econometrica* 60: 323–351.

Aghion, P., and P. Howitt. 1998. A Schumpeterian Perspective on Growth and Competition. In *New Theories in Growth and Development,* ed. F. Coricelli, M. Di Matteo, and F. Hahn, chap. 1, 9–49. Basingstoke: Palgrave Macmillan.

Aldrich, H.E. 2005. Entrepreneurship. In *The Handbook of Economic Sociology,* ed. N.J. Smelser and R. Swedberg, chap. 20, 2nd ed., 451–477. Princeton, NJ: Princeton University Press.

Aldrich, H.E., and M.A. Martinez. 2007. Many are Called, But Few are Chosen: An Evolutionary Perspective for the Study of Entrepreneurship. *Entrepreneurship Theory and Practice* 3: 293–311.

Barabási, A.-L. 2016. *Network Science.* Cambridge: Cambridge University Press.

Barker, J. 2014. *England, Arise: The People, the King and the Great Revolt of 1381.* London: Little, Brown Publishers.

Baumol, W.J. 1968. Entrepreneurship in Economic and Theory. *American Economic Review* 58: 64–71.

Baumol, W. 1983. Contestable Markets: An Uprising in the Theory of Industry Structure. *American Economic Review* 72: 1–15.

Baumol, W. 1990. Entrepreneurship: Productive, Unproductive, and Destructive. *Journal of Political Economy* 98: 893–921.

Baumol, W. 2002. *The Free-Market Innovation Machine: Analyzing the Growth Miracle of Capitalism*. Princeton, NJ: Princeton University Press.

Baumol, W.J., R.E. Litan, and C.J. Schramm. 2007. *Good Capitalism, Bad Capitalism, and the Economics of Growth and Prosperity*. New Haven, CT: Yale University Press.

Becker, M.C., and T. Knudsen. 2003. The Entrepreneur at a Crucial Juncture in Schumpeter's Work: Schumpeter's 1928 Handbook Entry. 'Entrepreneur'. *Advances in Austrian Economics* 6: 199–233.

Becker, M.C., T. Knudsen, and J.G. March. 2006. Schumpeter, Winter, and the Sources of Novelty. *Industrial and Corporate Change* 15: 353–371.

Boettke, P.J., and C.J. Coyne. 2009. Context Matters: Institutions and Entrepreneurship. *Foundations and Trends in Entrepreneurship* 5 (3): 135–209.

Brownlow, G. 2015. Back to the Failure: An Analytic Narrative of the DeLorean Debacle. *Business History* 57 (1): 156–181.

Buchanan, J.M. 1980. Rent Seeking and Profit Seeking. In *Toward a Theory of the Rent-Seeking Society*, ed. J.M. Buchanan, R.D. Tollison, and G. Tullock, 3–15. College Station: Texas A & M University Press.

Buchanan, J.M., and G. Tullock. 1965. *The Calculus of Consent: Logical Foundations of Constitutional Democracy*. Ann Arbor: University of Michigan Press.

Burt, R.S. 1976. Positions in Networks. *Social Forces* 55: 93–122.

Burt, R.S. 1992. *Structural Holes: The Social Structure of Competition*. Cambridge, MA: Harvard University Press.

Burt, R.S. 2004. Structural Holes and Good Ideas. *American Journal of Sociology* 110: 349–399.

Burt, R.S. 2005. *Brokerage and Closure: An Introduction to Social Capital*. Oxford: Oxford University Press.

Burt, R.S. 2010. *Neighbour Networks: Competitive Advantages Local and Personal*. Oxford: Oxford University Press.

Cagetti, M., and M. De Nardi. 2009. Estate Taxation, Entrepreneurship, and Wealth. *American Economic Review* 99 (1): 85–111.

Chaplin, D. 2016. *The Medici: Rise of a Parvenu Dynasty, 1360–1537*. London: CreateSpace Independent Publishing Platform.

Coase, R.H. 1937. The Nature of the Firm. *Economica* 4: 386–405.

Crotty, J. 2009. Structural Causes of the Global Financial Crisis: A Critical Assessment of the 'New Financial Architecture'. *Cambridge Journal of Economics* 33: 563–580.

Dahl, R. 1961. *Who Governs?*. New Haven, CT: Yale University Press.

De Jong, A., D. Higgins, and H. van Driel. 2012. *New Business History? An Invitation to Discuss*, Mimeo. Rotterdam School of Management, Erasmus University.

de Roover, R. 1946. The Medici Bank Financial and Commercial Operations. *Journal of Economic History* 6: 153–172.

Debreu, G. 1959. *Theory of Value*. New York, NY: Wiley.

DiMaggio, P. 1988. Interest and Agency in Institutional Theory. In *Institutional Patterns and Organizations: Culture and Environment*, ed. L.G. Zucker. Cambridge: HarperBusiness.

Eisenstadt, S.N. 1980. Cultural Orientations, Institutional Entrepreneurs and Social Change: Comparative Analysis of Traditional Civilizations. *American Journal of Sociology* 85: 840–869.

Emerson, R.M. 1962. Power-Dependence Relations. *American Sociological Review* 27: 31–41.

Evans, D., and B. Jovanovic. 1989. An Estimated Model of Entrepreneurial Choice Under Liquidity Constraints. *Journal of Political Economy* 97: 808–827.

Gilles, R.P., and D. Diamantaras. 2003. To Trade or Not to Trade: Economies with a Variable Number of Tradeables. *International Economic Review* 44: 1173–1204.

Gilles, R.P., E.A. Lazarova, and P.H.M. Ruys. 2015. Stability in a Network Economy: The Role of Institutions. *Journal of Economic Behavior and Organization* 119: 375–399.

Granovetter, M. 1973. The Strength of Weak Ties. *American Journal of Sociology* 78: 1360–1380.

Granovetter, M. 1983. The Strength of Weak Ties: A Network Theory Revisited. *Sociological Theory* 1: 201–233.

Grossman, H., and O.D. Hart. 1983. An Analysis of the Principal-Agent Problem. *Econometrica* 51: 7–45.

Hart, O.D., and J. Moore. 1990. Property Rights and the Nature of the Firm. *Journal of Political Economy* 98: 1119–1158.

Henrekson, M., and T. Sanandaji. 2011. The Interaction of Entrepreneurship and Institutions. *Journal of Institutional Economics* 7: 47–75.

Hibbert, C. 1980. *The House of Medici: Its Rise and Fall.* Paperback ed. New York, NY: Morrow Quill.

Hindle, T. 2008. *Guide to Management Ideas and Gurus.* London: Profile Books Ltd.

Howitt, P., and P. Aghion. 1998. Capital Accumulation and Innovation as Complementary Factors in Long-Run Growth. *Journal of Economic Growth* 2: 111–130.

Hwang, H., and W.W. Powell. 2005. Institutions and Entrepreneurship. In *Handbook of Entrepreneurship Research*, ed. S.A. Alvarez, R. Agarwal, and O. Sorenson, 179–210. Amsterdam: Kluwer Publishers.

Kihlstrom, R.E., and J.-J. Laffont. 1979. A General Equilibrium Entrepreneurial Theory of Firm Formation Based on Risk Aversion. *Journal of Political Economy* 87: 719–748.

Kirzner, I.M. 1979. *Perception, Opportunity and Profit.* Chicago, IL: University of Chicago Press.

Knight, F.H. 1921. *Risk, Uncertainty and Profit.* Boston, MA: Houghton Mifflin.

Knight, F. 1935. *The Ethics of Competition.* New Brunswick, NJ: Harper Press.

Krakovsky, M. 2015. *The Middleman Economy: How Brokers, Agents, Dealers, and Everyday Matchmakers Create Value and Profit.* New York: Palgrave Macmillan.

Lazear, E.P. 2002. Entrepreneurship. NBER Working Papers, No. 9109.

Lazear, E. 2004. Balanced Skills and Entrepreneurship. *American Economic Review* 94 (2): 208–211.

Lucas, R.E. 1978. On the Size Distribution of Business Firms. *The Bell Journal of Economics* 9: 508–523.

März, E. 1991. *Joseph Schumpeter: Scholar, Teacher and Politician.* New Haven, CT: Yale University Press.

Murphy, K.M., A. Shleifer, and R.W. Vishny. 1991. The Allocation of Talent: Implications for Growth. *The Quarterly Journal of Economics* 106: 503–530.

Newman, M.E.J. 2010. *Networks: An Introduction.* Oxford: Oxford University Press.

Padgett, J.F., and C.K. Ansell. 1993. Robust Action and the Rise of the Medici, 1400–1434. *American Journal of Sociology* 98: 1259–1319.

Peretto, P.F. 1998. Technological Change, Market Rivalry, and the Evolution of the Capitalist Engine of Growth. *Journal of Economic Development* 3: 53–80.

Sanandaji, T., and P.T. Leeson. 2013. Billionaires. *Industrial and Corporate Change* 22 (1): 313–337.

Sanders, M. 2007. Scientific Paradigms, Entrepreneurial Opportunities, and Cycles in Economic Growth. *Small Business Economics* 28: 339–354.

Schmitz, J.A. 1989. Imitation, Entrepreneurship, and Long-Run Growth. *Journal of Political Economy* 97: 721–739.

Schumpeter, J. 1926. *Theorie der wirtschaftlichen Entwicklung: Eine Untersuchung über Unternehmergewinn, Kapital, Kredit, Zins und den Konjunkturzyklus.* 2nd ed. Berlin: Duncker und Humblot.

Schumpeter, J. 1928. The Instability of Capitalism. *The Economic Journal* 38: 361–386.

Schumpeter, J. 1929. Der Unternehmer in der Volkswirtschaft von heute. In *Strukturwandlungen der Deutschen Volkswirtschaft, Vol. 1*, ed. B. Harms, 303–326. Berlin: Reimar Hobbing.

Schumpeter, J. 1934. *The Theory of Economic Development: An Inquiry into Profits, Capital, Credit, Interest and the Business Cycle.* Cambridge, MA: Harvard University Press.

Schumpeter, J. 1942. *Capitalism, Socialism and Democracy.* 3rd ed. New York, NY: HarperPerennial.

Schumpeter, J. 2003. The Theory of Economic Development. In *Joseph Alois Schumpeter: Entrepreneurship, Style and Vision*, ed. J.G. Backhaus, chap. 3, 61–116. Berlin: Springer.

Schumpeter, J. 2005. Development. *Journal of Economic Literature* 43: 108–120.

Shane, S., E.A. Locke, and C.J. Collins. 2003. Entrepreneurial Motivation. *Human Resource Management Review* 13: 257–279.

Sims, O. 2017. *Entrepreneurship and Wealth Generation in Socially Structured Economies.* Ph.D. thesis, Queen's University, Belfast.

Smelser, N.J., and R. Swedberg. 2005. *The Handbook of Economic Sociology.* 2nd ed. Princeton, NJ: Princeton University Press.

Smith, A. 1759. *The Theory of Moral Sentiments*, ed. by K. Haakonssen. Cambridge Texts in the History of Philosophy. Cambridge: Cambridge University Press. Reprint 2002.

Smith, A. 1776. *An Inquiry into the Nature and Causes of the Wealth of Nations.* Chicago, IL: University of Chicago Press. Reprint 1976.

Wennekers, S., and R. Thurik. 1999. Linking Entrepreneurship and Economic Growth. *Small Business Economics* 13: 27–55.

Witt, U. 2002. How Evolutionary Is Schumpeter's Theory of Economic Development? *Industry and Innovation* 9: 7–22.

# INDEX

Printed by Printforce, the Netherlands